DESIRE IN LANGUAGE

THE KRISTEVA LIBRARY

DESIRE IN LANGUAGE

A Semiotic Approach to Literature and Art

JULIA KRISTEVA

EDITED BY LEON S. ROUDIEZ
TRANSLATED BY THOMAS GORA, ALICE JARDINE, AND LEON S. ROUDIEZ

COLUMBIA UNIVERSITY PRESS   NEW YORK

COLUMBIA UNIVERSITY PRESS

Publishers Since 1893

New York   Chichester, West Sussex

cup.columbia.edu

Séméiôtiké: Recherches pour une sémanalyse © 1969 Éditions du Seuil

"Polylogue" © 1977 Éditions du Seuil

Copyright © 2024, 1980 Columbia University Press

Library of Congress Cataloging-in-Publication Data

Names: Kristeva, Julia, 1941– author. | Roudiez, Leon S. (Leon Samuel),
1917–2004, editor, translator. | Gora, Thomas, translator. | Jardine,
Alice, translator. | Kristeva, Julia, 1941– Polylogue. Selections.
English. | Kristeva, Julia, 1941– Sēmelōtikē. Selections. English.

Title: Desire in language : a semiotic approach to literature and art / by
Julia Kristeva ; edited by Leon S. Roudiez ; translated by Thomas Gora,
Alice Jardine, and Leon S. Roudiez.

Description: New York : Columbia University Press, 2024. |
Series: European perspectives | Includes bibliographical references and index.

Identifiers: LCCN 2023040263 | ISBN 9780231214551 (trade paperback) | ISBN
9780231561426 (e-book)

Subjects: LCSH: Semiotics and literature. | Semiotics and art. |
Criticism. | LCGFT: Essays.

Classification: LCC PN98.S46 K7413 2024 | DDC
808/.001/41—dc23/eng/20230928

LC record available at https://lccn.loc.gov/2023040263

Book design: Chang Jae Lee

Cover design: Julia Kushnirsky

CONTENTS

PREFACE

The essays that have been collected here for English-language readers were written over a span of some ten years; to the extent that their aim does not presuppose the writer's neutrality but, on the contrary, her involvement, presenting them today amounts to a test of *memory* for me. Furthermore, as they embody a form of research that recasts several disciplines traditionally kept apart and therefore proceeds with effort, tension, and a kind of passion familiar to pioneers—presenting them in another language, within a different culture, surely leads one to measure, more than one ordinarily would, the *difference* in mental and intellectual habits that persist in spite of recently increased cultural exchanges between the United States and Europe.

The memory I alluded to is of course a personal one, but it is also historical. Following upon the phenomenological and existentialist shock of the postwar period, the sixties witnessed a theoretical ebullience that could roughly be summarized as leading to the discovery of the determinative role of *language* in all human sciences. If it be true that the light thrown on the enigma constituted by *meaning* as well as by *society* came from the relationships discovered between them and the structures of language (to the extent that it is an object of linguistics), one did nevertheless, from then on and in parallel fashion, question the metaphysical premises on which rest not only the sciences of language but their exportation to other domains. Thus, next to structuralism, a critique of Hegelian, Heideggerian, Marxian, or Freudian derivation jolted its occasionally simplistic elegance and carried theoretical thought to an intensity of white heat that set categories and concepts ablaze—sparing not even discourse itself. *Semanalysis*, as I tried to define it and put it to work in Σημειωτιχή, meets that requirement to describe the signifying phenomenon, or signifying phenomena, while analyzing, criticizing, and dissolving "phenomenon," "meaning," and "signifier."

Two radical instrumentalities occurred to me as being germane to such a project in analytical semiology.

The first, located within that selfsame theoretical thought, involved a questioning of meaning and its structures, giving heed to the underlying *speaking subject.* Such an insertion of subjectivity into matters of language and meaning unfailingly led one to confront a semiology stemming from Saussure or Peirce with Hegelian logic and with Husserl's phenomenology as well; in a more specifically linguistic fashion, it resumed Benveniste's masterly undertaking and necessarily led to a linguistics of enunciation. Finally, mindful of the splitting of subjectivity implied by the discovery of the unconscious, and taking advantage of the breakthrough accomplished by Lacan in French psychoanalysis, semanalysis attempted to draw out its consequences with respect to the different practices of discourse (in literature and particularly in the novel and in the contemporary novel). That means that references to "dialectics," "practice," "subject," etc., are to be understood as *moments* within an analytical process, one involving the analysis of meaning, structure, their categories and relationships—not at all in the purity of the source from which they sprang.

I envisioned the second instrumentality of this analytical project as having to be made up of the *specific object* it needed to assign itself in order to emphasize the limits of a positivist knowledge of language and to induce research, harried by the specificity that the subject of the theory believes it can detect in that object, to attempt to modify its very theoretical apparatus. That uncanny object, pre-text and foil, weak link in human sciences and fascinating otherness for philosophy, is none other than art in general, modern art and literature even more particularly. The essays of *Σημειωτιχή* (1969) and even more so those of *Polylogue* (1977) are committed to it (and to works by Céline, Beckett, and Sollers among others).

One will perhaps better understand, now, why the essays presented here, even though they often deal with literature or art, do not amount to either "art criticism" or "literary criticism." Their concern remains intratheoretical: they are based on art and literature, or more precisely on a desire for art and literature on the part of their writer, in order to try to subvert the very theoretical, philosophical, or semiological apparatus. I hope the reader will also perceive, in this ambitious clarification, a confession of humility: considering the complexity of the signifying process, no belief in an all-powerful theory is tenable; there remains the necessity to pay attention to the ability to deal with the desire for language, and by this I mean paying attention to art and literature, and, in even more poignant fashion, to the art and literature of our time, which remain alone, in our world of technological rationality, to impel us not toward the absolute but toward a quest for a little more truth, an impossible truth, concerning the meaning of speech, concerning our condition as speaking beings. That, after all, is in my opinion the fundamental lesson taught us by Roman Jakobson, who reached one of the high points of language learning in this century by never losing sight of Russian futurism's scorching odyssey through a revolution that ended up strangling it.

Readers will also notice that a change in writing takes place as the work progresses. The starker style, tending toward a kind of formalization, of the earlier essays changes progressively as a psychoanalytic trend is accentuated (as well as interest in literary and artistic practices), making way for a more personal style. And yet, this does not go so far as identifying theoretical discourse with that of art—causing theory to be written as literary or para-literary fiction. If there is a strong post-Heideggerian temptation leading in that direction, the choice I have made is entirely different.

It assumes the necessity of adopting a stance involving otherness, distance, even limitation, on the basis of which a structure, a logical discourse, is sutured, hence demonstrable—not in a banal sense but by giving serious consideration to the new post-Freudian rationality that takes two stages into account, the conscious and the unconscious ones, and two corresponding types of performances. Such a theoretical stance could well be termed metaphysical. Still, if contemporary thought is often reluctant to adopt it, one must recognize that such a stance is the only guarantee of ethics, that of knowledge as well as of all discourse. Why should this be so?

The most telling answer to that question is provided by what will also be the second argument in favor of such a theoretical discourse, one resting on the brink of fiction without ever completely toppling over into it: it is provided by my experience as an analyst. The daily attention given to the discourse of the other confirms, if need be, that the speaking being maintains himself or herself as such to the extent that he/she allows for the presence of two brinks. On the one hand, there is pain—but it also makes one secure—caused as one recognizes oneself as the subject of (others') discourse, hence tributary of a universal Law. On the other, there is pleasure—but it kills—at finding oneself different, irreducible, for one is borne by a simply singular speech, not merging with the others, but then exposed to the black thrusts of a desire that borders on idiolect and aphasia. In other words, if the overly constraining and reductive meaning of a language made up of universals causes us to suffer, the call of the unnamable, on the contrary, issuing from those borders where signification vanishes, hurls us into the void of a psychosis that appears henceforth as the solidary reverse of our universe, saturated with interpretation, faith, or truth. Within that vise, our only chance to avoid being neither master nor slave of meaning lies in our ability to insure our mastery of it (through technique or knowledge) as well as our passage through it (through play or practice). In a word, jouissance.

Having recourse to psychoanalysis, as I attempt to do, in this work, in order to shed light on a number of borderline-practices of meaning and signification (practices of art and literature), bears, I hope, no relation to that "plague" that Freud, once more the prophet, promised America when he brought his discovery of the unconscious to its shores. Grafted on to semiology, analysis here is not restricted to themes or phantasms; rather, it scrutinizes the most subtle, the most deeply buried logic of those unities and ultimate relations that weave an identity for subject, or sign, or sentence.

What was necessary was undoubtedly a *desire for language* (is this another way of saying, "sublimation"?), a passion for ventures with meaning and its materials (ranging from colors to sounds, beginning with phonemes, syllables, words), in order to carry a theoretical experience to that point where apparent abstraction is revealed as the apex of archaic, oneiric, nocturnal, or corporeal concreteness, to that point where meaning has not yet appeared (the child), no longer is (the insane person), or else functions as a restructuring (writing, art).

It was perhaps also necessary to be a *woman* to attempt to take up that exorbitant wager of carrying the rational project to the outer borders of the signifying venture of men. . . . But that is another matter, of which this volume nevertheless bears the discreet trace.

In short, the problem of truth, truth of language but also of the discourse that attempts to account for it, makes up the fundamental epistomelogical concern of a journey, a portion of which American readers can see today. Such a "scientific" truth in general, and more so in the presence of language, comes to us from mastery. Saint Augustine knew that already when he noted that the possibility for language to speak the truth could not come from outside, but it "governs the inner workings of the mind itself." In 389 (*De Magístro*) he continues, "Now, the one we consult in such a manner, he is the master, the one of whom it is said that he dwells within the inner man, Christ, that is, the immutable Power of God and eternal wisdom." Such "magistrality" upholds faith as much as science and interpretations—that is what strikes the ear of the semiotician psychoanalyst who tries to articulate an utterance of truth (one should say a style) without censoring what has been learned over a period of two thousand years, but without being confined to it either. Without censoring: for there is language there, and devices dependent on scientific thought can describe it more or less masterfully. But without being confined to it: for there is more than a language object in the heterogeneous process of signifiance. The conjunction of those two propositions has a dramatic impact on thought and, more generally, on the speaking subject. Analytic discourse, by holding to it, is perhaps the only one capable of addressing this untenable place where our speaking species resides, threatened by madness beneath the emptiness of heaven.

Julia Kristeva

Translators' Note

Julia Kristeva's work at once demands and defies translation. In responding to that challenge, our primary concern has been to make her work as accessible as possible to an English-speaking audience. It may be that in spite of our efforts a number of awkwardnesses remain. If our undertaking has proved to be at all successful, it is in no small part due to the editorial sensibility of Leon S. Roudiez. We would like to thank him and Julia Kristeva herself for their continued encouragement and support in bringing this project to completion.

Tom Gora and Alice Jardine

ACKNOWLEDGMENTS

For assistance given, in matters large or small, scriptural or factual, much appreciation is due to the following friends and colleagues who cheerfully gave whatever information or time was requested: Robert Austerlitz, James A. Coulter, Robert D. Cumming, Arthur C. Danto, Howard McP. Davis, Richard F. Gustafson, William T. H. Jackson, Bert M-P. Leefmans, Marie-Rose Logan, Sidney Morgenbesser, Luciano Rebay, Alan Roland, Meyer Schapiro, and Marsha Wagner.

Particular gratitude goes to Julia Kristeva for taking time to respond to many questions and for going over the translation of a number of her essays; quite a few erroneous interpretations were thus avoided. I must, of course, bear responsibility for any that remain and for all other infelicities as well.

L. S. R.

DESIRE IN LANGUAGE

INTRODUCTION

For nothing is secret, that shall not be made manifest: neither any thing hid, that shall not be known and come abroad.

—Luke 8:17

At a colloquium on psychoanalysis and politics held in Milan in December of 1973, Julia Kristeva responded to a question concerning her own paper by saying, "I never intended to follow a correct Marxist line, and I hope I am not *correctly* following any other line whatsoever."[1] Indeed, when dealing with concepts borrowed from various disciplines, be they called Marxism, linguistics, philosophy, phychoanalysis, or semiology (with the latter two now the main derivations), she has fitted them to the object of her investigations. Not "applying" a theory, but allowing practice to test theory, letting the two enter into a dialectical relationship. She cannot claim originality in following such a procedure; just the same, her approach is, intellectually speaking, the only fruitful way leading to original discovery. I suspect Roland Barthes had in mind something of the sort when he credited her with delivering a new knowledge; he wrote, in 1970, "Julia Kristeva always destroys the latest preconception, the one we thought we could be comforted by, the one of which we could be proud."[2] The impact her articles and books have had in France (and are beginning to have elsewhere) testifies to the effectiveness of her strategy.

Born in Bulgaria in 1941 to a middle-class family, she received her early schooling from French nuns. Then came the inevitable Communist Party children's groups, and, later, the party youth organizations. As Kristeva put it in an interview published by *Le Nouvel Observateur*, "I learned [Lenin's] *Materialism and Empiriocriticism* at the same time as I did the square of the hypotenuse."[3] At one point, she wanted to pursue a career in astronomy or physics, but the main research and training center was in the Soviet Union, and only children of party cadres could aspire to enroll there. As it turned out, the first job she held was that of journalist; she worked on a newspaper for communist youth while pursuing literary studies at the university. This happened at a time when Eastern Europe was still reaping benefits from the "thaw" that followed the Twentieth Congress denunciation of the late Stalin by Krushchev, and as a result she was able to meet newspaper correspondents from many countries, receive books from abroad, and discuss those idea that came from the West. It was, however, as a doctoral-fellowship holder that she went to Paris early in 1966—and stayed.

Tzvetan Todorov, who had emigrated from Bulgaria a few years earlier, steered her to Lucien Goldmann's seminar; there began a research and writing process that has already resulted in publication of an impressive array of theoretical works. Her first (although not the first to be published) was *Le Texte du roman* (1970), an analysis of the birth of the novel in late medieval times. Using Antoine de La Sale's *Le Petit Jehan de Saintré* (1456) as emblematic paradigm, and drawing from what she calls the "postformalism" of Mikhail Bakhtin, Kristeva presents an original view of the concept of "genre"; putting that traditional concept aside, she sees what we call the novel as a narrative texture, woven together with strands borrowed from other verbal practices such as carnivalesque writing, courtly lyrics, hawkers' cries, and scholastic treatises. She also showed, among other things, how this texture is intertwined with something akin to what Michel Foucault has called *episteme*, for which she coined the neologism "ideologeme." The texture of the novel, as it slowly evolved, managed to become free of the "ideologeme" of symbolism (within which the medieval epic had flourished); in that process, however, it became caught up in the "ideologeme" of signs, which she sees as weighing heavily on its entire history; it has resulted in a gradual and nonconscious elaboration of concepts such as "author" (a person having final "authority" over the "meaning" of his achievement), "literature," "reading public," and *"oeuvre"*; such concepts, together with adherence to the sign-system, tied it to bourgeois class values— all of which reached the apex of their development or acceptance in the nineteenth century. Her essay, "The Bounded Text," a translation of which is included here, develops a number of these points.

Kristeva arrived in Paris when literary "structuralism" was most fashionable in avant-garde circles and also (as Jean Piaget remarked) at cocktail parties.[4] The term, where literary criticism is concerned, does belong within inverted commas, for I agree with Piaget's observation, made in the late sixties, that "one can only be disturbed by the current modishness of structuralism, which weakens and distorts it."[5] Kristeva's bent of mind, which I emphasized at the very outset, together with an experience of Russian postformalism dating back to her Sofia days, preserved her from uncritical acceptance of that fashionable trend. Rather than cocktail parties, she frequented the Ecole Pratique des Hautes Etudes, and the Centre National de Recherche Scientifique; she held the position of research assistant at Claude Lévi-Strauss's Laboratory of Social Anthropology. Possibly, too, Goldmann's example played a part; his own "genetic structuralism" managed to maintain the presence of factors such as genesis, history, and subject (i.e., the writing agent), which many literary "structuralists" ignored. At any rate, the volume of essays published in 1969, Σημείωτίχὴ / *Recherches pour une sémanalyse*, manifests both the presence of genuine structuralist thought and her own critical distance from its literary distortions.

This book, appearing with the *Tel Quel* imprint, also emphasized an association with that group that actually began two years earlier when her "Pour une sémiologie des paragrammes" appeared in the Spring, 1967, issue of *Tel Quel*. The review, under the forceful editorship of Philippe Sollers, had by the end of the sixties become quite influential among avant-garde writers and intellectuals.[6] From the title of Kristeva's collection of essays, it is now clear that semiotics, the science of signs, provided her with an important research tool. This came about, it would seem, because of an awareness of the role, both necessary and insufficient, played by linguistics in a scientific approach to the text. Necessary, because a writer obviously works with and within language; insufficient, because he is involved in a signifying process that operates through language and cannot be assimilated to its everyday function as instrument of simple communication. The term "semiotics" (and its Greek counterpart as used in the title) comes from Charles S. Peirce; "semiology" was defined by Ferdinand de Saussure; and Roland Barthes had first published his "Eléments de sémiologie" in the November, 1964, issue of *Communications.* But Kristeva did not merely follow a path that had been cleared by others. Characteristically, she introduced a new word into the second half of her title—"sémanalyse," defined as a "critique of meaning, of its elements and its laws."[7] Two essays from that collection have been translated for the present volume; the already mentioned "Bounded Text," and "Word, Dialogue, and Novel," in which she expands on ideas introduced by Mikhail Bakhtin and presents the often misunderstood concept of "intertextuality."

Perhaps more than modish "structuralism," what marked the year of Kristeva's arrival in Paris was the appearance of the nine-hundred-page volume of Jacques Lacan's *Ecrits.* And indeed, in conjunction with Marxism and linguistics, psychoanalysis was to have a determining influence in the development of her theories. She considered it so important that, some years later, in order to provide a material basis for her speculations, she underwent psychoanalytic training and started a practice that she fitted in with her obligations as a member of the faculty at the University of Paris VII. Earlier, in *Le Texte du roman,* her major references were Marx, Engels, Lukács, Saussure, Jakobson, Benveniste, Chomsky, Peirce, and Bakhtin; Lacan is only mentioned once, in passing. In Σημειωτιχὴ he is, with Freud, the object of frequent footnotes. That she was headed in that direction might well have been deduced from a reading of the previously mentioned essay, "Pour une sémiologie des paragrammes," written at the same time as her *Texte du roman*. Her emphasis on Saussure's anagrams, which were virtually unknown until Jean Starobinski brought them to light in the early sixties,[8] clearly reveals a convergence with Lacan's linking of language to the unconscious. Lacan referred to the dual planes on which language operates, to the possibility we have "of using it in order to signify *something quite other* than what it says."[9] Matters are more complex than the simple ambiguity suggested here, but briefly stated, that duality is such as to make it possible for semanalysis to be a critique of meaning (assuming that meaning is part of a fixed, symbolic system). Put another way, it is what enables instincts to challenge authority without producing anarchy—what enables authority to contain instincts without resorting to concentration camps.

Testifying to Kristeva's early training in the sciences, there are in Σημειωτιχὴ a number of references, metaphors, and formulas borrowed from mathematics. While they are pertinent to her argument, they do tend to complicate or even obscure matters for those readers who do not share her intellectual background. Fortunately for the latter, surface displays of mathematical knowledge subside in subsequent works, while the scientific urge to make the secret manifest remains ever present.

In a major work, *La Révolution du langage poétique* (1974), she brings together many of the strands that run through earlier theoretical essays. While her specific aim is to analyse the alteration, already noted by Foucault in *The Order of Things* and previously discussed in detail by Maurice Blanchot from a literary point of view, that marked several writers' relation to language during the late nineteenth century (and she does examine, in detail, works by Lautréamont and Mallarmé), the most valuable portion of this book, in my opinion, lies in its first two hundred pages entitled "Préliminaires théoriques." The object of her investigation in these pages is not called literature, for this is an ideologically loaded term that enables one to exclude any number of writings (for ethical, political, social, or even medical reasons) and exalt others by placing them in an untouchable category (something like "masterpieces of all time"): rather, she starts from the concept of "poetic language" as introduced by Russian formalists. Poetic language is distinct from language as used for ordinary communication—but not because it may involve a so-called departure from a norm; it is almost an otherness of language. It is the language of materiality as opposed to transparency (where the word is forgotten for the sake of the object or concept designated), a language in which the writer's effort is less to deal rationally with those objects or concepts words seem to encase than to work, consciously or not, with the sounds and rhythms of words in transrational fashion (in Ossip Brik's phrase) and effecting what Victor Shklovski called "semantic displacements."[10] Poetic language includes the language of Shakespeare, Racine, or Mallarmé; it also includes that of the Marquis de Sade, Antonin Artaud, Louis Wolfson, and of psychotics as well; and, of course, many more in between.

Summarizing the contribution Kristeva has made in *La Révolution du langage poétique* is beyond the scope of this introduction. Still, one of the basic working concepts of that volume needs to be presented; I shall do so briefly, and readers should be cautioned that brevity necessarily entails a modicum of distortion.

Here, as in other essays, she often refers to the "speaking subject." One should always bear in mind that this is a split subject—divided between unconscious and conscious motivations, that is, between physiological processes and social constraints. It can never be identified with anything like Husserl's transcendental ego. The activities and performances of the speaking subject are the result of a dialectical process, something previous linguistic theories, as she examines them, tended to ignore by emphasizing either one at the expense of the other. Linguists, by and large, have elaborated systems where one should analyze a process (and those who do, like Chomsky, tend to preserve a Cartesian or phenomenological subject); they have described stability where one should acknowledge mobility, unity where there is contradiction. On the one hand, what we have been offered so far are systems of meaning depending on consciousness; on the other, she proposes to analyze a signifying process, which presupposes a split subject—hence two heterogeneous levels. To state this in different terms, the object of her investigations is no longer language (as in structuralism), or discourse (as in phenomenology would have it), or even enunciation; rather, it is the discourse of a split subject—and this again involves her in psychoanalysis.

Allowing her to account for such splitting, Kristeva has posited two types of signifying processes to be analyzed within any production of meaning: a "semiotic" one and a "symbolic" one. The semiotic process relates to the *chora*, a term meaning "receptacle," which she borrowed from Plato, who describes it as "an invisible and formless being which receives all things and in some mysterious way partakes of the intelligible, and is most incomprehensible."[11] It is also anterior to any space, an economy of primary processes articulated by Freud's instinctual drives (*Triebe*) through condensation and displacement, and where social and family structures make their imprint through the mediation of the maternal body. While the *chora*'s articulation is uncertain, undetermined, while it lacks thesis or position, unity or identity, it is the aim of Kristeva's practice to remove what Plato saw as "mysterious" and "incomprehensible" in what he called "mother and receptacle" of all things—and the essays presented in this collection also proceed in the direction of such an elucidation. The symbolic process refers to the establishment of sign and syntax, paternal function, grammatical and social constraints, symbolic law. In short, the signifying process, as increasingly manifest in "poetic language," results from a particular articulation between symbolic and semiotic dispositions; it could be termed "catastrophe," given the meaning the word has in René Thom's theory. The speaking subject is engendered as belonging to both the semiotic *chora* and the symbolic device, and that accounts for its eventual split nature.

The signifying process may be analyzed through two features of the text, as constituted by poetic language: a phenotext, which is the language of communication and has been the object of linguistic analysis; a genotext, which may be detected by means of certain aspects or elements of language, even though it is not linguistic per se. Different kinds of writing are variously affected by this heterogeneous process. A theoretical treatise in mathematics is almost pure phenotext; some of Artaud's pages display a genotext that is nearly visible to the naked eye; fiction, in its traditional narrative guise, was dominated by the symbolic (it was mainly a phenotext), but in recent times it has increasingly been affected by the semiotic (i.e., the genotext plays a greater role; see Kristeva's discussion of a Sollers text, in "The Novel as Polylogue," and of Céline's writing, in "From One Identity to an Other," both translated here); and poetic language covers that wide body of texts where the signifying process can be seen at work—provided one uses the proper tools of analysis.

In the meantime, Kristeva had joined the editorial board of *Tel Quel* where her name appeared on the masthead for the first time in the summer issue of 1970. In the public eye, she can no longer be considered apart from the philosophical and political stances assumed by the review, especially those of Philippe Sollers, who, for practical purposes, *is* the review. In fact, I believe matters are a bit more complex; for if one can obviously not dissociate her from *Tel Quel*, one cannot completely identify her with it either, and there is a constant dialectical process at work, one of intellectual action and interaction. Thus, in the late sixties, she was as involved as other members of the group (which then included Jean-Louis Baudry, Jean Pierre Faye, Marcelin Pleynet, Jean Ricardou, Jacqueline Risset, Denis Roche, Pierre Rottenberg, and Jean Thibaudeau) in a dialogue with the French Communist Party; there was the possibility that such a party, having developed within the political and cultural framework of French democracy, would be more open to interior discussions or even challenges, and would not follow the path taken by Eastern European parties. Unlike others, however, Kristeva had a direct experience of Eastern communism; this may have been a factor in the arguments that must have taken place at the time. At any rate, after developments that were uncomfortably reminiscent of the Surrealists' affair with communism forty years earlier, the break came in 1971, causing a split within the ranks of *Tel Quel*. The break was abundantly publicized when an independent-minded Italian communist, Maria-Antonietta Macciochi, published *De la Chine* late in 1971, a book ignored by the pro-USSR French Communist Party but heralded by *Tel Quel*. Apparently the Italians were more like what the French were supposed to be: one recalls that, two decades earlier or so, Jean-Paul Sartre had found it possible to have open discussions with Italian communists but not with French ones. Rejection of the Communist Party signaled for *Tel Quel* the beginning of a period of considerable interest in, occasionally verging on enthusiasm for, Mao Zedong's version of communism; this lasted until the Chinese leader's death in 1976.

In 1974 Kristeva went to China with Philippe Sollers, Roland Barthes, Marcelin Pleynet, and François Wahl. What strikes me most, in her writings about that journey, is her sense of total estrangement.

> A large crowd is seated in the sun; they are waiting for us without a word, without a motion. Their eyes are calm, not really inquisitive but slightly amused or uneasy, piercing at any rate, and sure of belonging to a community with which we shall never have anything in common. They do not stare at the man or at the woman in our group, at the young or the old, at the blond or the brunette, at some specific feature of face or body. It is as though they had discovered bizarre and amusing animals, harmless but mad.[12]

Questions about the relevancy of the Chinese experiment, relevancy to Europeans that is, undoubtedly found a way into the meditations. André Malraux, in 1926, had already understood that the West could not hope to apply Chinese practice or concepts to solving its problems. That one can learn from China only in a complex, mediated fashion may well have been the postulate she took with her on her journey. In specific terms, she was curious to find out what happened when the anarchist and Taoist strands of Chinese culture (she was there at the height of the anti-Confucius campaign) were grafted on a Chinese version of Marxism. In other words, she went to China as a semanalyst.

After Mao's death, when one considers the almost immediate reaction of the party apparatus, an impression was made (or confirmed) that communists the world over, differences between national parties notwithstanding, had merely succeeded in replacing the oppressive regimes they overthrew with others equally or more oppressive and "concentrationary." Such at least, was Sollers's reaction: he spoke of a Chinese "drama" (an American might have said "tragedy") and asked whether this was what "Marxism" (his quotation marks) always added up to.[13] Kristeva, however, owing to her Bulgarian experience, probably did not feel the shattering disillusion some former Maoists went through in 1977. Some of those who called themselves "new philosophers" had turned Marxism into an ideal or a mystique. For her, I believe it was more a conceptual tool towards social truth, and now it was blunted. As with the French Communist Party a few years earlier, a sort of honeymoon with socialism was over. Nevertheless, she held on to Mao's saying about going from defeat to defeat until victory is won—modifying it to read, "Until truth is attained." Some form of Socialism is also to be preferred, in her view, over practical alternatives available to the French people; an intellectual, however, can no longer be counted on as an uncritical ally of the Left, and his or her position should be one of dissent. Dissenting from all political power groups, be they in the government or in the opposition, the intellectual's position should be one of continuously challenging all orthodoxies. He or she is in exile, "among which I include myself: exiled from socialism and a Marxist rationality but, without bitterly rejecting these, attempting to analyse them, to dissolve them—assuming that they are the forceful ideas, the very strength of our times."[14]

Late in the same year that saw her in China, Kristeva published *Des Chinoises*—the first book of hers to have been translated into English (*About Chinese Women*, 1977). It is no doubt significant that she focused on that aspect of the situation in China; subsequently she explained that "the history of Chinese communism is at one with a history of women's liberation."[15] To understand this, we need both historical and cultural perspective; we need to realize on the one hand how little Western women have in common with Chinese women from a social and cultural standpoint, and on the other what it must have meant for Chinese women to emerge out of a feudal age, of which bound feet and forced marriages were the most visible symbols. And Mao himself is reported to have said that "man could not be free unless woman was also liberated."

Kristeva's feminist position is no more orthodox than her other stands. Since this is a domain through which I am hardly qualified to roam, I shall let her speak for herself:

I am quite dedicated to the feminist movement but I think feminism, or any other movement, need not expect unconditional backing on the part of an intellectual woman. I think the time has come to emerge out of the "for-women-only" practice, out of a kind of mythicizing of femininity. [. . .] I have the impression [some feminists] are relying too much on an existentialist concept of woman, a concept that attaches a guilt complex to the maternal function. Either one has children, but that means one is not good for anything else, or one does not, and then it becomes possible to devote oneself to serious undertakings.

As far as I am concerned, childbearing as such never seemed inconsistent with cultural activity, and that is the point I try to make when talking to feminist groups. [. . .] Mallarmé asked, "What is there to say concerning childbirth?" I find that question much more pungent than Freud's well-known, "What does a woman want?" Indeed, what does it mean to give birth to a child? Psychoanalysts do not much talk about it. [. . .] The arrival of a child is, I believe, the first and often the only opportunity a woman has to experience the Other in its radical separation from herself, that is, as an object of love.[16]

Essays written between 1973 and 1976 and collected in *Polylogue* (1977) add the problem of sexual difference and that of child development (especially its language-learning aspect) to the concerns that were present in the earlier ones. The scope of her investigation also widens, as analyses of paintings are added to those of written texts. Of the seventeen essays in *Polylogue*, eight are included here.

The essay on Bellini deals with a man's relationship to the mother and to woman as mother by means of an original analysis of that painter's Madonnas. In "Giotto's Joy," Kristeva examines painting as she did poetic texts in *La Révolution du langage poétique*—at least in part. As phonic effects were seen to contribute, in nonconscious fashion, to the signifying process in the texts of Lautréamont and Mallarmé, likewise the retinal perception of the various colors of light (e.g., which color is perceived first as darkness recedes, which first as the child develops) is taken into consideration when accounting for the significance of Giotto's frescoes. Not that alone, of course: readers will soon be aware of the complex, interrelated fashion in which different fields of knowledge are brought to bear, and necessarily so, on literary and artistic exegesis.

I believe each one of the ten essays I selected for this volume sheds light not only on the object of analysis but on Kristeva's method as well. The discussion of Roland Barthes's criticism, in particular, gives her the opportunity to stress what, to her, are the positive aspects of his approach; in so doing, she provides us with a summary of her own point of view. For a capsuled statement of the basic principles that underlie her critical theory, I would go to the "triple thesis" set forth in the subsection entitled "Two Channels of Discovery: Dialectics and Sociology."

Kristeva brings to our own critical practice and textual theory something that is unmistakably alien but also, if one is willing to give this some thought, absolutely necessary. The article Roland Barthes devoted to her first collection of essays was given an ambiguous title; it could be translated either as "The Stranger" or "The Alien." (French language, with its more restricted vocabulary, sometimes allows for pregnant polysemy.) Barthes's specific reference is to semiotics, a feminine noun in French, whose "historical role presently is to be the intruder, the third element, the one that disturbs. . . ."[17] His implicit reference is also to Kristeva's own status, for which the trivial notion of nationality is little more than emblematic. (Ionesco and Adamov, Todorov and Greimas, Tzara and Beckett, Gris and Picasso, to name a few, are or were practically indigenous to the French scene.) She is the stranger because her writing does not conform to standard French theoretical writing (just as it is markedly different from other contemporary versions of it, like Foucault's or Derrida's), and because she confronts French writing practice with those emanating from other cultures, French theory with that issuing from other countries. Her status as stranger proved to have been an asset in France; it should be an asset in this country as well.

English-language critics have, until recently, been reluctant to confront literary texts with theory; rather, the emphasis has been on practical criticism (to borrow I. A. Richards's classic title) or on taxonomy (Northrop Frye); in our occasional forays into theory, we have been inclined to look for models (as Angus Fletcher did, for his study on allegory, in Freud's *Totem and Taboo*). To theory, we often prefer method, as the latter bears a greater likelihood of practical application—forgetting, perhaps, that this can lead to sclerosis.

Now, however, there are signs pointing to a possible change in this state of affairs. A perusal of articles published in a periodical such as *Diacritics* does reveal an increasing interest in theoretical writing;[18] and there are other journals moving in the same direction. At this juncture, lest such a growing appeal turn into fascination and lead to purely abstract speculation, Kristeva's work reminds us that theory is inseparable from practice—that theory evolves out of practice and is modified by further practice; and that the disciplines that enable us to undertake a scientific investigation of written texts, that will make their secret manifest, can never exclude the writing subject who undertakes the investigation from the results of that investigation.

Notes on the Translation and on Terminology

Well, here it is, the result of much labor. What else can translators say after working away at a set of original, groundbreaking essays?

There were days, perhaps only euphoric hours, when, contemplating the work that lay ahead, they might have entertained hopes of having Julia Kristeva come out, in English, reading like Edmund Wilson. Obviously she does not; the chances are that she never will— and probably should not anyway. If the translation is faithful, and that much, I believe, has been accomplished, the next thing to wish is that it be readable (even though not always easy to read) and still preserve some of the particular flavor that characterizes the French original.

I should emphasize that, in most instances, Kristeva's writing is not a "text" in the strong sense the word has acquired in recent (mainly French) critical theory. It was not conceived as "poetic language," it is not a body of words in a state of ferment and *working*, like "beer when the barm is put in" (Bacon, as quoted in *Webster 2*). And yet, there are sequences here and there that come pretty close to it.

In the main, nevertheless, it is a form of expository prose that has something specific to communicate. Concepts, a method, and, quite significantly, a choice of position, situation, or place from which to speak (or write). She is nearly always, if ever so slightly, off-centered in relation to all established doctrines (Marxian, Freudian, Saussurian, Chomskian, for instance). To put it another way, while she may borrow terminology from several disciplines and theoretical writers, her discourse is not the orthodox discourse of any one of them: the vocabulary is theirs but the syntax is her own. Such a stance carries inevitable consequences in return for the terminology, which at first gives the impression of having been thrown off balance by the shift in discourse—and related difficulties crop up for the translators, who may be tempted to render matters more conventionally logical, more commonplace.

The following glossary was not really prepared with a view to solving such problems; the point is rather to identify some of them and explain why a particular word or phrase was chosen in translating an expression used by Kristeva. One should keep in mind that, with few exceptions, these are not neologisms; they are also, on occasion, used with their everyday meanings. Unusual words that are defined within the essays where they appear have not, as a rule, been listed here; nor have those that are part of accepted technical or scientific vocabularies—such as, to name but a few, base, superstructure (Marxism); power of the continuum, next-larger (set theory); catastrophe, fold (catastrophe theory); signifier/signified, deep structure (linguistics); primal scene, cathexis (psychoanalysis); for psychoanalytic terms, the translation is that given by J. Laplanche and J.-B. Pontalis, *Vocabulaire de la psychanalyse* (Paris: Presses Universitaires de France, 1967; revised ed., 1976).

ANAGRAM (*anagramme*). See GRAM.
AUTHOR (*auteur*). When used, it means that the discussion takes place
within a specific ideological context where the writer is seen as
endowed with "authorial" attributes, such as full conscious control
of the writing process and "authority" over the meaning of what has

been written. Whenever possible the term has been avoided and replaced with the more neutral "writer."

BOUNDED (*clos*). The verb *clore* is father formal and even slightly archaic; in everyday usage it has survived in a number of set phrases such as *clore les débats* (formally bring a discussion to an end) or *huis-clos* ("in camera"). Our verb "to close" corresponds to the French *fermer*; "to bound" is less usual and its connotations are not far from those of *clore*, while "to limit" would convey (especially in the past participle) the unwanted connotation of something lacking. William Faulkner, recalling how he wrote *As I Lay Dying*, gave his description of what Kristeva calls a "bounded" novel: "Before I ever put pen to paper and set down the first word, I knew what the last word would be and almost where the last period would fall."

BEING, BEINGS (*être, étant*). Translating such philosophical distinction as conveyed in German by *Sein* vs. *Seiende* is easy for the French who can talk of *être* vs. *étant* but rather awkward when it comes to English. Translators of Heidegger apparently agree that *Sein* should be rendered as (capitalized) "Being"; there is less agreement as to *Seiende*. Rather than "entity," it would seem preferable to choose, as in German and French, another form of the verb "to be"—here practically the same form, "beings," but lower-case and set in the plural to avoid any possible confusion with the ordinary use of "being."

DIALECTICS (*dialectique*). Those unfamiliar with Marxist theory should keep in mind that Marx's "dialectics" is the opposite of Hegel's, and that Kristeva refers both to Marx and Hegel in her essays. (Marx: "My dialectical method is not only different from the Hegelian, but is its direct opposite.") In a nutshell, and considering *only one* aspect of dialectics as emphasized by Lenin, with Hegel there is thesis, then antithesis, and finally synthesis; with Marx there is contradiction inherent in all things, which results in a cleavage, a struggle between the two elements of the contradiction, elimination of the weaker element, and then, within the victorious one, there is a contradiction, etc. (Lenin: "The splitting of a single whole and the cognition of its contradictory parts . . . is the *essence* . . . of dialectics.") Marx often stressed that he was giving a naturalistic or materialistic account of dialectical development. One should note that Kristeva also takes into account a post-Heideggerian critique of dialectics, introducing the concept of heterogeneity and referring to catastrophe theory.

DRIVE (*pulsion*). This corresponds to Freud's *Trieb*, which has been mistranslated, in the *Standard Edition*, as "instinct." For those accustomed to the latter, in order to ease the transition, I have often qualified "drive" with "instinctual." To translate *pulsionnel*, however, since "drive" does not have an appropriate adjectival form, I have had to use "instinctual" (as opposed to "instinctive") in a number of instances. As there are no references to "instinct" as such in these essays, that should not cause any confusion.

GRAM (*gramme*). From the Greek *gramma*, that which is written. Used, especially in Kristeva's earlier essays, to designate the basic, material element of writing—the marking, the trace. It is the root of both the familiar "grammar" and the more recent "grammatology," the science of writing, defined as such by I. J. Gelb (*A Study of Writing*, 1952). Both "gram" and "grammatology" have been given wide dissemination by Jacques Derrida. More significantly for Kristeva's work, the same root is at the basis of Ferdinand de Saussure's "anagrams," which he thought he discovered in ancient Latin Saturnian verse (Cf. Jean Starobinski, *Les Mots sous les mots*), and which was the starting point for her essay, "Pour une sémiologie des paragrammes" (*Tel Quel*, Spring 1967). This was an early statement of her concern for the nonrational, nonsymbolic operation of signifying practice in poetic language. "Paragrams" refer not merely to changing letters (*Webster's* definition) but to the infinite possibilities of a text seen as an open network of indicial connections.

IDEOLOGY (*idéologie*). The term is used in the contemporary Marxist sense. The concept, posited by Marx and Engels, was used by them in a variety of interconnected senses. Louis Althusser has defined "ideology" as a system of representations (images, myths, ideas, or concepts) endowed with a specific historical context and functioning within a given society. It is related to the culture (in its sociological rather than humanistic sense) of that society, and to the sum of its prejudices and preconceptions. In most cases "ideology" is transmitted on a preconscious level, since it is usually taken for granted, considered as "natural," hence neither repressed (unconscious) nor intentionally propounded (conscious). "Dominant ideology" is the ideology existing and operating within the dominant class of a given society so as to further the economic and political interests of that class.

INTERTEXTUALITY (*intertextualité*). This French word was originally introduced by Kristeva and met with immediate success; it has since been much used and abused on both sides of the Atlantic. The concept, however, has been generally misunderstood. It has nothing to do with matters of influence by one writer upon another, or with the sources of a literary work; it does, on the other hand, involve the components of a *textual system* such as the novel, for instance. It is defined in *La Révolution du langage poétique* as the transposition of one or more *systems* of signs into another, accompanied by a new articulation of the enunciative and denotative position. Any SIGNIFYING PRACTICE (*q.v.*) is a field (in the sense of space traversed by lines of force) in which various signifying systems undergo such a transposition.

JOUISSANCE (*jouissance*). The English word "jouissance" rests in dictionaries, forgotten by all save a few Renaissance scholars. The OED attests that it was still used by eighteenth-century poets—e.g., William Dodd, in a 1767 poem. In *Webster 2*, one of the words used to define "jouissance" is "enjoyment." Indeed, the two words share a common etymology, and a few centuries ago both French and English cognates had similar denotations covering the field of law and the activity of sex. While the English term has lost most of its sexual connotations, the French one has kept *all* of its earlier meanings. Kristeva gives "jouissance" a meaning closely related to that given the word by Jacques Lacan, who discussed it in his 1972–73 seminar, which, when published in France, bore a photograph of Bernini's sculpture, the *Ecstasy of St. Teresa*, on its cover. What is significant is the *totality* of enjoyment that is covered by the word "jouissance," both in common usage and in Lacan; what distinguishes common usage from Lacan's usage (and Kristeva's as well) is that in the former the several meanings are kept separate and precipitated, so to speak, by the context, whereas in the latter they are simultaneous—"jouissance" is sexual, spiritual, physical, conceptual at one and the same time. Lacan speaks of *jouissance sexuelle* and of *jouissance phallique*, but in each case "jouissance" is both grammatically and conceptually qualified; and that sort of "jouissance" "does not involve the Other as such," for it merely deals with the OTHER (*q.v.*) and its (her/his) sexual attributes. The "jouissance" of the Other "is fostered only through infinitude" (*ne se promeut que de l'infinitude*). In Kristeva's vocabulary, sensual, sexual pleasure is covered by *plaisir*; "jouissance" is total joy or ecstasy (without any mystical connotation); also, through the working of the signifier, this implies the presence of meaning (*jouissance = j'ouïs sens* = I heard meaning), requiring it by going beyond it.

MATERIALISM (*matérialisme*). A brief reminder: just about everyone knows that there are various forms of materialism, but when dealing with Kristeva's essays (and even though she also deals with Greek materialism), two of these should be kept in mind. First, there is dialectical materialism, that of authentic Marxism; second, there is mechanistic materialism, which is related to determinism, argues from cause to effect in linear, nonreversible fashion, and is sometimes called vulgar Marxism.

NEGATIVITY (*négativité*). A Hegelian concept. "The dissimilarity that obtains in consciousness between the ego and the substance constituting its object is their inner distinction, the factor of negativity in general ... it is their very soul, their moving spirit" (from the Preface to *The Phenomenology of Mind*). It needs to be distinguished from both "nothingness" and "negation"; it is concrete mediation of what it reveals as mere stases—the pure abstractions of Being and nothingness; it can be seen as characterizing the very motion of heterogeneous matter, an "affirmative negativity," a "productive dissolving." Kristeva has reinterpreted such Hegelian notions in *La Révolution du langage poétique*.

OTHER, OTHER (*autre, Autre*). The distinction between the capitalized and the noncapitalized "other" is about the same in Kristeva as in Lacan. The "other" has either commonplace or philosophical meaning (e.g., what exists as an opposite of, or excluded by, something else). When capitalized, the "Other" refers to a hypothetical place or space, that of the pure signifier, rather than to a physical entity or moral category. Lacan: "The unconscious of the subject is the discourse of the other" versus "The Other is, therefore, the place in which is constituted the I who speaks with him who hears." This, however, does not apply to early essays such as "The Bounded Text."

PLACE (*lieu*). The word "place" has been preferred over the more mathematical "locus" (*lieu géométrique*), for it does not convey the latter's precise localization. Kristeva's *lieu* is a hypothetical place, even though constrained by actual forces or presences.

PROCESS (*procès*). Both the English term and its French equivalent cover two areas of meaning. On the one hand, they convey the idea of a continued forward motion possibly accompanied by transformations; on the other, they have a legal meaning that has remained strong in French (*procès*: a legal suit or proceedings), while in English surviving mainly in a few phrases such as "due process" or "process server." Since, in Kristeva's text, the word is used with varying nuances, an attempt has been made to render such nuances according to the context, either by using the word "process" alone or qualifying it with either or both "unsettling" and "questionable"—especially when the subject is in "process." For the subject is "questionable" (in the legal sense) as to its identity, and the process it undergoes is "unsettling" as to its place within the semiotic or symbolic disposition.

SEMIOTIC, SEMIOTICS (*sémiotique*). The French language has had for centuries the possibility of shifting an abstract word's meaning to its concrete counterpart by merely changing gender. Thus *la physique*, meaning the science of physics, becomes *le physique*, meaning bodily or physical attributes. In similar fashion, *la sémiotique* is "semiotics," the science of signs, a fashionable and somewhat overworked term (what semiotics is may be discovered in works such as Umberto Eco's *A Theory of Semiotics*; Kristeva's concerns have sometimes led her to prefer "semanalysis" to "semiotics"—owing to the etymology of "analysis": *analyein*, to dissolve; dissolving the sign, taking it apart, opens up new areas of signification); *le sémiotique* refers to the actual organization, or disposition, within the body, of instinctual drives (hence the "semiotic disposition") as they affect language and its practice, in dialectical conflict with *le symbolique*, i.e., the SYMBOLIC (*q.v.*). See also the introduction to this volume.

SIGNIFIANCE (*signifiance*). "Meaning" corresponds to *sens* and "signification" to *signification*; "significance" thus being available for *signifiance*,
it might seem unnecessary to resurrect the obsolete "signifiance,"
especially since "significance" carries the connotation of covert
rather than ostensible meaning ("The Rubicon . . . was a very
insignificant stream to look at; its significance lay entirely in certain invisible conditions"—George Eliot, as quoted in *Webster 2*).
"Signifiance," nevertheless, has been retained, partly to avoid other
connotations of "significance," partly because of its very obsolete-
ness. *Signifiance*, as Kristeva uses this term, refers to operations that
are both fluid and archaic—with the latter word restricted to its
Freudian sense (see *Introductory Lectures on Psychoanalysis*, Lecture 13).
It refers to the work performed in language (through the heterogeneous articulation of semiotic and symbolic dispositions) that
enables a text to signify what representative and communicative
speech does not say.

SIGNIFYING PRACTICE (*pratique signifiante*). "I shall call signifying practice the establishment and the countervailing of a sign system.
Establishing a sign system calls for the identity of a speaking subject within a social framework, which he recognizes as a basis for
that identity. Countervailing the sign system is done by having the
subject undergo an unsettling, questionable process; this indirectly
challenges the social framework with which he had previously identified, and it thus coincides with times of abrupt changes, renewal,
or revolution in society" (Julia Kristeva, in *La Traversée des signes*).

SPLIT (*clivé*). *Cliver* is used mostly in mineralogy, and it means to split
mica, for instance, into thin leaves—or a diamond according to
its cleavage planes; in either case the division is inherent and natural. All this is important for the metaphorical meaning it has in
Kristeva's work where *clivé* is applied mostly (but not exclusively)
to the SUBJECT (*q.v.*). "Split" is therefore, in theory at least, not the
most appropriate rendering of that term; it has been adopted, nevertheless, because of widespread psychoanalytic usage (the German
Spaltung translates both "cleavage" and "splitting"). Primal repression,
in founding the subject, also effects its first "splitting" into the conscious and the unconscious, and it institutes the signifier/signified

distinction. Both, in Kristeva's theory, are overridden by the dialectical opposition between the SEMIOTIC and the SYMBOLIC (*qq. v.*).

SYMBOLIC, SYMBOLICS (*symbolique*). See general remarks under SEMIOTIC. For Kristeva, *le symbolique* ("the symbolic") is a domain of position and judgment. Genetically speaking, it comes into being later than the semiotic, at the time of the mirror stage; it involves the thetic phase, the identification of subject and its distinction from objects, and the establishment of a sign system. Synchronically speaking, it is always present, even in the semiotic disposition, which cannot exist without constantly challenging the symbolic one.

SUBJECT (*sujet*). Here, this word is constantly used with the meaning it has in psychoanalysis, linguistics, and philosophy, i.e., the thinking, speaking, acting, doing, or writing agent. It is never used to suggest the topic or theme of a work.

TEXT, GENOTEXT, PHENOTEXT (*texte, génotexte, phénotexte*). See the Introduction to this volume.

UNARY SUBJECT (*sujet unaire*). The "unary subject" is closely related to traditional concepts of consciousness, where the self is seen as a homogeneous, consistent whole. It is the subject implicitly posited by science, society, and most political theory and practice. Marx still accepted that notion of the subject, which he inherited from Feuerbach. The phrase, however, was introduced by Kristeva in the wake of Freud's theory of the unconscious and Lacan's elaboration of the same. The "unary subject" is thus not an outdated notion, but it is seen as a momentary stasis or damming up of instinctual drives and the transverbal process; the concept is opposed to those of "split subject" and "subject in process."

WRITING (*écriture*). This word must unfortunately convey two distinct meanings as it corresponds both to *écrit* and to *écriture* (in the recent, stronger sense of the latter term). The situation is somewhat confusing in French, but worse in English. *Ecriture* is what produces "poetic language" or "text" (in the strong sense of *that* word; see the prefatory statement to this glossary). One could possibly use the word "scription" to convey the sense of contemporary *écriture*. But other translators seem to have stood by the word "writing," we have here enough unusual vocabulary as it is, and "writing," in that special sense, is used mainly in the essay on Barthes. Wherever it is used, the context should make the meaning clear. Edmund Wilson once complained that the novels of John Steinbeck were not "written": he came close to using that verb with the meaning described here.

Leon S. Roudiez

The Essays

NOTE

All translations are published here for the first time, with the two following exceptions: (1) a portion of the essay "The Novel as Polylogue" was translated by Carl R. Lovitt and Ann Reilly and published as "Polylogue" in *Contemporary Literature* (Summer 1978), 19(3):336–50 (the present translation was done independently); and (2) an earlier version of "Place Names" appeared in *October* (Fall 1978), 6:93–111.

1

THE ETHICS OF LINGUISTICS

Should a linguist, today, ever happen to pause and query the ethics of his own discourse, he might well respond by doing something else, e.g., engaging in political activity; or else, he might accommodate ethics to the ingenuousness of his good conscience—seeking socio-historical motives for the categories and relations involved in his model. One could thus account for the Janus-like behavior of a prominent modern grammarian; in his linguistic theories he sets forth a logical, normative basis for the speaking subject, while in politics he claims to be an anarchist. Then there are scholars, quite numerous but not so well known, who squeeze into modern linguistic theory a few additional considerations on the role of ideology; or who go no further than to lift their examples out of leftist newspapers when illustrating linguistic propositions.

Now, since the end of the nineteenth century, there have been intellectual, political, and, generally speaking, social ventures that have signaled the outbreak of something quite new within Western society and discourse, which is subsumed in the names of Marx, Nietzsche, and Freud, and their primary goal has been to reformulate an ethics. Ethics used to be a coercive, customary manner of ensuring the cohesiveness of a particular group through the repetition of a code—a more or less accepted apologue. Now, however, the issue of ethics crops up wherever a code (mores, social contract) must be shattered in order to give way to the free play of negativity, need, desire, pleasure, and jouissance, before being put together again, although temporarily and with full knowledge of what is involved. Fascism and Stalinism stand for the barriers that the new adjustment between a law and its transgression comes against.

Meanwhile, linguistics is still bathed in the aura of *systematics* that prevailed at the time of its inception. It is discovering the rules governing the coherence of our fundamental social code: language, either system of signs or strategy for the transformation of logical sequences. The ethical foundations for this belong to the past: in their work, contemporary linguists think like seventeenth-century men, while structuralist logic can be made to work only with primitive societies or their surviving elements. As wardens of repression and rationalizers of the social contract in its most solid substratum (discourse), linguists carry the Stoic tradition to its conclusion. The epistemology underlying linguistics and the ensuing cognitive processes (structuralism, for example), even though constituting a bulwark against irrational destruction and sociologizing dogmatism, seem helplessly anachronistic when faced with the contemporary mutations of subject and society. Even though "formalism" might have been right, contrary to Zhdanov, neither can think the rhythm of Mayakovsky through to his suicide or Khlebnikov's glossolalias to his disintegration—with the young Soviet state as backdrop.

For, as soon as linguistics was established as a science (through Saussure, for all intents and purposes), its field of study was thus hemmed in [*suturé*]; the problem of *truth* in linguistic discourse became dissociated from any notion of the *speaking subject*. Determining *truth* was reduced to a seeking out of the object-utterance's internal coherence, which was predetermined by the coherence of the particular metalinguistic theory within which the search was conducted.

Any attempt at reinserting the "speaking subject," whether under the guise of a Cartesian subject or any other subject of enunciation more or less akin to the transcendental ego (as linguists make use of it), resolves nothing as long as that subject is not posited as the place, not only of structure and its regulated transformation, but especially, of its loss, its outlay.

It follows that formulating the problem of linguistic ethics means, above all, compelling linguistics to change its object of study. The speech practice that should be its object is one in which signified structure (sign, syntax, signification) is defined within boundaries that can be shifted by the advent of a semiotic rhythm that no system of linguistic communication has yet been able to assimilate. It would deflect linguistics toward a consideration of language as articulation of a heterogeneous process, with the speaking subject leaving its imprint on the dialectic between the articulation and its process. In short, this would establish *poetic language* as the object of linguistics' attention in its pursuit of truth in language. This does not necessarily mean, as is often said today, that poetic language is subject to *more* constraints than "ordinary language." It does mean that we must analyze those elements of the complex operation that I shall call poetic language (in which the dialectics of the subject is inscribed) that are screened out by ordinary language, i.e., *social constraint.* I shall then be talking about something other than language—a practice *for which any particular language is the margin.* The term "poetry" has meaning only insofar as it makes this kind of studies acceptable to various educational and cultural institutions. But the stakes it entails are totally different; what is implied is that language, and thus sociability, are defined by boundaries admitting of upheaval, dissolution, and transformation. Situating our discourse near such boundaries might enable us to endow it with a current ethical impact. In short, the ethics of a linguistic discourse may be gauged in proportion to the poetry that it presupposes.

A most eminent modern linguist believed that, in the last hundred years, there had been only two significant linguists in France: Mallarmé and Artaud. As to Heidegger, he retains currency, *in spite of everything*, because of his attentiveness to language and "poetic language" as an opening up of beings; as an openness that is checked but nonetheless occurs; as a struggle between world and earth; artistic creations are all conceived in the image of poetic language where the "Being" of "beings" is fulfilled and on which, as a consequence, "History" is grounded. If modern art, which is post-Hegelian, sounds a rhythm in language capable of stymieing any subjugated work or logic, this discredits only that closure in Heidegger's reflections that systematizes Being, beings and their historial veracity. But such discredit does not jeopardize poetry's logical stake, inasmuch as poetry is a practice of the speaking subject, consequently implying a dialectic between limits, both signified and signifying, and the setting of a pre- and trans-logical rhythm solely within this limit. Similarly, modern art's odyssey nevertheless remains the field where the possibility of History and dialectic struggle can be played out (before these become a particular history and a concrete struggle), since this artistic practice is the laboratory of a minimal signifying structure, its maximum dissolution, and the eternal return of both.

One might submit that Freud's discovery of the unconscious provided the necessary conditions for such a reading of poetic language. This would be true for the history of *thought*, but not for the history of *poetic practice*. Freud himself considered writers as his predecessors. Avant-garde movements of the twentieth century, more or less unaware of Freud's discovery, propounded a practice, and sometimes even a knowledge of language and its subject, that kept pace with, when they did not precede, Freudian breakthroughs. Thus, it was entirely possible to remain alert to this avant-garde laboratory, to perceive its experiments in a way that could be qualified only as a "love" relationship—and therefore, while bypassing Freud, to perceive the high stakes of any language as *always-already* poetic. Such, I believe, was the path taken by Roman Jakobson. It should not be surprising, then, that it is his discourse and his conception of linguistics, and those of no other linguist, that could contribute to the theory of the unconscious—allowing us to see it being made and unmade—*poiein* [ποιεῖν]—like the language of any subject.

There is no denying Jakobson's contributions toward establishing phonology and structural linguistics in general, toward Slavic studies and research into language acquisition, and toward epistemology and the history of linguistic discourse in its relationship to contemporary or past philosophy and society. But beyond these contributions lies *foremost* the heed given by Jakobson to poetic language; this constitutes the uniqueness of his research, providing its ethical dimension, while at the same time maintaining the openness of present-day linguistic discourse, pointing out, for example, those blockings that cause it to have problems with semantics. Consequently, by virtue of its equally historical and poetic concern, Jakobson's linguistics appears to bracket the technical nature of some contemporary tendencies (such as generative grammar), and to leap from the beginning of our century, when linguistics was not yet hemmed in, to the contemporary period when it must open up in order to have something to say about the speaking subject. Precursor and predecessor, Jakobson nevertheless also accepted the task of providing a concrete and rigorous description, thereby maintaining science's limitative requirements; in this way, he defined the origin and the end of the linguistic episteme, which in recent years has taken upon itself to oversee all thinking, although, in fact, it is merely a symptom of the drama experienced by the Western subject as it attempts to master and structure not only the logos but also its pre- and trans-logical breakouts. *Irony*, alone, piercing through the linguist's metalanguage, is the timid witness to this drama. There is, however, an *other*, modestly filed away among the "objects" of research, as if to safeguard the sovereignty of the scholar-warden, standing watch over the structures of communication and sociality; there is an *other* besides the irony of the learned man; there is the poem, in the sense that it is *rhythm, death, and future*. The linguist projects himself into it, identifies with it, and in the end, extracts a few concepts necessary for building a new model of language. But he also and foremost comes away suspecting that the signifying process is not limited to the language system, but that there are also speech, discourse, and, within them, a causality other than linguistic: a heterogeneous, destructive causality.

It is quite an experience to listen to Harvard University's recording of Roman Jakobson's 1967 lecture, "Russian Poetry of My Generation"—he gave a reading of Mayakovsky and Khlebnikov, imitating their voices, with the lively, rhythmic accents, thrust out throat and fully militant tone of the first; and the softly whispered words, sustained swishing and whistling sounds, vocalizations of the disintegrating voyage toward the mother constituted by the "trans-mental" ("zaum") language of the second. To understand the real conditions needed for producing scientific models, one should listen to the story of their youth, of the aesthetic and always political battles of Russian society on the eve of the Revolution and during the first years of victory, of the friendships and sensitivities that coalesced into lives and life projects. From all this, one may perceive what initiates a science, what it stops, what deceptively ciphers its models. No longer will it be possible to read any treatise on phonology without deciphering within every phoneme the statement, "Here lies a poet." The linguistics professor doesn't know this, and that is another problem, allowing him blithely to put forward his models, never to invent any new notion of language, and to preserve the sterility of theory.

I shall not, then, summarize the linguistic models, much less the tools of poetic analysis, proposed by Jakobson. I shall only review a few themes, or mythemes, inherent in his listening to futurist poetry, insofar as they are hidden recesses—silent causality and ethics—of the linguistic process.

The Struggle Between Poet and Sun

Two tendencies seem to dominate Mayakovsky's poetic craft: *rhythmic* rapture and the simultaneous affirmation of the *"ego."*

Rhythm: "I walk along, waving my arms and mumbling almost wordlessly, now shortening my steps so as not to interrupt my mumbling, now mumbling more rapidly in time with my steps. So the rhythm is trimmed and takes shape—and rhythm is the basis of any poetic work, resounding through the whole thing. Gradually individual words begin to ease themselves free of this dull roar. . . . When the fundamentals are already there, one has a sudden sensation that the rhythm is strained: there's some little syllable or sound missing.

You begin to shape all the words anew, and the work drives you to distraction. It's like having a tooth crowned. A hundred times (or so it seems) the dentist tries a crown on the tooth, and it's the wrong size; but at last, after a hundred attempts, he presses one down, and it fits. The analogy is all the more apposite in my case, because when at last the crown fits, I (quite literally) have tears in my eyes, from pain and relief. Where this basic dull roar of a rhythm comes from is a mystery. In my case, it's all kinds of repetitions in my mind of noises, rocking motions or in fact, of any phenomenon with which I can associate a sound. The sound of the sea, endlessly repeated, can provide my rhythm, or a servant who slams the door every morning, recurring and intertwining with itself, trailing through my consciousness; or even the rotation of the earth, which in my case, as in a shop full of visual aids, gives way to, and inextricably connects with, the whistle of a high wind."[1]

On the one hand, then, we have this rhythm; this repetitive sonority; this thrusting tooth pushing upwards before being capped with the crown of language; this struggle between word and force gushing with the pain and relief of a desperate delirium; the repetition of this growth, of this gushing forth around the crown-word, like the earth completing its revolution around the sun.

On the other hand, we have the "ego," situated within the space of language, crown, system: no longer rhythm, but sign, word, structure, contract, constraint; an "ego" declaring itself poetry's sole interest (cf. the poem "I Am Alone"), and comparing itself to Napoleon ("Napoleon and I": "Today, I am Napoleon / I am the chief of armies and more. / Compare / him and me!"). Trotsky called this erection of the poetic "I" a "Mayakomorphism," which he opposed to anthropomorphism (one can think of other word associations on the basis of *mayak* = "beacon").

Once the rhythm has been centered in the fixed position of an all powerful "ego," the poetic "I" thrusts at the sun—a paternal image that is coveted but also feared, murderous, and sentenced to die, a legislative seat which must be usurped. Thus: "one more minute / and you will meet / the monarch of the skies / if I want, I'll kill him for you, the sun!" ("Napoleon and I"); "Sun! / My father! / Won't you melt and stop torturing me! / My blood spilled by you runs along the road" ("A Few Words about Myself").

I could give many references, evoke Lautréamont, Bataille, Cyrano, or Schreber; the struggle between poet and sun, which Jakobson brought out, runs through such texts. We should understand it as a summary leading from the poet's condition to poetic formulation. Sun: agency of language since it is the "crown" of rhythmic thrust, limiting structure, paternal law abrading rhythm, destroying it to a large degree, but also bringing it to light, out of its earthy revolutions, to enunciate itself. Inasmuch as the "I" is poetic, inasmuch as it wants to enunciate rhythm, to socialize it, to channel it into linguistic structure if only to break the structure, this "I" is bound to the sun. It is a part of this agency because it must master rhythm, it is threatened by it because solar mastery cuts off rhythm. Thus, there is no choice but to struggle eternally against the sun; the "I" is successively the sun and its opponent, language and its rhythm, never one without the other, and poetic formulation will continue as long as the struggle does. The essential point to note is that there would be no struggle but for the sun's agency. Without it, rhythm incapable of formulation, would flow forth, growling, and in the end would dig itself in. Only by vying with the agency of limiting and structuring language does rhythm become a contestant—formulating and transforming.

Khlebnikov evokes another aspect of this solar contest; a mother, coming to the aid of her children in their fight against the sun. "The otter's children" are squared off against three suns, one white, one purple, the other dark green. In "The God of the Virgins," the protagonist is "the daughter of the sun prince." The poem "Ka" calls forth the "hairy-armed sun of Egypt." All of Khlebnikov's pagan mythology is underlain with a contest against the sun supported by a feminine figure, all-powerful mother or forbidden virgin, gathering into one representation and thus substantifying all that which, with Mayakovsky, hammered in sonorous thrusts within and against the system of language—that is, rhythm.

Here, pagan mythology is probably nothing more than rhythm become substantive: this *other* of the linguistic and/or social contract, this ultimate and primordial leash holding the body close to the mother before it can become a social speaking subject. In any case, what in Khlebnikov Tynanov called "infantilism" or "the poet's pagan attitude regarding words"[2] is essentially manifest in the *glossolalias* unique to Khlebnikov. He invented words by onomatopoeia, with a great deal of alliteration, demanding of him an acute awareness of the articulatory base and instinctual charge of that articulation. This entire strategy broke up the lexicon of the Russian language, drawing it closer to childhood soliloquy. But above all, it threaded through metaphor and metonymy a network of meaning supplementary to the normative signifying line, a network of phonemes or phonic groups charged with instinctual drives and meaning, constituting what for the author was a *numerical* code, a *ciphering*, underlying the verbal signs: for example, "Veterpenie / kogo i o chëm? / neterpenie—mecha stat' mjachom" (Wind-song / of whom and for what? / Impatience / of the sword to become a bullet). Jakobson notes the phonic displacement *mech-mjach* (sword-bullet) dominating several lines of Khlebnikov's poetry, where one notices also a tendency toward infantile regression and/or toward lessening of tension on the level of pronunciation as well as on the more general level of sexualized semantic areas. The vocalization of language thus becomes a way of deflecting the censorship that, for rhythm, is constituted by the structuring agency. Having become "trans-mental," Khlebnikov's instinctual, ciphered language projects itself as prophetic and seeks for homologues within this tradition: for example, "Through Zarathustra's golden mouth let us swear / Persia shall become a Soviet country, thus has the prophet spoken."[3]

Rhythm and Death

"But how do we speak about the poetry of Mayakovsky, now that what prevails is not rhythm but the poet's death . . . ?" asks Jakobson in "The Generation That Wasted Its Poets."[4] We tend to read this article as if it were exclusively an indictment of a society founded on the murder of its poets. This is probably true; when the article first appeared in 1931, even psychoanalysts were not all convinced that "society was now based on complicity in the common crime," as Freud had written in *Totem and Taboo*.[5] On the basis of his work on Mayakovsky, Jakobson suggested that the crime was more concretely the murder of poetic language. By "society," he probably meant more than just Russian or Soviet society; there are frequent and more general allusions to the "stability of the unchanging present," to "life, hardened along narrow and rigid models," and to "daily existence." Consequently we have this Platonistic acknowledgment on the eve of Stalinism and fascism: a (any) society may be stabilized only if it excludes poetic language.

On the other hand, but simultaneously, poetic language alone carries on the struggle against such a death, and so harries, exorcises, and invokes it. Jakobson is fascinated by murder and suicide as themes with poets of his generation as well as of all time. The question is unavoidable: if we are not on the side of those whom society wastes in order to reproduce itself, where are we?

Murder, death, and unchanging society represent precisely the inability to hear and understand the signifier as such—as ciphering, as rhythm, as a presence that precedes the signification of object or emotion. The poet is put to death because he wants to turn rhythm into a dominant element; because he wants to make language perceive what it doesn't want to say, provide it with its matter independently of the sign, and free it from denotation. For it is this *eminently parodic* gesture that changes the system.

> The word is experienced as word and not as a simple substitute for a named object nor as the explosion of emotion [. . .] beside the immediate consciousness of the identity existing between the object and its sign (A is A), the immediate consciousness of the absence of this identity (A is not A) is necessary; this antinomy is inevitable, for, without contradiction, there is no interplay of concepts, no interplay of signs, the relationship between the concept and the sign becomes automatic, the progress of events comes to a halt, and all consciousness of reality dies [. . .] Poetry protects us from this automatization, from the rust that threatens our formulation of love, hate, revolt and reconciliation, faith and negation.[6]

Today, the analyst boasts of his ability to hear "pure signifiers." Can he hear them in what is known as "private life"? There is good reason to believe that these "wasted poets" are alone in meeting the challenge. Whoever understands them cannot "practice linguistics" without passing through whole geographic and discursive continents as an impertinent traveler, a "faun in the house" [*faune au logis* = *phonologie*—Ed.].

The Futurists' Future

According to Jakobson, Mayakovsky was interested in resurrection. It is easy, at that, to see that his poems, like those of Khlebnikov and other futurists, take up the theme of Messianic resurrection, a privileged one in Russian Medieval poetry. Such a theme is a very obvious and direct descendant of the contest against the sun myth that I mentioned earlier. The son assumes from his sun-father the task of completing the "self" and "rhythm" dialectic within the poem. But the irruption of semiotic rhythm within the signifying system of language will never be a Hegelian *Aufhebung*, that is, it will not truly be experienced in the present. The rigid, imperious, immediate present kills, puts aside, and fritters away the poem. Thus, the irruption within the order of language of the anteriority of language evokes a later time, that is, a forever. The poem's time frame is some "future anterior" that will never take place, never come about as such, but only as an upheaval of present place and meaning. Now, by thus suspending the present moment, by straddling rhythmic, meaningless, anterior memory with meaning intended for later or forever, poetic language structures itself as the very nucleus of a monumental historicity. Futurism succeeded in making this poetic law explicit solely because it extended further than anyone else the signifier's autonomy, restored its instinctual value, and aimed at a "trans-mental language." Consequently attuned to a scene preceding the logical systematicity of communication, Futurism managed to do so without withdrawing from its own historical period; instead, it paid strong attention to the explosion of the October Revolution. It heard and understood the Revolution only because its present was dependent on a future. Mayakovsky and Khlebnikov's pro-Soviet proposals and leaps into mythology came from a nonexistent place in the future. Anteriority and future join together to open that historical axis in relation to which concrete history will always be wrong: murderous, limiting, subject to regional imperatives (economic, tactical, political, familial . . .). Although, confronted with such regional necessities, poetic language's future anterior is an impossible, "aristocratic" and "elitist" demand, it is nonetheless the only signifying strategy allowing the speaking animal to shift the limits of its enclosure. In "As for the Self," Khlebnikov writes:

> Short pieces are important when they serve as a break into the future, like a shooting star, leaving behind a trail of fire. They should move rapidly enough so that they pierce the present. While we wait, we cannot yet define the reason for this speech. But we know the piece is good when, in its role as a piece of the future, it sets the present ablaze. [. . .] the homeland of creation is the future. The wind of the gods of the word blows from that direction.[7]

Poetic discourse measures rhythm against the meaning of language structure and is thus always eluded by meaning in the present while continually postponing it to an impossible time-to-come. Consequently, it is assuredly the most appropriate *historical* discourse, if and only if we attribute to this word its new resonance; it is neither flight in the face of a supposed metaphysics of the notion of "history," nor mechanistic enclosure of this notion within a project oblivious to the violence of the social contract and evolution's being, above all, a refinement of the various forms of dissipating the tension we have been calling "poetic language."

It should come as no surprise that a movement such as the October Revolution, striving to remain antifeudal and antibourgeois, should call forth the same mythemes that dominated feudalism and were suppressed by the bourgeoisie, in order to exploit solely their dynamics producing exchange value. Beyond these mythemes, however, futurism stressed equally its participation in the anamnesis of a culture as well as a basic feature of Western discourse. "You have to bring the poem to the highest pitch of expressiveness" (Mayakovsky, "How Are Verses Made"). At that point the code becomes receptive to the rhythmic body and it forms, in opposition to present meaning, another meaning, but a future, impossible meaning. The important element of this "future anterior" of language is "the word perceived as word," a phenomenon in turn induced by the contest between rhythm and sign system.

Mayakovsky's suicide, Khlebnikov's disintegration, and Artaud's incarceration prove that this contest can be prevented. Does this mean there is no future (no history) for this discourse, which found its own "anteriority" within the "poetic" experience of the twentieth century? Linguistic ethics, as it can be understood through Jakobson's practice, consists in following the resurgence of an "I" coming back to rebuild an ephemeral structure in which the constituting struggle of language and society would be spelled out.

Can contemporary linguistics hear this conception of language of which Jakobson's work is the major token?

The currently dominant course, generative grammar, surely rests on many of Jakobson's approaches, notably phonological, in the study of the linguistic system. Nonetheless, it is hard to see how notions of elision, metaphor, metonymy, and parallelism (cf. his study on biblical and Chinese verse) could fit into the generative apparatus, including generative semantics, except perhaps under the rubric of "additional rules," necessitating a cutoff point in the specific generation of a language. But the dramatic notion of language as a risky practice, allowing the speaking animal to sense the rhythm of the body as well as the upheavals of history, seems tied to a notion of signifying process that contemporary theories do not confront. Jakobson's linguistic ethics therefore unmistakably demands first a *historical epistemology of linguistics* (one wonders which Eastern or Western theories linked with what ideological corpus of Antiquity, the Middle Ages, or the Renaissance were able to formulate the problematic of language as a place of structure as well as of its bodily, subjective, and social outlay). Secondly, it demands a *semiology*, understood as moving beyond simple linguistic studies toward a typology of signifying systems composed of semiotic materials and varied social functions. Such an affirmation of Saussurian semiological exigencies in a period dominated by generative grammar is far from archaistic; rather, it is integrated into a tradition where linguistics is inseparable from concepts of subject and society. As it epitomizes the experiences of language and linguistics of our entire European century, it allows us to foresee what the discourse on the signifying process might be in times to come.

2

THE BOUNDED TEXT

The Utterance as Ideologeme

1. Rather than *a discourse*, contemporary semiotics takes as its object *several semiotic practices* which it considers as *translinguistic*; that is, they operate through and across language, while remaining irreducible to its categories as they are presently assigned.

In this perspective, the *text* is defined as a trans-linguistic apparatus that redistributes the order of language by relating communicative speech, which aims to inform directly, to different kinds of anterior or synchronic utterances. The text is therefore a *productivity*, and this means: first, that its relationship to the language in which it is situated is redistributive (destructive-constructive), and hence can be better approached through logical categories rather than linguistic ones; and second, that it is a permutation of texts, an intertextuality: in the space of a given text, several utterances, taken from other texts, intersect and neutralize one another.

2. One of the problems for semiotics is to replace the former, rhetorical division of genres with *a typology of texts*; that is, to define the specificity of different textual arrangements by placing them within the general text (culture) of which they are part and which is in turn, part of them.[1] The ideologeme is the intersection of a given textual arrangement (a semiotic practice) with the utterances (sequences) that it either assimilates into its own space or to which it refers in the space of exterior texts (semiotic practices). The ideologeme is that intertextual function read as "materialized" at the different structural levels of each text, and which stretches along the entire length of its trajectory, giving it its historical and social coordinates. This is not an interpretative step coming after analysis in order to explain "as ideological" what was first "perceived" as "linguistic." The concept of text as ideologeme determines the very procedure of a semiotics that, by studying the text as intertextuality, considers it as such within (the text of) society and history. The ideologeme of a text is the focus where knowing rationality grasps the transformation of *utterances* (to which the text is irreducible) into a totality (the text) as well as the insertions of this totality into the historical and social text.[2]

3. The *novel*, seen as a text, is a semiotic practice in which the synthesized patterns of several utterances can be read.

For me, the *utterance* specific to the novel is not a minimal sequence (a definitely set entity). It is an *operation*, a motion that links, and even more so, *constitutes* what might be called the *arguments* of the operation, which, in the study of a written text, are either words or word sequences (sentences, paragraphs) as sememes.[3] Instead of analyzing entities (sememes in themselves), I shall study the *function* that incorporates them within the text. That function, a dependent variable, is determined along with the independent variables it links together; more simply put, there is univocal correspondence between words or word sequences. It is therefore clear that what I am proposing is an analysis that, while dealing with linguistic units (words, sentences, paragraphs), is of a translinguistic order. Speaking metaphorically, linguistic units (and especially semantic units) will serve only as springboards in establishing different *kinds of novelistic utterances as functions*. By bracketing the question of semantic sequences, one can bring out the *logical practice* organizing them, thus proceeding at a *suprasegmental* level.

Novelistic utterances, as they pertain to this suprasegmental level, are linked up within the totality of novelistic production. By studying them as such, I shall establish a typology of these utterances and then proceed to investigate, as a second step, their origins outside of the novel. Only in this way can the novel be defined in its unity and/or as ideologeme. To put it another way, the functions defined according to the extra-novelistic textual set (Te) take on value within the novelistic textual set (Tn). The ideologeme of the novel is precisely this *intertextual* function defined according to Te and having value within Tn.

Two kinds of analyses, sometimes difficult to distinguish from each other, make it possible to isolate the *ideologeme of the sign* in the novel: first, a suprasegmental analysis of the utterances contained within the novel's framework will reveal it as a bounded text (with its initial programming, its arbitrary ending, its dyadic figuration, its deviations and their concatenation); second, an *intertextual* analysis of these utterances will reveal the relationship between writing and speech in the text of the novel. I will show that the novel's textual order is based more on speech than on writing and then proceed to analyze the topology of this "phonetic order" (the arrangement of speech acts in relation to one another).

Since the novel is a text dependent on the ideologeme of the sign, let me first briefly describe the particularities of the sign as ideologeme.

From Symbol to Sign

1. The second half of the Middle Ages (thirteenth to fifteenth centuries) was a period of transition for European culture: thought based on the sign replaced that based on the symbol. A semiotics of the symbol characterized European society until around the thirteenth century, as clearly manifested in this period's literature and painting. It is, as such, a semiotic practice of cosmogony: these elements (symbols) refer back to one (or several) unrepresentable and

unknowable universal transcendence(s); univocal connections link these transcendences to the units evoking them; the symbol does not "resemble" the object it symbolizes; the two spaces (symbolized-symbolizer) are separate and do not communicate.

The symbol assumes the symbolized (universal) as irreducible to the symbolizer (its markings). Mythical thought operates within the sphere of the symbol (as in the epic, folk tales, chansons de geste, et cetera) through symbolic units—*units of restriction* in relation to the symbolized universals ("heroism," "courage," "nobility," "virtue," "fear," "treason," etc.). The symbol's function, in its vertical dimension (universals—markings), is thus one of *restriction*. The symbol's function in its horizontal dimension (the articulation of signifying units among themselves) is one of escaping paradox; one could even say that the symbol is horizontally *antiparadoxical*: within its logic, two opposing units are exclusive.[4] The good and the bad are incompatible—as are the raw and the cooked, honey and ashes, et cetera. The contradiction, once it appears, immediately demands resolution. It is thus concealed, "resolved," and therefore put aside.

The key to symbolic semiotic practice is given from the very beginning of symbolic discourse: the course of semiotic development is circular since the end is programmed, given in embryo, from the beginning (whose end *is* the beginning) because the symbol's function (its ideologeme) antedates the symbolic utterance itself. Thus are implied the general characteristics of a symbolic semiotic practice: the *quantitative limitation* of symbols, their *repetition, limitation,* and *general nature.*

2. From the thirteenth to the fifteenth century, the symbol was both challenged and weakened, but it did not completely disappear. Rather, during this period, its passage (its assimilation) into the sign was assured. The transcendental unity supporting the symbol—its otherworldly casing, its transmitting focus—was put into question. Thus, until the end of the fifteenth century, theatrical representations of Christ's life were based on both the canonical and apocryphal Gospels or the Golden legend (see the Mysteries dated c. 1400 published by Achille Jubinal in 1837 and based on the manuscript at the Library of Sainte-Geneviève). Beginning in the fifteenth century, the theater as well as art in general was invaded by scenes devoted to

Christ's public life (as in the Cathedral of Evreux). The transcendental foundation evoked by the symbol seemed to capsize. This heralds a new signifying relation between two elements, both located on the side of the "real" and "concrete." In thirteenth-century art, for example, the prophets were contrasted with the apostles; whereas in the fifteenth century, the four great evangelists were no longer set against the four prophets, but against the four fathers of the Latin Church (Saint Augustine, Saint Jerome, Saint Ambrose, and Gregory the Great as on the altar of Notre Dame of Avioth). Great architectural and literary compositions were no longer possible: the miniature replaced the cathedral and the fifteenth century became the century of the miniaturists. The serenity of the symbol was replaced by the strained ambivalence of the *sign's* connection, which lays claim to resemblance and identification of the elements it holds together, while first postulating their radical difference. Whence the obsessive insistence on the theme of *dialogue* between two *irreducible* but *similar* elements (dialogue—generator of the pathetic and psychological) in this transitional period. For example, the fourteenth and fifteenth centuries abound in dialogues between God and the human soul: the Dialogue of the Crucifix and Pilgrim, Dialogue of the Sinful Soul and Christ, et cetera. Through this movement, the Bible was moralized (see the famous moralized Bible of the Duke of Burgundy's library). It was even replaced by pastiches that bracketed and erased the transcendental basis of the symbol (the Bible of the Poor and the Mirror of Human Salvation).[5]

3. The sign that was outlined through these mutations retained the fundamental characteristic of the symbol: irreducibility of terms, that is, in the case of the sign, of the referent to the signified, of the signified to the signifier, and, in addition, all the "units" of the signifying structure itself. The ideologeme of the sign is therefore, in a general way, like the ideologeme of the symbol: the sign is dualist, hierarchical, and hierarchizing. A difference between the sign and the symbol can, however, be seen vertically as well as horizontally: within its vertical function, the sign refers back to entities both of lesser scope and more *concretized* than those of the symbol. They are *reified* universals become *objects* in the strongest sense of the word.

Put into a relationship within the structure of sign, the entity (phenomenon) under consideration is, at the same time, transcendentalized and elevated to the level of theological unity. The semiotic practice of the sign thus assimilates the metaphysics of the symbol and projects it onto the "immediately perceptible." The "immediately perceptible," valorized in this way, is then transformed into an *objectivity*—the reigning law of discourse in the civilization of the sign.

Within their horizontal function, the units of the sign's semiotic practice are articulated as a *metonymical concatenation of deviations from the norm* signifying a *progressive creation of metaphors*. Oppositional terms, always exclusive, are caught within a network of multiple and always possible deviations (surprises in narrative structures), giving the illusion of an *open* structure, impossible to finish, with an *arbitrary* ending. In literary discourse the semiotic practice of the sign first clearly appeared, during the Renaissance, in the adventure novel, which is structured on what is unforeseeable and on *surprise* as reification (at the level of narrative structure) of the deviation from the norm specific to every practice of the sign. The itinerary of this concatenation of deviations is practically infinite, whence the impression of the work's *arbitrary* ending. This is, in fact, the *illusory* impression which defines all "literature" (all "art"), since such itinerary is programmed by the ideologeme constituting the sign. That is, it is programmed by a closed (finite), dyadic process, which, first, institutes the referent-signified-signifier hierarchy and, secondly, interiorizes these oppositional dyads all the way to the very level of the articulation of terms, put together—like the symbol—as resolution of contradiction. In a semiotic practice based on the symbol, contradiction was resolved by *exclusive disjunction* (nonequivalence)— ≠ —or by nonconjunction— | —; in a semiotic practice based on the sign, contradiction is resolved by nondisjunction—V̄—.

The Ideologeme of the Novel: Novelistic Enunciation

Every literary work partaking of the semiotic practice of the sign (all "literature" before the epistemological break of the nineteenth/

twentieth centuries) is therefore, as ideologeme, closed and terminated in its very beginnings. It is related to conceptualist (antiexperimental) thought in the same way as the symbolic is to Platonism. The novel is one of the characteristic manifestations of this ambivalent ideologeme (closure, nondisjunction, linking of deviations) — the sign. Here I will examine this ideologeme in Antoine de La Sale's *Jehan de Saintré*.

Antoine de La Sale wrote *Jehan de Saintré* in 1456, after a long career as page, warrior, and tutor, for educational purposes and as a lament for a departure (for puzzling reasons, and after forty-eight years of service, he left the Kings of Anjou to become tutor of the Count of Saint Pol's three sons in 1448). *Jehan de Saintré* is the only novel to be found among La Sale's writings, which are otherwise presented as compilations of edifying narratives (*La Salle*, 1448–1451), as "scientific" tracts, or as accounts of his travels (*Lettres à Jacques de Luxembourg sur les tournois*, 1459; *Réconfort à Madame de Fresne*, 1457) — all of these being constructed as historical discourse or as heterogeneous mosaics of texts. Historians of French literature have neglected this particular work—perhaps the first writing in prose that could be called a novel (if one labels as such those works that depend on the ambiguous ideologeme of the sign). The few studies that have been devoted to it[6] concentrate on its references to the mores of the time, attempt to find the "key" to the characters by identifying them with personalities La Sale might have known, accuse the author of underestimating the historical events of his time (the Hundred Years War, et cetera) as well as of belonging—as a true reactionary—to a world of the past, and so on. Literary history, immersed in referential opacity, has not been able to bring to light the *transitory structure* of this text, which situates it at the threshold of the two eras and shows, through La Sale's naive poetics, the articulation of this ideologeme of the sign, which continues to dominate our intellectual horizon.[7] What is more, Antoine de La Sale's narrative confirms the narrative of his own writing: La Sale speaks but also, writing, enunciates *himself*. The story of Jehan de Saintré merges with the book's story and becomes, in a sense, its rhetorical representation, its other, its inner lining.

1. The text opens with an introduction that shapes (shows) the entire itinerary of the novel: La Sale *knows* what his text *is* ("three stories") and *for what* reason it exists (a message to Jehan d'Anjou). Having thus uttered his purpose and named its addressee, he marks out within twenty lines the *first loop*[8] that encloses the textual set and programs it as a means of exchange and, therefore, as sign: this is the loop *utterance* (exchange object)/*addressee* (the duke or, simply, the reader). All that remains is to tell, that is, to fill in, to detail, what was already conceptualized, known, before any contact between pen and paper—"the story as word upon word it proceeds."

2. The *title* can now be presented: "And first, the story of the Lady of the Beautiful Cousins (of whom I have already spoken) and of Saintré," which requires a second loop—this one found at the thematic level of the message. La Sale gives a shortened version of Jehan de Saintré's life from beginning to end ("his passing away from this world," p. 2). We thus *already* know how the story will end: the end of the narrative is given before the narrative itself even begins. All anecdotal interest is thus eliminated: the novel will play itself out by rebuilding the distance between life and death; it will be nothing other than an inscription of *deviations* (surprises) that do not destroy the certainty of the thematic loop (life-death) holding the set together. The text turns on a thematic axis: the interplay between two exclusive oppositions, whose names might change (vice-virtue, love-hate, praise-criticism; for example, the Apology of the widow in the Roman texts is directly followed by the misogynist remarks of Saint Jerome). But the semic axis of these oppositions remains the same (positive-negative); they will alternate according to a trajectory limited by nothing but the initially presupposed *excluded middle*; that is, the inevitable choice of one *or* the other term (with the "or" being exclusive).

Within the ideologeme of the novel (as with the ideologeme of the sign), the irreducibility of opposite terms is admitted only to the extent that the empty space of rupture separating them is provided with ambiguous semic combinations. The initially recognized opposition, setting up the novel's trajectory, is immediately repressed within a *before*, only to give way—within a *now*—to a network of paddings, to a concatenation of deviations oscillating between two opposite poles, and, in an attempt at synthesis, resolving within a figure of *dissimulation* or *mask*. Negation is thus repeated in the affirmation of duplicity. The exclusiveness of the two terms posited by the novel's thematic loop is replaced by a *doubtful positivity* in such a way that the *disjunction* which both opens and closes the novel is replaced by a *yes-no* structure (nondisjunction). This function does not bring about a para-thetic silence, but combines carnivalistic play with its nondiscursive logic; all figures found in the novel (as heir to the carnival) that can be read in two ways are organized on the model of this function: ruses, treason, foreigners, androgynes, utterances that can be doubly interpreted or have double destinations (at the level of the novelistic signified), blazonry, "cries" (at the level of the novelistic signifier), and so on. The trajectory of the novel would be impossible without this nondisjunctive function—*this double*—which programs it from its beginning. La Sale first introduces it through the Lady's doubly oriented utterance: as a message destined to the Lady's female companions and to the Court, this utterance connotes aggressivity towards Saintré; as a message destined to Saintré himself, it connotes a "tender" and "testing" love. The nondisjunctive function of the Lady's utterance is revealed in stages that are quite interesting to follow. At first, the message's duplicity is known only to the speaker herself (the Lady), to the author (subject of the novelistic utterance), and to the reader (addressee of the novelistic utterance). The Court (neutrality = objective opinion), as well as Saintré (passive object of the message), are dupes of the Lady's univocal aggressivity towards the page. In the second stage, the duplicity is displaced: Saintré becomes part of it and accepts it; but in the same gesture, he ceases to be the object of a message and becomes the subject of utterances for which he assumes authority. In a third stage, Saintré forgets the nondisjunction; he completely transforms into something positive what he knew to be *also* negative; he loses sight of the dissimulation and is taken in by the game of a univocal (and therefore erroneous) interpretation of a message that remains double. Saintré's defeat—and the end of the narrative—are due to this error of substituting an utterance accepted as disjunctive and univocal for the nondisjunctive function of an utterance.

Negation in the novel thus operates according to a double modality: *alethic* (the opposition of contraries is necessary, possible, contingent, or impossible) and *deontic* (the reunion of contraries is obligatory, permissible, indifferent, or forbidden). The novel becomes possible when the *alethic* modality of opposition joins with the *deontic* modality of reunion.[9] The novel covers the trajectory of deontic synthesis in order to condemn it and to affirm, in the alethic mode, the opposition of contraries. The double (dissimulation, mask), as fundamental figure of the carnival,[10] thus becomes the pivotal springboard for the deviations filling up the silence imposed by the disjunctive function of the novel's thematic-programmatic loop. In this way, the novel absorbs the duplicity (the dialogism) of the carnivalesque scene while submitting it to the univocity (monologism) of the symbolic disjunction guaranteed by a transcendence—the author—that subsumes the totality of the novelistic utterance.

3. It is, in fact, precisely at this point in the textual trajectory—that is, after the enunciation of the text's toponymical (message-addressee) and thematic (life-death) closure (loop)—that the word "*actor*" is inscribed. It reappears several times, introducing the *speech* of he who is writing the narrative as being the *utterance* of a character in this *drama* of which he is also the *author*. Playing upon a homophony (Latin: *actor-auctor*, French: *acteur-auteur*), La Sale touches upon the very point where the speech *act* (work) tilts towards discursive *effect* (product), and thus, upon the very constituting process of the "literary" object. For La Sale, the writer is both actor and author; that means that he conceived the text of the novel as both practice (actor) and product (author), process (actor) and effect (author), play (actor) and value (author); and yet, the already set notions of oeuvre (message) and owner (author) do not succeed in pushing the play that preceded them into oblivion.[11] Novelistic speech is thus inserted into the novelistic utterance and accounted for as one of its elements. (I have examined elsewhere the topology of speech acts in the text of the novel.)[12] It unveils the writer as principal actor in the speech play that ensues and, at the same time, binds together two modes of the novelistic utterance, *narration* and *citation*, into the single speech of he who is both *subject* of the book (the author) and object of the

spectacle (actor), since, within novelistic nondisjunction, the message is both discourse and representation. The author-actor's utterance unfolds, divides, and faces in two directions: first, towards a referential utterance, *narration*—the speech assumed by he who inscribes himself as actor-author; and second, toward textual premises, *citation*—speech attributed to an other and whose authority he who inscribes himself as actor-author acknowledges. These two orientations intertwine in such a way as to merge. For example, La Sale easily shifts from the story as "lived" by the Lady of the Beautiful Cousins (to which he is witness, i.e., witness to the narration) to the story of Aeneas and Dido as read (cited), and so on.

4. In conclusion, let me say that the modality of novelistic enunciation is *inferential*: it is a process within which the subject of the novelistic utterance affirms a sequence, as *conclusion of the inference*, based on other sequences (referential—hence narrative, or textual—hence citational), which are the *premises of the inference* and, as such, considered to be true. The novelistic inference is exhausted through the naming process of the two premises and, particularly, through their concatenation, without leading to the syllogistic conclusion proper to logical inference. The function of the author/actor's enunciation therefore consists in binding his discourse to his readings, his speech act to that of others.

The words that mediate this inference are worth noting: "*it seems to me* at first view that she wished to imitate the widows of ancient times . . ." "if, *as* Vergil says . . ." "and *thereupon* Saint Jerome *says* . . ." and so on. These are empty words whose functions are both *junctive* and *translative*. As junctive, they tie together (totalize) two minimal utterances (narrative and citational) within the global, novelistic utterance. They are therefore internuclear. As translative, they transfer an utterance from one textual space (vocal discourse) into another (the book), changing its ideologeme. They are thus intranuclear (for example, the transposition of hawkers' cries and blazons into a written text).[13]

These inferential agents imply the juxtaposition of a *discourse* invested in a subject with another *utterance* different from the author's. They make possible the deviation of the novelistic utterance from its subject and its self-presence, that is, its displacement from a discursive (informational, communicative) level to a textual level (of productivity). Through this inferential gesture, the author refuses to be an objective "witness"—possessor of a truth he symbolizes by the word—in order to inscribe himself as reader or listener, structuring his text through and across a permutation of *other* utterances. He does not so much *speak* as *decipher*. The inferential agents allow him to bring a referential utterance (narration) back to textual premises (citations) and vice versa. They establish a similitude, a resemblance, an equalization of two different discourses. The ideologeme of the sign once again crops up here, at the level of the novelistic enunciation's inferential mode: it admits the existence of an *other* (discourse) only to the extent that it makes it *its own*. This splitting of the mode of enunciation did not exist in the epic: in the chansons de geste, the speaker's utterance is univocal; it names a referent ("real" object or discourse); it is a signifier symbolizing transcendental objects (universals). Medieval literature, dominated by the symbol, is thus a "signifying," "phonetic" literature, supported by the monolithic presence of signified transcendence. The scene of the carnival introduces the split speech act: the *actor* and the *crowd* are each in turn simultaneously subject and addressee of discourse. The carnival is also the bridge between the two split occurrences as well as the place where each of the terms is acknowledged: the author (actor + spectator). It is this third mode that the novelistic inference adopts and effects within the author's utterance. As irreducible to any of the premises constituting the inference, the mode of novelistic enunciation is the invisible focus where the phonetic (referential utterance, narration) and written (textual premises, citation) intersect. It is the hollow, unrepresentable space signaled by "*as*," "*it seems to me*," "*says thereupon*," or other inferential agents that refer back, tie together, or bound. We thus uncover a third programming of the novelistic text which brings it to a close before the beginning of the actual story: novelistic enunciation turns out to be a nonsyllogistic inference, a compromise between testimony and citation, between the voice and the book. The novel will be performed within this empty space, within this unrepresentable trajectory bringing together two types of utterances with their *different* and *irreducible* "subjects."

The Nondisjunctive Function of the Novel

1. The novelistic utterance conceives of the opposition of terms as a nonalternating and absolute opposition between two groupings that are competitive but never solidary, never complementary, and never reconcilable through indestructible rhythm. In order for this nonalternating disjunction to give rise to the discursive trajectory of the novel, it must be embodied within a negative function: nondisjunction. It is this nondisjunctive function that intervenes on a secondary level and instead of an *infinity complementary to bipartition* (which could have taken shape within another conception of negation one might term radical, and this presupposes that the opposition of terms is, *at the same time,* thought of as communion or symmetrical reunion) it introduces the figure of dissimulation, of ambivalence, of the *double.* The initial nonalternating opposition thus turns out to be a pseudo-opposition—and this at the time of its very inception, since it doesn't integrate its own opposition, namely, the solidarity of rivals. Life is opposed to death in an absolute way (as is love to hate, virtue to vice, good to bad, being to nothingness) without the opposition's complementary negation that would transform bipartition into rhythmic totality. The negation remains incomplete and unfinished unless it includes this doubly negative movement that reduces the *difference* between two terms to a radical *disjunction* with permutation of those terms; that is, to an empty space around which they move, dying out as entities and turning into an alternating rhythm. By positing two opposing terms without affirming their identity in the same gesture and simultaneously, such a negation splits the movement of *radical negation* into two phases: disjunction and nondisjunction.

2. This division introduces, first of all, *time*: temporality (history) is the *spacing* of this splitting negation, i.e., what is introduced between two isolated and nonalternating scansions (opposition-conciliation). In other cultures, it has been possible to develop an irrevocable negation that ties the two scansions into an equalization, thus avoiding the spacing of the negative process (duration) and substituting in its place an emptiness (space) that produces the permutation of contraries.

Rendering negation ambiguous brings about, in the same way, a finality, a theological principle (God, "meaning"). To the extent that disjunction is recognized as an initial phase, there imposes itself at a second stage a syntheses of the two into *one*, presented as a unification that "forgets" opposition in the same way that the opposition did not "assume" unification. If God appears at the second stage to mark the bounding of a semiotic practice organized according to nonalternating negation, it is obvious that this closure is already present at the first stage of the simple, absolute opposition (nonalternating opposition).

It is within this split negation that all *mimesis* is born. Nonalternating negation is the law of narrative: every narration is made up, nourished by time, finality, history, and God. Both epic and narrative prose take place within this spacing and move toward the theology produced by nonalternating negation. We would have to look to other civilizations to find a nonmimetic discourse—whether scientific or sacred, moral or ritual—constructed through a process of deletion by rhythmic sequences, enclosing antithetical semic couplings within an orchestrated movement.[14] The novel is no exception to that narrative law. It is a particular case within the plurality of narratives where the nondisjunctive function is concretized at all levels (thematic, syntagmatic, actants, et cetera) of the entire novelistic utterance. It is precisely the second stage of nonalternating negation—that is, nondisjuction—that determines the ideologeme of the novel.

3. Indeed, disjunction (the thematic loops: life-death, love-hate, fidelity-treason) frames the novel, as was found to be the case in the bounded structures programming the novel's beginning. But the novel is not possible unless the disjunction between two terms can be denied while all the time being there, confirmed, and approved. It is presented, now, as *double* rather than as *two irreducible elements*. The figures of traitor, scoffed-at sovereign, vanquished warrior, and unfaithful woman stem from this nondisjunctive function found at the novel's origin.

The epic, on the other hand, was organized according to the symbolic function of exclusive disjunction or nondisjunction. In the *Song of Roland* and the Round Table Cycles, hero and traitor, good and evil, duty and love pursue one another in irreconcilable hostility from beginning to end, without any possibility of compromise. The "classical" epic, by obeying the law of nonconjunction (symbolic), can therefore engender neither personalities nor psychologies.[15] Psychology will appear along with the nondisjunctive function of the sign, finding in its ambiguity a terrain conducive to its meanderings. It would be possible, however, to trace the appearance of the *double* as precursor to the conception of personality within the evolution of the epic. Near the end of the twelfth century—and especially in the thirteenth and fourteenth centuries—there spreads an ambiguous epic: emperors are ridiculed, religion and barons become grotesque, heroes are cowardly and suspect ("Charlemagne's Pilgrimage"), the king is worthless, virtue is no longer rewarded (the Garin de Monglan Cycle), and the traitor becomes a principal actant (the Doon de Mayence Cycle or the "Raoul de Cambrai" poem). Neither satirical, laudatory, stigmatizing, nor approving, this epic is witness to a dual semiotic practice, founded on the resemblance of contraries, feeding on miscellany and ambiguity.

4. The courtly literature of Southern France is of particular interest within this transition from symbol to sign. Recent studies have demonstrated the analogies between the cult of the Lady in these texts and those of ancient Chinese poetry.[16] There would be evidence showing influence of a hieroglyphic semiotic practice based on "conjunctive disjunction" (dialectical negation) upon a semiotic practice based on nondisjunctive opposition (Christianity, Europe). Such hieroglyphic semiotic practice is also and above all a conjunctive disjunction of the two sexes as irreducibly differentiated and, at the same time, alike. This explains why, over a long period, a major semiotic practice of Western society (courtly poetry) attributed to the *Other* (Woman) a *primary* structural role. In our civilization—caught in the passage from the symbol to the sign—hymn to conjunctive disjunction was transformed into an apology for only *one* of the opposing terms: the Other (Woman), within which is projected and with which is *later* fused the Same (the Author, Man). At the same time there was produced an exclusion of the Other, inevitably presented

as an exclusion of woman, as nonrecognition of sexual (and social) opposition. The rhythmic order of Oriental texts organizing the sexes (differences) within conjunctive disjunction (hierogamy) is here replaced by a centered system (Other, Woman) whose center is there only so as to permit those making up the Same to identify with it. It is therefore a pseudo-center, a mystifying center, a blind spot whose value is invested in the Same giving the Other (the center) to itself in order to live as one, alone, and unique. Hence, the exclusive positivity of this blind center (Woman), stretching out to infinity (of "nobility" and "qualities of the heart"), erasing disjunction (sexual difference), and dissolving into a series of images (from the angel to the Virgin). The unfinished negative gesture is, therefore, *already* theological: it is stopped before having designated the *Other* (Woman) as being *at the same time* opposed and equal to the *Same* (Man, Author), before being denied through the correlation of contraries (the identity of Man and Woman *simultaneous* to their disjunction). It eventually identified with religious attitudes, and in its incompletion it evokes Platonism.

Scholars have interpreted the theologization of courtly literature as an attempt to save love poetry from the persecutions of the Inquisition;[17] or, on the contrary, as evidence of the infiltration in Southern French society of the Inquisition Tribunals' activity, or that of the Dominican and Franciscan orders, after the debacle of the Albigenses.[18] Whatever the empirical facts may be, the spiritualization of courtly literature was already a given within the structure of this semiotic practice characterized by pseudo-negation as well as nonrecognition of the conjunctive disjunction of semic terms. Within such an ideologeme, the idealization of woman (of the Other) signifies the refusal of a society to constitute itself through the recognition of the *differential* but *nonhierarchizing* status of opposed groups. It also signifies the structural necessity for this society to give itself a permutative center, an *Other* entity, which has no value except as an *object of exchange* among members of the *Same*. Sociology has described how women came to occupy this permutational center (as object of exchange).[19] This devalorizing valorization prepared the terrain for, and cannot be fundamentally distinguished from, the explicit devalorization of women beginning with fourteenth-century bourgeois literature (in fabliaux, soties, and farces).

5. Antoine de La Sale's novel, situated halfway between these two types of utterances, contains both: the Lady is a dual figure within the novel's structure. She is no longer only the deified mistress required by the code of courtly poetry, that is, the valorized term of a nondisjunctive connection. She is also disloyal, ungrateful, and infamous. In *Jehan de Saintré*, the two attributive terms are no longer semically opposed through nonconjunction as would be required in a semiotic practice dependent on the symbol (the courtly utterance); rather, they are nondisjunctive within a single ambivalent unity connoting the ideologeme of the sign. Neither deified nor ridiculed, neither mother nor mistress, neither enamored of Saintré nor faithful to the Abbot, the Lady becomes the nondisjunctive figure par excellence in which the novel is centered.

Saintré is also part of this nondisjunctive function: he is both child and warrior, page and hero, the Lady's fool and conqueror of soldiers, cared for and betrayed, lover of the Lady and loved either by the king or a comrade in arms—Boucicault (p. 141). Never masculine, child-lover for the Lady or comrade-friend sharing a bed with the king or Boucicault, Saintré is the accomplished androgyne; the sublimation of sex (without sexualization of the sublime). His homosexuality is merely the narrativization of the nondisjunctive function peculiar to the semiotic process of which he is a part. He is the pivot-mirror within which the other arguments of the novelistic function are projected in order to fuse with themselves: the Other is the Same for the Lady (the man is the child, and therefore the woman herself finds there her self-identity nondisjoined from the Other, while remaining opaque to the irreducible *difference* between the two). He is the *Same* who is also the *Other* for the king, the warriors, or Boucicault (as the man who is also the woman who possesses him). The Lady's nondisjunctive function, to which Saintré is assimilated, assures her a role as object of exchange in male society. Saintré's own nondisjunctive function assures him a role as object of exchange between the masculine and feminine of society; together, they tie up the elements of a cultural text into a stable system dominated by nondisjunction (the sign).

The Agreement of Deviations

The novel's nondisjunctive function is manifested, at the level of the concatenation of its constituent utterances, as an *agreement of deviations*: the two originally opposed arguments (forming the thematic loops life-death, good-evil, beginning-end, etc.) are connected and mediated by a series of utterances whose relation to the originally posited opposition is neither explicit nor logically necessary. They are concatenated without any major imperative putting an end to their juxtaposition. These utterances, as deviations in relation to the oppositional loop framing the novelistic utterance, are *laudatory descriptions* of either objects (clothes, gifts, and weapons) or events (the departures of troops, banquets, and combats); such are the descriptions of commerce, purchases, and apparel (pp. 51, 63, 71–72, 79) or of weapons (p. 50), etc. These kinds of utterances reappear with obligatory monotony and make of the text an aggregate of recurrences, a succession of closed, cyclical utterances, complete in themselves. Each one is centered in a certain *point*, which can connote space (the tradesman's shop, the Lady's chamber), time (the troops' departure, Saintré's return), the subject of enunciation, or all three at once. These descriptive utterances are minutely detailed and return periodically according to a *repetitive* rhythm placing its grid upon the novel's temporality. Indeed, La Sale does not describe events evolving over a period of time. Whenever an utterance assumed by an Actor (Author) intervenes to serve as a temporary connecting device, it is extremely laconic and does nothing more than link together *descriptions* that first place the reader before an army ready to depart, a shopkeeper's place, a costume or piece of jewelry and then proceed to praise these objects put together according to no causality whatsoever. The imbrications of these deviations are apt to open up—praises could be repeated indefinitely. They are, however, *terminated* (bounded and determined) by the fundamental function of the novelistic utterance: nondisjunction. Caught up within the novel's totality—that is, seen in reverse, from the end of the novel where exaltation has been transformed into its contrary (desolation) before ending in death—these laudatory descriptions become relativized, ambiguous, deceptive, and double: their univocity changes to duplicity.

2. Besides laudatory descriptions, another kind of deviation operating according to nondisjunction appears along the novel's trajectory: Latin *citations* and moral precepts. Examples include Thales of Miletus, Socrates, Timides, Pittacus of Misselene, the Gospels, Cato, Seneca, Saint Augustine, Epicurus, Saint Bernard, Saint Gregory, Saint Paul, Avicenna, etc.; in addition to acknowledged borrowings, a considerable number of plagiarisms have also been pointed out.

It is not difficult to find the extranovelistic sources of these two kinds of deviations: the laudative description and the citation.

The first comes from the fair, marketplace, or public square. It is the utterance of the merchant vaunting his wares or of the herald announcing combat. Phonetic speech, oral utterance, sound itself, become text: less than writing, the novel is thus the transcription of vocal communication. An arbitrary *signifier* (the word as phone) is transcribed onto paper and presented as adequate to its signified and referent. It represents a "reality" that is already there, preexistent to the signifier, duplicated so as to be integrated into the circuit of exchange; it is therefore reduced to a *representamen* (sign) that is manageable and can be circulated as an element assuring the cohesion of a communicative (commercial) structure endowed with *meaning* (value).

These laudatory utterances, known as *blazons*, were abundant in France during the fourteenth and fifteenth centuries. They come from a communicative discourse, shouted in public squares, and designed to give direct information to the crowd on wars (the number of soldiers, their direction, armaments, etc.), or on the marketplace (the quality and price of merchandise).[20] These solemn, tumultuous, or monumental enumerations belong to a culture that might be called phonetic. The culture of exchange, definitively imposed by the European Renaissance, is engendered through the *voice* and operates according to the structures of the discursive (verbal, phonetic) circuit, inevitably referring back to a reality with which it identified by duplicating it (by "signifying it"). "Phonetic" literature is characterized by these kinds of laudatory and repetitive utterances-enumerations.[21]

The blazon later lost its univocity and became ambiguous; praise and blame at the same time. In the fifteenth century, the blazon was already the nondisjunctive figure par excellence.[22]

Antoine de La Sale's text captures the blazon just before this splitting into praise and/or blame. Blazons are recorded into the book as univocally laudatory. But they become ambiguous as soon as they are read from the point of view of the novelistic text's general function: the Lady's treachery skews the laudatory tone and shows its ambiguity. The blazon is transformed into blame and is thus inserted into the novel's nondisjunctive function as noted earlier: the function established according to the extratextual set (Te) changes within the novelistic textual set (Tn) and in this way defines it as ideologeme.

This splitting of the utterance's univocity is a typically oral phenomenon which can be found within the entire discursive (phonetic) space of the Middle Ages and especially in the carnival scene. The splitting that makes up the very nature of the sign (object/sound, referent/signified/signifier) as well as the topology of the communicative circuit (subject-addressee, Same-pseudo Other), reaches the utterance's logical level (phonetic) and is presented as nondisjunctive.

3. The second kind of deviation—the citation—comes from a written text. Latin as well as *other* books (already read) penetrate the novel's text either as directly copied (citations) or as mnesic traces (memories). They are carried intact from their own space into the space of the novel being written; they are transcribed within quotation marks or are plagiarized.[23]

While emphasizing the phonetic and introducing into the cultural text the (bourgeois) space of the fair, marketplace, and street, the end of the Middle Ages was also characterized by a massive infiltration of the written text: the book ceased to be the privilege of nobles or scholars and was democratized.[24] As a result, phonetic culture claimed to be a scriptural one. To the extent that every book in our civilization is a transcription of oral speech,[25] citation and plagiarism are as phonetic as the blazon even if their extrascriptural (verbal) source goes back to a few books before Antoine de La Sale's.

4. Nevertheless, the reference to a written text upsets the laws imposed on the text by oral transcription: enumeration, repetition,

and therefore temporality (cf. *supra*). The introduction of writing has two major consequences.

First, the temporality of La Sale's text is less a discursive temporality (the narrative sequences are not ordered according to the temporal laws of the verb phrase) than what we might call a *scriptural* temporality (the narrative sequences are oriented towards and rekindled by the very activity of writing). The succession of "events" (descriptive utterances or citations) obeys the motion of the hand working on the empty page—the very economy of inscription. La Sale often interrupts the *course* of discursive time to introduce the *present time* of his work on the text: "To return to my point," "to put it briefly," "as I will tell you," and "here I will stop speaking for a bit of Madame and her Ladies to return to little Saintré," etc. Such junctives signal a temporality other than that of the discursive (linear) chain: the *massive present* of inferential enunciation (of the scriptural work).

Second, the (phonetic) utterance having been transcribed onto paper and the foreign text (citation) having been copied down, both of them form a written text within which the very act of writing shifts to the background and appears, in its *totality*, as *secondary*: as a transcription-copy, as a sign, as a "letter," no longer in the sense of inscription but of exchange object ("which I send to you in the manner of a letter").

The novel is thus structured as dual space: it is both phonetic utterance and scriptural level, overwhelmingly dominated by discursive (phonetic) order.

Arbitrary Completion and Structural Finitude

I. All ideological activity appears in the form of utterances compositionally *completed*. This completion is to be distinguished from the *structural finitude* to which only a few philosophical systems (Hegel) as well as religions have aspired. The structural finitude characterizes, as a fundamental trait, the object that our culture consumes as a finished product (effect, impression) while refusing to read the process of its productivity: "literature"—within which the novel occupies a privileged position. The notion of literature coincides with the notion of the novel, as much on account of chronological origins as of structural bounding.[26] Explicit completion is often lacking, ambiguous, or assumed in the text of the novel. This incompletion nevertheless underlines the text's structural finitude. Every genre having its own particular structural finitude, I shall try to isolate that of *Jehan de Saintré*.

2. The initial programming of the book is already its structural finitude. Within the figures described earlier, the trajectories close upon themselves, return to their point of departure, or are confirmed by a censoring element in such a way as to outline the limits of a closed discourse. The book's compositional completion nevertheless reworks the structural finitude. The novel ends with the utterance of the author who, after having brought the story of his character, Saintré, to the point of the Lady's punishment, interrupts the narrative to announce the end: "And here I shall begin the end of this story . . ." (p. 307).

The story can be considered finished as soon as there is completion of one of the loops (resolution of one of the oppositional dyads), the series of which was opened by the initial programming. This loop is the condemnation of the Lady, signifying a condemnation of ambiguity. The *narrative* stops there. I shall call this completion of the narrative by a concrete loop a reworking of the structural finitude.

But the structural finitude, once more manifested by a concretization of the text's fundamental figure (the oppositional dyad and its relation to nondisjunction) is not sufficient for the bounding of the author's discourse. Nothing in speech can put an end—except arbitrarily—to the infinite concatenation of loops. The real arresting act is performed by the appearance, within the novelistic utterance, of the very work that produces it, here, on the actual page. Speech ends when its subject dies, and it is the act of writing (of work) that produces this murder.

A new rubric, the "*actor*" signals the second—the actual—reworking of the ending: "And here I shall give an ending to the book of the most valiant knight who . . ." (p. 308). A brief narrative of the narrative follows, terminating the novel by bringing the utterance back to the act of writing ("Now, most high, and most powerful and excellent prince and my most feared lord, if I have erred in any way either by *writing* too much or too little [. . .] I have made this book, said Saintré, which I send to you in the manner of a *letter*"—p. 309, emphasis mine) and by substituting the present of script for the past of speech ("And in conclusion, for the *present*, my most feared lord, I write you nothing else" [p. 309]—emphasis mine).

Within this dual surface of the text (story of Saintré—story of the writing process)—the scriptural activity having been narrated and the narrative having been often interrupted to allow the act of production to surface—(Saintré's) death as rhetorical image coincides with the stopping of discourse (erasure of the actor). Nevertheless— as another retraction of speech—this death, repeated by the text at the moment it becomes silent, cannot be spoken. It is asserted by a (tomblike) writing, which writing (as text of the novel) places in quotation marks. In addition—another retraction, this time of the place of *language*—this citation of the tombstone inscription is produced in a dead language (Latin). Set back in relation to French, the Latin reaches a standstill where it is no longer the narrative that is being completed (having been terminated in the preceding paragraph: "And here I shall begin the end of this story . . .") but rather the *discourse* and its product—"literature"/the "letter" ("And here I shall give an ending to the book . . .").

3. The narrative could again take up Saintré's adventures or spare us several of them. The fact remains nevertheless that it is bounded, born dead: what terminates it structurally are the bounded functions of the sign's ideologeme, which the narrative repeats with variation. What bounds it compositionally and as cultural artifact is the expliciting of the narrative as a written text.

Thus, at the close of the Middle Ages and therefore before consolidation of "literary" ideology and the society of which it is the superstructure, Antoine de La Sale doubly terminated his novel: as narrative (structurally) and as discourse (compositionally). This compositional closure, by its very naiveté, reveals a major fact later occulted by bourgeois literature.

The novel has a double semiotic status: it is a linguistic (narrative) *phenomenon* as well as a discursive *circuit* (letter, literature). The fact

that it is a *narrative* is but one aspect—an anterior one—of this particularity: it *is* "*literature.*" That is the difference characterizing the
novel in relation to narrative: the novel is already "literature"; that is,
a product of speech, a (discursive) object of exchange with an owner
(author), value, and consumer (the public, addressee). The narrative's
conclusion coincides with the conclusion of one loop's trajectory.[27]
The novel's finitude, however, does not stop at this conclusion. An
instance of speech, often in the form of an epilogue, occurs at the end
to slow down the narration and to demonstrate that one is indeed
dealing with a verbal construction under the control of a subject
who speaks.[28] The narrative is presented as a story, the novel as a
discourse (independent of the fact that the author—more or less
consciously—recognizes it as such). In this, it constitutes a decisive
stage in the development of the speaking subject's critical consciousness in relation to his speech.

To terminate the novel as *narrative* is a rhetorical problem consist-
ing of reworking the bounded ideologeme of the sign which opened
it. To complete the novel as literary artifact (to understand it as discourse or sign) is a problem of social practice, of cultural text, and it
consists in confronting speech (the product, the Work) with its own
death—writing (textual productivity). It is here that there intervenes a third conception of the book as *work* and no longer as a phenomenon (narrative) or as literature (discourse). La Sale, of course,
never reaches this stage. The succeeding social text eliminates all
notions of production from its scene in order to substitute a product
(effect, value): the reign of *literature* is the reign of *market value* occult-
ing even what La Sale practiced in a confused way: the discursive
origins of the literary event. We shall have to wait for a reevaluation
of the bourgeois social text in order for a reevaluation of "literature"
(of discourse) to take place through the advent of scriptural work
within the text.[29]

4. In the meantime, this function of writing as work destroying
literary representation (the literary artifact) remains latent, misunderstood, and unspoken, although often at work in the text and made
evident when deciphered. For La Sale, as well as for any so-called
"realist" writer, writing *is* speech as law (with no possible transgression).

Writing is revealed, for him who thinks of himself as "author," as a function that ossifies, petrifies, and blocks. For the *phonetic* consciousness—from the Renaissance to our time[30]—writing is an artificial limit, an arbitrary law, a subjective finitude. The intervention of writing in the text is often an excuse used by the author to justify the arbitrary ending of his narrative. Thus, La Sale inscribes himself as writing in order to justify the end of his writing: his narrative is a letter whose death coincides with the end of his pen work. Inversely, Saintré's death is not the narration of an adventure: La Sale, often verbose and repetitive, restricts himself, in announcing this major fact, to the transcription from a tomb in two languages—Latin and French.

There we have a paradoxical phenomenon that dominates, in different forms, the entire history of the novel: the devalorization of writing, its categorization as pejorative, paralyzing, and deadly. This phenomenon is on a par with its other aspect: valorization of the oeuvre, the Author, and the literary artifact (discourse). Writing itself appears only to bound the book, that is, discourse. What opens it is speech: "of which the first shall tell of the Lady of the Beautiful Cousins." The act of writing is the differential act par excellence, reserving for the text the status of *other*, irreducible to what is different from it; it is also the correlational act par excellence, avoiding any bounding of sequences within a finite ideologeme, and opening them up to an infinite arrangement. Writing, however, has been suppressed, evoked only to oppose "objective reality" (utterance, phonetic discourse) to a "subjective artifice" (scriptural practice). The opposition phonetic/scriptural, utterance/text—at work within the bourgeois novel with devalorization of the second term (of the scriptural, textual)—misled the Russian Formalists. It permitted them to interpret the insertion of writing into narrative as proof of the text's "arbitrariness" or of the work's so-called "literariness." It is evident that the concepts of "arbitrariness" or "literariness" can only be accepted within an ideology of valorization of the oeuvre (as phonetic, discursive) to the detriment of writing (textual productivity); in other words, only within a bounded (cultural) text.

1966–1967

3

WORD, DIALOGUE, AND NOVEL[1]

If the efficacy of scientific approach in "human" sciences has always been challenged, it is all the more striking that such a challenge should for the first time be issued on the very level of the structures being studied—structures supposedly answerable to a logic *other* than scientific. What would be involved is the logic of language (and all the more so, of poetic language) that "writing" has had the virtue of bringing to light. I have in mind that particular literary practice in which the elaboration of poetic meaning emerges as a tangible, *dynamic gram*.[2] Confronted with this situation, then, literary semiotics can either abstain and remain silent, or persist in its efforts to elaborate a model that would be isomorphic to this other logic; that is, isomorphic to the elaboration of poetic meaning, a concern of primary importance to contemporary semiotics.

Russian Formalism, in which contemporary structural analysis claims to have its source, was itself faced with identical alternatives when reasons beyond literature and science halted its endeavors. Research was nonetheless carried on, recently coming to light in the work of Mikhail Bakhtin. His work represents one of that movement's most remarkable accomplishments, as well as one of the most powerful attempts to transcend its limitations. Bakhtin shuns the linguist's technical rigor, wielding an impulsive and at times even prophetic pen, while he takes on the fundamental problems presently confronting a structural analysis of narrative; this alone would give currency to essays written over forty years ago. Writer as well as "scholar," Bakhtin was one of the first to replace the static hewing out of texts with a model where literary structure does not simply *exist* but is generated in relation to *another* structure. What allows a dynamic dimension to structuralism is his conception of the "literary word" as an *intersection of textual surfaces* rather than a *point* (a fixed meaning), as a dialogue among several writings: that of the writer, the addressee (or the character), and the contemporary or earlier cultural context.

By introducing the *status of the word* as a minimal structural unit, Bakhtin situates the text within history and society, which are then seen as texts read by the writer, and into which he inserts himself by rewriting them. Diachrony is transformed into synchrony, and in light of this transformation, *linear* history appears as abstraction. The only way a writer can participate in history is by transgressing this abstraction through a process of reading-writing; that is, through the practice of a signifying structure in relation or opposition to another structure. History and morality are written and read within the infrastructure of texts. The poetic word, polyvalent and multi-determined, adheres to a logic exceeding that of codified discourse and fully comes into being only in the margins of recognized culture. Bakhtin was the first to study this logic, and he looked for its roots in *carnival*. Carnivalesque discourse breaks through the laws of a language censored by grammar and semantics and, at the same time, is a social and political protest. There is no equivalence, but rather, identity between challenging official linguistic codes and challenging official law.

The Word Within the Space of Texts

Defining the specific status of the word as signifier for different modes of (literary) intellection within different genres or texts puts poetic analysis at the sensitive center of contemporary "human" sciences—at the intersection of *language* (the true practice of thought)[3] with *space* (the volume within which signification, through a joining of differences, articulates itself). To investigate the status of the word is to study its articulations (as semic complex) with other words in the sentence, and then to look for the same functions or relationships at the articulatory level of larger sequences. Confronted with this spatial conception of language's poetic operation, we must first define the three dimensions of textual space where various semic sets and poetic sequences function. These three dimensions or coordinates of dialogue are writing subject, addressee, and exterior texts. The word's status is thus defined *horizontally* (the word in the text belongs to both writing subject and addressee) as well as *vertically* (the word in the text is oriented toward an anterior or synchronic literary corpus.[4]

The addressee, however, is included within a book's discursive universe only as discourse itself. He thus fuses with this other discourse, this other book, in relation to which the writer has written his own text. Hence horizontal axis (subject-addressee) and vertical axis (text-context) coincide, bringing to light an important fact: each word (text) is an intersection of words (texts) where at least one other word (text) can be read. In Bakhtin's work, these two axes, which he calls *dialogue* and *ambivalence*, are not clearly distinguished. Yet, what appears as a lack of rigor is in fact an insight first introduced into literary theory by Bakhtin: any text is constructed as a mosaic of quotations; any text is the absorption and transformation of another. The notion of *intertextuality*[5] replaces that of intersubjectivity, and poetic language is read as at least *double*.

The word as minimal textual unit thus turns out to occupy the status of *mediator*, linking structural models to cultural (historical) environment, as well as that of *regulator*, controlling mutations from diachrony to synchrony, i.e., to literary structure. The word is spatialized; through the very notion of status, it functions in three dimensions (subject-addressee-context) as a set of *dialogical*, semic elements or as a set of *ambivalent* elements. Consequently the task of literary semiotics is to discover other formalisms corresponding to different modalities of word-joining (sequences) within the dialogical space of texts.

Any description of a word's specific operation within different literary genres or texts thus requires a *translinguistic* procedure. First, we must think of literary genres as imperfect semiological systems "signifying beneath the surface of language but never without it"; and secondly, discover relations among larger narrative units such as sentences, questions-and-answers, dialogues, et cetera, not necessarily on the basis of linguistic models—justified by the principle of semantic expansion. We could thus posit and demonstrate the hypothesis that *any evolution of literary genres is an unconscious exteriorization of linguistic structures at their different levels.* The novel in particular exteriorizes linguistic dialogue.[6]

Word and Dialogue

Russian Formalists were engrossed with the idea of "linguistic dialogue." They insisted on the dialogical character of linguistic communication[7] and considered the monologue, the "embryonic form" of *common* language,[8] as subsequent to dialogue. Some of them distinguished between monological discourse (as "equivalent to a psychic state")[9] and narrative (as "artistic imitation of monological discourse").[10] Boris Eikhenbaum's famous study of Gogol's *The Overcoat* is based on such premises. Eikhenbaum notes that Gogol's text actively refers to an oral form of narration and to its linguistic characteristics (intonation, syntactic construction of oral discourse, pertinent vocabulary, and so on). He thus sets up two modes of narration, *indirect* and *direct*, studying the relationship between the two. Yet, he seems to be unaware that before referring to an *oral* discourse, the writer of the narrative usually refers to the discourse of an *other* whose oral discourse is only secondary (since the other is the carrier of oral discourse).[11]

For Bakhtin, the dialogue-monologue distinction has a much larger significance than the concrete meaning accorded it by the Russian Formalists. It does not correspond to the *direct/indirect* (monologue/dialogue) distinction in narratives or plays. For Bakhtin, dialogue can be monological, and what is called monologue can be dialogical. With him, such terms refer to a linguistic infrastructure that must be studied through a *semiotics* of literary texts. This semiotics cannot be based on either linguistic methods or logical givens, but rather, must be elaborated from the point where they leave off.

> Linguistics studies "language" and its specific logic in its *commonality* ("*obshchnost*") as that factor which makes dialogical intercourse *possible*, but it consistently refrains from studying those dialogical relationships themselves. [. . .] Dialogical relationships are not reducible to logical or concrete semantic relationships, which are in and of *themselves* devoid of any dialogical aspect. [. . .] Dialogical relationships are totally impossible without logical and concrete semantic relationships, but they are not reducible to them; they have their own specificity.[12]

While insisting on the difference between dialogical relationships and specifically linguistic ones, Bakhtin emphasizes that those structuring a narrative (for example, writer/character, to which we would add subject of enunciation/subject of utterance) are possible because dialogism is inherent in language itself. Without explaining exactly what makes up this double aspect of language, he nonetheless insists that "dialogue is the only sphere possible for the life of language." Today we can detect dialogical relationships on several levels of language: first, within the *combinative* dyad, langue/parole; and secondly, within the systems either of langue (as collective, monological contracts as well as systems of correlative value actualized in dialogue with the other) or of parole (as essentially "combinative," not pure creation, but individual formation based on the exchange of signs).

On still another level (which could be compared to the novel's ambivalent space), this "double character of language" has even been demonstrated as syntagmatic (made manifest through extension, presence, and metonymy) and systematic (manifested through association, absence, and metaphor). It would be important to analyze linguistically the dialogical exchanges between these two axes of language as basis of the novel's ambivalence. We should also note Jakobson's double structures and their overlappings within the code/message relationship,[13] which help to clarify Bakhtine's notion of dialogism as inherent in language.

Bakhtin foreshadows what Émile Benveniste has in mind when he speaks about *discourse*, that is, "language appropriated by the individual as a practice." As Bakhtin himself writes, "In order for dialogical relationships to arise among [logical or concrete semantic relationships], they must clothe themselves in the word, become utterances, and become the positions of various subjects, expressed in a word."[14] Bakhtin, however, born of a revolutionary Russia that was preoccupied with social problems, does not see dialogue only as language assumed by a subject; he sees it, rather, as a *writing* where one reads the *other* (with no allusion to Freud). Bakhtinian dialogism identifies writing as both subjectivity and communication, or better, as intertextuality. Confronted with this dialogism, the notion of a "person-subject of writing" becomes blurred, yielding to that of "ambivalence of writing."

Ambivalence

The term "ambivalence" implies the insertion of history (society) into a text and of this text into history; for the writer, they are one and the same. When he speaks of "two paths merging within the narrative," Bakhtin considers writing as a reading of the anterior literary corpus and the text as an absorption of and a reply to another text. He studies the polyphonic novel as an absorption of the carnival and the monological novel as a stifling of this literary structure, which he calls "Menippean" because of its dialogism. In this perspective, a text cannot be grasped through linguistics alone. Bakhtine postulates the necessity for what he calls a *translinguistic* science, which, developed on the basis of language's dialogism, would enable us to understand intertextual *relationships*; relationships that the nineteenth century labeled "social value" or literature's moral "message." Lautréamont wanted to write so that he could submit himself to a *high morality*. Within his practice, this morality is actualized as textual ambivalence: *The Songs of Maldoror* and the *Poems* are a constant dialogue with the preceding literary corpus, a perpetual challenge of past writing. Dialogue and ambivalence are borne out as the only approach that permits the writer to enter history by espousing an ambivalent ethics: negation as affirmation.

Dialogue and ambivalence lead me to conclude that, within the interior space of the text as well as within the space of *texts*, poetic language is a "double." Saussure's poetic *paragram* ("Anagrams") extends from *zero* to *two*: the unit "one" (definition, "truth") does not exist in this field. Consequently, the notions of definition, determination, the sign " = " and the very concept of sign, which presuppose a vertical (hierarchical) division between signifier and signified, cannot be applied to poetic language—by definition an infinity of pairings and combinations.

The notion of *sign* (Sr-Sd) is a product of scientific abstraction (identity-substance-cause-goal as structure of the Indo-European sentence), designating a vertically and hierarchically linear division. The notion of *double*, the result of thinking over poetic (not scientific) language, denotes "spatialization" and correlation of the literary (linguistic) sequence. This implies that the minimal unit of poetic language is at least *double*, not in the sense of the signifier/signified dyad, but rather, in terms of *one and other*. It suggests that poetic language functions as *a tabular model*, where each "unit" (this word can no longer be used without quotation marks, since every unit is double) acts as a multi-determined *peak*. The *double* would be the minimal sequence of a paragrammatic semiotics to be worked out starting from the work of Saussure (in the "Anagrams") and Bakhtin.

Instead of carrying these thoughts to their conclusion we shall concentrate here on one of their consequences: the inability of any logical system based on a zero-one sequence (true-false, nothingness-notation) to account for the operation of poetic language.

Scientific procedures are indeed based upon a logical approach, itself founded on the Greek (Indo-European) sentence. Such a sentence begins as subject-predicate and grows by identification, determination, and causality. Modern logic from Gottlob Frege and Giuseppe Peano to Jan Lukasiewicz, Robert Ackermann, and Alonzo Church evolves out of a 0–1 sequence; George Boole, who begins with set theory, produces formulae that are more isomorphic with language—all of these are ineffective within the realm of poetic language, where 1 is not a limit.

It is therefore impossible to formalize poetic language according to existing logical (scientific) procedures without distorting it. A literary semiotics must be developed on the basis of a *poetic logic* where the concept of the *power of the continuum* would embody the 0–2 interval, a continuity where 0 denotes and 1 is implicitly transgressed.

Within this "power of the continuum" from 0 to a specifically poetic double, the linguistic, psychic, and social "prohibition" is 1 (God, Law, Definition). The only linguistic practice to "escape" this prohibition is poetic discourse. It is no accident that the shortcomings of Aristotelian logic when applied to language were pointed out by, on the one hand, twentieth-century Chinese philosopher Chang Tung-sun (the product of a different linguistic heritage— ideograms—where, in place of God, there extends the Yin-Yang "dialogue") and, on the other, Bakhtin (who attempted to go beyond the Formalists through a dynamic theorization accomplished in revolutionary society). With Bakhtin, who assimilates narrative discourse into epic discourse, narrative is a prohibition, a *monologism*, a subordination of the code to 1, to God. Hence, the epic is religious and theological; all "realist" narrative obeying 0–1 logic is dogmatic. The realist novel, which Bakhtin calls monological (Tolstoy), tends to evolve within this space. Realist description, definition of "personality," "character" creation, and "subject" development—all are descriptive narrative elements belonging to the 0–1 interval and are thus *monological*. The only discourse integrally to achieve the 0–2 poetic logic is that of the carnival. By adopting a dream logic, it transgresses rules of linguistic code and social morality as well.

In fact, this "transgression" of linguistic, logical, and social codes within the carnivalesque only exists and succeeds, of course, because it accepts *another law*. Dialogism is not "freedom to say everything," it is a *dramatic* "banter" (Lautréamont), an *other* imperative than that of 0. We should particularly emphasize this specificity of dialogue as *transgression giving itself a law* so as to radically and categorically distinguish it from the pseudo-transgression evident in a certain modern "erotic" and parodic literature. The latter, seeing itself as "libertine" and "relativizing," operates according to a principle of *law anticipating its own transgression*. It thus compensates for monologism, does not displace the 0–1 interval, nor has anything to do with the architectonics of dialogism, which implies a categorical tearing from the norm and a relationship of nonexclusive opposites.

The novel incorporating carnivalesque structure is called *polyphonic*. Bakhtin's examples include Rabelais, Swift, and Dostoievski. We might also add the "modern" novel of the twentieth century—Joyce, Proust, Kafka—while specifying that the modern polyphonic novel, although analogous in its status, where monologism is concerned, to dialogical novels of the past, is clearly marked off from them. A break occurred at the end of the nineteenth century: while dialogue in Rabelais, Swift, and Dostoievski remains at a representative, fictitious level, our century's polyphonic novel becomes "unreadable" (Joyce) and interior to language (Proust, Kafka). Beginning with this break—not only literary but also social, political, and philosophical in nature—the problem of intertextuality (intertextual dialogue) appears as such. Bakhtin's theory itself (as well as that of Saussure's "Anagrams") can be traced historically to this break: he was able to discover textual dialogism in the writings of Mayakovsky, Khlebnikov, and Andrei Bely, to mention only a few of the Revolution's writers who made the outstanding imprints of this scriptural break. Bakhtin then extended his theory into literary history as a principle of all upheavals and defiant productivity.

Bakhtin's term *dialogism* as a semic complex thus implies the double, language, and another logic. Using that as point of departure, we can outline a new approach to poetic texts. Literary semiotics can accept the word "dialogism"; the logic of *distance* and *relationship* between the different units of a sentence or narrative structure, indicating a *becoming*—in opposition to the level of continuity and substance, both of which obey the logic of being and are thus monological. Secondly, it is a logic of *analogy* and *nonexclusive opposition*, opposed to monological levels of causality and identifying determination. Finally, it is a logic of the "transfinite," a concept borrowed from Georg Cantor, which, on the basis of poetic language's "power of the continuum" (0–2), introduces a second principle of formation: a poetic sequence is a "next-larger" (not causally deduced) to all pre-ceeding sequences of the Aristotelian chain (scientific, monologi-cal, or narrative). The novel's ambivalent space thus can be seen as regulated by two formative principles: monological (each following sequence is determined by the preceding one), and dialogical (trans-finite sequences that are next-larger to the preceding causal series).[15]

Dialogue appears most clearly in the structure of carnivalesque language, where symbolic relationships and analogy take precedence over substance-causality connections. The notion of *ambivalence* per-tains to the permutation of the two spaces observed in novelistic structure: dialogical space and monological space.

From a conception of poetic language as dialogue and ambivalence, Bakhtin moves to a reevaluation of the novel's structure. This investi-gation takes the form of a classification of words within the narrative—the classification being then linked to a typology of discourse.

Classification of Words Within the Narrative

According to Bakhtin, there are three categories of words within the narrative.

First, the *direct* word, referring back to its object, expresses the last possible degree of signification by the subject of discourse within the limits of a given context. It is the annunciating, expressive word of the writer, the *denotative* word, which is supposed to provide him with direct, objective comprehension. It knows nothing but itself and its object, to which it attempts to be adequate (it is not "conscious" of the influences of words foreign to it).

Second, the *object-oriented* word is the direct discourse of "characters." It has direct, objective meaning, but is not situated on the same level as the writer's discourse; thus, it is at some distance from the latter. It is both oriented towards its object and is itself the object of the writer's orientation. It is a foreign word, subordinate to the narrative word as object of the writer's comprehension. But the writer's orientation towards the word as object does not penetrate it but accepts it as a whole, changing neither meaning nor tonality; it subordinates that word to its own task, introducing no other signification. Consequently, the object-oriented word, having become the object of an other (denotative) word, is not "conscious" of it. The object-oriented word, like the denotative word, is therefore univocal.

In the third instance, however, the writer can use another's word, giving it a new meaning while retaining the meaning it already had. The result is a word with two significations: it becomes *ambivalent*. This ambivalent word is therefore the result of a joining of two sign systems. Within the evolution of genres, ambivalent words appear in Menippean and carnivalesque texts. (I shall return to this point.) The forming of two sign systems relativizes the text. Stylizing effects establish a distance with regard to the word of another—contrary to *imitation* (Bakhtin, rather, has in mind *repetition*), which takes what is imitated (repeated) seriously, claiming and appropriating it without relativizing it. This category of ambivalent words is characterized by the writer's exploitation of another's speech—without running counter to its thought—for his own purposes; he follows its direction while relativizing it. A second category of ambivalent words, *parody* for instance, proves to be quite different. Here the writer introduces a signification opposed to that of the other's word. A third type of ambivalent word, of which the *hidden interior polemic* is an example, is characterized by the active (modifying) influence of another's word on the writer's word. It is the writer who "speaks," but a foreign discourse is constantly present in the speech that it distorts. With this *active* kind of ambivalent word, the other's word is represented by the word of the narrator. Examples include autobiography, polemical confessions, questions-and-answers, and hidden dialogue. The novel is the only genre in which ambivalent words appear; that is the specific characteristic of its structure.

The Inherent Dialogism of Denotative or Historical Words

The notion of univocity or objectivity of monologue and of the epic to which it is assimilated, or of the denotative object-oriented word, cannot withstand psychoanalytic or semantic analysis of language. Dialogism is coextensive with the deep structures of discourse. Notwithstanding Bakhtin and Benveniste, dialogism appears on the level of the Bakhtinian denotative word as a principle of every enunciation, as well as on the level of the "story" in Benveniste. The story, like Benveniste's concept of "discourse" itself, presupposes an intervention by the speaker within the narrative as well as an orientation toward the other. In order to describe the dialogism inherent in the denotative or historical word, we would have to turn to the psychic aspect of writing as trace of a dialogue with oneself (with another), as a writer's distance from himself, as a splitting of the writer into subject of enunciation and subject of utterance.

By the very act of narrating, the subject of narration addresses an other; narration is structured in relation to this other. (On the strength of such a communication, Francis Ponge offers his own variation of "I think therefore I am": "I speak and you hear me, therefore we are." He thus postulates a shift from subjectivism to ambivalence.) Consequently, we may consider narration (beyond the signifier/signified relationship) as a dialogue between the *subject* of narration (S) and the *addressee* (A)—the other. This addressee, quite simply the reading subject, represents a doubly oriented entity: signifier in his relation to the text and signified in the relation between the subject of narration and himself. This entity is thus a dyad $(A_1$ and $A_2)$ whose two terms, communicating with each other, constitute a code system. The subject of narration (S) is drawn in, and therefore reduced to a code, to a nonperson, to an *anonymity* (as writer, subject of enunciation) mediated by a third person, the *he/she* character, the subject of utterance. The writer is thus the subject of narration transformed by his having included himself within the narrative system; he is neither nothingness nor anybody, but the possibility of permutation from S to A, from story to discourse and from discourse to story. He becomes an anonymity, an absence, a blank space, thus permitting the structure to exist as such. At the very origin of narration, at the very moment when the writer appears, we experience emptiness. We see the problems of death, birth, and sex appear when literature touches upon this strategic point that writing becomes when it exteriorizes linguistic systems through narrative structure (genres). On the basis of this anonymity, this zero where the author is situated, the *he/she* of the character is born. At a later stage, it will become a *proper name* (N). Therefore, in a literary text, o does not exist; emptiness is quickly replaced by a "one" (a *he/she*, or a *proper name*) that is really twofold, since it is subject and addressee. It is the addressee, the other, exteriority (whose object is the subject of narration and who is at the same time represented and representing) who transforms the subject into an *author*. That is, who has the S pass through this zero-stage of negation, of exclusion, constituted by the author. In this coming-and-going movement between subject and other, between writer (W) and reader, the author is structured as a signifier and the text as a dialogue of two discourses.

The constitution of characters (of "personality") also permits a disjunction of S into S_r (subject of enunciation) and S_d (subject of utterance). A diagram of this mutation would appear as diagram 1. This diagram incorporates the structure of the pronominal system[16] that psychoanalysts repeatedly find in the discourse of the object of psychoanalysis (see diagram 2).

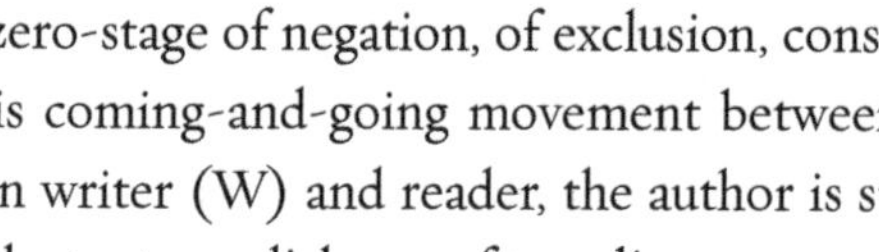

$$\frac{S}{A} \to W \text{ (zero)} \to he \to N = S \Big\langle \begin{matrix} S_r \\ S_d \end{matrix}$$

$$A \Big\langle \begin{matrix} A_1 \\ A_2 \end{matrix}$$

Diagram 1

$$\frac{\text{I}}{\text{he}_1} \qquad \frac{\text{S}}{\text{N}}$$
$$\frac{\text{he}_0}{\text{(some) one}} \qquad \frac{S_r}{S_d}$$

Diagram 2

At the level of the text (of the signifier)—in the S_r-S_d relationship—we find this dialogue of the subject with the addressee around which every narration is structured. The subject of utterance, in relation to the subject of enunciation, plays the role of addressee with respect to the subject; it inserts the subject of enunciation within the writing system by making the latter pass through emptiness. Mallarmé called this operation "elocutionary disappearance."

The *subject of utterance* is both representative of the subject of enunciation and represented as object of the subject of enunciation. It is therefore commutable with the writer's anonymity. A *character* (a personality) is constituted by this generation of a double entity starting from zero. The subject of utterance is "dialogical," both S and A are disguised within it.

The procedure I have just described in confronting narration and the novel now abolishes distinctions between signifier and signified. It renders these concepts ineffective for that literary practice operating uniquely within dialogical signifier(s). "The signifier represents the subject for another signifier" (Lacan).

Narration, therefore, is always constituted as a dialogical matrix by the receiver to whom this narration refers. Any narration, including history and science, contains this dialogical dyad formed by the narrator in conjunction with the other. It is translated through the dialogical S_r/S_d relationship, with S_r and S_d filling the roles of signifier and signified in turns, but constituting merely a permutation of two signifiers.

It is, however, only through certain narrative structures that this dialogue—this hold on the sign as double, this ambivalence of writing—is exteriorized in the actual organization of poetic discourse on the level of textual, literary occurrence.

Toward a Typology of Discourses

Bakhtin's radical undertaking—the dynamic analysis of texts resulting in a redistribution of genres—calls upon us to be just as radical in developing a typology of discourses.

As it is used by the Formalists, the term *"narrative"* is too ambiguous to cover all of the genres it supposedly designates. At least two different types of narrative can be isolated.

We have on the one hand *monological discourse*, including, first, the representative mode of description and narration (the epic); secondly, historical discourse; and thirdly, scientific discourse. In all three, the subject both assumes and submits to the rule of 1 (God). The dialogue inherent in all discourse is smothered by a *prohibition*, a censorship, such that this discourse refuses to turn back upon itself, to enter into dialogue with itself. To present the models of this censorship is to describe the nature of the differences between two types of discourse: the epic type (history and science) and the Menippean type (carnivalesque writings and novel), which transgresses prohibition. Monological discourse corresponds to Jakobson's systematic axis of language, and its analogous relationship to grammatical affirmation and negation has also been noted.

On the other hand, *dialogical discourse* includes carnivalesque and Menippean discourses as well as the polyphonic novel. In its structures, writing reads another writing, reads itself and constructs itself through a process of destructive genesis.

Epic Monologism

The *epic*, structured at the limits of syncretism, illustrates the double value of words in their postsyncretic phase: the utterance of a subject ("I") inevitably penetrated by language as carrier of the concrete, universal, individual, and collective. But in an epic, the speaker (subject of the epic) does not make use of another's speech. The dialogical play of language as correlation of signs—the dialogical permutation of two signifiers for one signified—takes place on the level of *narration* (through the denotative word, or through the inherency of the text). It does not exteriorize itself at the level of textual *manifestation* as in the structure of novels. This is the scheme at work within an epic, with no hint as yet of Bakhtin's problematic—the ambivalent word. The organizational principle of epic structure thus remains monological. The dialogue of language does not manifest itself except within a narrative infrastructure. There is no dialogue at the level of the apparent textual organization (historical enunciation/discursive enunciation); the two aspects of enunciation remain limited by the narrator's absolute point of view, which coincides with the wholeness of a god or community. Within epic monologism, we detect the presence of the "transcendental signified" and "self presence" as highlighted by Jacques Derrida.

It is the systematic mode of language (similarity, according to Jakobson) that prevails within the epic space. Metonymic contiguity, specific to the syntagmatic axis of language, is rare. Of course, association and metonymy are there as rhetorical figures, but they are never a principle of structural organization. Epic logic pursues the general through the specific; it thus assumes a hierarchy within the structure of substance. Epic logic is therefore causal, that is, theological; it is *a belief* in the literal sense of the word.

The Carnival: A Homology Between the Body, Dream, Linguistic Structure, and Structures of Desire

Carnivalesque structure is like the residue of a cosmogony that ignored substance, causality, or identity outside of its link to the whole, *which exists only in or through relationship*. This carnivalesque cosmogony has persisted in the form of an antitheological (but not antimystical) and deeply popular movement. It remains present as an often misunderstood and persecuted substratum of official Western culture throughout its entire history; it is most noticeable in folk games as well as in Medieval theater and prose (anecdotes, fables, and the *Roman de Renart*). As composed of distances, relationships, analogies, and nonexclusive oppositions, it is essentially dialogical.

It is a spectacle, but without a stage; a game, but also a daily undertaking; a signifier, but also a signified. That is, two texts meet, contradict, and relativize each other. A carnival participant is both actor and spectator; he loses his sense of individuality, passes through a zero point of carnivalesque activity, and splits into a subject of the spectacle and an object of the game. Within the carnival, the subject is reduced to nothingness, while the structure of *the author* emerges as anonymity that creates and sees itself created as self and other, as man and mask. The cynicism of this carnivalesque scene, which destroys a god in order to impose its own dialogical laws, calls to mind Nietzsche's Dionysianism. The carnival first exteriorizes the structure of reflective literary productivity, then inevitably brings to light this structure's underlying unconscious: sexuality and death. Out of the dialogue that is established between them, the structural dyads of carnival appear: high and low, birth and agony, food and excrement, praise and curses, laughter and tears.

Figures germane to carnivalesque language, including repetition, "inconsequent" statements (which are nonetheless "connected" within an infinite context), and nonexclusive opposition, which function as empty sets or disjunctive additions, produce a more flagrant dialogism than any other discourse. Disputing the laws of language based on the 0–1 interval, the carnival challenges God, authority, and social law; insofar as it is dialogical, it is rebellious. Because of its subversive discourse, the word "carnival" has understandably acquired a strongly derogatory or narrowly burlesque meaning in our society.

The scene of the carnival, where there is no stage, no "theater," is thus both stage and life, game and dream, discourse and spectacle. By the same token, it is proffered as the only space in which language escapes linearity (law) to live as drama in three dimensions. At a deeper level, this also signifies the contrary: drama becomes located in language. A major principle thus emerges: all poetic discourse is dramatization, dramatic permutation (in a mathematical sense) of words. Within carnivalesque discourse, we can already adumbrate that "as to mental condition, it is like the meanderings of drama" (Mallarmé). This scene, whose symptom is carnivalesque discourse, is the only dimension where "theater might be the reading of a book, its writing in operation." In other words, such a scene is the only place where discourse attains its "potential infinity" (to use David Hilbert's term), where prohibitions (representation, "monologism") and their transgression (dream, body, "dialogism") coexist. Carnivalesque tradition was absorbed into Menippean discourse and put into practice by the polyphonic novel.

On the omnified stage of carnival, language parodies and relativizes itself, repudiating its role in representation; in so doing, it provokes laughter but remains incapable of detaching itself from representation. The syntagmatic axis of language becomes exteriorized in this space and, through dialogue with the systematic axis, constitutes the ambivalent structure bequeathed by carnival to the novel. Faulty (by which I mean ambivalent), both representative and antirepresentative, the carnivalesque structure is anti-Christian and antirationalist. All of the most important polyphonic novels are inheritors of the Menippean, carnivalesque structure: those of Rabelais, Cervantes, Swift, Sade, Balzac, Lautréamont, Dostoïevski, Joyce, and Kafka. Its history is the history of the struggle against Christianity and its representation; this means an exploration of language (of sexuality and death), a consecration of ambivalence and of "vice."

The word "carnivalesque" lends itself to an ambiguity one must avoid. In contemporary society, it generally connotes parody, hence a strengthening of the law. There is a tendency to blot out the carnival's *dramatic* (murderous, cynical, and revolutionary in the sense of *dialectical transformation*) aspects, which Bakhtin emphasized, and which he recognized in Menippean writings or in Dostoievski. The laughter of the carnival is not simply parodic; it is no more comic than tragic; it is both at once, one might say that it is *serious*. This is the only way that it can avoid becoming either the scene of law or the scene of its parody, in order to become the scene of its *other*. Modern writing offers several striking examples of this omnified scene that is both *law* and *other*—where *laughter* is silenced because it is not parody but *murder* and *revolution* (Antonin Artaud).

The epic and the carnivalesque are the two currents that formed European narrative, one taking precedence over the other according to the times and the writer. The carnivalesque tradition of the people is still apparent in personal literature of late antiquity and has remained, to this day, the life source reanimating literary thought, orienting it towards new perspectives.

Classical humanism helped dissolve the epic monologism that speech welded together so well, and that orators, rhetoricians, and politicians, on the one hand, tragedy and epic, on the other, implemented so effectively. Before another monologism could take root (with the triumph of formal logic, Christianity, and Renaissance humanism),[17] late antiquity gave birth to two genres that reveal language's dialogism. Situated within the carnivalesque tradition, and constituting the yeast of the European novel, these two genres are *Socratic dialogue* and *Menippean discourse*.

Socratic Dialogue: Dialogism as a Destruction of the Person

Socratic dialogue was widespread in antiquity: Plato, Xenophon, Antisthenes, Aeschines, Phaedo, Euclid, and others excelled in it, although only the dialogues of Plato and Xenophon have come down to us. Not as much rhetorical in genre as popular and carnivalesque, it was originally a kind of memoir (the recollections of Socrates's discussions with his students) that broke away from the constraints of history, retaining only the Socratic process of dialogically revealing truth, as well as the structure of a recorded dialogue framed by narrative. Nietzsche accused Plato of having ignored Dionysian tragedy, but Socratic dialogue had adopted the dialogical and defiant structure of the carnivalesque scene. According to Bakhtin, Socratic dialogues are characterized by opposition to any official monologism claiming to possess a ready-made truth. Socratic truth ("meaning") is the product of a dialogical relationship among speakers; it is correlational and its relativism appears by virtue of the observers' autonomous points of view. Its art is one of *articulation* of fantasy, *correlation* of signs. Two typical devices for triggering this linguistic network are syncrisis (confronting different discourses on the same topic) and anacrusis (one word prompting another). The subjects of discourse are nonpersons, anonyms, hidden by the discourse constituting them. Bakhtin reminds us that the "event" of Socratic dialogue is of the nature of discourse: a questioning and testing, through speech, of a definition. This speech practice is therefore organically linked to the man who created it (Socrates and his students), or better, speech *is* man and his activity. Here, one can speak of a practice possessing a synthetic character; the process separating the *word* as act, as apodeictic practice, as articulation of difference from the *image* as representation, as knowledge, and as idea was not yet complete when Socratic dialogue took form. But there is an important "detail" to Socratic dialogism; it is the exclusive position of a subject of discourse that provokes the dialogue. In the *Apology* of Plato, Socrates's trial and the period of awaiting judgment determine his discourse as the confessions of a man "on the threshold." The exclusive situation liberates the word from any univocal objectivity, from any representative function, opening it up to the symbolic sphere. Speech affronts death, measuring itself against another discourse; this dialogue counts the *person* out.

The resemblance between Socratic dialogue and the ambivalent word of the novel is obvious.

Socratic dialogue did not last long, but it gave birth to several dialogical genres, including *Menippean discourse*, whose origins also lie in carnivalesque folklore.

Menippean Discourse: The Text as Social Activity

I. Menippean discourse takes its name from Menippus of Gadara, a philosopher of the third century B.C. His satires were lost, but we know of their existence through the writings of Diogenes Laertius. The term was used by the Romans to designate a genre of the first century B.C. (Marcus Terentius Varro's *Satirae Menippeae*).

Yet, the genre actually appeared much earlier; its first representative was perhaps Antisthenes, a student of Socrates and one of the writers of Socratic dialogue. Heraclitus also wrote Menippean texts (according to Cicero, he created an analogous genre called *logistoricus*); Varro gave it definite stability. Other examples include Seneca the Younger's *Apocolocynthosis*, Petronius's *Satyricon*, Lucan's satires, Ovid's *Metamorphoses*, Hippocrates' *Novel*, various samples of Greek "novels," classical utopian novels, and Roman (Horatian) satire. Within the Menippean sphere there evolve diatribe, soliloquy, and other minor genres of controversy. It greatly influenced Christian and Byzantine literature; in various forms, it survived through the Middle Ages, the Renaissance, and the Reformation through to the present (the novels of Joyce, Kafka, and Bataille). This carnivalesque genre—as pliant and variable as Proteus, capable of insinuating itself into other genres—had an enormous influence on the development of European literature and especially the formation of the novel.

Menippean discourse is both comic and tragic, or rather, it is *serious* in the same sense as is the carnivalesque; through the status of its words, it is politically and socially disturbing. It frees speech from historical constraints, and this entails a thorough boldness in philosophical and imaginative inventiveness. Bakhtin emphasizes that "exclusive" situations increase freedom of language in Menippean discourse. Phantasmagoria and an often mystical symbolism fuse with macabre naturalism. Adventures unfold in brothels, robbers' dens, taverns, fairgrounds, and prisons, among erotic orgies and during sacred worship, and so forth. The word has no fear of incriminating itself. It becomes free from presupposed "values"; without distinguishing between virtue and vice, and without distinguishing itself from them, the word considers them its private domain, as one of its creations. Academic problems are pushed aside in favor of the "ultimate" problems of existence: this discourse orients liberated language towards philosophical universalism. Without distinguishing ontology from cosmogony, it unites them into a practical philosophy of life. Elements of the fantastic, which never appear in epic or tragic works, crop forth here. For example, an unusual perspective from above changes the scale of observation in Lucan's *Icaro-menippea*, Varro's *Endymion*, and later in the works of Rabelais, Swift, and Voltaire. Pathological states of the soul, such as madness, split personalities, daydreams, dreams, and death, become part of the narrative (they affect the writing of Shakespeare and Calderon). According to Bakhtin, these elements have more structural than thematic significance; they destroy man's epic and tragic unity as well as his belief in identity and causality; they indicate that he has lost his totality and no longer coincides with himself. At the same time, they often appear as an exploration of language and writing: in Varro's *Bimarcus*, the two Marcuses discuss whether or not one should write in tropes. Menippean discourse tends towards the scandalous and eccentric in language. The "inopportune" expression, with its cynical frankness, its desecration of the sacred, and its attack on etiquette, is quite characteristic. This discourse is made up of contrasts: virtuous courtesans, generous bandits, wise men that are both free and enslaved, and so on. It uses abrupt transitions and changes; high and low, rise and fall, and misalliances of all kinds. Its language seems fascinated with the "double" (with its own activity as graphic *trace*, doubling an "outside") and with the logic of opposition replacing that of identity in defining terms. It is an all-inclusive genre, put together as a pavement of citations. It includes all genres (short stories, letters, speeches, mixtures of verse and prose) whose structural signification is to denote the writer's distance from his own and other texts. The multi-stylism and multi-tonality of this discourse and the dialogical status of its word explain why it has been impossible for classicism, or for any other authoritarian society, to express itself in a novel descended from Menippean discourse.

Put together as an exploration of the body, dreams, and language, this writing grafts onto the topical: it is a kind of political journalism of its time. Its discourse exteriorizes political and ideological conflicts of the moment. The dialogism of its words *is* practical philosophy doing battle against idealism and religious metaphysics, against the epic. It constitutes the social and political thought of an era fighting against theology, against law.

2. Menippean discourse is thus structured as ambivalence, as the focus for two tendencies of Western literature: representation through language as staging, and exploration of language as a correlative system of signs. Language in the Menippean tradition is both representation of exterior space and "an experience that produces

its own space." In this ambiguous genre appear, first, the *premises of realism* (a secondary activity in relation to what is lived, where man describes himself by making of himself an exhibition, finally creating "characters" and "personalities"); and secondly, the *refusal to define* a psychic universe (an immediately present activity, characterized by images, gestures, and word-gestures through which man lives his limits in the impersonal). This second aspect relates Menippean structure to the structure of dreams and hieroglyphic writing or, possibly, to the theater of cruelty as conceived by Artaud. His words apply equally; Menippean discourse "is not equal to individual life, to that individual aspect of life where characters triumph, but rather to a kind of liberated life that sweeps away human individuality and where man is no more than a reflected image." Likewise, the Menippean experience is not cathartic; it is a festival of cruelty, but also a political act. It transmits no fixed message except that itself should be "the eternal joy of becoming," and it exhausts itself in the act and in the present. Born after Socrates, Plato, and the Sophists, it belongs to an age when thought ceases to be practice; the fact that it is considered as a *techne* shows that the *praxis-poiesis* separation has already taken place. Similarly, literature becoming "thought" becomes conscious of itself as *sign*. Man, alienated from nature and society, becomes alienated from himself, discovering his "interior" and "reifying" this discovery in the ambivalence of Menippean writing. Such tokens are the harbingers of realist representation. Menippean discourse, however, knows nothing of a theological principle's monologism (or of the Renaissance man-God) that could have consolidated its representative aspect. The "tyranny" it is subjected to is that of text (not speech as reflection of a preexisting universe), or rather its own structure, constructing and understanding itself through itself. It constructs itself as a *hieroglyph*, all the while remaining a spectacle. It bequeaths this ambivalence to the novel, above all to the polyphonic novel, which knows neither law nor hierarchy, since it is a plurality of linguistic elements in dialogical relationships. The conjunctive principle of the different parts of Menippean discourse is certainly *similitude* (resemblance, dependence, and therefore "realism"), but also contiguity (analogy, juxtaposition, and therefore "rhetoric"—not in Benedetto Croce's sense of ornament, but rather, as justification through and in language). Menippean ambivalence consists of communication between two spaces:[18] that of the scene and that of the hieroglyph, that of representation *by* language, and that of experience *in* language, system and phrase, metaphor and metonymy. This ambivalence is the novel's inheritance.

In other words, the dialogism of Menippean and carnivalesque discourses, translating a logic of relations and analogy rather than of substance and inference, stands against Aristotelian logic. From within the very interior of formal logic, even while skirting it, Menippean dialogism contradicts it and points it towards other forms of thought. Indeed, Menippean discourse develops in times of opposition against Aristotelianism, and writers of polyphonic novels seem to disapprove of the very structures of official thought founded on formal logic.

The Subversive Novel

1. In the Middle Ages, Menippean tendencies were held in check by the authority of the religious text; in the bourgeois era, they were contained by the absolutism of individuals and things. Only modernity—when freed of "God"—releases the Menippean force of the novel.

Now that modern, bourgeois society has not only accepted, but claims to recognize itself in the novel,[19] such claim can only refer to the category of monological narratives, known as realistic, that censor all carnivalesque and Menippean elements, whose structures were assembled at the time of the Renaissance. To the contrary, the Menippean, dialogical novel, tending to refuse representation and the epic, has only been tolerated; that is, it has been declared unreadable, ignored, or ridiculed. Today, it shares the same fate as the carnivalesque discourse practiced by students during the Middle Ages outside of the Church.

The novel, and especially the modern, polyphonic novel, incorporating Menippean elements, embodies the effort of European thought to break out of the framework of causally determined identical

substances and head toward another modality of thought that proceeds through dialogue (a logic of distance, relativity, analogy, nonexclusive and transfinite opposition). It is therefore not surprising
that the novel has been considered as an inferior genre (by neo-
classicism and other similar regimes) or as subversive (I have in
mind the major writers of polyphonic novels over many centuries—
Rabelais, Swift, Sade, Lautréamont, Kafka, and Bataille—to mention
only those who have always been and still remain on the fringe of
official culture). The way in which European thought transgresses its
constituent characteristics appears clearly in the words and narrative
structures of the twentieth-century novel. Identity, substance, causality, and definition are transgressed so that others may be adopted:
analogy, relation, opposition, and therefore dialogism and Menippean ambivalence.[20]

Although this entire historical inventory that Bakhtin has undertaken evokes the image of a museum or the task of an archivist, it
is nonetheless rooted in our present concerns. Everything written
today unveils either the possibility or impossibility of reading and
rewriting history. This possibility is evident in the literature heralded
by the writings of a new generation, where the text is elaborated as
theater and as *reading*. Mallarmé, one of the first to understand the
Menippean qualities of the novel (let it be emphasized that Bakhtin's
term has the advantage of situating a certain kind of writing within
history), said that literature "is nothing but the flash of what should
have been produced previously or closer to the origin."

2. I would now suggest two models for organizing narrative
signification, based on two dialogical categories: (1) Subject (S) ⇆
Addressee (A); and (2) Subject of enunciation ⇆ Subject of utterance.

The first model implies a dialogical relationship, while the second presupposes modal relationships within this dialogical formation. The first model determines genre (epic poem, novel) while the
second determines generic variants.

Within the polyphonic structure of a novel, the first dialogical model (S ⇆ A) plays itself out entirely within the writing discourse; and it presents itself as perpetually challenging this discourse.

The writer's interlocutor, then, is the writer himself, but as reader of another text. The one who writes is the same as the one who reads. Since his interlocutor is a text, he himself is no more than a text rereading itself as it rewrites itself. The dialogical structure, therefore, appears only in the light of the text elaborating itself as ambivalent in relation to another text.

In the epic, on the other hand, A is an extratextual, absolute entity (God or community) that relativizes dialogue to the point where it is canceled out and reduced to monologue. With this in mind, it is easy to understand why not only the so-called "traditional" novel of the nineteenth century, but also any novel with any ideological thesis whatsoever, tends towards an epic, thus constituting a deviation in the very structure of the novel; this is why Tolstoy's monologism is epic and Dostoievski's dialogism novelistic.

Within the framework of the second model, several possibilities may be detected:

a. The subject of utterance (S_d) coincides with the zero degree of the subject of enunciation (S_r), which can be designated either by the "he/she" nonperson pronoun or a proper name. This is the simplest technique found at the inception of the narrative.

b. The subject of utterance (S_d) coincides with the subject of enunciation (S_r). This produces a first person narrative: "I."

c. The subject of utterance (S_d) coincides with the addressee (A). This produces a second person narrative: "you": as for example with Raskolnikov's object-oriented word in *Crime and Punishment*. Michel Butor insistently explored this technique in *A Change of Heart*.

d. The subject of utterance (S_d) coincides both with the subject of enunciation (S_r) and the addressee (A). In such a case the novel becomes a questioning of writing and displays the staging of its dialogical structure. At the same time, the text becomes a reading (quotation and commentary) of an exterior literary corpus and is thus constructed as ambivalence. Through its use of personal pronouns and anonymous quotations, Philippe Sollers's *Drame* is an example of this fourth possibility.

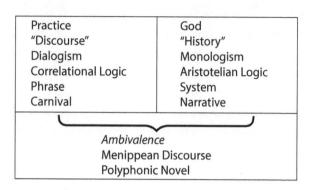

Practice	God
"Discourse"	"History"
Dialogism	Monologism
Correlational Logic	Aristotelian Logic
Phrase	System
Carnival	Narrative

Ambivalence
Menippean Discourse
Polyphonic Novel

Figure I

A reading of Bakhtin therefore leads to the paradigm shown in figure I.

I should finally like to insist on the importance of Bakhtin's concepts (on the status of the word, dialogue, and ambivalence), as well as on the importance of certain new perspectives opened up through them.

By establishing the status of the word as *minimal unit* of the text, Bakhtin deals with structure at its deepest level, beyond the sentence and rhetorical figures. The notion of *status* has added to the image of the text as a corpus of atoms that of a text made up of relationships, within which words function as quantum units. If there is a model for poetic language, it no longer involves lines or surfaces, but rather, *space* and *infinity*—concepts amenable to formalization through set theory and the new mathematics. Contemporary analysis of narrative structure has been refined to the point where it can delineate functions (cardinal or catalytic), and indices (as such or as information); it can describe the elaboration of a narrative according to particular logical or rhetorical patterns. Without gainsaying the undisputed value of this kind of research,[21] one might wonder whether the presuppositions of a metalanguage that sets up hierarchies or is heterogeneous to narrative do not weigh too heavily upon such studies. Perhaps Bakhtin's naive procedure, centered on the word and its unlimited ability to generate dialogue (commentary of a quotation) is both simpler and more productive.

The notion of dialogism, which owes much to Hegel, must not be confused with Hegelian dialectics, based on a triad and thus on struggle and projection (a movement of transcendence), which does not transgress the Aristotelian tradition founded on substance and causality. Dialogism replaces these concepts by absorbing them within the concept of relation. It does not strive towards transcendence but rather toward harmony, all the while implying an idea of rupture (of opposition and analogy) as a modality of transformation.

Dialogism situates philosophical problems *within* language; more precisely, within language as a correlation of texts, as a reading-writing that falls in with non-Aristotelian, syntagmatic, correlational, "carnivalesque" logic. Consequently, one of the fundamental problems facing contemporary semiotics is precisely to describe this "other logic" without denaturing it.

The term "ambivalence" lends itself perfectly to the current transitory stage of European literature—a coexistence (an ambivalence) of "the double of lived experience" (realism and the epic) and "lived experience" itself (linguistic exploration and Menippean discourse)—a literature that will perhaps arrive at a form of thought similar to that of painting: the transmission of essence through form, and the configuration of (literary) space as revealing (literary) thought without "realist" pretensions. This entails the study, through language, of the novel's space and of its transmutations, thereby establishing a close relationship between language and space, compelling us to analyze them as modes of thought. By examining the ambivalence of the spectacle (realist representation) and of lived experience (rhetoric), one might perceive the line where the rupture (or junction) between them takes place. That line could be seen as the graph of a motion through which our culture forsakes itself in order to go beyond itself.

The path charted between the two poles of dialogue radically abolishes problems of causality, finality, et cetera, from our philosophical arena. It suggests the importance of the dialogical principle for a space of thought much larger than that of the novel. More than binarism, dialogism may well become the basis of our time's intellectual structure. The predominance of the novel and other ambivalent literary structures; the communal, carnivalesque phenomena attracting young people; quantum exchanges; and current interest in the correlational symbolism of Chinese philosophy—to cite only a few striking elements of modern thought—all confirm this hypothesis.

1966

4

HOW DOES ONE SPEAK TO LITERATURE?

. . . a Passion of writing, which recounts stage by stage the disintegration of bourgeois consciousness.

—Roland Barthes, *Writing Degree Zero*[1]

As capitalist society is being economically and politically choked to death, discourse is wearing thin and heading for collapse at a more rapid rate than ever before. Philosophical finds, various modes of "teaching," scientific or aesthetic formalisms follow one upon another, compete, and disappear without leaving either a convinced audience or noteworthy disciples. Didacticism, rhetoric, dogmatism of any kind, in any "field" whatsoever, no longer command attention. They have survived, and perhaps will continue to survive, in modified form, throughout Academia. Only one language grows more and more contemporary: the equivalent, beyond a span of thirty years, of the language of *Finnegans Wake*.

It follows that the literary avant-garde experience, by virtue of its very characteristics, is slated to become the laboratory of a new discourse (and of a new subject), thus bringing about a mutation, "perhaps as important, and involving the same problem, as the one marking the passage from the Middle Ages to the Renaissance" (*Critique et vérité*, p. 48). It also rejects all discourse that is either stagnant or eclectically academic, preempts its knowledge where it does not impel it, and devises another original, mobile, and transformative knowledge. In so doing, it stimulates and reveals deep ideological changes that are currently searching for their own accurate political formulation, as opposed to the break-down of a bourgeois "liberalism" that never ceases to exploit and dominate, to the revisionism and hasty integration of a dogmatism that never ceases to be repressive and me-too-ist under its [revolutionary] disguise.

How does literature achieve this positive subversion of the old universe? How does there emerge, through its practical experience, a negativity germane to the subject as well as to history, capable of clearing away ideologies and even "natural" languages in order to formulate new signifying devices? How does it condense the shattering of the subject, as well as that of society, into a new apportionment of relationships between the symbolic and the real, the subjective and the objective?

The investigation of these contemporary ideological upheavals hinges on a knowledge of the literary "machine." My review of the work of Roland Barthes is situated in this perspective. He is the precursor and founder of modern literary studies precisely because he located literary practice at the intersection of subject and history; because he studied this practice as symptom of the ideological tearings in the social fabric; and because he sought, within texts, the precise mechanism that symbolically (semiotically) controls this tearing. He thus attempted to constitute the concrete object of a learning whose variety, multiplicity, and mobility allow him to ward off the saturation of old discourses. This knowledge is in a way already a writing, a text.

I shall now review what I consider a major portion of the work of Roland Barthes, which aims at specifying the key role of literature in the system of discourses: the notion of *writing*; language seen as *negativity*; the desubstantification of linguistic ideals; the operation of inscribing the a-symbolized real into the fabric of writing; the desire of the subject in writing; the impetus of the body and, ultimately, the reckoning of history within the written text; and the status of metalanguage within the possible knowledge of literature (the split between "science" and "criticism").

This will be a "classical," indeed a didactic review, whose only ambition is to *call attention* and *refer* to the texts of Roland Barthes; how could I match his talents as a writer? Intending to write neither a scientific analysis of any one specific text, nor a global evaluation, I shall attempt to choose a "point of view"—a displacement that perhaps justifies this undertaking. In other words, since I shall necessarily effect a sifting of the whole of Barthes's texts, I shall do so from the standpoint of avant-garde texts, of current avant-garde tendencies often subsequent to the writing of Barthes, thus displacing his framework. My "point of view," therefore, is that the avant-garde allows us to read in Barthes's work (itself part of that movement) contemporary elements of the current discursive-ideological mutation.

The Discovery

The notion of writing (*Writing Degree Zero*) fashioned the concept of *literary* practice as well as the possible *knowledge* of this practice.

"Literature" becomes *writing*; "knowledge" or "science" becomes the *objective formulation of the desire to write*, their interrelationship implicating both the "literary" person and the quibbling "scientific" specialist, thus setting the stakes where the subject is—within language through his experience of body and history. Writing then is a section effected by history in the language already worked on by a subject. Realizing the desire for writing requires of the subject (of metalanguage) the double motion of adhesion and of distancing wherein he curbs his desire for the signifier through the *sanction* of a code (linguistic, semiological, et cetera), itself dictated by an (utopian?) ethics. This is to insert within society a practice that it censors; to communicate what it cannot understand or hear; and thus to reconstitute the cohesion and harmony of a social discourse, inherently ruptured.

The knot is thus tied by which literature will be considered from various viewpoints at *the same time*; language, subject-producer, history, subject of metalanguage. These are all "entries" into it for sciences that are either established or in the process of being established, such as linguistics, psychoanalysis, sociology, and history. They are not only *inseparable* from one another, but their specific mode of blending is the very condition of this possibility of knowledge. The originality of Barthes's writings probably lies in this double necessity: (1) that scientific approaches be simultaneous and that they form an ordered set giving rise to Barthes's concept of semiology; (2) that they be controlled by the discreet and lucid presence of the subject of this "possible knowledge" of literature, by the *reading* that he gives of texts today, situated as he is within contemporary history.

The Technicist Illusion

Without the first of those necessities, we witness the fragmentation of the literary entity into "disciplines," grafting themselves onto literary practice, living off it (history, sociology, but also, in a more modern and devious way, the various formalisms, either linguistic or not, Russian or New-Critical). Literature confirms all the hypotheses of all the human sciences; it gives the linguist as well as the historian its surplus value, on the condition that it remain in the shadows of knowledge as a passive thing, never as an agent. This means that, not specified as a *precise object*, delineated in its totality by an autonomous, circumscribed theory looking for its truth, literature does not give rise to specific knowledge, but to *applications* of doctrines that are nothing but ideological exercises since they are empirical and fragmented.

Without the second necessity, we have the technicist illusion that "literary science" need only reproduce the norms of Science (if possible, of linguistics, or even more "rigorously," of phonology, structural semantics, or generative grammar) in order to insert itself into the dignified but amorphous domain of "studies in mass communication."

Possibly, not all of Barthes's writings obey (or at least not all in the same way) these necessities extracted from the whole of his work. It is rather certain that his colleagues or disciples tend to neglect them. Nonetheless, compliance takes place in the aggregate of Barthes's texts. These writings, often appearing as "essays," model literature and make of it the object of a new kind of objective discourse; but the same discourse fails in the works of those—more scientific or more essayistic—who, in the wake of Barthes, omit one or the other components of the operation. The term "essays" should not be perceived either as showing rhetorical humility or as admission of weak theoretical discourse (as the wardens of "rigor" in the human sciences might be tempted to think), but as a methodological exigency of the most serious kind; the science of literature is an always infinite discourse, an always open enunciation of a *search* for the laws of the practice known as literature. The *objective* of this search is to make *manifest* the very *procedure* through which this "science," its "object," and their relationship are brought about, rather than to apply empirically such and such a technique to an indifferent object.

The Axis of Recasting: The Historical Subject

What epistemological, ideological, or other requirement does Barthes's discovery meet—a discovery that amounts to a *recasting*? Would it not be more prudent to manage with modestly coupled divisions: literature *and* linguistics, literature *and* psychoanalysis, literature *and* sociology, literature *and* ideology, and so forth. The list goes on and on.

If the contribution of Barthes, who seeks to identify what is specific and incomparable in literary practice, seems to heed the technocratic requirements of our time (to constitute a specialized discourse for all of the so-called "human" domain), and to follow empirio-critical postulates (all signifying practices can be subsumed under a formalism borrowed from an exact science), in fact, it goes counter to these appearances, matching them so as to overturn them. For subjects of a civilization who are alienated in their language and blocked by their history, the work of Barthes shows that literature is precisely the place where this alienation and this blockage are thwarted each time in a specific way.

As the borderline between a signifier where the subject is lost and a history that imposes its laws on him, literature appears as a specific mode of *practical knowledge*. Here is concentrated what verbal communication and social exchange put aside, since they obey the rules of econo-technical evolution. This concentration, this deposit, is thus, by definition, a nonexistent object for the sciences of communication or social exchange. Its place is transversal to the one the sciences assign themselves. It goes through them and locates itself elsewhere. The current stage of capitalist, industrialist society, having delineated, if not dominated, the global possibilities of communication and technology, has allowed a portion of its analytical activity to grapple with this "absence of place."

Whether decadent or worked upon by what it has repressed, our society can see that art is as much, if not more, an index for the underlying rules governing it as is the structuration of kinship for so-called primitive societies. It can then make of this "art" an object of "science" in order to see that it cannot be simply reduced, like the myths of antiquity, to a *techne*-procedure of cogitation (to be manufactured according to this or that linguistic device) or to social *functions* (to be related to some economic need). But on the contrary, "art" reveals a specific *practice*, crystallized in a mode of production with highly diversified and multiplied manifestations. It weaves into language (or other "signifying materials") the complex relations of a subject caught between "nature" and "culture," between the immemorial ideological and scientific *tradition*, henceforth available, and the *present*, between *desire* and the *law*, the body, language, and "metalanguage."

What we discover, then, within this texture, is the function of the subject caught between instinctual drives and social practice within a language that is today divided into often incommunicable, multiple systems: a Tower of Babel that literature specifically breaks open, refashions, and inscribes in a new series of perpetual contradictions. This is the *subject* that has reached its apex in the Christian-capitalist era, to the point of being its secret motor, powerful and unknown, repressed and innovative; literature distills its birth and its struggles. The science whose possibilities Barthes outlines seeks the subject's lines of force within this literature, that is, this writing.

We have not yet grasped the importance of a change of venue that involves thinking about the subject on the basis of literary practice rather than on the basis of neurosis or psychosis. The project outlined by Roland Barthes, while in fact sanctioned by psychoanalysis, nonetheless opens out on a different "subject," which, as we know, psychoanalysis stumbled against while examining the meanderings between "I" and "other." "Literary" and generally "artistic" practice transforms the dependence of the subject on the signifier into a test of its freedom in relation to the signifier and reality. It is a trial where the subject reaches both its limits (the laws of the signifier) and the objective possibilities (linguistic and historic) of their displacement, by including the tensions of the "ego" within historical contradictions, and by gradually breaking away from these tensions as the subject includes them in such contradictions and reconciles them to their struggles. It is precisely this *inclusion*, an essential specificity of the "arts," by which an asserted "ego" becomes outside-of-self, objectivized, or better, neither objective nor subjective, but both at the same time, and consequently, their "other," to which Barthes has given its name: writing. As infra- and ultra-language, as translanguage, writing is the ridge where the historical becoming of the subject is affirmed; that is, an a-psychological, a-subjective subject—an historical subject. Writing thus posits another subject, for the first time a definitively antipsychological one, for what determines it *ultimately* isn't the problematic of *communication* (relationship to an other) but that of an excess of "ego" within an *experience*—a necessary practice. Barthes can say, therefore, that "art is a certain conquest of chance" (*Critical Essays*, p. 218) and that, like the structuralist project, it "speaks the place of meaning but does not name it" (*Critical Essays*, p. 219).

LITERATURE: THE MISSING LINK OF HUMAN SCIENCE

Because it focuses on the *process* of meaning within language and ideology—from the "ego" to history—literary practice remains the missing link in the socio-communicative or subjective-transcendental fabric of the so-called human sciences. Nothing more "natural," for this "place" of meaning that it enunciates but does not *name* is the very place of the materialist dialectic that no human science has yet approached.

The insertion of this practice into the social science corpus necessitates a modification of the very notion of "science," so that an analogous dialectic may operate. That is, an area of chance will be reserved and delineated within the procedure, whose purpose is to understand this practice: a localized chance as condition of objective understanding, a chance to be uncovered in the relationship of the subject of metalanguage to the writing under study, and/ or to the semantic and ideological means of constitution of the subject. Once this area has been determined, literary practices can be considered as the object of a possible knowledge: the discursive possibility emerges out of a *reality* impossible *for* it although localizable *by* it. What is involved here is the problem of impossible metalanguage, which makes up the second panel of Barthes's inaugural work. On the subject of literature, Barthes is the first to demonstrate this impossibility, thus opening the way for philosophers or semioticians.

This device in fact calls for the introduction of linguistics, psychoanalysis, et cetera, but only if they respect the constraints of the device. Barthes's work has proposed a new field—a new object, a new knowing subject—for these sciences. They are just beginning, sporadically, to notice it.

Language and Writing

Discovering a new object through a metalanguage elaborated halfway between chance and necessity seems to be the rule today in all the sciences. These limits, in themselves, appear frequently to be the ideological alibi for a barely modernized Kantianism, whose intrascientific productivity topples, having barely crossed the threshold of the "exact sciences," into a gnoseological dam holding back the scientific theory of the speaking and knowing *subject* (psychoanalysis) and of *history* (historical materialism).

At the same time, it is clear that it is the Hegelian dialectic (whose transcendence veils the objective progress it has achieved since Descartes, Kant, and the Enlightenment) that first pointed to the masterly lines of this interplay between limit and infinity, rationale and objectivity—a stumbling block for contemporary sciences. It succeeded in this by imposing at its foundations the *knots*, invisible without it, where the opposites—*subject* and *history*—are interwoven. They are indeed the ones that we encounter at the crossroads of Barthian reflection.

KNOWLEDGE IN THE TEXT

For already a century, literature has unfolded and held these opposites, with purposeful insistence, through language and within the ideology of our society, thereby wielding a "knowledge" that it does not necessarily reflect. If it thereby operates on the side of discursive reason, it avoids, above all, Hegelian transcendence by practicing contradiction within the material element of language as the generator of ideas or meaning through the biological and historical body of a concrete subject. Any phonic unit is thus number and infinity, plethora and as such signifying, because at the same time it is a differential of infinity. Any sentence is both syntax and nonsentence, normative unicity and disorderly multiplicity; any sequence is both myth and the melting pot where it is engendered and dies through its own history, the history of the subject, and the objective history of superstructures. Any chain of language is invested with a sending-focus that links the body to its biological and social history. Specific subjects cipher the normative language of everyday communication by means of extralinguistic, biological, and socially unforeseeable, chancy codes, which cannot be evidenced by a finite number of deductive or "rational" operations but operate within the necessity of "objective laws." This particular subject—neither of cogitation nor of Saussurian language, but of *a text*, shattered and coherent, legislated by an unforeseeable necessity—this "subject" is precisely the object that Barthes is looking for in the literature called *writing*. It is then clear that the practice of writing and its subject are immediate contemporaries, indeed forerunners, of the modern, scientific upheaval; their ideological and practical correspondents; the units that ensure coherence between the way in which the subject enunciates, "feels," and "lives," and what objective knowledge achieves without him elsewhere; operative symbols that suture the rifts between archaic subjectivist ideology on the one hand, and the development of productive forces and means of knowledge on the other, while both preceding and exceeding these rifts.

Two Channels of Discovery: Dialectics and Sociology

Brought to our attention by Maurice Blanchot through his studies on Hegel, Mallarmé, and Kafka, writing and its subject secure with Barthes a new epistemological status. They abandon the speculative labyrinth of absolute mind and the contemplation of the essence of language to achieve—with Fourier, Sade, Balzac; mythic, political, and journalistic discourse; the new novel; *Tel Quel*; and, thanks to an alliance between sociology (Marxism, Sartre), structuralism (Lévi-Strauss), and the literary avant-garde—a new status based on an implicit triple thesis:

(a) the materiality of writing (objective practice within language) insists on confronting the sciences of language (linguistics, logic, semiotics), but also on a *differentiation* in relation to them;

(b) its immersion in history entails the *taking into account of social and historical conditions*;

(c) its *sexual overdetermination* orients it toward psychoanalysis, and through it toward the set of a corporeal, physical, and substantial "order."

Writing as an object of knowledge emerges out of the transformation of dialectics in the field of language (meaning), and Barthes is the rational empiricist who comes to make a science of it. The productive ambiguity of Barthes's writings resides, it seems, precisely there. It is from that position that he radically opposes himself to any transcendent or positivist phenomenology; just as it is true that this same ambiguous stance can sometimes proffer a "naive" formalist temptation toward total symbolization of the real and symbolic world.

Signifying systems, according to Barthes, both *do and do not* pertain to linguistics. The deep unity of such seemingly divergent books as *Writing Degree Zero, Elements of Semiology*, and *Le Système de la mode*, evidence this constantly operative contradiction in Barthes.

Signifying systems are so strongly linguistic that Barthes proposes to modify Saussure's well-known position accordingly: "Linguistics is not a part of the general science of signs, even a privileged part, it is semiology which is a part of linguistics" (*Elements of Semiology*, p. 11). The need for this is visibly dictated by a concern for rigor and positivity, since language is the primary signifying system and the most easily apprehended.

But *at the same time*, signifying systems are *trans-linguistic*. They are articulated as large units that run across phonetic, syntactic order, and even stylistic order, to organize an *other* combinative system with the help of these same linguistic categories operating to the second power in that other system impelled by another subject.

The loop is looped: the passage through Russian Formalism served only to return us more firmly than ever to the translinguistic and even antilinguistic positions of *Writing Degree Zero* ("There exists fundamentally in writing a 'circumstance' foreign to language"— p. 20), and to enable us to substantiate them.

We might criticize the "ideology" of this procedure if we see it only as a reduction of complex signifying practice to a neutral and universal intelligibility. But that would amount to neglecting Barthes's itinerary, which is dictated by the desire to specify a topology (communication does not equal writing) and thus confronts semiological systematization with a critical writing (we shall return to this point) that breaks with the "neutral and universal" status of metalanguage.

Barthes's semiological texts—they all are semiological texts if we choose to retain the term to designate not formalization, but research into the dialectical laws of the signifying process—demand above all a desubstantification of signifying ideality. Their bearing is negative at first ("No semiology exists which cannot, in the last analysis, be acknowledged as *semioclasm*" [*Mythologies*, p. 9]); this negativity works against the transparence of language and of symbolic function in general. The phenomenological idealities that a linguistic approach discovers there are, for Barthes, a facade concealing another order that, precisely, remains to be established. Behind substantified, opaque linguistic categories and structures, there functions a scene where the subject, defined by the topos of its communication with an other, begins by *denying* this communication in order to formulate another device. As negative of the earlier so-called "natural" language, this new "language" is consequently no longer communicative. I shall call it *transformative*, or even *mortal*, for the "I" as well as for the "other": it leads, in borderline experiences, to an antilanguage (Joyce), to a sacrifical language (Bataille), indicating in other respects but simultaneously a disrupted social structure. Although it is still understood as signifying, this other scene is only partially linguistic. That is, it only partially depends on the idealities established by linguistic science, since it is only partially communicative. On the contrary, it has access to the formative process of its linguistic idealities by *unfolding* their phenomenal substance. Linguistic units and structures no longer determine writing, since it is not *only* or not *specifically* discourse directed at someone else. Displacements and facilitations of energy, discharges, and quantitative cathexes that are logically anterior to linguistic entities and to their subject mark the constitution and the movements of the "self," and are manifested by the formulation of symbolic-linguistic order.[2] Writing would be the recording, through symbolic order, of this dialectic of displacement, facilitation, discharge, cathexis of drives (the most characteristic of which is the death drive) that operates-constitutes the signifier but also exceeds it; adds itself to the linear order of language by using the most fundamental laws of the signifying process (displacement, condensation, repetition, inversion); has other supplementary networks at its disposal; and produces a sur-meaning. As Barthes wrote,

Writing on the contrary is always rooted in something beyond language, it develops like a *seed, not like a line*, it manifests an essence and holds the threat of a secret, it is an *anticommunication*, it is intimidating. All writing will therefore contain the ambiguity of an object which is both language and coercion: there exists fundamentally in writing a "circumstance" foreign to language, there is, as it were, the weight of a gaze conveying an intention which is no longer linguistic. This gaze may well express a passion of language, as in literary modes of writing; it may also express the threat of retribution, as in political ones [. . .] literary modes of writing, in which *the unity of the signs is ceaselessly fascinated by zones of infra- or ultra-language.* (*Writing Degree Zero*, p. 20; emphasis mine).

Written in 1953, these lines were to become the analytical method of S/Z in 1969.

MYTH, HISTORY, AESTHETICS

An analogous desubstantification is undergone by mythic idealities, reconstructed like crystals from the practice of subjects in history. "Myth is not defined by the object of its message, but by the *way* in which it utters this message: there are formal limits to myth, there are no *substantial* ones" (*Mythologies*, p. 109).

Although this position has a marked affinity to the structuralist procedure with which Barthes readily happened to fall in, his project is radically different. While it may be a structure, myth is intelligible only as historical production; its laws will thus be found not in phonology, but in history. "One can conceive of very ancient myths, but there are no eternal ones; for it is human history which conveys reality into speech, and it alone rules the life and death of mythical language. Ancient or not, mythology can only have an *historical foundation,* for myth is a type of speech chosen by history: it cannot possibly evolve from the 'nature of things' " (*Mythologies*, p. 110; emphasis mine). Contrary then to a structuralism that seeks in myths the "permanent structures of the human mind" and perhaps closer to a recently reasserted Lévi-Strauss,[3] Barthes pursues, through and beyond the discursive phenomenon, its social and historical overdetermination. But because he begins with another experience, Barthes's position differs from that of structuralism: history, with him, is inseparable from the *unfolding in depth of the signifying subject* through which, precisely, it is legible. "History, then, confronts the writer with a necessary option between several moral attitudes connected with language; it forces him to *signify* Literature in terms of possibilities outside his control" (*Writing Degree Zero*, p. 2; emphasis mine).

This compulsory but not masterable necessity that commands the obligation *to signify* is delivered by a privileged experience: "structuralist" reflection leads to it by unfolding the symbolic function "in depth," thanks to the subject and to history. This is the "aesthetic." "Structuralism does not withdraw history from the world: it seeks to link history not only to contents (this has been done a thousand times) but also to certain forms, not only the material but also the intelligible, not only the ideological but also the aesthetic" (*Critical Essays*, p. 219).

TO FASCINATE AND OBJECTIFY: BLANCHOT AND SARTRE

Two different confrontations will perhaps help us to perceive more clearly the strategy of this desubstantification that produces writing in Barthes. As a translinguistic formulation, it comes close to Blanchot's "fascinated" "act of writing" as well as to Sartre's "work as objectification of the person." Between these apparently irreconcilable limits, Barthes points out the dialectical kinship, or rather, the common element of a transformed dialectic; he posits writing in the space of their separation, as an *operation* admitting of being clarified by understanding.

The notion of writing, first formulated in *Writing Degree Zero* and continually analyzed in its various modes, partakes (as literally seen in the previous quotation from p. 20 of that work) of the "fascination" that Blanchot contemplates in an "act of writing" "committed to absence of time" and which, crossing through the negative and the affirmative, posits itself outside of dialectics, in a "loss of Being, where Being is lacking," in a blinding light, without figure, unfigurable, an impersonal "One" whose Oedipal mother seems to be the substratum.[4] Writing, according to Barthes, is familiar with this return of teleological dialectics, a return that allows the negative mode to be absorbed into a semblance of affirmation (the moment of inscription), but only a semblance, because what is inscribed is always already broken up within the ungraspable, impersonal, trans-subjective, anonymous, musical plurality of the paragrammatized text.[5] Such a text is *S/Z*, whose semiotic network, by means of the representative cut of castration, simultaneously veils and reveals the voice of the castrate, the music and the art that appear as lights freed by an incision. Yet, if this break permits the dazzling light of the scriptural position to flash "where space is the vertigo of spatial positioning,"[6] by suggesting that it is a maternal beaming that activates the subject of writing, then such a light can only be thrown on the horizon of the investigation. Sheltered by this dazzling light, the semiotician carries on his survey on this side of blindness, in the opaque night of the form he is to illuminate. For Barthes then, writing is less a dazzlement where the subject faints into the mother than an *operation* logically "preceding" this fainting: he follows its performance through the semantic volume of language and presents it in the rigor of its formalisms.

It is precisely upon the traces of this semantic operation that fascination appears as objectivation. The subjectal cloud crystallizes into the praxis of a "person" with a story and in history, and the text emerges as the work of a subject (Michelet, Balzac, Loyola, Sade, Fourier), a work that exceeds life, but whose life shares its structures. Formalism is thus tempered by the introduction of an objective subject for whom this formalism is the *practice*. A double approach is consequently necessary to deal with the text: it must be seen through the *linguistic* network, but also through *biography*. The proportion of each is already weighted in favor of the *written* element, which nevertheless merely releases, inscribes, and understands "lived experience."

Thus, there is no "absolute" anonymity of the text, except in the first stages of research and only inasmuch as the impersonal constitutes the "upper" limit of the *operation* involved. But there is objectivation of spacing within a subject, endowed with biography, body, and history, which are to be inserted in the text in order to define its "lower" limit.

This dialectical conception of writing as objective praxis is again sought after if not achieved in Sartre.[7] Barthes first substantiated it in his essay on Michelet. Language thus becomes not only a germination of empty and infinite meaning making its way through linguistic and semiological relationships and units, but at the same time it becomes a practice, a relationship to heterogeneity, to materiality.[8]

And yet, if writing is the objectivation of the "person," surpassing it and bequeathing to it its historical intelligibility, and if by the same token, it serves as the basis for the largely semiological conception of "praxis" (and not for an interpretation of semiosis based on a theory of "praxis," as seems to be the generally accepted existential approach), Barthes's goals are radically analytical and dissolve those entities characteristic of existential thought and inherited from speculative philosophy. In their place, mentioned in passing, it inaugurates a signifying *work* through which these entities are constituted. The "totality" (of "work" and "person") as well as "expression" and "lived experience" are doubtless the existential pillars that suffer the greatest damage in that kind of procedure. It is henceforth naive, if not impossible, to try to generalize from the seesaw motion linking biography and works without having minutely scrutinized the devices that the signifying texture offers to the semiotician's gaze.

CLARITY, NIGHT, AND COLOR

Caught between objectivation and fascination, between involvement and a-theism, writing will be exposed to the light of scientific investigation. The modelization proposed by Barthes, apparent in his strictly semiological writings as well as in the systematizing layer inherent in all his texts, operates for and through this light. Deductive, prudent, consequent, patient, it proceeds by demonstration, analysis, and synthesis; it explains, proves, and elucidates. The symbolic process is affected in its articulations.

The light that Barthes throws on the praxis of writing on the edge of the impersonal avoids the flight of meaning—its *night*-side, at one with anonymous dazzlement—as well as the historical juggernaut— the eventful *sequence* of "forms" accompanying the sequence of base and superstructure in *time*. The light of such a semiological reason leaves in the shadows the loss of the subject into nonsense as well as his loss into what is beyond meaning. This rationalism knows neither negativity as *poetry* nor objectivity as *movement*.

The light of understanding that animates this semiotic and ethical discourse pushes the poet aside, "He who hears a language without understanding" (Blanchot). Is this because the poetic work, as Hegel would say, is withdrawn from ethical substance? A work where any fixed definition is absorbed into the unconscious and where any (linguistic or subjective) substance is fluid and incandescent, like an ink that is eaten away? A work where the subject is not "empty" under the appearance of multiple meaning, but is a "surplus of subject" exceeding the subject through nonsense, in contradiction to which a symbolic formality comes along to posit the meaning(s) as well as the subject?[9] Faced with this form's night spreading across poetic surplus, faced with this nocturnal form not illuminated by a subject master of language, Barthes's light fails. Of the subject's dark appearance within the impersonal, within the maternal "One," it retains only the classic systematicness, but not the repressed poetic intensity of their struggle; the pluralized domination, but not the pluralizing negative. In analogous fashion, history as a succession is partitioned into experiences. Sketched out, it is replaced by *atoms* of flux, full of desires that are legible through their oral (Fourier) or object-related (Sarrasine) attachment. These atoms are present in their own time, but in a time that does not flow, a time that brings them or takes them away but does not transport them, does not bind them, does not empty them except to fill them up all the more. History (real or literary), then, is what Barthes calls in his essay on Michelet a "cordial history," a softening of the rigid legislature of social or literary systems, a supplement of intimacy that Barthes sees, with Michelet, taking the shape of "virtue hatching the ambisexual Masses" (*Michelet par lui-même*, p. 53). Sifted by understanding, time and motion are incarnated by "personalities" or "utterances": a historicity peppered with timeless "types"—"in it, there is no more duration: a minute equals a century," or rather, "no more centuries, nor years, nor months, nor days, nor hours [. . .] Time no longer exists; time has perished" (*ibid.*, p. 55).

And yet, this supplement of night and motion that escapes the light of *semiological* understanding will be produced by the *critic's* writing within the very linguistic texture that gives rise to light, mixes into writing, shadowing it and coloring it.

LANGUAGE AS NEGATIVITY: DEATH AND IRONY

Consequently drained of substance and ideality, language becomes the border between subjective and objective, and also between the symbolic and the real. It is understood as the material limit against which the one and the other are dialectically constituted: "The language functions negatively, as the initial limit of the possible" (*Writing Degree Zero*, p. 13).

From within "structuralism," Barthes was probably the first to consider language as negativity, less because of a philosophical option (deconstruction, antimetaphysics, etc.) than by reason of the very object of his investigation. Literature is for him the experience and proof of the negativity specific to the linguistic process: "A writer is someone for whom language is a problem, who experiences its profundity, not its instrumentality nor its beauty" (*Critique et vérité*, p. 46). Experiencing the trajectory of this negativity, writing is contestation, rupture, flight, and irony. Negativity operates within it upon the unity of Language and upon the agent of this unity. Acting with the subject, it breaks its individual, contingent, and superficial representations and makes of them an *inorganic nature*,[10] a pulverization of fragmented elements. "There is no language site outside bourgeois ideology. [. . .] The only possible rejoinder is neither confrontation nor destruction, but only theft; fragment the old text of culture, science, literature, and change its features according to formulas of disguise"; writing is able to "exceed the laws that a society, an ideology, a philosophy establish for themselves in order to agree among themselves in a fine surge of historical intelligibility" (*Sade, Fourier, Loyola*, p. 10).

Yet, this negativity reaches the edges of a positivity because it operates within language and the subject. By obeying strict, abstract rules also involving corporeal and historical materiality, signifying materiality stops the movement of absolute negativity that might exist in the signified alone and by means of a negative theology. In writing, the negative is formulated. The new signifying process welcomes negativity in order to remodel language into a universal, international, and transhistoric writing-language. The writers that Barthes chooses are classifiers, inventors of codes and languages, topologists, logothetes. They enumerate, count, synthesize, articulate, formulate; they are architects of new languages. This, at least, is the axis that Barthes seeks in them, from *Writing Degree Zero* through *S/Z* into *Sade, Fourier, Loyola*, threading his way in and out of the "flesh" of their writing to find new syntheses of new languages.

As for the critic, he brushes against and then passes by this shattering of meaning in language with no pole of transference other than linguistic and/or self-referential. But the formulating operation of critical writing needs to be distinguished from that of the writer. The operating negativity of writing is grasped, in criticism, by *One Affirmation*. It is ultimately blocked by *one* meaning clearly revealing the critic's writing as being entirely triggered, sustained, and determined by the discourse of the other. That is, it operates within the dialectic of transferential relationship. "Although we don't know how the reader *speaks* to a book, the critic himself is obliged to produce a particular 'tone'; and this tone, in the final analysis cannot be anything but affirmative" (*Critique et vérité*, p. 78). The critic "openly assumes at his own risk the intention of giving a precise meaning to a work" (*ibid.*, p. 56). Unable to dissolve the "self" into this whirling and self-regulated *inorganic nature* that produces logothetes, the critic remains riveted to his "I" that hoards polyvalences, and *signs* them. "The critic is he who is incapable of producing the novel's *He*, but who is also incapable of tossing back the *I* into pure, private life, that is, who cannot give up writing. This is an aphasia of the *I*, while the rest of his language remains, intact, yet marked by the infinite detours that (as in aphasia) the constant blocking of a particular sign imposes on speech" (*ibid.*, p. 17). Through a perfectly *homonymic* course, starting from his opaque "I" and moving towards the writings of an other, he returns to this same "I," which, in the process, has become *language*: the critic "confronts [. . .] his own language"; "it is not the object which must be opposed to the subject in criticism, but its predicate" (*ibid.*, p. 69); "The symbol must go looking for the symbol" (*ibid.*, p. 73).

Implicating himself, therefore, in the negative operation that is language, through the intermediary of the other, the critic retains from scriptural negativity a weakened, but persistent, effect. The *death drive* of the writer becomes *irony* in the critic, because there is irony each time an ephemeral meaning crystallizes for such a reader. Freud demonstrated precisely this economy of laughter in *Jokes and Their Relation to the Unconscious*: it is a discharge with two meanings between sense and nonsense. In order for this to happen, a semblance of meaning must appear at a fugitive moment. It is the critic's task, and there is hardly a more comical one, to coagulate an island of meaning upon a sea of negativity. Thus, for Barthes, the critic may "develop what is precisely lacking in science and could be summed in one word: irony"; "Irony is nothing more than a question put to language by language" (*Critique et vérité*, p. 74). This irony, by which the critic, sure of his *I* and without abandoning it, participates in the scriptural operation, constitutes only *one* moment (among others) of the operation. For Rabelais, Swift, Lautréamont, and Joyce are ironic only when we posit them (or when they posit themselves) as subjects tapping a meaning that is always already old, always already out of date, as funny as it is ephemeral.

THE OBJECTIFICATION OF THE NEGATIVE

Since language is negativity, a movement exceeding its subjective center and encompassing the enlarged center making up the object, it is amenable—even in its negative mobility—to laws. Writing would be the inscription of *other* laws, although they be inseparable from the rules of negativity inherent in the symbolic function. Barthes points to these laws when he speaks of "*formal truth*," "equation," "necessity," and indeed "law." "The man is put on show and delivered up by his language, betrayed by *a formal reality* which is beyond the reach of his lies, whether they are inspired by self-interest or generosity" (*Writing Degree Zero*, p. 81). "If the writing is really *neutral*, and if language, instead of being a cumbersome and recalcitrant act, reaches the state of a pure equation, which is no more tangible than an *algebra* when it confronts the innermost part of man, then Literature is vanquished" (*ibid.*, p. 78); "social or mythical characters of a language are abolished in favor of a *neutral* and inert state of form" (*ibid.*, p. 77). "If Flaubert's writing enshrines a *Law*, if that of Mallarmé postulates a silence, and if others, that of Proust, Céline, Queneau, Prévert, each in its own way, is founded on the existence of a social nature, if all these modes of writing *imply an opacity of form* and presuppose a problematic of language and society, thus establishing speech as an *object which must receive treatment* at the hands of a craftsman, a magician or a sculptor" (*ibid.*; all emphases mine).

Dialectical Law, Scriptural Law: Writing of the Real

The practice of writing becomes the edge separating and uniting the subjectivity to which style attests—"starting from a sublanguage elaborated where flesh and external reality come together" (*ibid.*, p. 11)—with the objectivity represented by social history. Writing, then, is considered as a kind of totality "in itself" and "for itself." Better defined than the negative unity of individual language, it denies it. More precise than an exterior objectivity that is nothing in itself, it specifies it precisely by returning through and across negative language to the singular speaking being. In short, it brings one back to the other, neither subjective individuality nor exterior objectivity, it is the very principle of Hegel's "self-movement" and offers the very element of law: "the *determinateness* of this animating principle, which is the difference if the Notion itself is *Law*."[11]

Although it is dialectical, the law inscribed by writing according to Barthes is not Hegelian. One will recall that in Hegel "law [as] the stable presentment or picture of unstable appearance"[12] must, in order to palliate this difference internal to the thing itself, and to place itself on a par with the phenomenon, appropriate infinity to itself. To do that, in a first stage, "understanding thus learns that it is a law in the sphere of appearance for distinctions to come about which are not distinctions. In other words, it learns that what is self-same

[Gleichnämige] is self-repulsive. . . ."[13] In a second stage, and after a precise course, an inverted world (the in-itself of the sensible world) is posited and remains present in the sensible world. Such a dialectic of inversion leads to Hegelian infinity, situated, because of this self-sameness, beyond representation.[14]

Writing establishes a different legality. Writing is upheld not by the subject of understanding, but by a divided subject, even a pluralized subject, that occupies, not a place of enunciation, but permutable, multiple, and mobile places; thus, it brings together in a *heteronomous* space the naming of phenomena (their entry into symbolic law) and the negation of these names (phonetic, semantic, and syntactic shattering). This supplementary negation (derivative negation, negation of the homonomic negation) leaves the homogeneous space of meaning (of naming or, if one prefers, of the "symbolic") and moves, without "imaginary" intermediary, toward the biological-societal "base" that is its excess, toward what cannot be symbolized (one might say, toward the "real").

In other terms, the heteronomical negativity of writing operates, on the one hand, between *naming* (utterance/enunciation) carried out by the subject of understanding (meaning) and *polynomia*, that is, the pluralization of meaning by different means (polyglottism, polysemia, etc.) traversing nonsense and indicating a suppression of the subject. *Writing Degree Zero* identifies this type of heteronomy by the term "writing"; *S/Z* analyzes in the text the contradiction between naming and polynomia, the subject and its loss. At the same time, but on the other hand, heteronomic negativity operates between *polynomia* and its *instinctual cathexis*. Polynomia is the index, the *ideogram* of biological and social orders. It is a kind of asymbolic memory of the body. In *Writing Degree Zero* it is *style* that represents this heteronomia included in writing. Indeed, style as a "frame of reference is biological or biographical, not historical [. . .] indifferent to society and transparent to it, a closed personal process [. . .] a *sublanguage* elaborated where flesh and external reality come together" (*Writing Degree Zero*, p. 11); "its secret is *recollection* locked within the *body* of a writer" (*ibid.*, p. 12). "By reason of its biological origin, style resides outside art, that is, outside the pact which binds the writer to society" (*ibid.*, p. 12; emphasis mine). Barthes's studies of Fourier and Sade suggest the possibilities open to this biological-corporeal, transsymbolic, and transhistorical cathexis.

In these two aspects (contradiction between naming and polynomia, contradiction between symbolic and asymbolized), scriptural heteronomia does not come into play between two "sames" that repulse one another or dissolve within one unity. So, too, it avoids Hegelian and post-Hegelian "aesthetic religion." Never producing *ex nihilo*, without an origin, it includes a production. "Without origins" means that it is a superimpression or a suppression of a first, primordial meaning, which is always for Barthes a neutral symbolic, an unmarked code, an unwritten language, a void meaning. "It includes a production" means that the polynomic superimpression (suppression of first and, when all is said and done, null meaning), identifiably within language, is a supercathexis of the symbolic "void" by a biological-social, instinctual substratum left intact by the first symbolization (by natural language) and thus, in a sense, *preceding* it so as to look back upon the scriptural act through the interplay of "primary processes," of the "signifier's logic," bursting across and through the language of a book-free dramatized subject. Thus, it appears that for literature, language is "the whole of History [. . .] unified and complete in the manner of a Natural Order" (*Writing Degree Zero*, p. 10). "A language is therefore on the hither side of literature. Style is almost beyond it" (*ibid.*); "another notion of writing is possible: neither decorative nor instrumental, i.e., in sum secondary but primal, antecedent to man, whom it traverses, founder of its acts like so many inscriptions" (*Sade, Fourier, Loyola*, p. 40).

Clearly, naming and its negation in writing operate on heterogeneous series and split the totality of One homonomic Meaning (prescribed by the first negation-symbolization) in order to reproduce the production of the subject between the real and the symbolic *backwards, after the fact*. The conditions for a theory of writing are thereby posited. Semiology could be this discourse if, by recognizing the heteronomy of meaning, it started from linguistics and went to meet with psychoanalysis and history; consequently, its name ("semiology") matters little.

The path is clearly marked along which writing organizes, but differently, into a new legislation the "phenomena" as "named." It appears to deny Hegelian phenomenon and law because it struggles against the "first" naming, which is the domain of *Law*. The text, as an other name (a pseudonym), an antiname and pronominal, "cuts obliquely through the instances of discourse as well as through 'genres.'" It effects the anamnesis of "literary history" only by dint of undertaking an analysis of the place of enunciation within the very element of language. The first study of Barthes that records the multiplications of the space of enunciation within writing, relying on Benveniste's linguistic analyses of the subject in language, was devoted to Philippe Sollers's novel *Drame* ("Drama, Poem, Novel").[15] Here, the drama of personal pronouns reveals the staging of a subject pluralized on the chessboard of writing. Neither lyric "I," ritual "you," nor epic—or more prosaically—novelistic "he," the "plural subject" of writing simultaneously traverses the sites of these three discursive agencies, invoking their conflicts and undergoing their divergent appearances.

Now, since writing breaks the "subject" apart into multiple doers, into possible places of retention or loss of meaning within "discourse" and "history," it inscribes, not the original-paternal law, but *other* laws that can enunciate themselves differently beginning with these pronominal, transsubstantive agencies. Its legitimacy is illegal, paradoxal, heteronymic; heteronomous in relation to Hegelian Law, it struggles with constancy and originality. Although one can discern in writing a movement that seems to recall ideated dialectics condensing the phenomenon and inverted infinity, scriptural logic brings it about specifically in a fragmented space that transforms the idealistic matrix. Writing provides the act of reading with an asymbolic "phenomenon," left unnamed because it is "real," and whose novelty is due to the infinity emanating from the rupture of the symbolic, unifying instance. A *process* of naming is substituted for this impossible to symbolize real, whose transformation and future nevertheless allow themselves to be inscribed (in the pronominal device, among others).

It is also in departing from totalizing homonymy that scriptural laws postulate, not a beyond of representation, but a transfusing and renewal of it. To the extent that they are inscribed through and across the enunciations emanating from the multiple and unnamable places of meaning occupied by the book-free subject, and to the extent that they combine these enunciations together with their agencies, they liberate new representations elaborated by the subject of these enunciations. Such new representations of a world "in progress" translate the suppression of the topos of *One Subject* of understanding (a new symbolic responds to the new topology articulated by the instinctual drives organized by desire) as well as a violent *criticism* of ideologies, habits, and *social* rules (a new world through and across the negation of the present world that writing denies according to its immanent logic).

For *semiological* metalanguage, this new representation appears as a "double coding,"[16] as a redistribution of language amenable to "extra" or supplementary rules. It presents itself as a simply nominal negation, and thus as a homonymic negation, rejecting the name outside of itself into other pluralized names. But what the literary avant-garde grasps of this rejection is situated outside of naming itself; it is no longer language, or is so only metaphorically, because what is involved is the material that—through drives—accomplishes in each writing according to a specific topos, a sentence always in the process of becoming.[17]

This warrants repeating. Although one can detect in Barthes's works a kinship with dialectical principles, portents of avant-garde activities, and the foundations of a program for a contemporary literary theory, it is largely because we read them in the light of what is being written today. The terminology we are using, the very problems that we keep facing with Barthes, are called forth by this avant-garde, whose epic rhythm breaks apart social and phantasmatic mythology by synthesizing in a new way a critical tradition whose subversive impact has been ignored (Rabelais, Joyce) with the formal experience of the avant-garde of this century and with a revolt against the language and order of a society on the wane.

Confronted with this text, and if one accepts the necessity of Barthes's ethical project, the question still remains: how does one constitute a new heterogeneous signifying body, for which literature, and even more so, this new "literature" that has us read in a new and different manner, can no longer be merely an "object"? No work other than Barthes's better opens up a path of investigation that might yield an answer to this question.

Science and Criticism: Music

In the place of a metalanguage generally recognized as powerless, the discourses of the "critic" and of the "scholar" become differentiated and linked to spell out the legislating heteronomy of writing.

"The scholar" describes negativity within a transrepresentative and transsubjective homogeneous system: his discourse detects the linguistic formality of a shattered, pluralized meaning as the *condition*, or rather, as the *index* of a heteronomous operation: "general discourse, whose object is not a particular meaning, but the very plurality of the work's meanings" (*Critique et vérité*, p. 56); "science of the contents' *conditions*, that is, science of forms: what will concern it are the variations in meanings engendered and, in a manner of speaking, *engenderable* by the works themselves. It will not interpret symbols, but their polyvalence alone; in a word, its object will no longer be the full meanings of a work but, on the contrary, the empty meaning that supports them all" (*ibid.*, p. 57); "We shall not classify the entirety of possible meanings as an immutable order but as the traces of an immense 'operating' arrangement [. . .] broadened from author to society" (*ibid.*, p. 58).

As for the "critic," he takes on the task of pointing out heteronomy. How? Through the presence of enunciation in the utterance, by introducing the agency of the subject, by assuming a representative, localized, contingent speech, determined by its "I" and thus by the "I" of its reader. Speaking in his *name* to an *other*, he introduces *desire*: "Clarity [. . .] is all this desire that lies within writing" (*Critique et vérité*, p. 33); one should ask the critic to "make me believe in your decision to speak" (*ibid.*, p. 75); "To move from reading to criticism is to change desires; it is no longer to desire the work but to desire one's own language" (*ibid.*, p. 79); "works crisscrossed by the great mythic writing in which humanity tries out its significations, that is, its desires" (*ibid.*, p. 61); "there is no other primary *significatum* in literary works than a certain desire: to write is a mode of Eros" (*Critical Essays*, p. xvi); "the same writing: the same sensual pleasure in classification, the same mania for cutting up [. . .]the same enumerative obsession [. . .] the same image practice [. . .] the same erotic and phantasmatic fashioning of the social system" (*Sade, Fourier, Loyola*, p. 3); "the accounting passion transmitted to the exercitant" (*ibid.*, p. 70); "the energy of language (of which the *Exercises* is one of the exemplary theaters) is a form—and the very form of a desire of the world" (*ibid.*, p. 68). "What is indeed remarkable about such an imagination, with desire as its purpose (and one would hope that semiological analysis shows this abundantly), is that its substance is essentially *intelligible*; a name prompts desire, an object does not; meaning prompts a sale, a dream does not" (*Système de la mode*, p. 10).

The network to be deciphered seems to split in half. *Desire*, where the subject is implicated (body and history), and *symbolic order*, reason, intelligibility. Critical knowledge ties and unties their imbrication.

DESIRE AS INDEX OF HETEROGENEITY

Desire causes the signifier to appear as heterogeneous and, inversely, indicates heterogeneity through and across the signifier. To posit that the subject is linked by its desire to the signifier is to say, therefore, that he has access through and across the signifier to what the symbolic does not make explicit, even if it translates it: instinctual drives, historical contradictions.

One can thus understand how Barthes's work is not only a translation into scientific law of the literary text. His knowledge of literature is precious precisely because it joins to these "traces of an immense operating device" that science punctuates, the irruption of desire in the signifier as an index of "real" hetero-geneity. Perhaps one can posit that, for Barthes, "desire" seems to signify the recognition of a heterogeneous element in relation to the symbolic—the space of a material contradiction where the "other" is another *topos* of the subject, an other *practice* of the sexes. Consequently, there is "desire" between language and writing, but also "desire" between writing and criticism-knowledge, and so on. Thus is made up not a hierarchy of overlapping metalanguages but a mobile system of free signifying devices, alert, in a state of per-petual initiative.

This revealer-desire of the *eteros* (ἕτερος) is not only a mode of *eros* (ἔρως) that then finds its categorial explanation. It is equally and simultaneously the mark of Barthes's prudence that brings together knowledge and the process of truth—a prudence whose moral con-notation is erased if we admit that the irruption within the neu-tral truth of science of a subject of enunciation does not invalidate this truth but calls attention to its *operation*, its objective genesis. The statements of all great scholars in the "human sciences," from Benveniste to Lévi-Strauss, statements supposedly legislative and lacking in any kind of subject, give evidence of being contaminated by this type of "modesty" and affected by "writing."

Within such a method, the unicity of the enunciating *rationale* contradicts the heteronomous development of writing. The "model" itself, a paragon of demonstration, becomes caught in this contradic-tion. Extracted from linguistics, for example, appropriated and thus transformed according to the object under scrutiny (a myth, poem, or novel), its intelligibility does not merely lie within the rules of pure mathesis or any other systematicness on which it depends in order to give coherence to metalanguage and a meaning to its object. The formal network that such a model *is* can only be the exterior facet of this mass whose hidden side made up of asymbolic "remnants" comes to light within the negativity of desire. Without the latter, the model does not touch upon the extrahomonymic objectivity of the signi-fying operation that the critical knowledge of Barthes proposes to address. With it, the eventuality of a possible understanding of this operation is preserved.

"The critic of verisimilitude," Barthes writes, "normally chooses the code of the letter," while the *nouvelle critique* "grounds the *objectivity* of its descriptions on their coherence" (*Critique et vérité*, p. 20).

The desire of a subject that ties him to the signifier obtains through this signifier an objective, extraindividual value, void-in-itself, other, without, for all that, ceasing (as it does in science) to be the desire of a subject. This happens only in literature. Writing is precisely this "spontaneous motion" that changes the formulation of desire for a signifier into objective law, since the subject of writing, specific like no other, is "in-itself-and-for-itself," the very place, not of division but, overcoming it, of motion. Consequently, it is the place where the subjective/objective distinction proves invalid, where it is erased, where it appears to be dependent on ideology. Since Freud noticed in the subject the failure of a desire for the signifier to achieve objective value, it is possible to conclude that literary practice is not situated within the field explored by psychoanalysis.

Barthes's work is not an investigation into *how* this "objective-becoming of desire" comes about within the literary text. Revealing literature as a possible science, by way of example, he paves the way for such a strictly scientific investigation. His own undertaking makes it clear that literature's specificity resides in the passage between this *desire* to signify the asymbolized and the asymbolizable, where the subject coalesces, and historically sanctioned *objectivity*.

That constitutes a radical discovery of which no literary history, no aesthetic or stylistic approach could ever conceive, as they remain limited by their fragmentation. Moreover, on each of these planes (desire/objectivity), Barthes seeks whatever can be mastered and experimented upon in schematic form; whatever is regularity, code, formality, necessity, and algebra: in short, semiology. Yet, we must never forget that these peaks of Barthes's semiological graph rise up from a base that cannot be made axiomatic and is summarized by *desire* and *history*. Thus, Balzac, Sade, and Loyola can be grasped within a semiological diagram that summarizes the regular objectivity of their writing, which permeates the biological subject and descriptive history. But, at the same time, each of these rules depends on corporeal, biological, vital, and historical elements. The empirical, *unmasterable*, aleatory, hazardous object appears from beyond the diagram—it supports it, gives it its buoyancy, and engenders it. The salience of Barthes's discovery lies precisely in this alliance between regularity and unclassifiable, objectival multiplicity; an alliance of unification and pluralism, a passion for objectivity simultaneous with a subjective desire for objects. The laws that Barthes taught us to bring to light from within literary practice always exhibit this duplicity, this assymmetry, and this dialectic. He discovers them to be the essential principles of texts, since, as we have already pointed out, they constitute his own way of proceeding.

LAWS AND RULES

What apparently begins to emerge from within Barthes's textual analyses is the rough draft of a dialectical conception of law. The laws that he formulates for signifying systems do not carry the weight of *rules* governing a formal, logical procedure; but they do convey a sense of the "precision" of a dialectics, a "motion," or a "limit" (these are Barthes's words) between the two levels that writing makes objective (symbolic/real; subject/history). Barthes's semiological laws delineate the objectivation of the subjective through and across history and within the signifying texture (language, image, et cetera). One can thus understand that Barthes's semiology is not a *formalization*; his formulations that so irritate the purist are all on the order of dialectical laws.

This kind of theoretical attitude allows Barthes to skirt psychoanalysis without making mistakes on writing. In his writings, his knowledge of literature, his reading of it, occupies the position of a theory of the unconscious and of its role in writing. But Barthes's conception and practice of "writing," as a *notion* substituted for "literature" and as a *procedure*, is not alien to the Freudian discovery. The being-in-itself-and-for-itself of the "objective" other that negates and determines the "subjective" is active within *language* and adheres to certain *laws*; stating this should be enough to establish a common ground for psychoanalytic and dialectical laws.

Yet, for Barthes, this position proves to be less a theoretical platform than what we might call a "practical knowledge" of writing.

MUSIC

The *reading of* a text is doubtlessly the first stage of theoretical elaboration. A reading, whose conceptual supports are muted, is the terrain of the reading subject's desire, his drives, sexuality, and attentiveness toward the phonematic network, the rhythm of the sentences, the particular semanteme bringing him back to a feeling, pleasure, laughter, an event or reading of the most "empirical" kind, abounding, enveloping, multiple. The identity of the reading *I* loses itself there, atomizes itself; it is a time of jouissance, where one discovers one text under another, its other. This rare capacity is a condition of Barthes's writings on the frontiers of "science" and "criticism" (Barthes is probably the only one who can read his students). "The text is an object of pleasure" (*Sade, Fourier, Loyola*, p. 7); "it is a matter of bringing into daily life the fragments of the unintelligible "formulas" that emanate from a text we admire" (*ibid.*).

At the same time, *already*, a regularity comes forth to gather these atoms: a grid lays out jouissance, and "makes pleasure, happiness, communication dependent on an inflexible order or, to be even more offensive, a combinative" (*Sade, Fourier, Loyola*, p. 3). A harmony organizes sounds around us. The "I" is not the one who reads: the impersonal time of regularity, of the grid, and of harmony takes hold of the "I," dispersed for having read. Then, one reads just as one listens to music: "the measure of critical discourse is its *accuracy*. Just as in music . . ." (*Critique et vérité*, p. 72). There is only one final step left before we reach explicative discourse. We must find a way to communicate this music by finding a *code*, while allowing what is said and what is not said to float haphazardly.

THE EXTERNAL INCLUSION

The goal here is to capture the law of desire that makes music, that produces writing. But it is also to experience the desire of the one who reads, to find its code and to note it down. Metalanguage, then, is not everything. Theoretical discourse is not the discourse of a repudiated subject, but of one searching for the laws of its desires, operating as a hinge between immersion in the signifier and repudiation (it is neither one nor the other), its status unknown. Its novelty is measured in the change of a preposition. He doesn't speak *about* literature, he speaks *to* literature as to his other as instigator. Through this change, Barthes's discourse posits itself outside the circumscribed discourse of the scholar and calls forth on his part the charge of "jargon" as an objective necessity: " 'jargon' is a product of imagination (it shocks as does the imagination), the approach to metaphorical language that intellectual discourse will one day need" (*Critique et vérite*, p. 34); " 'jargon' is the language of the other; the other (and not others) is what is not self; whence the trying character of its language" (*ibid.*, p. 31). But where, then, is objectivity? What "guarantee" have we against the possibility of desire to "deform" the "truth" of the "object" itself, the literary text?

The *dialectical* objectivity of this discourse stems from its "truth," constructing itself in the *operation* of an *inclusion exterior* to its "object." Its *truth* is to produce the *motion of* this *inclusion* (contrary to the excluding procedure of classical science) that posits and goes beyond its subjective center (repudiated in science, hypostasized in ideology) by addressing itself to a *difference* (writing) recognized and always maintained as external (heterogeneous) to knowing discourse, while revealing the dialectical laws formulated by this discourse. Thus, this new continent of knowledge that approaches ideology, religions, and the "arts" articulates itself through an external inclusion in its object.

Through its function, which Barthes calls "critical," that is, by reason of the desire and heteronomy it brings to light and into play, this possible understanding of literature heralded by Barthes possesses a knowledge that science does not attain. It implicates the knowing subject within an analytic relationship to language, within a constant questioning of the symbolic and of its subject, with a perpetual struggle with no possible philosophical relaxation. Such a discourse announces what seems required by an eventual ideological renewal: the awakening of subjects.

This awakening occurs simultaneously with the putting into play of the desire for a signifier to symbolize a "real" that has fallen into the subject's past or is questionable for society. It is also simultaneous with the opening up of the homonymic corral of the totalizing and repudiated subject toward the questioning of active, corporeal, and social materiality. This simultaneity is accomplished in literature and especially in the literature of the contemporary avant-garde. Indeed, on account of that, such a literature assumes its efficacy in present time.

What can literature accomplish today? This ethical and political question has never failed to be present under the formalist appearances that journalistic and academic rumors have pasted onto the avant-garde. What can literature accomplish? Perhaps no one knows, but one is nonetheless obliged to draw up an answer if one does not want to abdicate time: the time of history as well as that microcosmic time, the other, where the text is elaborated. An answer: Where from? When? Barthes's work and the trend that he initiated, and which still carries him, are perhaps the symptom indicating that this power of writing penetrates, in our time and according to historical necessity, all discourses that do not shirk their topicality: "knowledge," "politics,"[18] and in general any art that carries meaning. The constitution of a possible knowledge of this writing is, for Barthes, the symptom of a deep social mutation, "as important, and involving the same problem, as the one marking the passage from the Middle Ages to the Renaissance" (*Critique et vérité*, p. 48).

5

FROM ONE IDENTITY TO AN OTHER

I shall attempt, within the ritual limits of a one-hour seminar, to posit (if not to demonstrate) that every language theory is predicated upon a conception of the subject that it explicitly posits, implies, or tries to deny. Far from being an "epistemological perversion," a definite subject is present as soon as there is consciousness of signification. Consequently, I shall need to outline an epistemological itinerary: taking three stages in the recent history of linguistic theory, I shall indicate the variable position these may have required of the speaking subject-support within their object language. This—on the whole, technical—foray into the epistemology of linguistic science will lead us to broach and, I hope, elucidate a problem whose ideological stakes are considerable but whose banality is often ignored. Meaning, identified either within the unity or the multiplicity of subject, structure, or theory, necessarily guarantees a certain transcendence, if not a theology; this is precisely why all human knowledge, whether it be that of an individual subject or of a meaning structure, retains religion as its blind boundaries, or at least, as an internal limit, and at best, can just barely "explain and validate religious sentiment" (as Lévi-Strauss observed, in connection with structuralism).[1]

Second, I shall deal with a particular signifying practice, which, like the Russian Formalists, I call "poetic language," in order to demonstrate that this kind of language, through the particularity of its signifying operations, is an unsettling process—when not an outright destruction—of the identity of meaning and speaking subject,[2] and consequently, of transcendence or, by derivation, of "religious sensibility." On that account, it accompanies crises within social structures and institutions—the moments of their mutation, evolution, revolution, or disarray. For if mutation within language and institutions finds its code through this signifying practice and its questionable subject in process that constitutes poetic language, then that practice and subject are walking a precarious tightrope. Poetic language, the only language that uses up transcendence and theology to sustain itself; poetic language, knowingly the enemy of religion, by its very economy borders on psychosis (as for its subject) and totalitarianism or fascism (as for the institutions it implies or evokes). I could have spoken of Vladimir Mayakovsky or Antonin Artaud; I shall speak of Louis-Ferdinand Céline.

Finally, I shall try to draw a few conclusions concerning the possibility of a *theory* in the sense of an *analytical discourse* on signifying systems, which would take into account these crises of meaning, subject, and structure. This for two reasons: first, such crises, far from being accidents, are inherent in the signifying function and, consequently, in sociality; secondly, situated at the forefront of twentieth-century politics, these phenomena (which I consider within poetic language, but which may assume other forms in the West as well as in other civilizations) could not remain outside the so-called human sciences without casting suspicion on their ethic. I shall therefore and in conclusion argue in favor of an analytical theory of signifying systems and practices that would search within the signifying phenomenon for the *crisis* or the *unsettling process* of meaning and subject rather than for the coherence or identity of either *one* or a *multiplicity* of structures.

Without referring back to the stoic sage, who guaranteed both the sign's triad and the inductive conditional clause, let us return to the congruence between conceptions of language and of subject where Ernest Renan left them. We are all aware of the scandal he caused among nineteenth-century minds when he changed a theological discourse (the Gospels) not into a *myth* but into the *history of* a man and a people. This conversion of *theological* discourse into *historical* discourse was possible thanks to a tool (for him, scientific) whose omnipotence he never ceased praising—philology. As used by Renan or Eugene Burnouf in Avestic Studies, for example, philology incorporates the *comparativism* of philologists Franz Bopp or August Schleicher. Whatever the difference between comparativists seeking those *laws* unique to *families* of languages and philologists deciphering the *meaning* of *one* language, a common conception of language as an *organic identity* unites them. Little does it matter that, as comparativists believed, this organic identity articulates itself thanks to *a law* that crosses national and historical language borders making of them one family (cf. Jacob Grimm's phonetic laws); or that, as philologists believed, this organic identity articulates itself thanks to *one meaning*—singular and unique—inscribed into a text still undeciphered or whose decipherability is debatable. In both cases this *organic identity* of law or meaning implies that language is the possession of a *homo loquens* within history. As Renan writes in *Averoés et l'Averroïsme*, "for the philologist, a text has only one meaning" even if it is through "a kind of necessary misinterpretation" that "the philosophical and religious development of humanity" proceeds.[3] Closer to the objectivity of the Hegelian "consciousness of self" for the comparativists, embodied into a singularity that, be it concrete, individual, or national, still owes something to Hegel for the philologists; language is always *one* system, perhaps even one "structure," always *one meaning*, and, therefore, it necessarily implies a subject (collective or individual) to bear witness to its history. If one has difficulty following Renan when he affirms that "rationalism is based on philology"—for it is obvious that the two are interdependent—it is no less obvious that philological reasoning is maintained through the identity of a historical subject: a subject in becoming. Why? Because, far from dissecting the internal logic of sign, predication (sentence grammar), or syllogism (logic), as did the universal grammar of Port Royal, the comparativist and philological reason that Renan exemplifies considers the signifying unit in itself (sign, sentence, syllogism) as an unanalyzable given. This signifying unit remains implicit within each description of law or text that philologists and comparativists undertake: linear, unidimensional descriptions—with no analysis of the sign's density, the logical problematic of meaning, etc.—but which, once technically completed, restore structural identity (for the comparativists) or meaning (for the philologists); in so doing they reveal the initial presupposition of the specifically linguistic undertaking as an ideology that posits either the people or an exceptional individual as appropriating this structure or this meaning. Because it is in itself unanalyzable (like the sign, sentence, and syllogism, it has no density, no economy), this subject-support of comparativist laws or of philological analysis does not lend itself to change, that is to say, to shifting from one law to another, from one structure to another, or from one meaning to another, except by postulating the movement of becoming, that is, of history. In the analysis of a signifying function (language or any "human," social phenomenon), what is censured at the level of semantic complexity reemerges in the form of a becoming: that obliteration of the density that constitutes sign, sentence, and syllogism (and consequently, the speaking subject), is compensated for by historical reasoning; the reduction of the complex signifying economy of the speaking subject (though obliquely perceived by Port Royal) produces without fail an opaque "I" that makes history. Thus, philological reasoning, while founding history, becomes a deadlock for language sciences, even though there actually is in Renan, beyond countless contradictions, an appreciation of universal grammar, a call for the constitution of a linguistics for an isolated language (in the manner of the ancient Indian grammarian Pāṇini), and even surprisingly modern proposals that advocate the study of crisis rather than normality, and in his Semitic studies the remarks on "that delirious vision transcribed in a barbaric and undecipherable style" as he calls the Christian gnostic texts, or on the texts of John the Apostle.[4]

Linguistic reasoning, which, through Saussure, succeeded philological reasoning, works its revolution precisely by affecting the constitutive unity of a particular language; a language is not a system, it is a system of signs, and this vertically opens up the famous gap between signifier and signified, thus allowing linguistics to claim a logical, mathematical formalization on the one hand, but on the other, it definitely prevents reducing a language or text to one law or one meaning. Structural linguistics and the ensuing structural movement seem to explore this epistemological space by eliminating the speaking subject. But, on a closer look, we see that the subject they legitimately do without is nothing but the subject (individual or collective) of historico-philological discourse I just discussed, and in which the Hegelian consciousness of self became stranded as it was concretized, embodied into philology and history; this subject, which linguistics and the corollary human sciences do without, is the "personal identity, miserable treasure."[5] Nevertheless, a subject of enunciation takes shape within the gap opened up between signifier and signified that admits both structure and interplay within; and structural linguistics ignores such a subject. Moreover, because it left its place vacant, structural linguistics could not become a linguistics of speech or discourse; it lacked a grammar, for in order to move from sign to sentence the place of the subject had to be acknowledged and no longer kept vacant. Of course, generative grammar does reinstate it by rescuing universal grammar and the Cartesian subject from oblivion, using that subject to justify the generative, recursive functions of syntactic trees. But in fact, generative grammar is evidence of what structural linguistics omitted, rather than a new beginning; whether structural or generative, linguistics since Saussure adheres to the same presuppositions, implicit within the structuralist current, explicit in the generative tendency that can be found summed up in the philosophy of Husserl.

I refer modern linguistics and the modes of thought which it oversees within the so-called human sciences back to this founding father from another field, but not for conjunctural reasons, though they are not lacking. Indeed, Husserl was invited to and discussed by the Circle of Prague; indeed, Jakobson explicitly recognized in him a philosophical mentor for post-Saussurian linguists; indeed, several American epistemologists of generative grammar recognize in Husserlian phenomenology, rather than in Descartes, the foundations of the generative undertaking. But it is possible to detect in Husserl the basis of linguistic reasoning (structural or generative) to the extent that, after the reduction of the Hegelian consciousness of self into philological or historical identity, Husserl masterfully understood and posited that any signifying act, insofar as it remains capable of elucidation by knowledge, does not maintain itself by a "me, miserable treasure" but by the *transcendental ego.*"

If it is true that the division of the Saussurian sign (signifier/signified), unknown to Husserl, also introduces the heretofore unrecognized possibility of envisioning language as a free play, forever without closure, it is also true that this possibility was not developed by Saussure except in the very problematic *Anagrammes.*[6] Moreover, this investigation has no linguistic followers, but rather, philosophical (Heideggerian discourse) and psychoanalytic (Lacan's signifier) contemporaries or successors, who today effectively enable us to appreciate and circumscribe the contribution of phenomenological linguistics from a Husserlian perspective. For post-Saussurian structural linguistics still encloses the signifier, even if nonmotivated, within patterns of a signification originally destined for faultless communication, either coinciding with the explicit signified or set off a short distance from it, but still fastened to the unalterable presence of meaning and, similarly, tributary to phenomenological reason.

It is therefore impossible to take up the congruence between conceptions of language and of subject where Renan left off without recalling how Husserl shifted ground by raising it above empiricism, psychologism, and incarnation theories typical of Renan. Let us examine for a moment the signifying act and the Husserlian transcendental ego, keeping in mind that linguistic reason (structural or generative) is to Husserl what philological reason was to Hegel: reduction perhaps, but also concrete realization, that is, failure made manifest.

As early as *Logical Investigations* of 1901, Husserl situates the sign (of which one could have naively thought that it had no subject) within the act of expressing meaning, constituted by a judgment on something: "The articulate sound-complex, the written sign, etc., first becomes a spoken word or communicative bit of speech, when a speaker produces it with the intention of 'expressing himself about something' through its means."[7]

Consequently, the thin sheath of the sign (signifier/signified) opens onto a complex architecture where intentional life-experience captures material (hylic) multiplicities, endowing them first with noetic meaning, then with noematic meaning, so that finally the result for the judging consciousness is the formation of an *object* once and for all signified as real. The important point here is that this real *object*, first signified by means of hylic data, through noesis and noemis, if it exists, can only be transcendental in the sense that it is elaborated in its identity by the judging consciousness of transcendental ego. The signified is transcendent as it is posited by means of certain concatenations within an experience that is always confined to judgment; for if the phenomenologist distinguishes between intuiting and endowing with meaning, then perception is already *cogitation* and the *cogitation* is transcendent to perception.[8] So much so that if the world were annihilated, the signified "*res*" would remain because they are transcendental: they "refer entirely to a consciousness" insofar as they are signified *res*. The *predicative* (syntactic) operation constitutes this judging consciousness, positing at the same time the signified *Being* (and therefore, the object of meaning and signification) and the *operating consciousness* itself. The ego as support of the predicative act therefore does not operate as the ego-cogito, that is, as the ego of a logically conceived consciousness and "fragment of the world"; rather, the transcendental ego belongs to the constituting operating consciousness, which means that it takes shape within the predicative operation. This operation is *thetic* because it simultaneously posits the thesis (position) of both Being *and* ego. Thus, for every signified transcendental object, there is a transcendental ego, both of which are givens by virtue of thetic operation—predication of judgment.

"Transcendental egology"[9] thus reformulates the question of the signifying act's subject: (1) the operating consciousness, through predication, simultaneously constitutes Being, the (transcendent) signified real object, and the ego (in so far as it is transcendental); the problematic of the sign is also bound up in this question; (2) even if intentionality, and with it, the judging consciousness, is already a given in material data and perceptions, as it "resembles" them (which allows us to say that the transcendental ego is always already in a way given), *in fact*, the ego constitutes itself only through the operating consciousness at the time of predication; the subject is merely the subject of predication, of judgment, of the sentence; (3) "belief" and "judgment" are closely interdependent though not identical: "The syntheses of belief (Glaubenssynthesen) find their 'expression' in the forms of stated meaning."[10]

Neither a historical individual nor a logically conceived consciousness, the subject is henceforth the operating thetic consciousness positing correlatively the transcendental Being and ego. Thus, Husserl makes clear that any linguistic act, insofar as it sets up a signified that can be communicated in a sentence (and there is no sign or signifying structure that is not already part of a sentence), is sustained by the transcendental ego.

It is perhaps not unimportant that the rigor of Judaism and the persecution it has been subjected to in our time underlie Husserl's extraordinarily firm elucidation of the transcendental ego, just as they are the foundation of the human sciences.

For the purposes of our discussion, we can draw two conclusions from this brief review:

1. It is impossible to treat problems of signification seriously, in linguistics or semiology, without including in these considerations *the subject thus formulated as operating consciousness*. This phenomenological conception of the speaking subject is made possible in modern linguistics by the introduction of logic into generative grammar and, in a much more lucid manner, through a linguistics (developing in France after Benveniste) which is attuned to the *subject of enunciation* and which includes in the latter's operating consciousness not only logical modalities, but also interlocutory relationships.

2. If it is true, consequently, that the question of signification and therefore of modern linguistics is dominated by Husserl, the attempts to criticize or "deconstruct" phenomenology bear concurrently on Husserl, meaning, the still transcendental subject of enunciation, and linguistic methodology. These criticisms circumscribe

the metaphysics inherent in the sciences of signification and there-fore in the human sciences—an important epistemological task in itself. But they reveal their own shortcomings not so much, as some believe, in that they prevent serious, theoretical or scientific research, but in that such "deconstructions" refuse (through discrediting the signified and with it the transcendental ego) what constitutes one function of language though not the only one: to express meaning in a communicable sentence between speakers. This function harbors coherence (which is indeed transcendental) or, in other words, social identity. Let us first acknowledge, with Husserl, this thetic charac-ter of the signifying act, which establishes the transcendent object and the transcendental ego of communication (and consequently of sociability), before going beyond the Husserlian problematic to search for that which produces, shapes, and exceeds the operating consciousness (this will be our purpose when confronting poetic language). Without that acknowledgement, which is also that of the episteme underlying structuralism, any reflection on significance, by refusing its thetic character, will continually ignore its constraining, legislative, and socializing elements: under the impression that it is breaking down the metaphysics of the signified or the transcendental ego, such a reflection will become lodged in a negative theology that denies their limitations.

Finally, even when the researcher in the field, beginning with what is now a descriptive if not scientific perspective, thinks he has discovered givens that may escape the *unity* of the transcendental ego (because each identity would be as if flaked into a multiplicity of qualities or appurtenances), the discourse of knowledge that deliv-ers this multiplied identity to us remains a prisoner of phenomeno-logical reason for which the multiplicities, inasmuch as they signify, are givens of consciousness, predicates within the same eidetic unity: the unity of an object signified by and for a transcendental ego. In an interpretive undertaking for which there is no domain hetero-geneous to meaning, all material diversities, as multiple attributes, revert to a real (transcendental) object. Even apparently psychoan-alytic interpretations (relationship to parents, et cetera), from the moment they are posited by the structuring learning as particularities of the transcendental real object, are false multiplicities; deprived of what is heterogeneous to meaning, these multiplicities can only produce a plural identity—but an identity all the same, since it is eidetic, transcendental. Husserl therefore stands on the threshold not only of modern linguistics concerned with a subject of enunciation, but of any science of man as signified phenomenon, whose objecthood, even if multiple, is to be restored.

To the extent that poetic language operates with and communicates meaning, it also shares particularities of the signifying operations elucidated by Husserl (correlation between signified object and the transcendental ego, operating consciousness, which constitutes itself by predication—by syntax—as thetic: thesis of Being, thesis of the object, thesis of the ego). Meaning and signification, however, do not exhaust the poetic function. Therefore, the thetic predicative operation and its correlatives (signified object and transcendental ego), though valid for the signifying economy of poetic language, are only one of its *limits*: certainly constitutive, but not all-encompassing. While poetic language can indeed be studied through its meaning and signification (by revealing, depending on the method, either structures or process), such a study would, in the final analysis, amount to reducing it to the phenomenological perspective and, hence, failing to see what in the poetic function departs from the signified and the transcendental ego and makes of what is known as "literature" something other than knowledge: the very place where social code is destroyed and renewed, thus providing, as Artaud writes, "A release for the anguish of its time" by "animating, attracting, lowering onto its shoulders the wandering anger of a particular time for the discharge of its psychological evil-being."[11]

Consequently, one should begin by positing that there is within poetic language (and therefore, although in a less pronounced manner, within any language) a *heterogeneousness* to meaning and signification. This *heterogeneousness*, detected genetically in the first echolalias of infants as rhythms and intonations anterior to the first phonemes, morphemes, lexemes, and sentences; this heterogeneousness, which is later reactivated as rhythms, intonations, glossalalias in psychotic discourse, serving as ultimate support of the speaking subject threatened by the collapse of the signifying function; this heterogeneousness to signification operates through, despite, and in excess of it and produces in poetic language "musical" but also nonsense effects that destroy not only accepted beliefs and significations, but, in radical experiments, syntax itself, that guarantee of thetic consciousness (of the signified object and ego)—for example, carnivalesque discourse, Artaud, a number of texts by Mallarmé, certain Dadaist and Surrealist experiments. The notion of *heterogeneity* is indispensable, for though articulate, precise, organized, and complying with constraints and rules (especially, like the rule of *repetition*, which articulates the units of a particular rhythm or intonation), this signifying disposition is not that of meaning or signification: no sign, no predication, no signified object and therefore no operating consciousness of a transcendental ego. We shall call this disposition *semiotic (le sémiotique)*, meaning, according to the etymology of the Greek *sémeion (σημεῖον)*, a distinctive mark, trace, index, the premonitory sign, the proof, engraved mark, imprint—in short, a *distinctiveness* admitting of an uncertain and indeterminate articulation because it does not yet refer (for young children) or no longer refers (in psychotic discourse) to a signified object for a thetic consciousness (this side of, or through, both object and consciousness). Plato's *Timeus* speaks of a *chora* (χώρα), receptacle (ὑποδοχεῖον), unnamable, improbable, hybrid, anterior to naming, to the One, to the father, and consequently, maternally connoted to such an extent that it merits "not even the rank of syllable." One can describe more precisely than did philosophical intuition the particularities of this signifying disposition that I have just named semiotic—a term which quite clearly designates that we are dealing with a disposition that is definitely heterogeneous to meaning but always in sight of it or in either a negative or surplus relationship to it. Research I have recently undertaken on child language acquisition in the prephonological, one could say prepredicative stages, or anterior to the "mirror stage," as well as another concomitant study on particularities of psychotic discourse aim notably at describing as precisely as possible—with the help of, for example, modern phono-acoustics— these semiotic operations (rhythm, intonation) and their dependence vis-à-vis the body's drives observable through muscular contractions and the libidinal or sublimated cathexis that accompany vocalizations. It goes without saying that, concerning a *signifying practice*, that is, a socially communicable discourse like poetic language, this semiotic heterogeneity posited by theory is inseparable from what I shall call, to distinguish it from the latter, the *symbolic* function of significance. The symbolic (*le symbolique*), as opposed to the semiotic, is this inevitable attribute of meaning, sign, and the signified object for the consciousness of Husserl's transcendental ego. Language as social practice necessarily presupposes these two dispositions, though combined in different ways to constitute *types of discourse*, types of signifying practices. Scientific discourse, for example, aspiring to the status of metalanguage, tends to reduce as much as possible the semiotic component. On the contrary, the signifying economy of poetic language is specific in that the semiotic is not only a constraint as is the symbolic, but it tends to gain the upper hand at the expense of the thetic and predicative constraints of the ego's judging consciousness. Thus in any poetic language, not only do the rhythmic constraints, for example, perform an organizing function that could go so far as to violate certain grammatical rules of a national language and often neglect the importance of an ideatory message, but in recent texts, these semiotic constraints (rhythm, phonic, vocalic timbres in Symbolist work, but also graphic disposition on the page) are accompanied by nonrecoverable syntactic elisions; it is impossible to reconstitute the particular elided syntactic category (object or verb), which makes the meaning of the utterance undecidable (for example, the nonrecoverable elisions in *Un Coup de Dés*).[12] However elided, attacked, or corrupted the symbolic function might be in poetic language, due to the impact of semiotic processes, the symbolic function nonetheless maintains its presence. It is for this reason that it is a language. First, it persists as an internal limit of this bipolar economy, since a multiple and sometimes even uncomprehensible signified is nevertheless communicated; secondly, it persists also because the semiotic processes themselves, far from being set adrift (as they would be in insane discourse), set up a new formal construct: a so-called new formal or ideological "writer's universe," the never-finished, undefined production of a new space of significance. Husserl's "thetic function" of the signifying act is thus re-assumed, but in different form: though poetic language unsettled the position of the signified and the transcendental ego, it nonetheless posits a thesis, not of a particular being or meaning, but of a signifying apparatus; it posits its own process as an undecidable process between sense and nonsense, between *language* and *rhythm* (in the sense of linkage that the word "rhythm" had for Aeschylus's *Prometheus* according to Heidegger's reading), between the symbolic and semiotic.

For a theory attuned to this kind of functioning, the language object itself appears quite differently than it would from a phenomenological perspective. Thus, a phoneme, as distinctive element of meaning, belongs to language as symbolic. But this same phoneme is involved in rhythmic, intonational repetitions; it thereby tends towards autonomy from meaning so as to maintain itself in a semiotic disposition near the instinctual drives' body; it is a sonorous distinctiveness, which therefore is no longer either a phoneme or a part of the symbolic system—one might say that its belonging to the set of the language is indefinite, between zero and one. Nevertheless, the set to which it thus belongs exists with this indefinition, with this fuzziness.

It is poetic language that awakens our attention to this undecidable character of any so-called natural language, a feature that univocal, rational, scientific discourse tends to hide—and this implies considerable consequences for its subject. The support of this signifying economy could not be the transcendental ego alone. If it is true that there would unavoidably be a speaking *subject* since the signifying set exists, it is nonetheless evident that this subject, in order to tally with its heterogeneity, must be, let us say, a questionable *subject-in-process*. It is of course Freud's theory of the unconscious that allows the apprehension of such a subject; for through the surgery it practiced in the operating consciousness of the transcendental ego, Freudian and Lacanian psychoanalysis did allow, not for (as certain simplifications would have it) a few typologies or structures that might accommodate the same phenomenological reason, but rather for heterogeneity, which, known as the unconscious, shapes the signifying function. In light of these statements, I shall now make a few remarks on the questionable subject-in-process of poetic language.

I. The semiotic activity, which introduces wandering or fuzziness into language and, *a fortiori*, into poetic language is, from a synchronic point of view, a mark of the workings of drives (appropriation/rejection, orality/anality, love/hate, life/death) and, from a diachronic point of view, stems from the archaisms of the semiotic body. Before recognizing itself as identical in a mirror and, consequently, as signifying, this body is dependent vis-à-vis the mother. At the same time instinctual and maternal, semiotic processes prepare the future speaker for entrance into meaning and signification (the symbolic). But the symbolic (i.e., language as nomination, sign, and syntax) constitutes itself only by breaking with this anteriority, which is retrieved as "signifier," "primary processes," displacement and condensation, metaphor and metonomy, rhetorical figures—but which always remains subordinate—subjacent to the principal function of naming-predicating. Language as symbolic function constitutes itself at the cost of repressing instinctual drive and continuous relation to the mother. On the contrary, the unsettled and questionable subject of poetic language (for whom the word is never uniquely sign) maintains itself at the cost of reactivating this repressed instinctual, maternal element. If it is true that the prohibition of incest constitutes, at the same time, language as communicative code and women as exchange objects in order for a society to be established, *poetic language would be* for its questionable subject-in-process the *equivalent of incest*: it is within the economy of signification itself that the questionable subject-in-process appropriates to itself this archaic, instinctual, and maternal territory; thus it simultaneously prevents the word from becoming mere sign and the mother from becoming an object like any other—forbidden. This passage into and through the forbidden, which constitutes the sign and is correlative to the prohibition of incest, is often explicit as such (Sade: "Unless he becomes his mother's lover from the day she has brought him into the world, let him not bother to write, for we shall not read him,"—*Idée sur les romans*; Artaud, identifying with his "daughters"; Joyce and his daughter at the end of *Finnegans Wake*; Céline who takes as pseudonym his grandmother's first name; and innumerable identifications with women, or dancers, that waver between fetishization and homosexuality). I stress this point for three reasons:

(*a*) To emphasize that the dominance of semiotic constraint in poetic language cannot be solely interpreted, as formalist poetics would have it, as a preoccupation with the "sign," or with the "signifier" at the expense of the "message"; rather, it is more deeply indicative of the instinctual drives' activity relative to the first structurations (constitution of the body as self) and identifications (with the mother).

(*b*) To elucidate the intrinsic connection between literature and breaking up social concord: because it utters incest, poetic language is linked with "evil"; "literature and evil" (I refer to a title by Georges Bataille) should be understood, beyond the resonances of Christian ethics, as the social body's self-defense against the discourse of incest as destroyer and generator of any language and sociality. This applies all the more as "great literature," which has mobilized unconsciousnesses for centuries, has nothing to do with the hypostasis of incest (a petty game of fetishists at the end of an era, priesthood of a would-be enigma—the forbidden mother); on the contrary, this incestuous relation, exploding in language, embracing it from top to bottom in such a *singular* fashion that it defies *generalizations*, still has this common feature in all outstanding cases: it presents itself as demystified, even disappointed, deprived of its hallowed function as support of the law, in order to become the cause of a permanent trial of the speaking subject, a cause of that agility, of that analytic "competency" that legend attributes to Ulysses.

(*c*) It is of course possible, as Lévi-Strauss pointed out to Dr. André Green, to ignore the mother-child relationship within a given anthropological vision of society; now, given not only the thematization of this relationship, but especially the mutations in the very economy of discourse attributable to it, one must, in discussing poetic language, consider what this presymbolic and trans-symbolic relationship to the mother introduces as aimless wandering within the identity of the speaker and the economy of its very discourse. Moreover, this relationship of the speaker to the mother is probably one of the most important factors producing interplay within the structure of meaning as well as a questioning process of subject and history.

2. And yet, this reinstatement of maternal territory into the very economy of language does not lead its questioned subject-in-process to repudiate its symbolic disposition. Formulator—logothete, as Roland Barthes would say—the subject of poetic language continually but never definitively assumes the thetic function of naming, establishing meaning and signification, which the paternal function represents within reproductive relation. Son permanently at war with father, not in order to take his place, nor even to endure it, erased from reality, as a symbolic, divine menace and salvation in the manner of *Senatspräsident* Schreber. But rather, to signify what is untenable in the symbolic, nominal, paternal function. If symbolic and social cohesion are maintained by virtue of a sacrifice (which makes of a *soma* a sign towards an unnamable transcendence, so that only thus are signifying and social structures clinched even though they are ignorant of this sacrifice) and if the paternal function represents this sacrificial function, then it is not up to the poet to adjust to it. Fearing its rule but sufficiently aware of the legislation of language not to be able to turn away from this sacrificial-paternal function, he takes it by storm and from the flank. In *Maldoror*, Lautréamont struggles against the Omnipotent. After the death of his son Anatole, Mallarmé writes a *Tombeau*, thanks to which a book replaces not only the dead son, his own father, mother, and fiancée at the same time, but also hallowed humanism and the "instinct of heaven" itself. The most analytical of them all, the Marquis de Sade, gives up this battle with, or for, the symbolic legislation represented by the father, in order to attack the power represented by a woman, Madame de Montreuil, visible figurehead of a dynasty of matrons toward whom he usurps, through writing, the role of father and incestuous son; here, the transgression is carried out and the transsymbolic, transpaternal function of poetic language reaches its thematic end by staging a simultaneously impossible, sacrificial, and orgastic society—never one without the other.

Here we must clearly distinguish two positions: that of the rhetorician and that of the writer in the strongest sense of the word; that is, as Céline puts it, one who has "style." The rhetorician does not invent a language; fascinated by the symbolic function of paternal discourse, he *seduces* it in the Latin sense of the verb—he "leads it astray," inflicts it with a few anomalies generally taken from writers of the past, thus miming a father who remembers having been a son and even a daughter of his father, but not to the point of leaving cover. This is indeed what is happening to the discourse of contemporary philosophers, in France particularly, when, hemmed in by the breakthroughs in social sciences on the one hand, and social upheavals on the other, the philosopher begins performing literary tricks, thus arrogating to himself a power over imaginations: a power which, though minor in appearance, is more fetching than that of the transcendental consciousness. The stylist's adventure is totally different; he no longer needs to seduce the father by rhetorical affectations. As winner of the battle, he may even drop the name of the father to take a pseudonym (Céline signs with his grandmother's first name), and thus, in the place of the father, assume a different discourse; neither imaginary discourse of the self, nor discourse of transcendental knowledge, but a permanent go-between from one to the other, a pulsation of sign and rhythm, of consciousness and instinctual drive. "I am the father of my imaginative creations," writes Mallarmé at the birth of Geneviève. "I am my father, my mother, my son, and me," Artaud claims. Stylists all, they sound a dissonance within the thetic, paternal function of language.

3. Psychosis and fetishism represent the two abysses that threaten the unstable subject of poetic language, as twentieth-century literature has only too clearly demonstrated. As to *psychosis*, symbolic legality is wiped out in favor of arbitrariness of an instinctual drive without meaning and communication; panicking at the loss of all reference, the subject goes through fantasies of omnipotence or identification with a totalitarian leader. On the other hand, where *fetishism* is concerned, constantly dodging the paternal, sacrificial function produces an objectification of the pure signifier, more and more emptied of meaning—an insipid formalism. Nevertheless, far from thus becoming an unpleasant or negligible accident within the firm progress of symbolic process (which, in the footsteps of science, would eventually find signified elements for all signifiers, as rationalists believe), these borderline experiences, which contemporary poetic language has undergone, perhaps more dramatically

than before or elsewhere, show not only that the Saussurian cleavage (signifier/signified) is forever unbridgeable, but also that it is reinforced by another, even more radical one between an instinctual, semioticizing body, heterogeneous to signification, and this very signification based on prohibition (of incest), sign, and thetic signification establishing signified object and transcendental ego. Through the permanent contradiction between these two dispositions (semiotic/symbolic), of which the internal setting off of the sign (signifier/signified) is merely a witness, poetic language, in its most disruptive form (unreadable for meaning, dangerous for the subject), shows the constraints of a civilization dominated by transcendental rationality. Consequently, it is a means of overriding this constraint. And if in so doing it sometimes falls in with deeds brought about by the same rationality, as is, for example, the instinctual determination of fascism—demonstrated as such by Wilhelm Reich—poetic language is also there to forestall such translations into action.

This means that if poetic economy has always borne witness to crises and impossibilities of transcendental symbolics, in our time it is coupled with crises of social institutions (state, family, religion), and, more profoundly, a turning point in the relationship of man to meaning. Transcendental mastery over discourse is possible, but repressive; such a position is necessary, but only as a limit open to constant challenge; this relief with respect to repression—establishing meaning—is no longer possible under the incarnate appearance of a providential, historical, or even rationalist, humanist ego (in the manner of Renan), but through a *discordance* in the symbolic function and consequently within the identity of the transcendental ego itself: this is what the literary experience of our century intimates to theoretical reason, thereby taking its place with other phenomena of symbolic and social unrest (youth, drugs, women).

Without entering into a technical analysis of the economy specific to poetic language (an analysis too subtle and specious, considering the purpose of this specific paper), I shall extract from Céline, first, several procedures and, second, several themes, which illustrate the position of the unsettled, questionable subject-in-process of poetic language. I shall not do this without firmly underlining that these themes are not only inseparable from "style," but that they are produced by it; in other words, it is not necessary "to know" them, one could have heard them by simply listening to Céline's staccato, rhythmic discourse, stuffed with jargon and obscenity.

Thus, going beyond semantic themes and their distributions, one ought to examine the functioning of poetic language and its questionable subject-in-process, beginning with constitutive linguistic operations: syntax and semantics. Two phenomena, among others, will become the focus of our attention in Céline's writing: *sentential rhythms* and *obscene words*. These are of interest not only because they seem to constitute a particularity of his discourse, but also because, though they function differently, both of them involve constitutive operations of the judging consciousness (therefore of identity) by simultaneously perturbing its clarity and the designation of an object (objecthood). Moreover, if they constitute a network of constraints that is added to denotative signification, such a network has nothing to do with classic poeticness (rhythm, meter, conventional rhetorical figures) because it is drawn from the drives' register of a desiring body, both identifying with and rejecting a community (familial or folk). Therefore, even if the so-called poetic codes are not recognizable within poetic language, a constraint that I have termed semiotic functions in addition to the judging consciousness, provokes its lapses, or compensates for them; in so doing, it refers neither to a literary convention (like our poetic canons, contemporary with the major national epics and the constitution of nations themselves) nor even to the body *itself*, but rather, to a signifying disposition, pre- or transsymbolic, which fashions any judging consciousness so that any ego recognizes its crisis within it. It is a jubilant recognition that, in "modern" literature, replaces petty aesthetic pleasure.

Sentential rhythms. Beginning with *Death on the Installment Plan*, the sentence is condensed: not only does Céline avoid coordination and embeddings, but when different "object-phrases" are for example numerous and juxtaposed with a verb, they are separated by the characteristic "three dots." This procedure divides the sentence into its constitutive phrases; they thus tend to become independent of the central verb, to detach themselves from the sentence's own signification, and to acquire a meaning initially incomplete and consequently capable of taking on multiple connotations that no longer depend on the framework of the sentence, but on a free context (the entire book, but also, all the addenda of which the reader is capable). Here, there are no syntactic anomalies (as in the *Coup de Dés* or the glossalalias of Artaud). The predicative thesis, constitutive of the judging consciousness, is maintained. By using three dots to space the phrases making up a sentence, thus giving them rhythm, he causes connotation to rush through a predication that has been striated in that manner; the denotated object of the utterance, the transcendental object, loses its clear contours. The elided object in the sentence relates to a hesitation (if not an erasure) of the *real object* for the speaking subject. That literature is witness to this kind of deception involving the object (object of love or transcendental object); that the existence of the object is more than fleeting and indeed impossible: this is what Céline's rhythms and syntactic elisions have recently evidenced within the stern humor of an experiment and with all its implications for the subject. This is also true of Beckett, whose recent play, *Not I*, spoken by a dying woman, sets forth in elided sentences and floating phrases the impossibility of God's existence for a speaking subject lacking any object of signification and/or love. Moreover, beyond and with connotation, with the blurred or erased object, there flows through meaning this "emotion" of which Céline speaks—the nonsemanticized instinctual drive that precedes and exceeds meaning.

The exclamation marks alternating with three dots even more categorically point to this surge of instinctual drive: a panting, a breathlessness, an acceleration of verbal utterance, concerned not so much with finally reaching a global summing up of the world's meaning, as, to the contrary, with revealing, within the interstices of predication, the rhythm of a drive that remains forever unsatisfied—in the vacancy of judging consciousness and sign—because it could not find an other (an addressee) so as to obtain meaning in this exchange. We must also listen to Céline, Artaud, or Joyce, and read their texts in order to understand that the aim of this practice, which reaches us as a language, is, through the signification of the nevertheless transmitted message, not only to impose a music, a rhythm—that is, a polyphony—but also to wipe out sense through nonsense and laughter. This is a difficult operation that obliges the reader not so much to combine significations as to shatter his own judging consciousness in order to grant passage through it to this rhythmic drive constituted by repression and, once filtered by language and its meaning, experienced as jouissance. Could the resistance against modern literature be evidence of an obsession with meaning, of an unfitness for such jouissance?

Obscene words. Semantically speaking, these pivotal words in the Célinian lexicon exercise a *desemanticization* function analogous to the fragmentation of syntax by rhythm. Far from referring, as do all signs, to an object exterior to discourse and identifiable as such by consciousness, the obscene word is the minimal mark of a situation of desire where the identity of the signifying subject, if not destroyed, is exceeded by a conflict of instinctual drives linking one subject to another. There is nothing better than an obscene word for perceiving the limits of a phenomenological linguistics faced with the heterogeneous and complex architectonics of significance. The obscene word, lacking an objective referent, is also the contrary of an autonym— which involves the function of a word or utterance as sign; the obscene word mobilizes the signifying resources of the subject, permitting it to cross through the membrane of meaning where consciousness holds it, connecting it to gesturality, kinesthesia, the drives' body, the movement of rejection and appropriation of the other. Then, it is neither object, transcendental signified, nor signifier available to a neutralized consciousness: around the object denoted by the obscene word, and that object provides a scanty delineation, more than a simple context asserts itself—the drama of a questioning process heterogeneous to the meaning that precedes and exceeds it. Childrens' counting-out rhymes, or what one calls the "obscene folklore of children," utilize the same rhythmic and semantic resources; they maintain the subject close to these jubilatory dramas that run athwart the repression that a univocal, increasingly pure signifier vainly attempts to impose upon the subject. By reconstituting them, and this on the very level of language, literature achieves its cathartic effects.

Several themes in Céline bring to light the relationships of force, at first within the family triangle, and then in contemporary society, that produce, promote, and accompany the particularities of poetic language to which I have just referred.

In *Death on the Installment Plan*, the most "familial" of Céline's writings, we find a paternal figure, Auguste: a man "of instruction," "a mind," sullen, a prohibitor, prone to scandal, full of obsessional habits like, for example, cleaning the flagstones in front of his shop. His anger explodes spectacularly once, when he shuts himself up in the basement and shoots his pistol for hours, not without explaining in the face of general disapproval, "I have my conscience on my side," just before falling ill. "My mother wrapped the weapon in several layers of newspaper and then in a cashmere shawl . . . 'Come, child . . . come!' she said when we were alone [. . .] We threw the package in the drink."[13]

Here is an imposing and menacing father, strongly emphasizing the enviable necessity of his position, but spoiling it by his derisive fury: undermined power whose weapon one could only take away in order to engulf it at the end of a journey between mother and son.

In an interview, Céline compares himself to a "society woman" who braves the nevertheless maintained family prohibition, and who has the right to her own desire, "a choice in a drawing room": "the whore's trade doesn't interest me"; before defining himself, at the end: "I am the son of a woman who restored old lace . . . [I am] one of those rare men who knows how to distinguish batiste from valencienne . . . I do not need to be taught. I know it."

This fragile delicacy, heritage of the mother, supports the language—or if you wish, the identity—of him who unseated what Céline calls the "heaviness" of men, of fathers, in order to flee it. The threads of instinctual drive, exceeding the law of the paternal word's own mastery, are nonetheless woven with scrupulous precision. One must therefore conceive of another disposition of the law, through signified and signifying identity and confronting the semiotic network: a disposition closer to the Greek *gnomon* ("one that knows," "carpenter's square") than to the Latin *lex*, which necessarily implies the act of logical and legal judgment. A device, then, a regulated discrimination, weaves the semiotic network of instinctual drives; if it thus fails to conform to signifying identity, it nevertheless constitutes another identity closer to repressed and gnomic archaisms, susceptible of a psychosis-inducing explosion, where we decipher the relationship of the speaker to a desiring and desired mother.

In another interview, this maternal reference to old lacework is explicitly thought of as an archeology of the word: "No! In the beginning was emotion. The Word came next to replace emotion as the trot replaces the gallop [. . .] They pulled man out of emotive poetry in order to plunge him into dialectics, that is, into gibberish, right?" Anyway, what is *Rigodon* if not a popular dance which obliges language to bow to the rhythm of its emotion.

A speech thus slatted by instinctual drive—Diderot would have said "musicated"—could not describe, narrate, or theatricalize "objects": by its composition and signification it also goes beyond the accepted categories of lyric, epic, dramatic, or tragic. The last writings of Céline, plugged in live to an era of war, death, and genocide, are what he calls in *North*, "the vivisection of the wounded," "the circus," "the three hundred years before Christ."

While members of the Resistance sing in alexandrine verse, it is Céline's language that records not only the institutional but also the profoundly symbolic jolt involving meaning and the identity of transcendental reason; fascism inflicted this jolt on our universe and the human sciences have hardly begun to figure out its consequences. I am saying that this literary discourse enunciates through its formal decentering, more apparent in Artaud's glossalalias, but also through the rhythms and themes of violence in Céline, better than anything else, the faltering of transcendental consciousness: this does not mean that such a discourse is aware of such a faltering or interprets it. As proof, writing that pretends to agree with "circus" and "vivisection" will nonetheless find its idols, even if only provisional; though dissolved in laughter and dominant nonsense, they are nevertheless posited as idols in Hitlerian ideology. A reading of any one of Céline's anti-semitic tracts is sufficient to show the crudely exhibited phantasms of an analysand struggling against a desired and frustrating, castrating, and sodomizing father; sufficient also to understand that it is not enough to allow what is repressed by the symbolic structure to emerge in a "musicated" language to avoid its traps. Rather, we must in addition dissolve its sexual determinations. Unless poetic work can be linked to analytical interpretation, the discourse that undermines the judging consciousness and releases its repressed instinctual drive as rhythm always turns out to be at fault from the viewpoint of an ethic that remains with the transcendental ego—whatever joys or negations might exist in Spinoza's or Hegel's.

Since at least Hölderlin, poetic language has deserted beauty and meaning to become a laboratory where, facing philosophy, knowledge, and the transcendental ego of all signification, the impossibility of a signified or signifying identity is being sustained. If we took this venture seriously—if we could hear the burst of black laughter it hurls at all attempts to master the human situation, to master language by language—we would be forced to reexamine "literary history," to rediscover beneath rhetoric and poetics its unchanging but always different polemic with the symbolic function. We could not avoid wondering about the possibility or, simultaneously, the legitimacy of a theoretical discourse on this practice of language whose stakes are precisely to render impossible the transcendental bounding that supports the discourse of knowledge.

Faced with this poetic language that defies knowledge, many of us are rather tempted to leave our shelter to deal with literature only by miming its meanderings, rather than by positing it as an object of knowledge. We let ourselves be taken in by this mimeticism: fictional, para-philosophical, para-scientific writings. It is probably necessary to be a woman (ultimate guarantee of sociality beyond the wreckage of the paternal symbolic function, as well as the inexhaustible generator of its renewal, of its expansion) not to renounce theoretical reason but to compel it to increase its power by giving it an object beyond its limits. Such a position, it seems to me, provides a possible basis for a theory of signification, which, confronted with poetic language, could not in any way account for it, but would rather use it as an indication of what is heterogeneous to meaning (to sign and predication): instinctual economies, always and at the same time open to bio-physiological sociohistorical constraints.

This kind of heterogeneous economy and its questionable subject-in-process thus calls for a linguistics other than the one descended from the phenomenological heavens; a linguistics capable, within its language object, of accounting for a nonetheless articulated *instinctual drive*, across and through the constitutive and insurmountable frontier of *meaning*. This instinctual drive, however, located in the matrix of the sign, refers back to an instinctual body (to which psychoanalysis has turned its attention), which ciphers the language with rhythmic, intonational, and other arrangements, nonreducible to the position of the transcendental ego even though always within sight of its thesis.

The development of this theory of signification is in itself regulated by Husserlian precepts, because it inevitably makes an *object* even of that which departs from meaning. But, even though abetting the law of signifying structure as well as of all sociality, this expanded theory of signification cannot give itself new objects except by positing itself as nonuniversal: that is, by presupposing that a questionable subject-in-process exists in an economy of discourse other than that of thetic consciousness. And this requires that subjects of the theory must be themselves subjects in infinite analysis; this is what Husserl could not imagine, what Céline could not know, but what a woman, among others, can finally admit, aware as she is of the inanity of Being.

When it avoids the risks that lie in wait for it, literary experience remains nevertheless something other than this analytical theory, which it never stops challenging. Against knowing thought, poetic language pursues an effect of *singular truth*, and thus accomplishes, perhaps, for the modern community, this solitary practice that the materialists of antiquity unsuccessfully championed against the ascendance of theoretical reason.

6

THE FATHER, LOVE, AND BANISHMENT

That one who on earth
usurps my place, my place which is vacant
in the sight of the Son of God,
has made of my cemetery a sewer

—Dante, *Paradiso*, XXVII, 22–25 (Trans. H. R. Huse, 1965)

What goes by the name of love is banishment.

—Beckett, *First Love*

Strangely enough, I needed a Venetian ambience—the complete opposite of Beckett's universe—to have a sense of grasping, within the parenthesis of *First Love* and *Not I*, both the strength and the limitations of a writing that comes across less as "aesthetic effect" than as something one used to situate close to the "sacred." No name exists today for such an "unnamable" interplay of meaning and jouissance.

This parenthesis, in my opinion quite adequately circumscribing that writer's known novels and plays, conveys back to me, in microcosmic fashion, the now carnivalized destiny of a once flourishing Christianity. It includes everything: a father's death and the arrival of a child (*First Love*), and at the other end, a theme of orality stripped of its ostentation—the mouth of a lonely woman, face to face with God, face to face with nothing (*Not I*). Beckett's *pietà* maintains a sublime appearance, even on her way to the toilet. Even though the mother is a prostitute, it doesn't matter who the actual father is since the child belongs solely to its mother (*First Love*). And the babblings of a seventy-year-old woman (*Not I*), the antonym of a hymn or of

Molly's monologue, are no less haloed, in all their nonsense, with a paternal aura, ironically but obstinately raising her toward that third person—God—and filling her with a strange joy in the face of nothingness. Raised, demystified, and for that very reason more tenacious than ever, the pillars of our imagination are still there. Some of them, at least ... And so:

1. A man experiences love and simultaneously puts it to the test on the death of his father. The "thing" he had heard of "at home, in school, in brothel and at church" finally appears in reality under the guise of a paternal corpse. Through it, he catches a glimpse of "some form of aesthetics relevant to man" (the only one!) and discovers a "great disembodied wisdom" (the unrivaled one!). *Father* and *Death* are united, but still split and separate. *On the one hand*, Death—the ideal that provides meaning but where the word is silent; *on the other*, the paternal corpse, hence a possible though trivial communication, waste, decay, and excrement mobilizing pleasure and leisure. A verbal find seals this junction of opposites: *chamber pot*, a term that, for the son-writer, evokes Racine, Baudelaire, and Dante all at once,[1] summarizing the sublimated obscenity that portrays him as consubstantial with his father, but only the *decayed* cadaver of his father, never leaving the black mourning of an inaccessible paternal function, which itself has found refuge on the side of *Death*. From afar, and constantly threatened with being obscured, it thus provides a meaning for the existence of living corpses.

Racked between the *father* (cadaverous *body*, arousing to the point of defecation) and *Death* (empty *axis*, stirring to the point of transcendence), a man has a hard time finding something else to love. He could hardly venture in that direction unless he were confronted with an undifferentiated woman, tenacious and silent, a prostitute to be sure, her singing voice out of tune in any case, whose name remains equally undifferentiated, just like the archaic breast (Lulu? or Lully? or Lolly?), exchangeable for another (Anna), with only one right: to be inscribed "in time's forgotten cowplats," and thus to blend into "history's ancient faeces." This will then be the only love—one that is possible, one that is true: neither satyric, nor Platonic, nor intellectual. But *banishment-love*.

2. Banishment: an attempt at separating oneself from the august and placid expanses where the father's sublime Death, and thus *Meaning*, merges with the son's "self" (but where a daughter can very easily become trapped), mummified, petrified, exhausted, "more dead than alive"; a banishment robbing this sensible but always already dead, filial self of its silence on the threshold of a rimy minerality, where the only opportunity is to become anyone at all, and moreover, without the means for fading away. So flee this permanence of meaning. Live somewhere else, but in the company of paternal Death.

Banishment: above/beyond a life of love. A life always off to one side, at an impassable distance, mourning a love. A fragile, uncertain life, where, without spending the saved-up, paternal capital in one's pockets, he discovers the price of warmth (of a hothouse, of a room, of a turd) and the boredom of those humans who provide it—but who waste it, too. It is a life apart from the paternal country where nonetheless lies the obsessed self's unshakable quiet, frozen forever, bored but solid.

To love is to survive paternal meaning. It demands that one travel far to discover the futile but exciting presence of a waste-object: a man or woman, fallen off the father, taking the place of his protection, and yet, the always trivial ersatz of this disincarnate wisdom that no object (of love, necessarily) could ever totalize. Against the modifying *whole* of the father's Death, on chooses banishment toward the *part* constituting a fallen object or an object *of* love (*of* being possessive and genitive partitive). How trivial, this object of love—transposition of love for the Other. And yet, without banishment, there is no possible release from the grip of paternal Death. This act of loving and its incumbent writing spring from the Death of the Father—from the Death of the third person (as *Not I* shows).

3. In other words, the primary, obsessed man never sees his father as dead. The corpse under his eyes is the waste-object, the fallen and thus the finally possible object, endlessly expected from the first cries on, from the first feces on, from the first words on; and so firmly condemned, pushed aside by paternal strength. This cadaverous object finally allows its son to have a "real" relationship with the world, a relationship in the image of this very object, this miserable downfall,

this disappointed mercy, this disabused realism, this sullen irony, this low-spirited action. Through this opening, he might look for woman. But the Other, the third-person father, is not that particular dead body. It is Death; it always was. It is the meaning of the narrative of the son, who never enunciated himself as anything else, save for and by virtue of this stretched out void of paternal Death, as ideal and inaccessible to any living being as it might seem. As long as a son pursues meaning in a story or through narratives, even if it eludes him, as long as he persists in his search he narrates in the name of Death for the father's corpses, that is, for you, his readers.

4. Now, how can one fail to see that if Death gives meaning to the sublime story of this first love, it is only because it has come to conceal barred incest, to take up all the space where otherwise we would imagine an unspoken woman: the (father's) wife, the (son's) mother? It is because he deduces this absence that the banished son, by analyzing his banishment, might not remain forever a bachelor—neither monk nor narcissistic lover of his peers, but a father in flight.

5. Indeed, with Beckett, the myth of the bachelor writer leaves behind the fascinated terror of Proust or Kafka and comes closer to Marcel Duchamp's dry humor. This banished lover, with all his calculations ("I thought of Anna then, long long sessions, twenty minutes, twenty-five minutes and even as long as half an hour daily. I obtain these figures by the addition of other, lesser figures.") and his nighttime "stewpan," keeping him bedtime company better than a bride, truly evokes the autoerotic mechanism and "Malic Molds" of the "Large Glass" Bachelor. Moreover, Lulu-Anna has all the qualities of *The Bride Stripped Bare by Her Bachelors, Even*—half robot, half fourth dimensional, a kind of "automobilism," automatically activating its "internal combustion engine" and setting forth again by "stripping-bare" movements. And even if Lulu isn't a virgin, even if she proves to be a woman with an unruly clientele, the "cooling cycle" that adjusts her amorous mechanism to that of the banished narrator places the two coital protagonists forever, as with Duchamp, into icy communication. In the manner of Duchamp, Beckett says, after and against the militant bachelors of the early twentieth century, that rather than avoid the sexual act, they should assume it but only as

an impossible relationship, whose participants are condemned to a perpetual banishment that confines them within autoeroticism. But Beckett writes against Joyce, too, ascetically rejecting the latter's joyous and insane, incestuous plunge summed up in Molly's jouissance or the paternal baby talk in *Finnegans Wake*.

Assumption of self through the dead father turns the banished writer into a father in spite of himself, a father under protest, a false father who doesn't want to be a father, but nonetheless believes in being one—tense in the elegance of permanent mourning. There remains for him to relish his grief, and even more so, the emptiness holding him up between Death and waste, between sublimity and pleasure, a balance of nothingness—on condition that it be written: "those instants when, neither drugged nor drunk, nor in ecstasy, one feels nothing." Living close to a woman who helps him survive in this banishment from the father's Death, he does not allow himself to be concerned about her own experience; fortified with this assumption of Death, he quickly gets away from her so as to devote himself entirely to his own "slow descents again, the long submersion," which expressly allows him to sketch out a new meaning, to write a narrative. Assuming the stance of his father's son inoculates him forever against any incestuous, that is, "poetic" endeavor.

In corresponding fashion, for his wife—the "married" spinster—the autoerotic autonomy of her universe is ensured by childbirth. This also accomplishes the impossible coexistence of two incommunicable entities, one male and one female.

First Love suggests that, for a woman, the counterpart of what the dead father is for the obsessed man is the child, substituting for the father; that, however, is a different matter. Because in a more immediate and direct sense, what the banished man needs most from a woman is simply someone to accompany him into Death's void, into the third person's void. He needs the gentle touch of a mute partner, renunciation of the body, waste, sublimation, and—in order to be faithful to his dead father to the end—a double suicide.

6. The banished young man has aged. Faithful to his paternal love, he has become an old lady (*Not I*). Yet, there are no ambiguities to suggest the slightest measure of perversion. The body is stiff, there

is no pleasure, except, in the field, the soft, solitary illumination of a head suffused by light and of a mouth, grasping at the same void, and continually asking questions. The father's Death, which enabled the son to experience love, is still with us, at the end of the act, in these light beams, this void, but now it does not even lead to a pseudofictional narrative. The father's presence that caused the son to narrate *First Love* has become for the old woman of *Not I* a rhetorical device: a questioning. Corpse and waste have been replaced by a syntactic occurrence: *elision.*

Questioning is the supreme judicial act, for the *I* who asks the questions, through the very act of asking these questions (apart from the meaning of the request) postulates the existence of the other. Here, since it is "not I," not *you* either, there must be a *He beyond communication.*

The *elision* of the object is the syntactic recognition of an impossible object, the disappearance not only of the addressee (*you*), but of all topic of discourse. In *First Love,* already, the object conceals itself, slipping out of the sentence, probably remaining in that unnamable domain of the father:

> It had something to do with lemon trees, or orange trees, I forget, that is all I remember, and for me that is no mean feat, to remember it had something to do with lemon trees, or orange trees, I forget, for of all the other songs I have ever heard in my life, and I have heard plenty, it being apparently impossible, physically impossible short of being deaf, to get through this world, even my way, without hearing singing, I have retained nothing, not a word, not a note, or so few words, so few notes, that, that what, that nothing, this sentence has gone on long enough.

What in this text still appears as a surplus of meaning, an overflow caused by an excess of internal subordination, often becomes, in *Not I*, a deletion of direct objects, and always a deletion of the object of discourse. A missing (grammatical or discursive) object implies an impossible subject: not I. And yet, it exists, she speaks; this de-oralized and frustrated mouth is nevertheless held to its trivial search: "not knowing what . . . what she was— . . . what? . . . who? . . .

no! . . . she! . . . SHE! . . ." "*Mouth* recovers from vehement refusal to relinquish third person."

Here, this means that the act of writing, without me or you, is in fact an obstinate refusal to let go of the third person: the element beyond discourse, the third, the "it exists," the anonymous and unnamable "God," the "Other"—the pen's axis, the father's Death, beyond dialogue, beyond subjectivism, beyond psychologism. A disappointed Mouth, seized by the desire to pour itself out as into a wash basin. And yet there is nobody in mind, no "you"—neither father, mother, man, nor child; alone with the flow of words that have lost their meaning, that are suspended, like pleasureless vowels, "askew," "tacky"; useless, dying Mouth, dying but persistent, tenacious, obstinate voice, sustained by the same first love, looking for, awaiting, pursuing, who? what? . . . The prerequisites of writing.

Yet, beyond this amorous association of the *banished writer* with the *mad*, seventy-year-old woman, pursuing a paternal shadow binding her to the body and to language, the gap between *writing* and *psychosis* bursts open. He, writing, fled his father so that the introjected superego, adhering to its meaning, might perpetuate itself as trace through a symbolic ascesis renouncing sexual jouissance. She, devastated by (paternal) love, which she incorporates into her impossibility to such a degree that she sacrifices her "self" to it, replaces a forbidden, permanently mourning vagina with a mouth, through which, madly but certainly, jouissance seeps—oral, tactile, visible, audible, and yet unnamable disgust, without link or syntax, permanently setting her off from socialized humans, either before or beyond their "works." He writes in a state of ascesis. She experiences jouissance in nonsense through repression. Two boundaries of paternal love, one for each sex. They are a fascinating and impossible couple, also sustained, on both sides, by censorship of the maternal body.

Beckett's tragic irony thus achieves its maximal resonance when the son's tenacious love of Death is uttered through the mouth of a woman. Impossible subjectivity ("if I have no object of love, I do not exist"), but an equally impossible femininity, an impossible genitality for both sexes, no escape from death for either. *Not I*: a heartrending statement of the loss of identity but also, discreet and resigned jubilation, a sweet relief produced by the most minute corruption of meaning in a world unfailingly saturated with it. In contrast with the overflowing Molly and Finnegan's negative awakening, stands a jouissance provoked by meaning's deception, which nevertheless inevitably perseveres through and beyond this unavoidable third person.

At the (phantasmatic?) dawn of religion, the sons of the primitive horde commemorated their share in the Death of the father by partaking of a totemic meal. In fact, the father's Death was a murder denied. Swallowing the totemic animal, the substitute for the father, reconciled them to his body as if it were a maternal breast; that was sexual ambiguity or travesty, and it exonerated them from any guilt in replacing the father and exercising the power they took from him. They thus incorporated into their reality what they had symbolically introjected.

But Beckett represents the other end of the process. Only refuse, "stewpans," and the "convenience" have replaced the totemic meal. Left with only failed or frustrated orality, the sons have given up any hope of either annexing, incorporating, or introjecting the father's power and/or Death. They will remain forever separated from him; but, forever subject to his hold, they will experience its fascination and terror, which continues to infuse meaning, dispersed as it might be, into their absurd existence as wastrels. The only possible community is then centered in a ritual of decay, of ruin, of the corpse-universe of Molloy, Watt, and the rest of their company, who nonetheless continue their most "Beckettian" of activities: questioning and waiting. Will he come? Of course not! But just the same, let us ask for Godot, this Father, this God, as omnipresent as he is incredible.

There probably has never been a keener eye directed at paternal Death in that it determines the son, our monotheistic civilization, and maybe even all granting of meaning: saying, writing, and doing. Carnivalesque excavations on the brink of a toppling over toward something else, which, nonetheless, remains impossible in Beckett. X-ray of the most fundamental myth of the Christian world: the love for the father's Death (a love for meaning beyond communication, for the incommunicable) and for the universe as waste (absurd communication).

In this way, *one of the components* of Christianity reaches its apex and the threshold leading to its reversal: its Judaic substratum and its Protestant branch, which, lucid and rigorous, have founded speech's meaning in the Death of the inaccessible father.

The fact remains that there is another component.

Christianity, according to Freud, seems to be on the verge of admitting that this Death was a Murder. But what is more, such an admission could surface or become bearable only if the communal *meaning*, thus linked to the murder, were compensated by jouissance. Both in its pagan beginnings or its Renaissance deviation, Christianity celebrates maternal fecundity and offsets the morbid and murderous filial love of paternal reason with mother-son incest. One needs only to glance through fifteenth-century art, or better yet, to see both— Pietà and serene jubilation of the mother—in the work of Giovanni Bellini, for example, to understand that the fascination and enduring quality of Mediterranean and Oriental Christianity are unthinkable without this conjunction.

True, these luminously fleshed Madonnas, holding their male infants with often ambiguous caresses, remain enigmatic because of an incommensurable distance separating them from their sons—a distance especially manifest in their averted gazes, close to fainting, disgust, or nothingness. As if to say that their love is not even the baby—still an object of banishment—but perhaps now as always, an elsewhere, the same incredulous and stubborn "God is love" that in *Not I* already opens up onto *nothing*. Their child is probably there, but its presence is only *one segment* of jouissance, the segment destined for others. What remains, in its immensity, can be expressed by neither narrative nor image, except, perhaps, through these oblique, dimmed, withheld, and always vacant glances; or through these oblivious heads, averted from the world in a frustrated and melancholy expectation. Illuminated by absence, nothingness; and nonetheless persistent, obstinate—like *Not I*.

And yet there is a *remnant*, which cannot be found in the glance soothed by the nothingness underlying "God is love," nor in the serenely positioned, maternal body, that discretely diverted body— intermediary and passageway between an exploded and absent head

and an infant to be given away. This remnant is precisely what constitutes the enigma of Christian maternity; by means of a quite *unnamable*
stance, it parallels the obsessional morbidity specific to Christianity
as it is to any religion, but which, in Christianity, has already been
eclipsed by the God in the Madonna's eyes as well as in Mouth of
Not I. Now, such an unnamable, unlike that of *Not I*, is not *less* but
more than Word and Meaning. Through the recovered memory of the
incestuous son—the artist—this jouissance imagines itself to be the
same as the mother's. It bursts out in a profusion of colors, a flood of
lights, and even more brutally, in the baby-angels and winged breasts
sculpted into the columns of Saint Mark's Church in Venice.

An attempt was made, at the beginning of the Renaissance, to save
the Religion of the Father by breathing into it, more than before,
what it represses: the joyous serenity of incest with the mother.
Bellini's classicism and, in another fashion, the lavishness of the
baroque testify to it. Far from feminist, they can be seen as a shrewd
admission of what in the feminine and maternal is repressed, and
which is always necessarily kept under the same veils of sacred terror
when faced with the father's Death—a Death that, nevertheless, had
henceforth become nothingness in the eyes of these early Western
women, looking at us from within a painting.

Too late. The Renaissance was to revive Man and his perversion beyond the mother thus dealt with and once again rejected.
Leonardo and Michelangelo replaced Giovanni Bellini. Humanism
and its sexual explosion, especially its homosexuality, and its bourgeois eagerness to acquire objects (products and money) removed
from immediate analysis (but not from the preconscious) the cult
of natality and its real and symbolic consequences. So much the better. For, through such scorn for femininity, a truly analytic solution
might, albeit very exceptionally, take shape at last. It was not until the
end of the nineteenth century and Joyce, even more than Freud, that
this repression of motherhood and incest was affirmed as risky and
unsettling in one's very flesh and sex. Not until then did it, by means
of a language that "musicates through letters," resume within discourse the rhythms, intonations, and echolalias of the mother-infant
symbiosis—intense, pre-Oedipal, predating the father—and this in

the third person. Having had a child, could a woman, then, speak another love? Love as object banished from paternal Death, facsimile of the third person, probably; but also a shattering of the object across and through what is seen and heard within rhythm: a polymorphic, polyphonic, serene, eternal, unchangeable jouissance that has nothing to do with death and its object, banished from love. In *Not I, Mouth*, leaving behind an obsessional labyrinth, becomes a mirage of this possible serenity, shielded from death, that is, incarnate in the mother. Here I see the averted, disillusioned eyes of radiant Madonnas . . .

But the colors of the paintings are lacking.

Is it because Beckett's written works, after Joyce and in different fashion, seem to have their sights on some archeology other than Christianity's? Using the Latins' most analytic language, French, a language nonetheless foreign to him, a language of banishment, a language of love, Beckett doesn't oblige them to experience the explosion of a nativity whose incestuous jouissance they celebrated. If he had, he would have been led to write *poetry*. On the contrary, having chosen the *narrative*, frustrated but obstinate, through monologue or dialogue, he has set forth the limitations and the means—the structure—that enabled him to probe the desacralized piety of the father's Death. And he made us a present of the calm discharge that it allows.

The result is a text that forces Catholics, Latins, to assume, if not to discover, what they have borrowed from the outside (Judaism) or what they have rejected (Protestantism). Such a text necessarily attracts a certain number of admirers or even accomplices from among the "others," the "dissimilar," the strange, foreigners, and exiles. On the other hand, those who refuse consciously to acknowledge their debt to the third person will listen to *Not I* and its portrayal of senseless, radiant death in the face of a fleeing God with a feeling of terror and lack of understanding. Beckett's lesson is thus one in morality, one of rigor and ironic seriousness.

Yet, at a glance and despite *Not I*, the community that Beckett so challenges quickly notices that the writer's work *does* leave something untouched: the jubilant serenity of the unapproached, avoided mother. So beyond the debris of the desacralized sacred that Beckett calls upon us to experience, if only as lucid and enlightened observers, does there not persist an *other*—untouched and fully seductive? The true guarantee of the last myth of modern times, the myth of the feminine—hardly the third person any longer, but, both beyond and within, more and less than meaning: rhythm, tone, color, and joy, within, through, and across the Word?

Therein lie both the strength and the limitations of Beckett's fiction, at least within Christianity's closed world.

And that will have to do until someone else comes in a burst of song, color, and laughter to conquer the last refuge of the sacred, still inaccessibly hidden in Bellini's remote Madonnas. To give them back to us transformed, secular, and corporeal, more full of language and imagination. Just as Beckett restored, above and beyond his mockery and for a humanity searching for a solitary community, the trivial rigor of paternal Death—for every speaking being, a disillusioned and hardly bearable, but permanent support of Meaning.

7

THE NOVEL AS POLYLOGUE

Unveiling is not reduction but passion. Logically, the reader of the Divine Comedy is Dante, that is, no one—he, too, is within "love," and knowledge is here but a metaphor for a far more radical experience: that of the letter, where life, death, sense, and nonsense become inseparable. Love is sense and nonsense, it is perhaps what allows sense to come out of nonsense and makes the latter obvious and legible. [. . .] Language is seen as the scene of the whole, the way to infinity: he who knows not language serves idols, he who could see his language would see his god.

—Philippe Sollers, *Logiques*

H is a music that is inscribed in language, becoming the object of its own reasoning, ceaselessly, and until saturated, overflowing, and dazzling sense has been exhausted. *H* asks for nothing—no deciphering, at any rate, no commentaries, no philosophical, theoretical, or political complement that might have been left in abeyance, unseen and forgotten. *H* sweeps you away. It whisks you from your comfortable position; it breathes a gust of dizziness into you, but lucidity returns at once, along with music, and you can watch your opacity being dissolved—into sounds; your blind, organic, murderous sexuality being unwound into a subtle, easy gesture, projected from the body into language; and your social animosities being released into a vision of time where Dionysius, the ancient land of Aquitaine, Nerval, Hölderlin, Epicurus, Chuang Tzu, the poets of Arabia, Webern ("Das Augenlicht"), the "Apocalypse," Augustine, Marx, Mao, the class struggle, Pompidou's France, and cultural revolution all find their place. So you must read, listen, immerse yourself in its language;

discover its music, its gestures, its dance; and have its time, its history, and all of history join in a dance.

Or else, you talk about it, because *H* sends you into analysis; you assume its writer as an object of transference, as a character on your Oedipal stage. And that is endless, undecidable. You go from *H* to Sollers, and from Sollers, back to *H*: Who is what? Does the text have a master? How do I go about killing what I assume is "master" and causes me to founder, dissects my language, my representation, and my history: *H*? You tend to see *H* as a person, to fashion its negativity into a psychological or sociological case, and to search for an identity that is a threat to itself—and a threat to you. How so? As musical and as active as all that? Impossible! It is not delirious enough, not sexed enough, not politicized enough. It is overpoliticized, oversexed, overdelirious. In a first phase, as protection from *H* (I mean, from the process that today writes *H* and tomorrow something else) you say, "This is a problem." In a second phase, "I don't want to know that this is a problem." In a third, "It gets at me just the same, but elsewhere and deferred."

The jolt of May '68: a call from the masses. For those who have long known that imagination is an absolute antipower, what was new was the concrete manifestation of this truth—the general strike immobilizing France. Were they mistaken? The time of history passes through the stories of individuals: their birth, their experience. . . .

Worldwide revisionism has collapsed—a foundering that is plain for all to see, henceforth, through the climax it has reached. The Cultural Revolution follows its course: socialism now attempts to transform itself, to find a new vitality, to reject dogmatism—politics-ideology-diplomacy moving forward, withdrawing, correcting themselves, thus giving evidence of a historical turning point having been arrived at, perhaps.

What about us, here, now, concretely, enclosed within a still-active bourgeoisie, living in a culture that is weakened but still capable of integration, at the peak of a rationality that is no longer Greek, but dialecticized, materialized, permeated by the unconscious, and structured by the reality principle laid down by social contradictions?

A language, a subject within language, seeks itself—it seeks one that might enunciate this turning point, this whirlwind, this reversal, this confrontation of the old within the new.

There is the violence of *Lois* ("Laws," 1972).

The laughing, singing, somber, and open logic of *H* (1973).

Would discussing it amount to resisting the tide?

One resistance against *others*?

Since people have been wondering why, since they have said so, for some time, and under various guises that change according to power relationships, I want to speak about it myself. In fact, to speak about it, to the extent that I am allowed to use the pronoun "I," is to speak about my right to speak, in French. Obviously, I shall not say all.

To put it bluntly, I speak in French and about literature because of Yalta. I mean that because of Yalta, I was obliged to marry in order to have a French passport and to work in France; moreover, because of Yalta I wanted to "marry" the violence that has tormented me ever since, has dissolved identity and cells, coveted recognition and haunted my nights and my tranquility, caused hatred to well within what is usually called love, in short, has raked me to death. Consequently, as you may have noticed, I have no "I" any more, no imaginary, if you wish; everything escapes or comes together in theory, or politics, or activism . . . But that is not the issue. You will perhaps understand if I tell you that Yalta has turned a portion of the earth into societies that are being built on the illusion that the negative—death, violence—does not concern them. That the negative is a remnant of the past (the not yet abolished bourgeois classes, parents) or an outside threat. But what we are proposing *will be*, or rather, *is* nothing more than understanding, exchange, and sociality, hence, socialism. Or perhaps, violence is a passing error (Stalin's prison camps); what one tends to accept before veering completely about and believing that such violence is fatal, irremediable, insuperable, but—alas!—such is our lot, while elsewhere, they do without it, and that is what is known as civilization. Read Hegel as one might, the "ego," once exposed to the negative, ignores it and escapes more or less unscathed; complicity with, if not basis for Stalinism. It all begins with dogmatizing ideological struggle, then abandoning it and, finally, making up little protectionist "I's"—the convenient narcissisms of backward bourgeois "subjects," very much protected, indeed; but such a protection, generally speaking and allowing for a few exceptions, shields them from innovation, analysis, and history. And yet, it sometimes happens: questions about sexuality, irregularity in a poem, sounds in a foreign language, eroticism that is forbidden, impossible, and yet all the more experienced and unremitting. You become someone who wonders if the communal euphoria is not a lie, a lie involving not only harvest-time enthusiasm, but something that no one talks about: devious words, dreams, the soreness in your throat, desires, death drive, wasted sentences, rhythms. Then, after you ask for information on the latest five-year plan, you listen to the figures, of course, but you also listen to the voice of the woman talking to you, and you look especially at the orange, purple, red, and green rugs she wove . . . Like something by Matisse, one might say. And you notice, returning to the capital, that the "abnormal" and "crazy" people, the "homosexuals," the "poets," the gadflies are there, their numbers are growing, and there is no way either to integrate them or to avoid integrating them into your thinking. Because of the well-known easing of oppression, the "thaw" . . .

You will say that Freud has given us a way of getting rid of all of these problems, be they juvenile or characteristic of developing societies (one and the same). It is easily said, but not quite certain. Above all, you must not forget that this all takes place within language. Hence, not possible in Bulgarian, once again because of Yalta, and, of course, past history. As a result, I had recourse to French: Robespierre, Sade, Mallarmé . . .

And I have since been wedded to a torrent. It is a desire to understand, to be sure, or, if you prefer, a laboratory of death. For what you take to be a shattering of language is really a shattering of the body, and the immediate surroundings get it smack on the chin. Besides, they exist for no other reason than to take it on the chin, and to resist, if they can. But above all, do not take yourself for someone or something; you "are" within the shattering, to be shattered. Woe unto him who thinks that you *are*—in good part or in bad, no matter. First, narcissism crumbles and the superego says, "So much the better, there's one problem out of the way." But the body seems to need an identity, and it reacts—matures, tightens, like stone, ebony. Or else it cracks, bleeds, decays. All according to the symbolic reaction that is more or less likely. Then, the symbolic covering (constituted by acquired knowledge, the discourse of others, and communal shelter) cracks, and something that I call instinctual drive (for lack of a better term) rides up to destroy any guarantees, any beliefs, any protection, including those comprised by father or professor. An aimless drifting ensues that reconciles me to everything that is being shattered— rejecting what is established and opening up an infinite abyss where there are no more words. That gives me a fractured appearance that fools the naive observer. In fact, it opens me up to a precise jouissance that few suspect even existed. That is a place one must rush away from; otherwise, two thousand years of nunneries illustrate what might happen. Words come to mind, but they are fuzzy, signifying nothing, more throbbing than meaning, and their stream goes to our breasts, genitals, and irridescent skin. That could be all there is to it—an "anonymous white conflict" as they said in the nineteenth century. But what would be the point? Now this is the point; my concern lies in the other, what is heterogeneous, my own negation erected as representation, but the consumption of which I can also decipher. This heterogeneous object is of course a body that invites me to identify with it (woman, child, androgyne?) and immediately forbids any identification; it is not me, it is a non-me in me, beside me, outside of me, where the me becomes lost. This heterogeneous object is a body, because it is a *text.* I have written down this much abused word and insist upon it so that you might understand how much risk there is in a text, how much nonidentity, nonauthenticity, impossibility, and corrosiveness it holds for those who chose to see themselves within it. A body, a text that bounces back to me echoes of a territory that I have lost but that I am seeking within the blackness of dreams in Bulgarian, French, Russian, Chinese tones, invocations, lifting up the dismembered, sleeping body. Territory of the mother. What I am saying to you is that if this heterogeneous body, this risky text provide meaning, identity, and jouissance, they do so in a completely different way than a "Name-of-the-Father." Not that they do not operate under the shield of a tyrannical, despotic Name-of-the-Father; I understand that, and we could engage in endless forensic contests. But it is only a question of power; the important thing is to see what exceeds it. So I listen to the black, heterogeneous territory of the body/text; I coil my jouissance within it, I cast it off, I sidestep its own, in a cold fire where murder is no longer the murder of the other, but rather, of the other who thought she was I, of me who thought I was the other, of me, you, us—of personal pronouns therefore, which no longer have much to do with all this. For neither body that has become liquid powder nor the shining mercury that founders me can ever abolish a vigil: paternal shadow, Being of language? It even calls on me to represent it. "I" continually makes itself over again, reposits itself as a displaced, symbolic witness of the shattering where every entity was dissolved. "I" returns then and enunciates this intrinsic twisting where it split into at least four of us, all challenged by it. "I" pronounces it, and so "I" posits myself—"I" socializes myself. This is an indispensable and imperative movement, an abrupt about-face when this heterogeneous negative that provoked me to jouissance/death *sets to work*, wants to know itself, to communicate, and consequently, loses itself. To communicate, to know . . . All that is, if I may say so, rather perverted. Language is affected by it, the concept is twisted, the murder is disguised as a request that others put some rigor in their thinking. No scholar, no orthodox theoretician can find his way through any of my essays, unless he has personally experienced this four-sided duel.

And yet, this already puts me on the other side, where society constitutes itself by denying the murder it inflicts on music—on instinctual drive—when it is founded on a *code*, that is, on a *language*. Having returned, "I" feels uncomfortable there, but not without a certain sense of gratification, having a tendency to accept the ambiguous and ephemeral praises due to the diver who was mischievous enough to bring back a few trophies. But ceaselessly drifting away, letting out slack, protesting: jealous of its exploration, fascinated by the danger of ever having to begin again . . . All the more so because the other, the "poet," the "actor" is there, coming and going, leaving, shattering, and forbidding any "I" to doze off within the realm where denial persists.

I feel that this path is determined by sexual difference. I think that for a woman, generally speaking, the loss of identity in jouissance demands of her that she experience the phallus that she simply is; but this phallus must immediately be established somewhere; in narcissism, for instance, in children, in a denial and/or hypostasis of the other woman, in narrowminded mastery, or in fetishism of one's "work" (writing, painting, knitting, et cetera). Otherwise, we have an underwater, undermaternal dive: oral regression, spasmodic but unspeakable and savage violence, and a denial of effective negativity. Remember Artaud's text where the black, mortal violence of the "feminine" is simultaneously exalted and stigmatized, compared to despotism as well as to slavery, in a *vertigo* of the phallic mother—and the whole thing is dedicated to Hitler. So then, the problem is to control this resurgence of phallic presence; to abolish it at first, to pierce through the paternal wall of the superego and afterwards, to reemerge still uneasy, split apart, asymmetrical, overwhelmed with a desire to know, but a desire to know more and differently than what is encoded-spoken-written. If a solution exists to what we call today the feminine problematic, in my opinion, it too passes over this ground.

I believe two conditions are necessary if this course is to be followed. The first is historical; it was satisfied much more rapidly in socialist countries and is already reaching the Christian, bourgeois West. It involves throwing women into all of society's contradictions with no hypocrisy or fake protection. The second condition is sexual and no social statute can ever guarantee it. As far as I am concerned, it involves coming to grips with one's language and body as others, as heterogeneous elements. The "author," as I perceive him through my reading *H*, keeps me awake during my negative vigil. For others, it might be something else; what is indispensable is the function carried out by *some One*, or—why not (but not yet)—by a *group*, having you, *through language too*, go through an infinite, repeated, multipliable dissolution, until you recover possibilities of symbolic restoration: having a position that allows your voice to be heard in real, social matters—but a voice fragmented by increasing, infinitizing breaks. In short, a device that dissolves all of your solutions, by they scholarly, ideological, familial, or protective, in order to point out to you that you do not take place as such, but as a *stance* essential to a practice. With this device, castration applies not to this or that person, but specifically to each individual in recurrent fashion. It applies to him as he experiences his phallic fixation; to her as she accedes to it, and the other way around, interchangeably.

The other that will guide you and itself through this dissolution is a rhythm, music, and within language, a text. But what is the connection that holds you both together? Counter-desire, the negative of desire, inside-out desire, capable of questioning (or provoking) its own infinite quest. Romantic, filial, adolescent, exclusive, blind and Oedipal: it is all that, but for others. It returns to where you are, both of you, disappointed, irritated, ambitious, in love with history, critical, on the edge and even in the midst of its own identity crisis; a crisis of enunciation and of the interdependence of its movements, an instinctual drive that descends in waves, tearing apart the symbolic thesis. There, before you, it breaks apart and recovers, building up its strength, quiescent, elsewhere. After the saccharine whirlwind of Jocastas and Antigones, next to a quietude fascinated with the self-indulgent whims of hysterics, the negative awakens within the body and language of the other so as to weave a fabric in which your role is tolerated only if it resembles that of women in Sade, Joyce, and Bataille. But you most certainly must not consider yourself either as the weaving or as the character against whom it is woven. What is important is to listen to it, in your own way, indefinitely, and to disappear within the movement of this attentiveness.

This means that the wife of a "poet," of this particular poet, no longer exists. Neither Mme. Mallarmé's knitting, nor Lou Salomé's subtle curiosity, nor Nora Joyce's proud and obedient excitement, nor Maria van Rysselbergh's asexual mythology, any more than the gratifying coupling that "virilized" the women of postwar existentialism or romantic-communism—henceforth, all that is impossible, antiquated, a dismal relic.

Since there is one man and one woman, but since they are "one" only to begin with, another "relationship" arises out of sexual difference and the impossible element it infers on both sides. This development has just barely begun, by virtue of a certain non-"uxorial" way of grasping the Freudian revolution; by virtue of communities that open up the family; by virtue of pop music; and H[ash][1] . . . A painful laboratory that entails mistakes, failures, and victims. But if you want to talk about it (and this is the only way to undergo its process) you find yourself once again face to face, two by two, bearing its and the other's familial, social, and linguistic constellation.

I am talking about it because it is my problem, a contemporary problem. There are men, enthralled by archaic mothers, who dream of being women or some unapproachable master; exasperated and frigid young women, confined within groups where what they take for lesbianism leads them into seclusion from society; others, classic hystericals, search for that impossible maternal fusion and are exalted in their frustration. We recognize them more clearly each day; they are precisely the subjects who involve themselves in class and ideological struggles, in scientific experimentation, in production . . . So that is why, where, and how I am searching for, hearing, reading, and dealing with H—taking H.

Beyond the Sentence: The Transfinite in Language

With no punctuation, H is not a sentence but it is not less than a sentence. The clauses are there: short and regular, with no syntactic or lexical anomalies to cloud their clarity. Sentences are easily "restored," and the simple clause kernels that constitute the running text are easily isolated and punctuated. In so doing, we lose semantic and logico-syntactic ambiguities, but we mainly lose a music. By *music*, I mean intonation and rhythm, which play only a subordinate role in everyday communication but here constitute the essential element of enunciation and lead us directly to the otherwise silent place of its subject. You yourself perceive this music when you let yourself be carried along by the unpunctuated, sentence fragments; you can check this, if you are so inclined, by listening to the writer read. You notice that whenever you expect his voice, ordinarily, to slow down, drop, and trail off so as to suggest a limit, a period, it in fact rises higher, releases the period and, instead of declaring, questions or requests. So that the sentence limits are there, *meaning* (the position of a subject of enunciation) and *significance* (possible, plausible, or actual denotation) remain, but the semiotic process does not stop there. Instead of serving as the upper limits of enunciation, the *sentence-meaning-significance* here acts as its lower limits. Through and in conjunction with these limits, but not below, there occurs a breakthrough of what may be called "primary" processes, those dominated by intonation and rhythm. When this involves morphemes, it produces "stylistic figures": metaphor, metonymy, elisions, etc. Here, this intonational, rhythmic, let us say "instinctual" breakthrough is situated at the most intense place of naming—at the thetic place of an inescapable syntax that abruptly halts the maternal body's vague, autoerotic jubilation—recognizes its reflection in a mirror and shifts instinctual motility into logically structurable signifiers. The *Aufhebung* of instinctual drive across this boundary, which nonetheless exerts its full impact, situates the semiotic experience beyond the sentence, and thus, beyond signification and meaning.

So-called "artistic" practices have always exerted fascination because they elude this boundary, owing to which signification— always already in the form of a sentence—comes into being, and they revive the uneasiness that goes with regressing to a time before the mirror stage. *H* moves us beyond these aesthetic regions, although they continue to upset commonplace logical order by setting in motion the most active, insurgent, modern practices. But these have found their most fruitful ground in music: Cage, La Monte Young, Kagel, and Stockhausen have made this clear.

Language, on the other hand, has a specificity that no other system based on differences possesses: it *divides* (signifier/signified) and *joins* (modifier/modified = sentence); it is sign-communication-sociality. "Musicating" this dividing-joining movement involves exploding rhythm *into division*, of course, but also, *into juncture*: into the metaphoric-metonymic slippage that corrugates lexemic items and lifts even the signifier/signified censorship; *but especially, into the juncture of logic and sentence* where socio-symbolic order is rebuilt and ignores anything having to do with the previous, underlying (semic, morphemic, phonic, instinctual) explosion. Intervening at the level where syntactic order renders opaque the outlay underlying the signifying practice; intervening at the point where sociality constitutes itself by killing, by throttling the outlay that keeps it alive—that means intervening precisely when the sentence pulls itself together and stops. The problem is to raise and transform this very moment, to allow it to sing.

Thus we are dealing with a composition where the sentence is a minimal unit and where a texture that surpasses but never belies it is elaborated on the basis of it: more-than-a-sentence, more-than-meaning, more-than-significance. If there is a loss, if an outlay is made, they never result in less, but always *more*: more-than-syntactic. There is no outlay of logical movement without the completion of its course. Finishing off reason is done only after the fullness of reason, (full)filling it and then ripping it: "a reason in hell" (p. 26).[2] Otherwise, reason remains as a power and demands its right to exercise control over the drifting that remains unaware of it. Otherwise, literature lends itself to the Hegelian challenge that discovered in it nothing more than a few pearls of wisdom in a sty. *H* reveals a practice where present and surpassed reason has no power; a practice where the antipower of instinctual drive is in turn deprived of its hallucinatory influence as it is filtered through the rigor of the sentence; a practice where logical superego and fetishist oralization neutralize each other without mastery and without regression.

Looking closely at the beginning of *H*, we notice that sentences, easily detachable from the textual whole, either dovetail or adjoin ambiguously because of the elision of determinants (conjunctions, relative pronouns, et cetera). This ambiguity is heightened when predicate phrases appear in surface structures, as nominative, attributive, adjoined phrases that can agree in many different ways with the noun-phrase subject. Or for reasons of semantics or of length, the predicative sequence itself breaks up into phrases that function as subjects and others that function as predicates. Equally applicable is the ambivalent value of those personal pronouns whose antecedent is unclear: the pronoun *elle* on the first page could refer equally to the feminine French words *machine, femme*, or *balle*. Networks of alliteration (the correlatives of "signifying differentials") establish trans-sentence paths that are superimposed over the linear sequences of clauses and introduce into the logical-syntactic memory of the text a phonic-instinctual memory. They set up associative chains that crisscross the text from beginning to end and in every direction: *son côté cata socle* (9:1–2), *accents toniques* (9:2), *cata cata catalyse* (9:10–11); *filtre philtre* (9:23), *phi flottant* (9:28), *philippe filioque procedit—l'fil* (10:23–24); *clé* (9:15), *claquement* (9:16); *glaïeul clocher clé de sol* (10:6–7); *sollers-sollus* (11:1), etc.

Through these ambiguities and polyvalances, *sentence sequences* still manage to become established, defined in reading by *a single breathing motion*, which results in a *generally rising intonation*. This breathing thus sustains a succession of sentences, simultaneously unified by meaning (a *position of the subject of enunciation*) and significance (*a virtual denotation*). A breathing movement thus coincides with the attitude of the speaking subject and the fluctuating range of denotation. The next breathing movement introduces the speaking subject's new attitude and a new sphere of denotation. The human body and meaning, inseparable as they are, thus fashion a dismembered score; a halt in breathing and syntactic finitude, also inseparable, are thus given a new start, but in a different logical realm, as if they were drawing support from some other region of the body-support.

The *borders* that define a *sequence* as a unit of breathing, meaning, and signification (grammatically made up as a concatenation of sentences) vary greatly and indicate the subject of enunciation's motility—his chances for resurgence and metamorphosis. Here are some that appear at the beginning of the text:

—The personal pronoun *elle* (9:3) marks the boundary of the preceding sequence and introduces another unit of breathing-meaning-signification. It is a reply to the initial question (*qui dit salut*), a reinvoking of the *machine*, or a reminder of a heterogeneous enunciation, of an *elle* who activates the *machine* and triggers its—or her—*tonic accents*. In any case, it is a displacement of the machine-like anonymity toward a *she*, a dream and motion cast. The second boundary is marked by the pronoun *elle*, now become *balle* and *bombe qui retombe*. Notice that the *je* representing the subject presenting the text appears for the first time within the dream of the pronoun *elle: "elle a rêvé cette nuit que je lançais la balle"* (9:3). The narration has begun; *elle* is at the same time the speaking and acting subject of the narrative, just like *je*. *Je/elle* marks the maximum sexual and discursive alteration—trauma and leap of the narrative's beginnings.

—After the *interrogative* enunciation gives way to the *declarative*, the latter is in turn cut and replaced by an *imperative*: *"tiens on est en pleine montagne y a d'la poudreuse regarde les cristaux blancs violets sens cet air"* ("hey we're way up in the mountains the stuff is powdery look white purple crystals feel that air"). *"Je"* begins to speak and takes charge of the narrative now under way.

—There follows a *metalinguistic* position that comments upon the course of a silent body brought into play by someone else's dream and henceforth placed in a position to control this narrative, phantasmatic, and hallucinatory alterity: *"pour la première fois l'hallucination goutte à goutte est vue du dedans découpée foulée"* ("for the first time the hallucination drop by drop is seen from within cut up crushed").

—There is an irruption of *onomatopoeias: cata cata catalyse* suggests the sound of a typewriter in action, marking infinitely a biological, electric, signifying current . . . Thus, a fracturing of the previously affirmed, metalinguistic mastery; reminder of lexical dissolution, of the bursts of instinctual drives working through phonemes: the metalinguistic position does not predominate.

—A new resumption of the *narrative*, with the pronoun *elle*; but does the pronoun refer to the machine or the woman?

—Again, a return to *metalanguage*: *"y a-t-il une autre forme non y aura-t-il réponse bien sûr que non personne et d'ailleurs le délire n'est pas le délire"* ("is there another form no will there be an answer certainly not no one and besides delirium isn't delirium").

—Within a few lines, we find several *new boundaries* analogous to the previous ones, introducing an explicit *I* ("I was not born to be quiet") who begins his "own" narrative. It again drifts away, however, is impossible to pinpoint, this time floating across new boundaries corresponding to historical and biographical references.

—The pronoun *I* is not seeking itself, it loses itself in a series of references to logical or political events that, within the framework of either the past or the present, determine a similar mobility of a subject propelled into the whirlwind of his own fragmentation and renewal—his *ex-schize* (p. 82).[3] It is a mortal, but "exquisite" scission (an ironic comment on Surrealist automatism's *cadavre exquis*, or "exquisite corpse") because it is anterior, a renewing and prophetic resumption. Thus we have the reference at the beginning of the text to the magic "filter" or "philtre," structuring and regenerating the intoxication of a shattered, but not lost, identity. Or similarly, this "phi floating on my lips like the other infant with the vultures' tail" reminding us of Freud's interpretation of one of Leonardo Da Vinci's dreams. Or the first and last paternal names generating through signifying series an infinitely open array of signifieds, where each element in turn gives rise to a mini-narrative, what I have called a "sequence"—a unit of breathing, meaning, and signification, gathering childhood memories or historical sketches by means of a swarm of homonymous kings. Or the references to the Bible: "in Hebrew the word for nude crafty awake is the same" (p. 11); or to the Koran: "he who accepts his book with his right hand that might be alright but he who accepts it behind his back zap flunked" (p. 12).

The reading voice marks the boundaries of each sequence by rising. Nothing is brought to completion, the enunciation is not finished, other semiotic procedures draw out the completion produced by syntactic operations. This intonation hangs on a clearly *interrogative* connotation, which, in addition, the interrogative sentence opening the text ("*qui dit salut...*") stimulates from the very beginning, and which several interrogative sentences frequently and throughout the text confirm. That questioning summons is less pronounced at the end, but it persists; interrogative segments are present up to the last sequences of the text: "*kílusu kílucru kíluentendu* [. . .] *que crierai-je* [. . .]*" ("hoocoudanown hoocoudabeleev'd hoocoudaherd [. . .] what shall I shout" (pp. 184–85). The summoning intonation also enters into the abundant imperatives near the end: "that's why go enter leave come back in leave again close yourself upon yourself hide yourself from yourself outside of yourself come back leave come back in quickly [. . .] shout to him" (p. 185). The set ends with a sequence held on a level rather than a descending intonation: "all flesh is like grass shadow the dew of time among voices" (p. 185).

As is well known, the lowering voice of the declarative sentence and the ensuing pause are essential and distinctive marks of a sentence. Children learning a language first learn the intonations indicating syntax structure—that is, melody or music—before they assimilate the rules of syntactic formation. Intonation and rhythm are the first markers of the finite in the infinity of semiotic process; they delineate the limited positions of a subject who first invokes but, soon thereafter, also signifies. Syntactic apprenticeship brings about and completes the subject's ability to become a speaking subject, but only to the extent that he has at his disposal an infinite system that can be made finite. This is what generative grammar attempts to represent through its system of recursive operations capable of reducing an infinite number of signifying procedures to the grammatical norms of any national language; and (within the specific infinity of any of these languages) of repeatedly producing finite but original and renewable utterances. We do not know, however, *what determines* that possibility for the speaking subject to confine the semiotic practice within the limits of the sentence normally described as noun phrase plus verbal phrase (Chomsky) or modified plus modifier (Kurylowicz) or the joining of nonlinguistic terms by means of nonrelational ties between the universal and the particular (Strawson), and so on. Although everyone agrees that there is neither meaning nor signification without a syntactic nucleus, we are still far from understanding which of the speaking subject's attitudes imposes this finitude and, even less, what happens on either side of it.

I shall assume that a precise type of signifying practice, based on a *request* and an *exchange of information*, embeds the speaking subject within the limits of sentence enunciation; but other signifying practices that have jouissance as their goal—that is, the *Aufhebung* of death and of outlay of signifying unit within the production of a new socio-symbolic device—would necessitate the pursuit of signifying operations beyond the limits of the sentence. We have seen that these signifying operations, for which the sentence serves as a basic component through which one must work one's way, can be either "primary" or "secondary," and they prevent the speaking subject from being fixed in a single or unified position—rather, they multiply it. Thus, instinctual rhythm becomes logical rhythm.

It is not enough to say that, thanks to these operations, the sentence gains access to a higher domain, that is, to *discourse*. For discourse might be (as in fact is the case) a simple concatenation of sentences (whose logic remains to be determined), without ever requiring of the subject of enunciation a shift *as to his position in relation to his speech act*. Yet, this is precisely what happens in *H*. Not only is there a juxtaposition of different ideological or communicative positions (sender, addressee, illocution, presupposition), but also a juxtaposition of utterances that record the various stratifications of the genotext (instinctual drive, resonant rhythm, syntactic and metalinguistic positions and their inversions).

Language possesses a transfinite element (if I may use this term in a different sense than Cantor's); it is the expanse beyond the sentence limits that, preserved, open up on a sundered continuity where a precise interval (the sentence) holds the value of meaning and signification—but their true power is built up only on the basis of the numerated, phrased infinity of a polylogical "discourse" of a multiplied, stratified, and heteronomous subject of enunciation. *H* generates this transfinite of language, one that is neither sentential monologue nor allocutionary dialogue, but rather, a raising of sentential (monological *or* dialogical) meaning to the power of an open infinity, to the extent that the possible attitudes of the subject in relation to his speech remain open. Because it is transfinite, the text of *H* functions not only as a plural dialogue between the subject of enunciation and his identity; not only is it a speech act imposing the fulfillment of this plural dialogism on the addressee subject (that is, an illocutionary, "juridic" act presupposing a direct effect on the reader, without which it cannot exist); but the text functions as a plural dialogue, an illocutionary act, *in relation to the very realm of language*: in relation to the sentence and its support-subject, in the sense that it takes them for granted, necessitates their position, but also appropriates them within the infinitely open "set" that it constitutes.

Therefore, we are no longer talking about *poetry* (a return to the near side of syntactic articulation, a pleasure of merging with a rediscovered, hypostatized maternal body); nor about *narrative* (the fulfillment of a request, the exchange of information, the isolation of an ego amenable to transference, imagining, and symbolizing). In the narrative, the speaking subject constitutes itself as the subject of a family, clan, or state group; it has been shown that the syntactically normative sentence develops within the context of prosaic and, later, historic narration. The simultaneous appearance of *narrative* genre and *sentence* limits the signifying process to an attitude of request and communication. On the other hand, since poetry works on the bar between signifier and signified and tends to erase it, it would be an anarchic outcry against the thetic and socializing position of syntactic language. It depletes all communities, either destroying them or identifying with the moment of their subversion. *H's* originality derives from playing these contradictions one against another; being neither. The breaking up of genres ("poetry," "narrative," and so on) isolates the protective zones of a subject who normally cannot totalize the set of signifying procedures. In *H*, on the contrary, all the strings of this prodigious instrument that language is are played together and simultaneously; no process is impeded, repressed, or put aside to give free rein to another. "Primary" processes confirm, interrupt, or rather, shorten "secondary processes," condensing and shifting them onto another level where, in the meantime, the subject of enunciation has turned around. Consequently, although the collision between *semiotic operations* (those involving instinctual drive, phonic differentials,[4] intonation, and so on) and *symbolic operations* (those concerned with sentences, sequences, and boundaries) may be thought of as a totalizing phenomenon, it actually produces an infinite fragmentation that can never be terminated: an "external polylogue."

I have attempted to "restore" standard punctuation to the transcription of the opening passages of *H*. A plus sign (+) marks syntactic ambiguities (indefinite embeddings and subordinations) that remain. A double virgule (//) marks the limits of each sequence, and the lines drawn above each sentence indicate the level of intonation.

The lines linking certain segments of the text mark a few of its pho-netic-signifying differential axes.

Intonation actually punctuates the text. A vocalic "scanning" of these two pages (figure 2) generally matches syntactic divisions, and, in this sense, eliminates some of the ambiguities that persist when one merely restores standard, written punctuation. Yet, my vocalic scanning cannot coincide with commonplace punctuation, for it sets up vocalic series whose arrangement *also* remains autonomous in relation to the signified sequence. For this rhythm is kept up inde-pendently, as if an enunciatory flight, marked off by the scope of one's breathing, went beyond sentence limits and sequence boundaries and called forth, within the phenotext, a "fundamental language"[5] that is quite simply rhythm. The regularity of these breathing periods that arise and stop short at precise intervals is striking. They appear as a sequence of short intervals, or as a long one followed by three short ones; sometimes, however, they are broken up, shortened, or highlighted by the insertion of tonic accents. This scanning, which is added to the underlying punctuation and points out the latter's inability to comprehend "the rhythmic fundamental language," strikes the unconscious as a calm and yet horrifying violence. Still, our conscious listening registers it as an invocative, lyric monotone—a kind of Tibetan Mozart.

Within the text taken as a whole, which is neither poem nor novel but *polylogue*, both pulverizing and multiplying unity through rhythm, the unpunctuated but metrical sentence finds its justification. The subject of enunciation's motility, converting prelogical rhythm or crumbling logic into a polylogical rhythm, requires a different mode of phrasing. There is no formal prejudgment that led to breaking up the sentence. The sentence is lifted away through a scanning that, while maintaining it, imbeds it into a new semiotic device. This is precisely the device that produces the limited-and-infinitized sen-tence. It evokes images of old, unpunctuated Chinese texts, which are impossible to decipher except when approached as a whole; for one must grasp the rhythm of the whole text, hence the poly-logic of the speaking subject, in order to pick out, in reverse fashion, the meaning of the smaller sentence or lexical units. *One does not begin with the part in order to reach the whole: one begins by infinitizing the totality in order to reach, only later, the finite meaning of each part.*

With this reversal of our logical habits, the sentence appears as a shelter, a finitude in which there huddles an ideational unit, plainly narrow-minded, refusing its infinitization—the metaphysical, transcendental ego, threatened by the negativity that produced it, denying that negativity and going on to a syntax seen as absolute. Keeping and converting this shelter within a poly-logue, where it would play the role of lower limit rather than absolute pinnacle, would thus amount to upsetting a metaphysical enunciation. When the most solid guarantee of our identity—syntax—is revealed as a limit, the entire history of the Western subject and his relationship to his enunciation has come to an end: "teach the tongue to sing and it will be ashamed to want anything else but what it sings" (p. 11); "what interests me is this brain dive below the sponge flip flop letting the clay run in it drop in pressure half-muted shreds who sees a sentence there you do yes oh really" (p. 32); "sentences should be misunderstood" (p. 89); "language is a finite or infinite grouping of sentences themselves sequences of discrete atoms" (p. 77); with and beyond the sentence, there is always a logical stubbornness: "alone the logical fire cipher of negation leaves no remnants" (p. 66).

Thus, when you allow yourself to be carried away by the poly-logue's fugue, you first hear a rhythm-sound-voice-scanning. But this is merely a bridge, like the bridge of a ship on the high seas, evoking Moby Dick and Melville (p. 42), taking you toward the dissolution of symbolic linking, toward the dissolution of rhythm after that of the sentence, toward empty and mute instinctual drive, toward the clashes of matter: "better to perish in this wailing infinity than to be thrown back to the lands" (p. 43); "there comes a time when i feel myself like i am the bearer of everything and nothing in everything it's maybe a cranked symphonic state" (p. 41) and "you have to treat yourself like a sonata" (p. 96), but "don't rush and give too full a contour to what comes back" (p. 98), because it is "sounds-words-sounds-not-words-sounds-nor-words-sounds" (155). The polylogue's first prerequisite: cause rhythm to emerge, hasten it, have it remove the symbolic surface: "you believe you can hold out at this

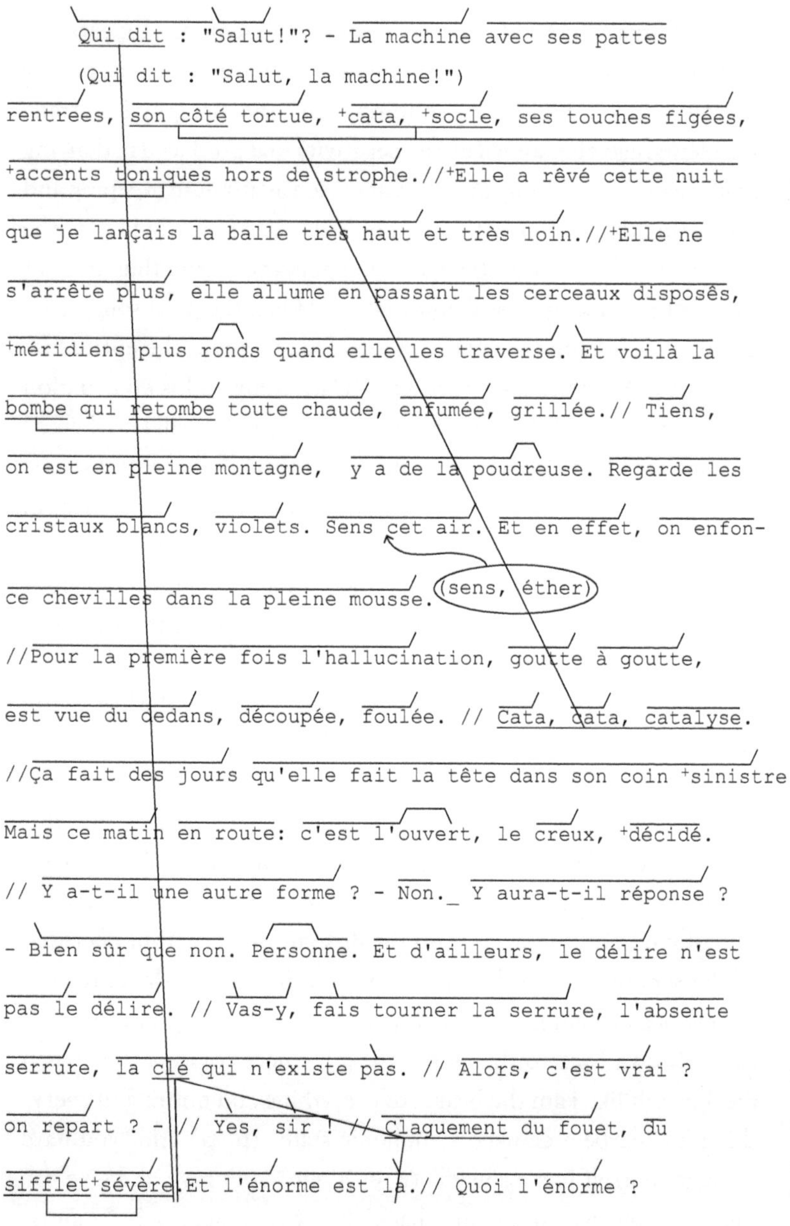

Qui dit : "Salut!"? - La machine avec ses pattes

(Qui dit : "Salut, la machine!")

rentrees, son côté tortue, +cata, +socle, ses touches figées,

+accents toniques hors de strophe.//+Elle a rêvé cette nuit

que je lançais la balle très haut et très loin.//+Elle ne

s'arrête plus, elle allume en passant les cerceaux disposés,

+méridiens plus ronds quand elle les traverse. Et voilà la

bombe qui retombe toute chaude, enfumée, grillée.// Tiens,

on est en pleine montagne, y a de la poudreuse. Regarde les

cristaux blancs, violets. Sens cet air. Et en effet, on enfon-

ce chevilles dans la pleine mousse. (sens, éther)

//Pour la première fois l'hallucination, goutte à goutte,

est vue du dedans, découpée, foulée. // Cata, data, catalyse.

//Ça fait des jours qu'elle fait la tête dans son coin +sinistre

Mais ce matin en route: c'est l'ouvert, le creux, +décidé.

// Y a-t-il une autre forme ? - Non._ Y aura-t-il réponse ?

- Bien sûr que non. Personne. Et d'ailleurs, le délire n'est

pas le délire. // Vas-y, fais tourner la serrure, l'absente

serrure, la clé qui n'existe pas. // Alors, c'est vrai ?

on repart ? - // Yes, sir ! // Claquement du fouet, du

sifflet+sévère. Et l'énorme est là.// Quoi l'énorme ?

Figure 2.

Quoi ?-//+ Le tourbillon, +radium, +carrefour. // Quoi encore ?

Et comment ? Qui ? Et quoi ? Et comment ? Pour qui et pour

quoi encore ? qui ? comment ? vers où ? pour où ? // Ça,

décidément, je ne suis pas né pour être tranquille. J'ai

pourtant fait ce que j'ai pu pour ne pas m'en apercevoir.

Enfin, cette fois ce sera peut-être la bonne. // On croit

toujours ça, en partant.// Invocation, début, désir d'âge d'or.

Transformer le filtre, se verser le philtre.// Que veux-tu ?

il y a là quelque chose d'inguérissable, double noeud qui te

défait l'un mais pas l'autre. Négation du self, de la mort.

//Bordel, je me dis, le moment est venu de s'enlever carrément

au fourreau des membres, de plus supporter la dictée par

séries volées, transvasées. //Après tout, j'ai ce phi flottant

sur les lèvres, comme l'autre infans avec la queue des

vautours.// Et si le huit revient sans fin quand je marche,

si je pense facilement à la liturgie, si un son m'apparaît

toujours accompagné, surmonté, ça vient du prénom impossible

en même temps latin, de mon père.// Non, tu ne trouveras pas.//

Je l'écris : .O.c.t.ave, oui, exactement comme in-octavo.Ce

qui lui donnait pour signer ce o tournant sur lui-même suivi

d'un point minuscule juste avant le j travaillé, brodé, genre

glaïeul, clocher, clé de sol ..."[1]

Figure 2. (*Continued*)

pace in the face of universal refusal you know i don't mind war i enjoy it" (p. 41); "you think i go too fast you think it has the shakes it might look hysterical of course not everyone has understood it was only a peaceful open kindly rhythm true meaning of the torrential spasm here i mimic the least possible music" (p. 64); "speech is a recessive phase of the respiratory cycle" (p. 78). But through music, through breathed rhythm, "everything crumbles at the same time without moving without water without substance while emptiness forces everything to flow while it goes plop by plopped matter only filaments on the surface" (pp. 32–33).

Music itself is a derivative. It is simply the sonorous indicator of a break, of a deaf, mute, mortal, and regenerative rhythm. It takes place where the body is gashed by the blows of biology and the shock of sexual, social, and historical contradiction, breaking through to the quick, piercing through the shield of the vocal and symbolic cover: "but as long as space and drives or the animated void push you on go on let yourself bloom begin again erase your get out again from there" (p. 129); "the guy who's got brakes he stops as if drive wasn't constant as if was enough time t'write comma semicolon and the whole mess as if it wasn't on the air 24 out of 24 it's up to you to transform yourself each to his own ditch" (p. 178); "what a choral group the whole body let me stick my ear against you cheek against your jaw that's where i want to listen to your silence in stifled noise not sound effects" (p. 94).

A measured language carried away into rhythm to a point beneath language: violent silence, instinctual drive, collided void; and back again—the path of jouissance, "it's the underside of language that turns over at the boiling point" (p. 64); "as far as i remember the hallucination was there alive patient its third dimension added listen I didn't invent the clock of language the point is to know who is master and that's it" (p. 64); "my words have begun to tremble in the shape of airplanes comets tendrils torches busy pouring out this sky toward the end of the day bursts of delirium you only have to find outside the raw triggering enemy wall of come coal-smeared ice axe entangled suck me or else i'll blow my brains out" (p. 147). Each syllable then becomes the support for a small portion of body, which is just as much inside (the body itself) as outside (the physical, cosmic space). Each syllable becomes a particle, a wave, a whirlwind of a pulverized "I" dissolved and reassembled within, violating and harmonizing, raising and lowering its voice, its language: "so my hypothesis is as follows wells of roaring orgasms tapped to the ten-thousandth thought to the ten-billionth thrust aside honestly with the force of a drop hammer" (p. 72); "once one has truly scaled the voice the names come back softly violently that is an experience that takes up delirium from way back" (p. 99).

Consciousness in rhythm and instinctual drive, instinctual drive and rhythm in consciousness: they are the repossession and representation of delirium and the loosening of this repossession and representation: "what distinguishes this style from the clinical document in the strictest sense is the absence of choking linked not linked no reason for the opening to sketch itself id is the representation of things nerved rather than nervous nervated narrated in the inert that is innate twice born never superannuated" (p. 139); "the schizo is as much a bircher as anyone" (p. 139).

Rhythmic language thus carries a representation, but it is indeed a striated representation and vision. The eye cannot be excluded by the ear; the representation reverberates, sound becomes image, invocative instinctual drive encounters the signifiable, realistic, polylogical object: "when the ear is penetrating it becomes an eye otherwise the lesson remains tangled in the ear without reaching the knot staccato outside" (p. 97). Language exists to have music burst into sight, otherwise music is exiled into an esoteric, mythic inside, and sight remains "one," opaque: "i said you have to exhaust sight spread hearing before letting it go in due time come on let's get this skull out for me gold meant sonority and jade glitter branch leaves flow smile all of this must be slipped into silk herbs light [. . .] you must exercise throat larynx lungs liver spleen the two sexes" (p. 81).

Under this totalizing-infinitizing condition, the equation *sex = politics* is satisfied, as the agent of this equation is a sonorous-representative, depleting-signifying language: "the sex and politics equation without the insertion of language remains metaphysical the indicator of an unmastered belief [. . .] how can one say that in what rhythm how does one transform written and spoken language in the sense of breathing dismantling of ideology verbal tartar now become mute orbital sometimes we are on the bank sometimes in the middle of the stream it is necessary that one feel that very strongly the stream the bank two and one on top of the other and one underneath the other and one separated from the other and one linked to the other stream bank stream bank stream bank stream leaving the thread to the current" (p. 83).

Spelled out here, there is a dialectics between limit and dismembered infinity, between sight and rhythm, between meaning and music, and between bank and stream: dialectics—epitome of language. Yet, the polylogue-text, which only this dialectics can construct, emphasizes music above all and, through it, the mute matter of language: it is a polemic with finitude, with pause, with totality, with the thesis of socialization that is also, and simultaneously, bounding and deadly. The polylogue destroys any symbolic "thesis" that it preserves by pelting it with a music that revives the deafened, if not ruptured, eardrum of socialized, educated, phrasemongering man: "there go your associative chains gnawing at the liver of yesterday yet this music should have massacred the memory struck the eardrum straight from the shoulder no no not the ear the eardrum cut out in the open no no not the old drum a whole lucid peeled vortex shined thawed colors now listen please be fair pick out the pieces the effort the crystals that yearned for no for what well that yearned yes that wanted oh yes that wanted would a complaint be hazardous an asshole of a man half-baked animal" (p. 162). To revive the animal, to rectify the failure, to stretch out the eardrum anew, the unreasoning resonance; all this is to push man aside and to refashion the animal within man—to make him sing like the birds of Josquin des Près: "hyt ys mornyng cum now herkyn the smale larke that sayeth lorde hyt ys day hyt ys day rede rede dil do rede dil do lee" (p. 145); drowning him in a burst of laughter: "we are the ashes of innumerable living beings while the problem is to experience it in the throat as if we had all become nobody what impalpable instrument dissolved in the wind" (p. 145).

Laugh through saturated-striated meaning, through affirmed-rhythmic identity. Laugh into a void composed of logical, syntactic, and narrative surplus. An unfamiliar, troubling, undefinable laugh. *H*'s laughter does not arise out of the Rabelaisian joy shaking up science and esotericism, marriage and Spirit, based on a full, recovered, promising body—the laughter of gigantic Man. Nor is it Swift's furious, disillusioned, and cruel fit, unearthing hell under social harmony and proving to Man that he is "Lilliputian." Since the Renaissance, the West has laughed only with the Enlightenment (with Voltaire and Diderot, laughter dethrones), or perhaps in the recesses of psychosis, where power and logic are experienced as ambivalent at first, and broken down in the end (laughter is black with burnt up meaning: Jarry, Roussel, Chaplin . . .). *H* laughs differently. Its laugh is heard only through and after the music of the text. All networks of possible meaning must be exhausted beneath common sense, banal, vulgar, obvious meaning, or cruel, threatening, and aggressive meaning—before we can understand that they are ungraspable, that they adhere to no axis, that they are "arbitrary" just like the sign, the name, and the utterance, but also pleasure and jouissance. The laughter of *H* isn't caused by a clash between signified values; nor is it caused by the eruption of nonsense within sense as appears to be the case in *Lois* ["Laws," 1972]. Rather, it is the *arbitrariness of the break establishing meaning*, which sets itself squarely against the flow of rhythm, intonation, and music, that provokes this laughter. We do not laugh because of what makes sense or because of what does not. We laugh because of possible meaning, because of the *attitude* that causes us to enunciate signification as it brings us jouissance; *H* does not avoid this attitude, rather it accepts it so as to pulverize it all the better. We laugh at the utterance that is not music, and/or at sexuality that is not a process of consumption. We laugh at castration. Neither happy nor sad, neither life nor death, neither sexual organicism nor sublimated renunciation, such a laughter is synonymous with musicated enunciation—a space where enunciation and rhythm, positioning and infinitization of meaning are inseparable.

We do not laugh, then, in order to judge the position that gives meaning; even less so in order to put ourselves out of judgment's reach, in some surreality where everything is equal. We laugh on account of the limit assumed in the very movement that enroots and uproots finitude within an endlessly centered and yet decentered process. Laughter of language, laughter of sociality itself. Laughter of a castration that moves us to name in a process that exceeds naming. Optimism or pessimism?—misplaced milestones that also cause laughter. Everything causes laughter since signifiance is motion. Oriental laughter: sensible and leading to the void.

The sonorous threads branch out until they disperse with loss in a body inebriated with a motion that is in no way personal to it, but rather, merges with the motion of nature as well as of an historical mutation: "you must swim in matter and the language of matter and the transformation of language into matter and matter into language tribe of matter feeling of the outing on swann's way the sun is still the same as before but chang hsü had the best cursive script under the t'ang he would get drunk the souse shouted ran every which way then took up his brush wrote at top speed it even happened that he dipped his hair into the ink to draw to the quick hsieh-huo means to write lively that's clearly evident in mao's characters 17 august 1966 hsin p'ei ta the first two jumbled the third aggressive resolute sure of the new and there it is that's the whole story the class struggle is part of nature and nature has plenty of time this seagull is the same as a thousand years ago but man is full of clouds" (p. 100).

What Is a Materialist Who Speaks?

I am reading Sollers's *H*, at the same time as I am reading his *Sur le matérialisme* [On materialism] (Paris: Seuil, 1974): two aspects of the same process. From a mechanistic point of view, materialism is a question of substance, or better, of the acknowledgement of the primacy of exterior over interior, of nature over society, of economy over ideology, et cetera. Language, the practice that causes the id to signify, the-id-to-signify-that-something-is, is left to the wardens of the logos positing-removing Being-beings-nothingness. *There is no such thing as materialist logic or materialist linguistics.* Logics and linguistics have each been based on an attitude that repudiates heterogeneity in the signifier and that, as such, conforms to the truth of a particular stance of the speaking subject: that of the transcendental ego, whose emergence through the game of hide-and-seek with the object was explained by Husserl. Moreover, any discourse that adheres to the postulates of a communicational logic and linguistics is at once a discourse that, in its very system, is foreign to materialism. Philosophy—be it logical, grammatical, or pedagogical—could never be materialist. Seen from the place of its enunciation—the same as that of the basic sentence (an utterance of request and exchange)—matter can be nothing but "transcendence," and Husserl said as much.

And yet, materialism was able to signify; it did in Heraclitus's elisions, in Epicurus's gestures declining the mores of the city-state, in Lucretius's poetic language. In spite of its prescientific shortcomings, naivetés, and errors, this classical materialism carries within itself a "truth" that contemporary mechanistic materialists are unable to match. Materialism is a knowledge of the world, to be sure, but this knowledge is inseparable from the attitude of the speaking subject within his language and/or within the world. Materialism is above all an enunciation *of* whatever you please, but that necessarily implies that whoever enunciates has an unconscious that beats within him as rhythm-intonation-music, before dissolving him within a cellular and biological, at the same time as a subjective, symbolic, and social explosion. An "I" that has undergone this process in order to return to his former position and give voice to its poly-logic—that is a *materialist* who *speaks*. Diderot speaks as a materialist when he performs as a one-man orchestra: Rameau's nephew. Marx and Lenin speak as materialists when they reject philosophical discourse and, through polemics or struggle, rediscover a multivalent "discourse" beneath surface speech; let us call it a discourse without words. It is a token of their involvement in a broader process, and this implies the masses' own involvement.

H investigates precisely this moment that so many philosophies and dogmatisms seek to cover up—the moment when materialism is able to utter itself. Not the "self" dissolving into some muted matter—schizophrenia adrift; not the flight of an ego subsumed by the predicative synthesis outside of any notion of what came before its logical position. Rather, it is the ordeal of an attack, instinctual separation, immobility, or death, at the same time as their reappearance at the heart of a logical, fragmented, and rhythmic polyvalence. The subject loses himself so as to immerse himself in the material and historical process; but he reconstitutes himself, regains his unity and rhythmically pronounces his own dissolution as well as his return.

When it is set forth in rhythm, a materialist discourse appears as joy ripped with pain. A rhythm that multiplies language and withdraws from its transcendental position is propelled by pain; rhythm is the enunciation of a pain that severs the "self," the body, and each organ. That pain is experienced as such as soon as a word (signified, signifier) is posited. It is drained only after having pelted all words circulating within, before, and after the enunciating subject. Only through this multiple schiztic pain can the process of the subject, matter, and history be formulated—spoken—as a dialectical process, that is, as *one* and *heterogeneous*. So Heraclitus was the misanthrope, the fragmenter, divider, and separator. And Sade was the stage director for pain as the scene of unconsciousness and jouissance—spoken at last, possible after all. And Lenin, torn between *Philosophical Notebooks* and *What Is To Be Done?*, who arrived during the night at [his] Smolny [headquarters in St. Petersburg] with his body crippled by pain, and that mysterious death . . . The protectionist, bargaining, social code, made up of opaque units that interchange without getting involved, subject-object irremediably lost to each other . . .—such a code cannot become cancelled—ecstatic—laughing—without hurting.

The instant the attack begins, there is loss of self and of knowledge, the pain of schism, a brush with death, and the absence of meaning: "there is an instant vertigo when you reach out your arm beyond absolute knowledge in order to find the flower" (p. 96); "a bone that is feeling a high" (p. 162); "it's like the intimate start of matter now me i refuse i refuse i refuse no no no [. . .] i won't accept the identity i feel much too amphibious bombing protein nucleotides hydrogen cloud initial iridescence of helium double helix" (p. 61); "it's true that that frightens them this daily crumbling of sensitive tissue pain of the gums in the kidneys of the liver in the shoulder there are some who would lock themselves up with math for no more reason than there are some who prefer rushing to a dance" (p. 26); "so there's the pain that rises again in the teeth the temples in the back of the neck the pain you know it's like extended tallied temporalized palpable jouissance who said it couldn't be written but of course by long suffering little fire sharp keen points that is where you see who works and who gossips [. . .] oh dusty conveyor belt" (p. 32); "i hurt everywhere when i am seized by this epilepsy from medical greek spilepsia properly attack yes it attacks me it takes hold of me inside-out skeleton" (p. 121). And then, there is this rewriting of Saint Paul: "oh but who shall deliver me from this body without death" (p. 39); "the grave you carry it everywhere with you" (p. 77).

Painful and deadly negative drive, capable of provoking schism, and immobility, does not stop this process. The "I" emerges again, speaking and musicating, so as to reveal the material truth of the process that brought it to the brink of its shattering into a whirlwind of mute particles. The schizoid regains consciousness: "the schizoid becomes diplomat enterprising unbeatable supple again post maso bird kind" (p. 113).

His shattering has multiplied him, deprived him of human characteristics, made him anonymous: "nature is for me a lake full of fish and me fish fish fish without a complex" (p. 63). The "I" has become a strange physicist for whom the quantum particle is not merely an "external" object to be observed, but also, an "internal" state of the subject and of experienced language: "the actor may indicate this by the wave function of his molecule to escape the cycle he must crush himself in the umbilical" (p. 105); "if you wish to maintain the boiling point in your room don't forget that each link is represented by a wave function with two centers occupied by a pair of electrons emanating from two linked atoms go on breathe your probability of presence the clouds now replace the trajectories we evolve with this spectral fog any ejaculation casts a thought not thought it really makes one burst with laughter" (p. 106). It cannot be pinned down but is liable to be present, logical, thought out—both wave and particle, matter coming through: "i don't paint being i paint the passing anyhow i don't paint anything at all i feel really bombed out when will we accept impermanence absence of signature disappearance of the seal inside feet close together and goodnight" (p. 46).

Only then does the speaking subject discover himself as subject of a body that is pulverized, dismembered, and refashioned according to the polylogue's bursts of instinctual drive—rhythm. As an area of heterogeneous strata (drive-sound-language) that can be multiplied and infinitized, materialist language is the language of a body never heard and never seen. Here, there are none of Spinoza's substances, no Cartesian extension, nor even Leibnitz's monads in tabular networks. This polylogical body is a permanent contradiction between substance and voice, as each one enters into a process of infinite fission that begins as they clash; substance is vocalized, voice is damped, as each is made infinite in relation to the other. But it finally recovers the unity of speaking consciousness in order to signify itself.

The subject is destabilized—Van Gogh, Artaud—and physical dislocation has become its metaphor. But—and this is what is so surprising—the subject returns. Sollers speaks of a "springing of the subject," occurring in order to arrange the shattering into a language, which it immediately provides with a dismembered, countless body. Because some One emerges from this schizophrenic pulverizing and has it go through our communal code (discourse), a new rhythm is perceived and our body appears as broken, refashioned, and infinite: "one body is not equivalent to another we are here to begin enlightening the scale of bodies within the stream how do you force the head to let it be to become conscious of all the registers" (p. 47); "this ability that sometimes an obstinate but fluid subject has to remove veil by veil to untie the knots to insist on its negation until the infinity in its always unexpected shape begins to well up nearby inside outside" (p. 70); "curious how the animal can get a hard on in its sleep while it is in the process of cutting itself up how it experiences itself at the same time compressed gaseous unit put away in drawer" (p. 68). An animal is a physical, vocal, perhaps codified whirlwind; but it is also cleft from its axis, from its subjective-signifying-symbolic control point. The test of radical heterogeneity comes when the signifying thesis finds itself outside of any multiplicative experience, while the taut stretch separating the two, liable to break at any moment, preventing any return to unity, makes of this suspended "unity" a dead entity: "i apply this treatment to myself by periodic massaged excitement each side occupied with crisscrossing itself striated zones on the whole the problem is this unit of equilibrium which causes the multiplicity to be thought outside on the basis of a unit that is firm on dead center" (p. 155); "never forget the right of the deadmost" (p. 110).[6]

In short, right belongs only to the "deadmost." The deadmost alone is capable of formulating something new. Formulation immediately becomes anteriority, death. It is the (primary) condition of this surprising rebound, which is itself a (secondary) condition causing the pulverization to speak, causing the once alientated unity to dance: "basically it is death that is afraid of us" (p. 87); "any spontaneous formulation that is not sought after will have to be paid for dearly" (p. 62).

I shall term "writer" that ability to rebound whereby the violence of rejection, in extravagant rhythm, finds its way into a multiplied signifier. It is not the reconstruction of a unary subject, reminiscing, in hysterical fashion, about his lacks in meaning, his plunges into an underwater body. It is rather the return of the limit-as-break, castration, and the bar separating signifier from signified, which found naming, codification, and language; they do this not in order to vanish at that point (as communal meaning would have it), but in order, lucidly and consciously, to reject and multiply them, to dissolve even their boundaries, and to use them again . . . A reminder of the *Vedas*: "here i am i i and again i first-born of the order before the gods in the navel of nondeath" (p. 99). This is a reaffirmed, indelible "I," tenaciously holding on to its unity, but busy going through it—going through itself—in all directions, crisscrossing itself with furrows, reaching over itself, appraising itself and conceiving of itself in terms of all the coordinates of "geometry": "that's a peculiar kind of horse this subject at a walk at a trot at a gallop before you behind you under you and above you forward motion backward motion swallowed up swimmer worker idler and dreamer and fudger liar and seeker and speaker pillager weeper listener fleer and unemployed" (p. 129); "how do you expect to live with an ungraspable sheet of water with a body that sees itself and sees itself that sees itself seeing itself seen visible invisible thus ceaselessly saying good-bye that's not a father ma'am that's not a mother" (p. 107); "there is the object of sexual gratification and someone who passes for the one who experiences it but he who while he experiences orgasm knows one and the other is not affected" (p. 99). So here, then, is "the sign of a more profound geometry that i feel in me behind me with the smell of the attic cross-roads of stitching fine network of stars dig dig unfasten unglue send back you get here a quick theory of envelopes algebra and arithmetic are the doubles of this tongued wind without effect" (p. 98).

This "I" speaks/sings the indecisive movement of its own coming. Its geometry—that is, the text, this "double of tongued wind"—gathers together into a single, formulated sequence rhythm and meaning, erased presence, and a reconstructed or mimed presence where it scans-and-signifies the truth of its production and death. It goes from the "subjective" to the "objective," then back again to the "subjective," and so forth without end: "i had nothing of the outside save an inter-rupted circular perception i wasn't able to determine if the water had a backdrop of vegetation the color green was perhaps simply the reflec-tion of the shutter" (p. 11); "i want to be alone understand alone when i want to as bathed aired as on the first morning" (p. 36).

But such an asserted "I," hypostasized and unshakeable in its twisted multiplications, conscious of the truth of its *practice*, does not insist on truth for its *speech*. This is not mysticism saying, "I am the truth." The polylogue says, "i truth i have a right to lie in the manner that suits me" (p. 35). For this polylogical "I" speaks of a *before*: before logic, before language, before being. A *before* that isn't even uncon-scious; a "before" all "before-unconsciousness"—*shock*, spurt, death; a collision, then—*stasis* of sound, then—*heterogeneity* of the "represen-tamen," the "other," "language," "I," "speech," . . . then—an inrush of shock, spurt, and death. One cannot even say that this "before" has in fact taken place, because if "it has taken place," it is only because "I" says so; otherwise, this before, in relation to the "I," constitutes a "knot," a "not," that is, negativity. Yet, any "I" that ventures into this "before" has no guarantee of "being" or of "truth" in its speech other than intonation, melody, song, and the twisting effect it inflicts on language by making it speak in a future tense that is menacing to those comfortably satisfied with the *present*—with "beings" commem-orating a "Being" that, nevertheless, remains presentable. In *H*, on the other hand, the present "I" is the crest of a melodious *before* and an *immediate, logical future*, flashing like lightning for whoever has not heard the echo of the *before* and has not gone there on his own. This "I" is just present enough to open the present into a double infinity: an immemorial *before* and an historically ravaging immediateness: "as for me I speak of misappropriation from before the before let him who has the spark be enlightened with the deduction at the source which they never viscerally suspected it's something entirely different a fight here with knives between what traverses me and the set brow that used to be called demonic don't believe for a minute the deluders who tell you that it isn't true at all the term prophet came into use around 980 concerning passion in its physical sense in the twelfth they said prophesy from the greek prophêtês literally he who says in advance check it out yourself at least those of you not too entrenched where do i get this insolence i don't know yes it is really limitless" (p. 30).

"Who says *hello*"?—hello, Yesha'yâhû, Isaiah. It is "I," present to signify the process that exceeds it, and only for that. It is neither One, paranoid, set in his mastery. Nor is it an Other, prophesying because he is cutting a dangerous *after* (logical, naming, castrating) away from an inaccessible *before* (instinctual, maternal, musical). But it is *the very process itself, where One and Other* are stases, moments of pause: a natural-semiotic—symbolic process, involving heterogeneity and contradiction: "i kind of like when malaise misunderstanding grow in thickness the whirlwind must come into being there maybe they'll make me kick myself off in the end accused as i am of wanting the two and at the same time proposing scission they see it as manichaeism while the rumbling in their stomachs doesn't make the multiple voice one and bound multiple divided bound saying the one multiple the non-one the always and never multiple oh my void you alone faithful i shall go so far as saying tender and faithful and cutting horrible soft punctual terrifying" (p. 35).

A floating signifier? A senseless flow that produces its own signifiance: "what a profession being the so-called floating signifier or rather the water that signifies itself by itself' (p. 59). Thus impersonal, in short, speaking (in) the name of no one—not even in its (own) "proper name," but *saying what is heard*: "he shall not speak on his own but everything he hears he shall say" (p. 181). This is the Augustinian formula referring to the "holy spirit" in *De Trinitate*. But, within this register, to what can "in the name of" refer? An excess in the function of the Father or of the Son; the ideal proceedings against the One and against Naming itself?

The transfinite in language, as what is "beyond the sentence," is probably foremost a going through and beyond the naming. This means that it is a going through and beyond the sign, the phrase, and linguistic finitude. But it is also and simultaneously that of one's "proper name"; an indexing that gives an identity to entity if, and only if, it has such entity proceed from a symbolic origin where the law of social contract is concealed.

H introduced proceedings against both naming and the (proper) Name by positing and then acknowledging their constraint. Proper Name—pseudonym—releasing the two in a burst of laughter that attacks the son's identity—but also that of the "artist." Sentence-sequence-narration—and an excess of their significations (in which so many readers of *Lois* became trapped) localizable in a process of indefinitely, infinitely movable centers. Nothing proceeds from anything; infinity is invented through colliding, heterogeneous, and contradictory bursts where "what proceeds" (naming and the Name) is only a set whose existence depends on infinity thrust aside; here, however, the logical *and* heterogeneous infinity is no longer kept out of the way, it returns and threatens all nominal existence.

Shattering the Family

There is a sober quality in *H* that consists in the light contour of music, an avoidance of overloading sequences with narrative, and a logical and permanent awakening in the very drift of syllables— frustrating the hysteric, disappointing the obsessed, getting on the fetishist's nerve, and intriguing the schizoid.

H says that what determines these reactions lies within the domain of the Phallic Mother. Any subject posits himself in relation to the phallus—that much everyone understands. That the phallus could be the mother is something often said, but here we are all stopped short by this "truth": the hysteric, the obsessed, the fetishist, and the schizoid. It is a focus of attention that drives us crazy or perhaps allows us to remain afloat when the thetic (the symbolic) lets go. The phallic mother has possession of our imaginaries because she controls the family, and the imaginary is familial. The alternatives used to seem set: either the Name-of-the-Father transcending the family within a signifier that, in fact, reproduces its dramas; or the phallic Mother who gathers us all into orality and anality, into the pleasure of fusion and rejection, with a few limited variations possible. Either you stay spastic and aphasic, or a fantasy takes root in you and clears the way for a polymorphism that eats away at accepted social codes—but can also be their repressed accomplice. Or you have this Phallic Mother enter into your language where she enables you to kill the master signifier—but also reconstitutes that ultimate and tenacious repression seizing you in the veils of the "genital mystery" (Nerval, Nietzsche, Artaud) . . .

No language can sing unless it confronts the Phallic Mother. For all that it must not leave her untouched, outside, opposite, against the law, the absolute esoteric code. Rather, it must swallow her, eat her, dissolve her, set her up like a boundary of the process where "I" with "she"—"the other," "the mother"—becomes lost. Who is capable of this? "I alone am nourished by the great mother," writes Lao Tzu. In the past, this was called "the sacred." In any case, within the experiencing of the phallic, maternal mirage, within this consummated incest, sexuality no longer has the gratifying appeal of a return to the promised land. Know the mother, first take her place, thoroughly investigate her jouissance and, without releasing her, go beyond her. The language that serves as a witness to this course is iridescent with a sexuality of which it does not "speak"; it turns it into rhythm—it is rhythm. What we take for a mother, and all the sexuality that the maternal image commands, is nothing but the place where rhythm stops and identity is constituted. Who knows? Who says so? Only rhythm, the de-signating and dissolving gesture, scans it.

The son's incest is a meeting with the other, the first other, the mother. It is the penetration of a heterogeneous terrain, the absorption of its bursting, and the alliance of the bursting of the "proper" that follows. The poet's jouissance that causes him to emerge from schizophrenic decorporealization is the jouissance of the mother: "who was able is able will be able to kiss his deep mother on the mouth and sense arising radiating the triple and one rejoicing" (p. 164); "i had my mother in a dream clearly silhouetted clean alluring" (p. 138); "what causes the poet to have first a definite taste of menstrua in the mouth and why it is not reasonable to ask him to talk as if he had not lost his baby teeth" (p. 143); "it's the whirlwind no need to insist to make one believe there is a thought on this side nervous non-thought read to me slowly it's not about a crisis we are in a mess in fact what remains here is always childish free fall the difficulty lies precisely in accepting that the mother be this slow oh so slowly broken from the species would that she were blind what here's the secret would that she were this slow blind fall and whore despite the appetite support but don't hope to see her without smashing yourself in" (p. 127).

It is a strange sort of incest where "Oedipus" comes out looking like Orpheus—singing—and where Jocasta remains blind. It involves a reversal of roles; the mother's power, engaged and directed towards refashioning a harmonious identity, is exhausted. Oedipus, made into a hero through the unconscious support from Jocasta, retraces his steps to a *before* all of this happened—so as to know; his is a refusal to accept blindness, a demystification of the female sphinx, and a forsaking of Antigone. The Greek myth is deflated, replaced by a non-Oedipal incest that opens the eyes of a subject who is nourished by the mother. The Phallic Mother—as blinding pillar of the *polis* and unconscious buttress of the laws of the city—is apprehended, comprehended, and thrust aside. The subject of this drama can in no way be a "citizen"—neither Orestes, murderer of his mother, nor Oedipus, castrated trustee of an invisible knowledge, occult wise man, tragic support of political religion. The "actor" subject, "poet" banished from the Republic because he has shot through his maternal pedestal, abides in the margins of society by wavering between the cult of the mother and the playful, laughing, stripping away of its mystery. By the same token, he eludes all codes; neither animal, god, nor man, he is Dionysius, born a second time for having had the mother.

His oracular discourse, split (signifier/signified) and multiplied (in its sentential and lyrical concatenations), carries the scar of not merely the *trauma* but also the *triumph* of his battle with the Phallic Mother: "you haven't sufficiently noticed that the double dimension of oedipal language reproduces in inverted form the double dimension of the oracle oidos swollen foot oida i know while sucking his thumb grapes of corinth they also say the laws at a higher moment's notice defining the animals below the gods above one and another pawns isolated on the chessboard of the polis out of play rupture of the game moral whoever wants to leave without for that matter buying glasses white cane while listening carefully to the whee whee when the animal finally falls without him we would know nothing what a view into backness true surpassing of the soothsayer in short there are two ways of being blind one in the future the other in the past [. . .] or else go take a walk in the schizoo when I say kill father sleep with mother go away eyeless from where one comes got to understand that it takes place on the same body right hand left hand [. . .] do you know what he does after having disappeared at colonus because antigone was beginning to get 'im pissed off he returns on the road to thebes he notices that the female sphinx is surfacing again oh well once again he kills it but forewarned by the previous experience he doesn't tell anyone and ye'know buzzes off far real far sometimes he's here among you aggrieved look for being so badly thought of badly understood" (p. 158).

The war, however, is never over and the poet shall continue indefinitely to measure himself against the mother, against his mirror image—a partially reassuring and regenerative experience, a partially castrating, legislating and socializing ordeal: "it's the old woman's vengeance furious at having been deciphered saying that's it isn't it it's finished buried once and for all that pig you are free my little darlings i squat on his grave reproduce the dead end ask your questions have respect for the bar it's me it's the law i anus in the superego i bring you the child of an inhumed guy's night" (p. 158).[7] The luster surrounding Mallarméan mystery is shattered, as is the tragedy

firmly and entirely anchored in class struggle. For the subject, however, this tragedy is primarily anchored in the somber and blinding
region of the maternal phallus. What follows is the aggressive and
musicated discourse of a knowledge that attacks phallic power each
time it sees it constituting itself under the aegis of the mother. Yet
it never forgets to draw forth the truth that this conflict lets escape.

Whence the warning that conjures up the *City of God*: "the great
mother tends to come back with her castrates as she does each
time the ground opens up before boiling" (p. 49); "when thought
is impeded it's because it has come and gathered around a name a
desire for a name for a navel" (p. 52). He who thinks he is a man is
merely the appendage of a mother. Does that make *Man* a fantasy of
the Phallic Mother? " . . . man as such does not exist [. . .] the shadow
of mama shaping her penis everywhere" (p. 113); just like the Primitive Father, by the way, "what is all this talk about a man who could
have every woman if not a woman's fantasy" (p. 137).

Procreation: the mother's pregnancy, that unshakable buttress of
every social code, insures continued repression: "as if science's postulate was at the beginning woman made pregnant" (p. 137); "mister
totem misses taboo the dessert à la stabat mater" (p. 137). It also
insures, by the same stroke, the power of the Phallic Mother underlying any tyrannical organization as she is present in any unconscious
desire: "the mama the mama of great big papa [. . .] mother on the
right father on the left and the right side has the left side killed
and the right side gets hold of the tip of the left side which it hides
under its litt'l skirt which generates the indefinite laying of the one
excluded from the middle" (p. 137); "the cult of the goddess reason
always seemed to me to be a negative argument against robespierre
there's still some of mama inside it reeks of a submissive son fine student still although the soprano on the altar that was daring from that
point of view we haven't progressed that much" (p. 70). The occult,
the esoteric, and the regressive rush in as soon as the symbolic surface
cracks and allows the shadow of the travestied mother to appear—its
secret and its ultimate support.

But why is the speaking subject incapable of uttering the mother
within her very self? Why is it that the "mother herself" does not

exist? Or that what *is* (what is *said*) has a mother who can only be phallic? And whence the insuperable oral stage? " . . . you're all stuck at the
oral" (p. 75).[8] The difficulties of gathering into a specular space the
motility of a premature human body, pulverized by instinctual drive:
that is the difficulty of identification that the mother is particularly
partial to—is that an unavoidable backdrop? Transforming this identifying support into an Other—into the place of a pure signifier—
maintains the presence of a maternal, substantial, and ego-related
opacity in the shadows. The mother reemerges as the archetype of
the infinitely interchangeable object of the desiring quest. Thus only
by puncturing this place of a "pure signifier" can we also and simultaneously deflate the maternal support upon which the signifier establishes itself, and vice versa. Then, what about the desiring quest? It
becomes a desire for appropriation by maternal language: "i'm not
talking to you in the name of the phallic anal this pisses you off like
me nor in the name of the father the son or the trading post nor in
the name of the thieving genital no but of genius spread the newness
of tomorrow the antisuperman the nongod nonman the nonunique
the excesses in dormitories because at last i ask you what becomes of
death in your neighborhood [. . .] your birth smacks you in the face
you hear breathing easier the rights of what was there before you
i pass through you i do not pass through you it's you who chooses my
amoeba" (pp. 75–76).

To rediscover the intonations, scansions, and jubilant rhythms
preceding the signifier's position as language's position is to discover
the voiced breath that fastens us to an undifferentiated mother, to
a mother who later, at the mirror stage, is altered into a *maternal language*. It is also to grasp this maternal language as well as to be free of
it thanks to the subsequently rediscovered mother, who is at a *stroke*
(a linguistic and logical *stroke*, mediated by the subject's position),
pierced, stripped, signified, uncovered, castrated, and carried away
into the symbolic. This is the text—detached from orality, set within
the symbolic thesis of a language already acquired before puberty.

Perhaps what is involved is the possibility of reactivating the
experience of early childhood (the Oedipal stage), after the period
of latency, into puberty, and undergoing the crisis of this particular

reactivation in the midst of language, with no delayed action, directly on the body "proper," and within the already ripe symbolic-logical system that the subject will have at its disposal in his future experience. This "second birth"—this Dionysiac birth—probably comes at the moment of puberty: then the subject and the Oedipal, maternal body come together again, her power collides with the *symbolic* (which the mature subject-body has already mastered during the period of latency), and the subject experiences the trauma of this collision. At that point, either the subject submits inextricably to a reactivated Oedipal experience, or he and his semiotic capability flee beyond the burnt out, distracting mother who threatens symbolic unity, but who is ultimately carried along within a semiotic process, where the subject is alternately put together and pulled apart.

From a careful reading of *Lois* and *H*, it becomes clear through the numerous evocations of childhood situations—the Gironde region, the garden, the family, the factory, sisters, workers, friends, and games—that Sollers grants a great deal of importance to the period of latency as a true laboratory where this storehouse of evocations, this semiotic, more-than-linguistic *stroke*, is worked out, which allows the subject to break through the pubescent reactivation of the Oedipal experience. This consequently lets the subject reconnect with his own oral, anal, and phallic stages and to function within the complete gamut of the body, language, and the symbolic. Does this, then, make the "poet" a subject who, toward the end of his childhood, did not simply stop and forget but now roams over his own backlands and, like an anamnestic child finds his phallic mother again, thus leaving a trace of their conflict in the very language he uses? As a result, that spoken incest places him on the brink where he could sink into the delirium of a schizoid that successfully breaks through everything but the mother; he could also, under the same momentum, although by dialecticizing the rediscovered mother, on the one hand, and the signifier ripened at the moment of latency, on the other, by pitting them against each other, produce what is *new* in "culture." The innovator, then, would be that child that doesn't forget. Neither blind Oedipus nor warring Orestes trampling the mother underfoot, but a subject who ceaselessly searches through his latent memory for whatever might allow him to resist an invoked and rejected mother.

From this moment, every "she" has a place in this configuration. Every hysterical woman, as symptom of symbolic weakness in relation to the overflowing instinctual drive, index of a poorly controlled phallus, and drama of the word/body separation whose flash-spasm the poet alone can hear and whose lesson he alone can integrate; "the hysterical woman's mouth is our radar" (p. 67); "it can feel in a flash what years could never have revealed" (p. 88); "resonant mercury separating the germs divergence of dye especially with women while man tends to bury himself under words because he still doesn't know how to let the words bury the words" (p. 117)—such is "Man's" mistake, which the "poet," who has learned from the hysterical woman, will not make.

The hysterical woman, as woman, as the other, heterogeneous to the "poet," represents what poetic discourse brings about but what man is not (to the extent that he does exist); "she" is this "disunited unity unified into the unique and multiplied multifold" (p. 130), which he experiences only in a text.

This is why he must necessarily and constantly measure himself against her, confront her by inventing a new meaning for love. Evoking Joyce: "the other one is right to say that finally a hero matters little if he has not also lived with a woman that lofty airs without this multiple experience in the minuscule allow the maximum amount of illusion to subsist" (p. 22). And love? " . . . what new relationship male female i've been looking for this forever at bottom alone with all quicker lighter brighter" (p. 102); "just the same i say love out of personal taste for paradox because of course little to do with the filth for sale under that label just the same we need revolutionary romanticism a particular serious new style brilliant resolute a vice that obeys us qualified partners [. . .] on the contrary i say that with that we settle at the heart of power we overthrow it if we hold firm on obscure points whatever the case may be i want to see people come while they're wondering why" (p. 56). Otherwise, we revert back to notions of God, the *exiled* negative, and mythical fusion. Opposed to this, and in support of the "new relationship," we must "*think*" love—that is, we must impregnate it with negativity, contradiction, and conflict; we must display, as a watermark, its constitutive hatred: "bearing the hate of someone who hates you is not unworthy and i am sick if it is so to hate your enemies hate is older than love" (p. 167). The "new relationship" involved here is consequently diametrically opposed to familial, mothering, and domestic tranquillity. The closest comparison would be "the big bang hypothesis inspiration expiration the galaxies move apart from each other as if they were located on a balloon that was being quickly inflated there is the sensation that we must ask of coitus without which what a bore the yarn about fusion captation the manger the stable the moo moo of the beauty and the beast" (p. 52). "He?" "She?" Each is split apart, twisted, infinitized, usurping the other's place, giving it back, an enemy, alone, incomprehensible, dissolved, harmonizing, making war again elsewhere, surer, truer: "thus the point is to mold oneself exactly on the enemy like the enemy in the spouse and the spouse in the enemy that's the way he himself offers you victory one wants the other and his other is other and you are alone with the sunset" (p. 124); "real netting of the bedmate who has become an accomplice in murder doesn't stop me from liking the horse in you galloping noble savage" (p. 96).

She?—"here there's a moment when the girl looks at you and says i am you you're happy that i'm you" (p. 144).

He?—"he the specialist in reverse pregnancies" (p. 110).

She-He?—as the crisscrossing of sexual differences, as the splitting of "I's," or as avoidance, since each one bestows deficiency on the other: "these women their parry is taut under rock toward childbearing the men want to avoid death theorem their desires cross" (p. 60); "you're my little boy and i'm you mother very depraved observing you young beautiful supple your living zipper" (p. 38); with death running the show, shattering every entity: "and each bone exploded by layers arms getting longer and longer [. . .] but there is the other's torture trusting and burning and i already know how she won't ever get to know i see her already eyes open incredulous crammed full of life and scents carried away blown out like a torch are you able to touch her punctured skull to weigh it to enter it in the race and to laugh just the same to continue isn't that the moment when you crack up" (p. 84).

Romeo? Juliet? They are dissonant: "it's true that i would kill you with too many caresses and he detestable matrix of death i damn well will force your rotten mouth open [. . .] they can't feel from in there this unexpected aspirated jouissance the one since ever on the horizon the retained excess flare let's go come and die where your life was" (pp. 84–85); and even more clearly: "shall i ever be a sharp parcel of her breath shall i ever succeed in making a bank dissolving of banks in its reflection i understand him who says no i'll stop when the last one has been freed until then i want to hear only dissonances i refuse to sign the prepared agreement" (p. 148).

Now we can understand that the logic of this place where negativity causes jouissance is foreign to the logic of genealogy and paternal-filial numeration, in short, foreign to procreation. This is a place of depletion, lying athwart that of the reproduction of the species, refusing its absolute regulation with a black ease that here, as elsewhere, avoids the tragic with a laugh: "i propose to provide for as of now a central area for reproduction with feminine interests set forth from head to foot national assemblies of huckstering fathers stock exchange of proper names [. . .] with a normalization of sundry homosexual practices [. . .] sgic sodom gomorrha international council" (69–70).

The reproductive function, sustained by a homosexuality (narcissism—tapping by the mother) that is unaware of itself, engenders the Father—the figure of a power against which the "actor" rebels and whose fissure precisely induces him to explore the maternal territory. Thus, next to the Phallic Mother, but more noticeable than she, and hence less dangerous than she, the Primitive Father arises. The Freudian vision in *Totem and Taboo* is deciphered as a homosexual conspiracy in which brothers kill the father to take the mother for themselves. But, before restoring paternal *power* in the form of a paternal *right*, they indulge in homosexual practices under the primal mother's imaginary grip: "finally the primordial father was simply a tall crazy woman and freud was right to recall that guys in exile base their organization on mutual feelings they foreswear the use of liberated women it scares them shitless they see again in their dreams that butchered father who is none other than mama knowing the ropes and diseased" (p. 128). Similarly, Laius, Oedipus's father, "disobeyed the oracle who forbade him to procreate but on the other hand as he was a fag like everyone else and as he's supposed to have forgotten himself one day in a woman you get the picture" (p. 163). The procreator, an unconscious genetrix, who accomplishes the Phallic Mother's desire, is thus the antonym of the "actor," of the "poet." The latter, preserved from the reproductive chain, is at the same time preserved from sociality and the social *sexual* code—normal or abnormal: "leave the ballroom where the judge dances glued to his favorite lawbreaker go deeper leave 'em alone you've got no truck with them" (p. 27). He is also preserved from *authority* and from coded mastership: "you should procreate how do you expect anyone to take your word without that" (p. 79). Whence, once again, the "poet's" complicity with the hysterical-phobic woman who suspects that the father is castrated: "enormous difference of the daughter who was able physically to ascertain the father's filthiness she can become exceptionally our ally how do we liberate the woman from woman that is the question likewise how do we rid the guy of the guy and maybe then everybody outside of their boundaries the real session could begin" (p. 37).

And yet, since the symbolic network not only resists the onrush of music, and since the subject's unity not only refrains from crumbling into the "schizoo" but, pluralized, sets up an analytical polylogue in all of his peregrinations, consequently, the *paternal function*—inasmuch as it is symbolic function, a guarantee of nomination, symbolization, and superegoistic (even pulverizable) resurgences—persists eternally. The father's death accelerates the analysis of the Phallic Mother; it reopens access to the negativity of drive; but it also probably favors its insertion in a signifier that was never so completely liberated and mastered at the same time. The father's first name shows up at the very beginning of *H*, just as, later on, one encounters the Asiatically calm image of the father planting orange trees (p. 139). They are an imaginary accomplishment, recognizing this symbolic, or one could say "paternal" function that the "I" henceforth assumes; yet, far from providing the subject with either family or power, this function makes of him an innumerable and infinitizable exile from social sets:

"and he puts his right hand on me i mean that i put it there myself but in a rather special way that would really take too long to explain but that in any case uses a rather significant qualitative jump to keep the two of the one divides into two and he tells me don't worry 'bout it i am the first and the last and so we have time to gas together i am living i was dead but now i am living in a way that you will never stop suspecting [. . .] anyhow they can't do anything against my missile ground ground ground air let him who has ears listen" (p. 28; ground air = *sol air* = Sollers [Ed.]).

The paternal function: internal structuration of the polylogical process, condition of separation from maternal rhythm, positing of an "I" that is stable and here, by means of a spoken incest, multipliable.

When all protagonists in what was the family become functions within the signifying process, and nothing more, the family loses its reason to exist. It withdraws before something else, something still invisible, an other social space serving the polylogizing subject; perhaps it withdrew before the contradictory association of jouissance and work?

Stratified Time: History as Infinitized Totality

Since the family has its familial time—the time of reproduction, generations, life and death, the linear-phallic time within which and in relation to which the familial son-daughter-subject thinks itself—shattering the family through rhythmic polylogue puts an end to that time.

Still, the time of the polylogue is not pause in time, either; some outside-of-time rediscovered by the "I" in analysis who breaks through his symbolic screen and plunges into a receptacle where the unconscious holds itself protected and in reserve, without time or negation, but who returns within the act of writing, outlining this division under the guise of an I/she-he contradiction. This timelessness, which is staged in *Drame* and, to a lesser degree, in *Nombres*,[9] is no longer called for with the "springing of the subject" in *Lois* and *H*. Here, time reappears and, with the logical-symbolic thesis, the "I" rediscovers the thread of succession, deduction, and evolution. But the rhythm that scans this thesis turns the thread into a broken path with multiple edges, an infinity of forks, returns to the same furrows, and departures into other dimensions. It turns it into an unlikely "topology" that totalizes every possible and imaginable zone (history of thought, history of art, history of conquests, history of revolutions, and history of class struggle), infinitizing them the one through the others. It is like a *Phenomenology of the Mind*, with chapters shuffled like playing cards, their piecing together revealing recursive determinations, trans-temporal causalities, and achronic dependencies that Hegel—a teleologist of the evolutionary finite who proceeded by closing cycles—could not have imagined. In *H*, there are no set cycles—they open up and crisscross.

This is not a Proustian "recovered time" where concatenation of sentences harkens the story back to its familial genesis, even if it allows itself to be broken or rhythmically measured by a panchronic and unconscious pro-ject. Time in *H* is stratified, polyphonic time; the genesis of the family plays only one score among many others, literally jolted by the sudden appearance of other paths, brief flashes, condensed echoes of otherwise interminable chronologies. Almost every sequence is recovered time, although it lasts but the time of a breath, of an intonation, or of one or more juxtaposed and imbricated sentences. Thereupon the subsequent sequence emerges out of another chronology, and condenses an entirely different time. The *rapidity* that *H* produces is in fact the rapidity with which temporal changes take place; it departs from logical mastership, the calm rigor of utterances, and the permanent rationality of the subject of enunciation, crossing unscathed the boundaries of each sequence. What moves quickly is not linguistic time nor intonational sequences; although brief, they in fact calm the text by means of their periodic flow, even to the point of making it monotonous, as some feel Indian music to be. What really moves along quickly is the perpetually dividable story. First, it is taken from different "domains," as can be seen from the list of names that are evoked: Goethe (*Dichtung und Wahreit*), Homer (*The Iliad*, p. 11), Overney (p. 12),[10] Hölderlin (p. 16), USSR-India-USA (p. 59), Stalin-Lenin-Lasalle–Hegel-Heraclitus (p. 67), an ailing Freud (p. 73), oppositions to Freud (p. 81), Don Juan (p. 86), Mozart and Nietzsche (p. 87), Rumi (p. 89), Mozart (p. 89), Purcell (p. 90), Joyce (p. 90), Charcot (p. 92), Mallarmé (p. 103), Marx (p. 107), Sade (p. 109), Nietzsche and Socrates (p. 113), Stalin's daughter (p. 114), Leibnitz (p. 114), Spinoza (p. 114), Marx-Engels and Nietzsche again, along with the Vietnam war (p. 115), Hölderlin (p. 119), Lenin–Epicurus (p. 119), Hegel and Plato (p. 119), Mallarmé rewritten (p. 125), the Greeks (p. 125), Melville (p. 126), Mao ("the infinite flow of absolute truth," p. 125), the Biturige people (p. 141), the child Goethe (p. 145), Gorgias (p. 110), Euripides and Pindar (p. 122), Aristotle, Aeschylus, Purcell (p. 122), Nerval (p. 123), Engels and Bachofen (p. 123), Copernicus (p. 156), Baudelaire as dealt with by *Le Figaro* (p. 162), Greek paeans (p. 165), again Mallarmé rewritten (p. 164), Pound (p. 172), Freud on homosexuality (p. 132), Nerval with the Prince of Aquitaine (p. 139), Monteverdi (*che gloria il morir per desio della vittoria*, p. 142), the Brahmins (pp. 142–43), Descartes-Napoleon (p. 143), Socrates (p. 148), Céline, Beckett, Burroughs (p. 151), Lautréamont (pp. 153–54), Van Gogh (p. 154), Lenin (p. 182) ... This list is far from complete, but it eventually provides an (approximate) idea of the meanderings of *H* through what is known as the history of philosophy, science, religion, and art. By means of these circuits and short-circuits, these separate fields cease to be the shreds of one "specific history" to become the heterogeneous moments of a poly-logical, poly-temporal subject; the reader is asked to refashion within his own semiotic process "specific temporalities" (art, science, politics, economics) and the exceptional adventures of "great men." These are indices of the "springing of the subject" into and through his own dissolution into the masses, among others, and they continue to weigh uncomfortably on the complex-ridden, neurotic consciousness of this or that political choice. Through time experienced and recast—heterogeneous and multiplied—the sub-ject who has been called forth, the twentieth-century subject, is a subject of more than twenty centuries of histories that ignored one another, within modes of production that excluded one another. Let us set history to rhythm, let us introduce history's rhythm into our discourses, so that we might become the infinitized subject of all histories—be they individual, national, or class histories—which henceforth nothing can totalize. Confronted with that practice in *H*, any historical, linear, and "specific" reconstitution seems narrow, penal, penalizing, and reductive of at least one of the lines that are competing here to sever, complement, and open themselves—avoiding the formation of a closed loop.

There is, however, an axis that insures the progression of this fragmentation of refashioned time: the critical political position in present-day history. To the logical thesis, disintegrated by semiotic rhythms within an infinite sentence, there corresponds, as concerns time, a critical practice within contemporary history. The stage is set with Overney from the outset, but one also recognizes passing figures or configurations of the political scene: Messmer;[11] Pompidou (p. 134); the Palestinians at the Munich Olympic Games (p. 155); fascists massacring Jews; Laurence, a childhood friend, and her yellow star (p. 140); Mao's reception of the Japanese Prime Minister (p. 172); the Lin Piao "affair" (p. 168); the idiocy of academic discourse ("that seven horned sheep of a reading expert," pp. 30, 148); the accelerated rhythm of the polylogue identifying with the pace of industrial work (p. 92); and so on. Class conflicts, the shifting of the historical axis, the entry of China into world history, and, gradually, the ideological struggle, here and now: thus is the historical space elaborated where the subject posits himself in order to refashion time—the time of subjectivity and, through it, a new historical time. Without this space, there can be no polylogue: neither rhythm, nor multiplied meaning, nor totalized, stratified, infinitized time.

By this I mean that *H* would not be conceivable if it were not political. There could be no polylogical subject without this new—stratified, multiplied, and recurring—political topos, which demonstrably has nothing to do with classical, dogmatic, and merely linear political positions that incarnate a familial time structure within a familial discourse. The inseparability of politics and polylogue appears as the guarantee of a meeting between the subject's unsettling process and that of history. Failing such meeting, there is either insanity or dogmatism—always solidary, like the two sides of a coin. Historically significant, the bourgeois class, the very one that was responsible for forging a notion of history, has had no poetry and has censured madness. Its successor, the petty bourgeoisie, at best rehabilitated madness, but it lacks a sense of history: "there is by definition no bourgeois poetry just as there is no petty bourgeois history" (p. 141). New historical forces, if they exist, will have no choice but to impose themselves in other ways; that is, through a polylogical politics: "a form of life has grown old it's done for bring on the next one" (p. 161).

The kind of upheaval now required involves more than a change in class power. We are now faced with a monumental requirement. We must transform the subject in his relationship to language, to the symbolic, to unity, and to history. Until recently, this kind of revolution took the form of religion: "as if the new subject was not primarily the one risen from the dead in other words he who absolutely doesn't give a damn forever and forever climbing out of potter's field with his little red and gold flag that's why Christianity is a tragic or comic misinterpretation" (p. 65). H also listens to *the time of Christianity*, perhaps more closely than anyone today, in order to grasp the truth of monotheism that it sets forth; namely, that neither subject nor history can exist without a confrontation between challenging process (semiotics, production, class struggle) and unity (symbolic, thetic, phallic, paternal, of the state). H does this with the aim of leading us through and beyond Christianity: "he'll come the new subject it's messianic thinking not really only that we move forward in disorder on all fronts strudel leaves" (p. 73).

H inserts us into the momentum of death held in abeyance—that is, of time. H splinters and refashions our language, our body, and our time. H infuses our identity with a sense of struggle to have us desire social conflict and no longer separate the one from the other. In France today, "death lives a human life you can check it out yourself every night just look at the newscaster on the tv absolute knowledge has come into being period" (p. 41). So "i accept completely the coming of class struggle it does not affect my interests no second thoughts about it no bank account no subjective obelisk to polish i'm looking for points at which to intervene little finger right foot earlobes wrists top of the shoulders i've been really on top of it for years now" (p. 27).

Traditionally, time has been divided into two opposing modes—irreducible, split, both symptom and cause of schizoid condition. The first is an atemporal "basis" from which there surges an infinitely repeatable, resounding impulse, cutting an inaccessible *eternity* into uniform or differentiated instants. The second is the, let me call it "biblical," *succession* of numbers, chronological development, evolution with an infinite goal; this is generally called *historical* time.

H releases from within the historical continuum certain eternally recurrent moments. Similarly, but inversely, by situating each rhythmic measure, each intonation, each narrative sequence, each sentence, and each eternal moment of personal experience within historical development and progression, *H* prevents any atemporal "basis" whatsoever from forming. Time as *rhythmic agency* and time as evolutive *duration* meet dialectically in *H*, just as they meet in language, even if every linguistic performance does not reveal it. Consequently, if historical duration operates on the basis of repression, locking the *ego* and the *superego* into an endless race toward death, seen as a race toward paradise, then rhythm—as metered time, spatialized, volume rather than line—crops up to remind one of what is at work beneath repression: the cost at which repression (duration—or history, to put it briefly) achieves its goal as the fulfillment of a sociocultural contract.

But it is an explosive encounter, for when rhythm gets rid of repressive duration, time can stop for the subject who has become the situs of the intersection. Rhythm causes this stop in order to cut duration short; duration plans it so as to impede rhythmic pain. Suicide: "write this down a hundred times rhythm is an inferior demon but sir if the general refers to itself it catches fire negation that makes up the basis of cause is the positive encounter of cause with itself and anyhow the reciprocal action being the causality of cause cause doesn't die out in the effect alone [. . .] what is the one a disqualifying limit and lenin says it in restrained fashion thought should emcompass all representation and so must be dialectical to wit divided by nature unequal altered i am thirsty [. . .] i've had enough enough or then the courage to want also this enough to the extreme in half a second it is gulped raw temptation for it is out of the question to express oneself here during the lecture light up no turn on the gas no jump go on come on now jump no swallow all of that no i said no the knife no the razor blades in hot water no now is the time when you're the ration" (pp. 182–83).

Suicide stands for the accident of this dialectical encounter between rhythm and duration; of the negativity that causes each stasis to be "deferred" and each instance of repression to be driven towards the limits where sociality and life disappear; and of the repression that serves as a foundation for the symbolic, for communication, and for the social juggernaut. Thus, it is easy to understand why striated, rhythmic, and transfinite discourses are cathected into social logic only at the moment of its ruptures—i.e., its revolutions. It should be equally understandable why suicide (in Mayakovsky's case, for example) marks the failure of a revolution; its settling down censures a rhythm that thought it could meet and recognize itself within it. But besides revolutions? Classically and traditionally, when there is no revolution, there is transcendence "rescuing" the subject from suicide. Divine, family oriented, humanitarian (the list could go on forever) transcendence shifts the rhythmic time of a polylogical subject into a signifying or symbolic elsewhere where he exists as a sheltered exile. Yet, there, surreptitiously, the eternal "basis" is reconstituted, along with phobic homogeneity, and once again, an eternal—support for the Eternal—Phallic Mother. Such a "rescue" is therefore impossible for the heterogeneous, material, and polylogical experience of the subject in unsettling process. But what about suicide? It is, indeed, the ultimate gesture, if one exists, and which is prevented only by the jouissance of regaining control—the recovery of the "I," this "springing of the subject" against (as one says, "leaning against") her, the other, as well as against the others, the other in itself; against the symbolic, structuring, regimenting, protective, historicizing *thesis*—to be shifted, traversed, exceeded, made negative, and be brought to jouissance.

The negativity that underlies historical duration is the rejection of the other but also of the "I," of the altered "I." The history that precedes us, that is being made all around us, that we invoke as ultimate justification and untouchable sublimation, is built upon negativity—rejection-death; and the fulcrum of this negativity is first and foremost the subject itself: put to death or suicided by society (as Artaud said of Van Gogh). This is what *H* sets forth by means of its series of "personal histories," its "case studies" (Nerval, Hölderlin, Artaud, et cetera), often invisible within "commonplace" renditions of history, and particularly that of class struggle. Having *durable* history listen to the murder over which it steps ahead; having those atempo- ral moments when duration was ruptured reason and resound, so as to extract whatever it represses and whatever renews it at the same time (new music, new poetry, new philosophy, new politics). The ruptured, inverted, and refashioned time of *H* induces us to grasp a new history.

We tend to forget that when a twentieth-century-minded per- son listens to the Eroica, for example, he/she is listening to time as Beethoven experienced it when he heard the armies of the French Revolution; the rhythmic hoofbeats of their horses, the borders they opened, and Europe brought together for the first time thanks to the canons . . .

Listening to the time that fills *H*, I hear a world finally spread out. Asia, Africa, America, and Europe are inextricably mingled by economy, politics, radio, television, and communications satellites. Each one bears a chronology that, instead of accepting to be qui- etly pigeonholed in proper order, calls on the other, pointing out its shortcomings, even though it wishes to be its partner. Each one admitting of different semiotic practices (myths, religions, art, poetry, politics) whose hierarchies are never the same; each system in turn questioning the values of the others. The subject who listens to this time could indeed and at least "treat himself as a sonata," as *H* puts it.

Is *H*, then a book? A text that exists only if it can find a reader who matches its rhythm—its sentential, biological, corporeal, and trans-familial rhythm, infinitely marked out within historical time. Already in *H*, as Artaud wanted it to be, "composition instead of hap- pening in the head of an author will happen in nature and real space with consequently immense objective wealth in addition impeding underhanded appropriation necessitating the risks of execution" (p. 104). This is all possible because *someone* refashioned his "I" and his language into a music adequate to the continuing, splintering times. But also and at the same time, this is possible because *H* has gone beyond the *One* in order to be written, and thus calls on every "one" to venture out into the explosion that surrounds us, moves through us, refashions us and that sooner or later we shall have to hear: "a form of life has grown old it's done for bring on the next one" (p. 161) or, if you take in some of *H*, you know that "all flesh is like grass shadow the dew of time among voices" (p. 185).

8

GIOTTO'S JOY

How can we find our way through what separates words from what is both without a name and more than a name: a painting? What is it that we are trying to go through? The space of the very act of naming? At any rate, it is not the space of "first naming," or of the incipient naming of the *infans;* nor is it the one that arranges into signs what the subject perceives as separate reality. In the present instance, the painting is already there. A particular "sign" has already come into being. It has organized "something" into a painting with no hopelessly *separate* referent; or rather, the painting is its own reality. There is also an "I" speaking, and any number of "I's" speaking differently before the "same" painting. The question, then, is to insert the signs of language into this already-produced reality-sign—the painting; we must open out, release, and set side by side what is compact, condensed, and meshed. We must then find our way through what separates the place where "I" speak, reason, and understand from the one where something functions in addition to my speech: something that is more-than-speech, a meaning to which space and color have been added. We must develop, then, a second-stage naming in order to name an excess of names, a more-than-name become space and color—a painting. We must retrace the speaking thread, put back into words that from which words have withdrawn.

My choice, my desire to speak of Giotto (1267–1336)—if justification be needed—relates to his experiments in architecture and color (his translation of instinctual drives into colored surface) as much as to his place within the history of Western painting. (He lived at a time when the die had not yet been cast, when it was far from sure that all lines would lead toward the unifying, fixed center of perspective.)[1] I shall attempt to relate that experience, that translation, that pivotal historic moment without verbal support from any of these—except for a few anecdotal although not insignificant points, drawn mostly from Giorgio Vasari.[2] This kind of endeavor locates my strategy somewhere between an immediate and subjective deciphering and a still incoherent, heteroclitic theoretical apparatus yet to be worked out. Primarily, I should emphasize that such an itinerary implicates its subject more than it repudiates it under the aegis of a scientific code. This is not an apology; rather, I am calling attention to the dialectical necessity and difficulty now facing any theory of painting that attempts to put forward an understanding of its own *practice*.

Narration and the Norm

Giotto's pictorial narrative follows biblical and evangelical canon, at Assisi as well as at Padua, deviating from it only to bring in the masses. In those works concerning St. Francis, the Virgin Mary, and Christ, mythical characters resemble the peasants of Giotto's time. This sociological aspect, however important it might be to the history of painting, shall not concern me here. Of course, it goes hand in hand with Giotto's disruption of space and color; it could not have come about without such a disruption and, in this sense, I could say that it followed.

Christian legend, then, provided the pictorial signified: the normative elements of painting, insuring both adherence to social code and fidelity to ideological dogma. The norm has withdrawn into the *signified*, which is a *narrative*. Painting as such would be possible as long as it served the narrative; within the framework of the narrative, it had free rein. A narrative signified cannot constrain the signifier (let us accept these terms for the moment) except through the imposition of *continuous representation*. Contrary to a certain kind of Buddhist or Taoist painting, Christian painting experienced the mass arrival of characters with their itineraries, destinies, and histories: in short, their epic.

The advent of "histories of subjects" or "biographies"—symbolizing both phylo- and ontogenetic mutations—as well as the introduction of the principle of *narrative* into Christian ideology and art are theoretically justified by Saint Francis and his exegete Saint Bonaventura. The latter's *The Mind's Road to God* is the philosophical enunciation of a subject's itinerary, of a series of trials, of biography, of *narrative*. If the principle of *itinerary* itself is not new (it appears in Greek epics, popular oral tradition, biblical legends, etc.), its formulation by Bonaventura is relatively so, favoring, or simply justifying, its entry into the Christian pictorial art of the time by disrupting twelve-centuries-old, rigid Christian canon. This theoretical and artistic phenomenon fits in with a new European society moving towards the Renaissance and breaks with the Byzantine tradition (portraits and detailed but isolated scenes, lacking sequences of images articulated within a totalizing continuity) that Orthodox Christianity, which had no Renaissance, preserved.

There are pictorial narrative *episodes* in the nave of Santa Maria Maggiore in Rome (fourth century), but it would seem that the oldest narrative *sequence* pertaining to the old Testament is in the Church of Sant' Apollinare Nuovo in Ravenna, dating from the time of Theodoric. In illustrated manuscripts of the sixth century, illuminations follow a logic of narrative episodes (cf. *The Book of Genesis* at Vienna). But Byzantine mosaics, including those at St. Mark's Church in Venice, depict detailed scenes and sequences of dramatic and pathetic scenes without any comprehensive narrative to seal the entire fate of a *particular* character.

To the contrary, the narrative signified of the Giotto frescoes at Padua (figure 3), through a simple and stark logic limited to the basic

Figure 3. Giotto, interior of the Arena Chapel, Padua, Italy.

© Mondadori Portfolio/Archivio Antonio Quattrone/Bridgeman Images

episodes of Mary's and Jesus' lives, suggests that the democratization of the Christian religion was effected by means of biography. On the walls of Padua we find a masterful expression of personal itineraries replacing Byzantine pathos. Within Giotto's pictorial narrative, the notion of individual history is, in fact, more developed in the Padua frescoes than in those at Assisi. The empty chairs suspended in a blue expanse (*The Vision of the Thrones at Assisi*) would be unimaginable in the secular narrative of the Padua frescoes.

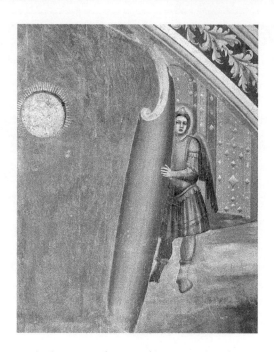

Figure 4. Detail of Giotto, *The Last Judgment*, Arena Chapel, Padua.

Photo: Scala

Yet, the narrative signified of the Arena Chapel's nave, support-ing the symbolism of teleological dogma (guarantee of the mythical Christian community) and unfolding in three superimposed bands from left to right in accordance with the Scriptures, is artificial. Abruptly, the scroll tears, coiling in upon itself from both sides near the top of the back wall facing the altar, revealing the gates of heaven and exposing the narrative as nothing but a thin layer of color (figure 4). Here, just under the two scrolls, facing the altar, lies another scene, outside the narrative: *Hell*, within the broader scope of the Last Judgment. This scene is the reverse of the narrative's symbolic sequence; three elements coexist there: historical charac-ters (Scrovegni [who is the donor of the chapel], and the painter himself), the Last Judgment, and the two groups of the blessed and the damned. With the representation of Hell the narrative sequence stops, is cut short, in the face of historical reality, Law, and fantasy (naked bodies, violence, sex, death)—in other words, in the face of the human dimension—the reverse of the divine continuity displayed in the narrative. In the lower right-hand corner, in the depiction of Hell, the contours of the characters are blurred, some colors disappear, others weaken, and still others darken: phosphorescent blue, black, dark red. There is no longer a distinct architecture; obliquely set masonry alongside angular mountains in the narrative scenes give way on the far wall to ovals, discontinuity, curves, and chaos.

It seems as if the narrative signified of Christian painting were upheld by an ability to point to its own dissolution; the unfolding narrative (of transcendence) must be broken in order for what is both extra- and anti-narrative to appear: nonlinear space of historical men, Law, and fantasy.

The representation of Hell would be the representation of narrative dissolution as well as the collapse of architecture and the disappearance of color. Even at this full stop in epic sequence, *representation* still rules as the only vestige of a transcendental norm, and of a signified in Christian art. Deprived of narrative, representation alone, as signifying device, operates as guarantee for the mythic (and here, Christian) community; it appears as symptomatic of this pictorial work's adherence to an ideology; but it also represents the opposite side of the norm, the antinorm, the forbidden, the anomalous, the excessive, and the repressed: Hell.

Only in this way is the *signifier* of the narrative (i.e., the particular ordering of forms and colors constituting the narrative as *painting*) released here, at the conclusion of the narrative; it finds its sign, and consequently, becomes symbolized as the reverse, negative, and inseparable other of transcendence. The history of individual subjects, the Last Judgment, and Hell capture in a transcendence (which is no longer recited, but rather, pinpointed; no longer situated in time but rather in space) this "force working upon form" that earlier was concatenated as narrative. In Hell, painting reaches its limit and breaks apart. The next move would be to abandon representation, to have nothing but color and form—or nothing at all. In Giotto's work, color and form "in themselves" are never liberated. But beginning with Giotto, with the emergence of the great Christian paintings of the Renaissance, the independence of color and form appears *in relation to* the signified (to theological norm): with respect to *narrative* and *representation*. It appears independent precisely because it constantly *pits itself* against the everpresent norm. It tears itself from the norm, bypasses it, turns away from it, absorbs it, goes beyond it, does something else—always in relation to it.

Certain Buddhist and Far Eastern paintings exclude the signified from representation and become depleted either through the way they are laid out (Tantric squares, for example) or inscribed (ideograms in Chinese painting). Giotto's practice, on the other hand, and the Christian tradition of art in general, show their independence of symbolic Law *by pitting themselves* against the represented narrative (parables of Christian dogma) as well as against the very economy of symbolization (color-form-representation). Thus, pictorial practice fulfills itself as freedom—a process of liberation *through and against the norm*; to be sure, we are speaking of a subject's freedom, emerging through an order (a signified) turned graphic while permitting and integrating its transgressions. For, the subject's freedom, as dialectics sets forth its truth, would consist precisely in its *relative* escape from the symbolic order. But, since this freedom does not seem to exist outside of what we agree to call an "artist," it comes about by modifying the role played by the systems of referent, signifier, and signified and their repercussions within the organization of signifiance into real, imaginary, and symbolic (both role and organization are patterned on the function of verbal communication—keystone of the religious arch) so as to organize them *differently*. Two elements, *color* and the organization of pictorial *space*, will help us, within Giotto's painting, to follow this movement towards relative independence from a signifying practice patterned on verbal communication.

The Triple Register of Color

In the search for a clue to artistic renewal, attention has often been given to the composition and geometrical organization of Giotto's frescoes. Critics have less frequently stressed the importance of color in the pictorial "language" of Giotto and of painters in general. This is probably because "color" is difficult to *situate* both within the *formal system* of painting and within painting considered as a *practice*—therefore, in relation to the painter. Although semiological approaches consider painting as a language, they do not allow an equivalent for color within the elements of language identified by linguistics. Does it belong among phonemes, morphemes, phrases, or lexemes? If it ever was fruitful, the language/painting analogy, when faced with the problem of color, becomes untenable. Any investigation of this question must therefore start from another hypothesis, no longer structural, but *economic*—in the Freudian sense of the term.

> What we have permissibly called the conscious presentation of the object can now be split up into the presentation of the *word* and the presentation of the *thing* [. . .] The system *Ucs.* contains the thing-cathexes of the objects, the first and true object-cathexes; the *Pcs.* comes about by this thing-presentation being hypercathected through being linked with the word-presentations corresponding to it. It is these hypercathexes, we may suppose, that bring about a higher psychical organization and make it possible for the primary process to be succeeded by the secondary process which is dominant in the *Pcs.*[3]

This hypercathexis of thing-presentations by word-presentations permits the former to become conscious, something they could never do without this hypercathexis, for "thought proceeds in systems so far remote from the original perceptual residues that they have no longer retained anything of the qualities of those residues, and, in order to become conscious, need to be reinforced by new qualities."[4]

Freud sees, then, a split between perception and thought process. Positing a qualitative disappearance of archaic perceptions (an assumption that seems wrong to us when we consider the subject as "artist," but we shall not argue this point here), Freud situates word-*presentations* in a position of relationship involving two categories: the perceptual and the verbal. Such an economy is particularly clear in the case of schizophrenia where word-presentations undergo a more intense cathexis in order to allow for recovery of "lost objects" separated from the ego (what Freud calls "taking the road of the object by way of its word element").

In interpreting Freud's terminology, it becomes clear that "thing-presentation" principally designates the pressure of the *unconscious* drive linked to (if not provoked by) objects. "Thought" denotes *conscious* processes (including secondary processes), and the various syntactical and logical operations; resulting from the imposition of repression, they hold at bay the "thing-presentations" and their corresponding instinctual pressures. The term "word-presentation" poses more of a problem. It seems to designate a complex state of drive that cathects the symbolic level,[5] where this instinctual drive will later be replaced, due to repression, by the sign represent-ing (erasing) it within the communicative system. Within "word-presentations" the drive's pressure: (1) is directed at an external object; (2) is a sign in a system; and (3) emanates from the biolog-ical organ that articulates the psychic basis of such sign (the vocal apparatus, the body in general). Freud in fact writes, "But word-presentations, for their part too, are derived from sense-perceptions, in the same way as thing-presentations are."[6]

Word-presentations would then be doubly linked to the body. First, as representations of an "exterior" object denoted by the word, as well as representations of the pressure itself, which, although intraorganic, nevertheless relates the speaking subject to the object. Second, as representations of an "interior object," an internal per-ception, an eroticization of the body proper during the act of for-mulating the word as a symbolic element. This bodily "duel," thus coupling the inside and the outside, as well as the two instinctual pressures linked to both, is the matter upon which repression is set—transforming this complex and heterogeneous pressure into a *sign* directed at someone else within a communicative system, i.e., trans-forming it into language.

The triple register is made up of a pressure marking an outside, another linked to the body proper, and a sign (signifier and pri-mary processes). This is then invested in the fragile, ephemeral, and compact phase of the symbolic function's genesis and constitutes the true requirement for this function. It is precisely this triple register that is cathected in an instinctual manner in cases of "narcissistic neuroses" where one has detected the "flight of the ego that manifests itself in the removal of conscious cathexis." That is, it forsakes the distance that kept apart "thought" from "drives" and "thing-presentations" and thus culminated in isolating the ego.

This triad also seems to be hypercathected on the artistic function, whose economy thus appears to be clearly distinct from that of communication. If, indeed, the signifier-signified-referent triangle seems methodologically sufficient to describe the communicative function, artistic practice adds what Freud calls "word-presentation." This implies the triple register of exterior drive, interior drive, and signifier. It in no way corresponds to the sign's triangle, but it affects the architecture of the latter. As a result, the artistic function introduces a pivotal order into the symbolic order (the order of "thought," according to Freud's terminology). This pivotal order—both an "energetic pressure" (instinctual drive) and an "imprint" (signifier)—modifies both the symbolic (because it cathects it with instinctual drive and thing-presentation) and thing-presentations (because it cathects them with signifying relationships that the perceptions themselves could not have insofar as their cathexes "correspond only to relationships between thing-presentations").[7]

This Freudian metapsychological triad frustrates both "representation" (as it rather involves taking in instinctual pressures) and the "word." It suggests an elementary *formal apparatus*, capable of setting in motion the phonemic order, a stock of lexemes, syntactic strategies (these to be determined for each subject through the process of language acquisition), and the presyntactic and prelogical primary processes of displacement, condensation, and repetition. This formal apparatus, subsuming instinctual pressures, is a kind of verbal *code* dominated by the two axes of metaphor and metonymy; but it uses, in a specific way (according to each subject) the general and limited possibilities of a given language.

Color can be defined, considering what I have just said, as being articulated on such a triple register within the domain of visual perceptions: an instinctual pressure linked to external visible objects; the same pressure causing the eroticizing of the body proper *via* visual perception and gesture; and the insertion of this pressure under the impact of censorship as a sign in a system of representation.

Matisse alludes to color having such a basis in instinctual drives when he speaks of a "*retinal sensation* [that] destroys the calm of the surface and the contour"; he even compares it to that of voice and hearing: "Ultimately, there is only a *tactile vitality* comparable to the 'vibrato' of the violin or voice."[8] And yet, although subjective and instinctual, this advent of color (as well as of any other "artistic device") is necessarily and therefore *objectively* occasioned and determined by the historically produced, formal system in which it operates:

> Our senses have an age of development which does not come from the immediate surroundings, but from a moment in civilization. We are born with the sensibility of a given period of civilization. And that counts for more than all we can learn about a period. The arts have a development which comes not only from the individual, but also from an accumulated strength, the civilization which precedes us. One can't do just anything. A talented artist cannot do just as he likes. If he used only his talents, he would not exist. We are not the masters of what we produce. It is imposed on us.[9]

One might therefore conceive color as a complex economy effecting the condensation of an excitation moving towards its referent, of a physiologically supported drive, and of "ideological values" germane to a given culture. Such values could be considered as the necessary historical decantation of the first two components. Thence, color, in each instance, must be deciphered according to: (1) the scale of "natural" colors; (2) the psychology of color perception and, especially, the psychology of each perception's instinctual cathexis, depending on the phases the concrete subject goes through with reference to its own history and within the more general process of imposing repression; and (3) the pictorial system either operative or in the process of formation. A preeminently composite element, color condenses "objectivity," "subjectivity," and the intrasystematic organization of pictorial practice. It thus emerges as a grid (of *differences* in light, energetic charge, and systematic value) whose every element is linked with several interlocking registers. Because it belongs to a painting's system, and therefore, to the extent that it plays a structural role in any subject-elaborated apparatus, color is an index of value (of an objective referent) and an instinctual pressure (an erotic implication of the subject); it hence finds itself endowed with new functions it does not possess outside this system and, therefore, outside pictorial practice. In a painting, color is pulled from the unconscious into a symbolic order; the unity of the "self" clings to this symbolic order, as this is the only way it can hold itself together. The triple register is constantly present, however, and color's diacritical value within each painting's system is, by the same token, withdrawn toward the unconscious. As a result, color (compact within its triple dimension) escapes censorship; and the unconscious irrupts into a culturally coded pictorial distribution.

Consequently, the chromatic experience constitutes a menace to the "self," but also, and to the contrary, it cradles the self's attempted reconstitution. Such an experience follows in the wake of the specular-imaginary self's formation-dissolution. Linked therefore to primary narcissism and to subject-object indeterminacy, it carries traces of the subject's instinctual drive toward unity (*Lust-Ich*) with its exterior surrounding, under the influence of the pleasure principle about to become reality principle under the weight of rejection, the symbolic function, and repression.[10] But chromatic experience casts itself as a turning point between the "self's" conservative and destructive proclivities; it is the place of narcissistic eroticism (autoeroticism) and death drive—never one without the other. If that experience is a revival of the "self" through and beyond the pleasure principle, such a revival never succeeds in the sense that it would constitute a subject *of* (or *under*) symbolic law. This is because the symbolic necessity, or the interdiction laid down by color, are never absolute. Contrary to delineated *form* and *space*, as well as to *drawing* and *composition* subjected to the strict codes of representation and verisimilitude, color enjoys considerable freedom. The color scale, apparently restricted by comparison with the infinite variation of forms and figures, is accepted as the very domain of whim, taste, and serendipity in daily life as much as in painting. If, nevertheless, the interplay of colors follows a particular historical necessity (the chromatic code accepted in Byzantine painting is not the same as that of the Renaissance) as well as the internal rules of a given painting (or any device whatsoever), still such a necessity is weak and includes its own transgression (the impact of instinctual drive) at the very moment it is imposed and applied.

Color might therefore be the space where the prohibition foresees and gives rise to its own immediate transgression. It achieves the momentary dialectic of law—the laying down of One Meaning so that it might at once be pulverized, multiplied into plural meanings. Color is the shattering of unity. Thus, it is through color—colors—that the subject escapes its alienation within a code (representational, ideological, symbolic, and so forth) that it, as conscious subject, accepts. Similarly, it is through color that Western painting began to escape the constraints of narrative and perspective norm (as with Giotto) as well as representation itself (as with Cézanne, Matisse, Rothko, Mondrian). Matisse spells it in full: it is through color—painting's fundamental "device," in the broad sense of "human language"—that revolutions in the plastic arts come about.

> When the means of expression have become so refined, so attenuated that their power of expression wears thin, it is necessary to return to *the essential principles which made human language.* They are, after all, the principles which "go back to the source," which relive, which give us life. Pictures which have become refinements, subtle gradations, dissolutions without energy, call for *beautiful blues, reds, yellows*—matters to stir the *sensual depths in men.*[11]

The chromatic apparatus, like rhythm for language, thus involves a shattering of meaning and its subject into a scale of differences. These, however, are articulated within an area beyond meaning that holds meaning's surplus. Color is not zero meaning; it is excess meaning through instinctual drive, that is, through death. By destroying unique normative meaning, death adds its negative force to that meaning in order to have the subject come through. As asserted and differentiating negativity, pictorial color (which overlays the practice of a subject merely speaking in order to communicate) does not erase meaning; it maintains it through multiplication and shows that it is engendered as the meaning of a singular being. As the dialectical space of a psycho-graphic equilibrium, color therefore translates an oversignifying logic in that it inscribes instinctual "residues" that the understanding subject has not symbolized.[12] It is easy to see how color's logic might have been considered "empty of meaning," a mobile grid (since it is subjective), but outside of semantics, and therefore, as dynamic law,[13] rhythm, interval,[14] gesture. We would suggest, on the contrary, that this "formal," chromatic grid, far from empty, is empty only of a "unique or ultimate signified"; that it is heavy with "semantic latencies" linked to the economy of the subject's constitution within significance.

Color, therefore, is not the black cast of form, an undefilable, forbidden, or simply deformable figure; nor is it the white of dazzling light, a transparent light of meaning cut off from the body, conceptual, instinctually foreclosed. Color does not suppress light but segments it by breaking its undifferentiated unicity into spectral multiplicity. It provokes surface clashes of varying intensity. Within the distribution of color, when black and white are present, they too are colors; that is to say, instinctual/diacritical/representational condensations.

After having made manifest and analyzed the "mystery" of light and the chemical production of colors, science will no doubt establish the objective basis (biophysical and biochemical) of color perception; just as contemporary linguistics, having discovered the phoneme, is seeking its corporeal, physiological and, perhaps, biological foundation. Psychoanalytic research will then make it possible, proceeding not only from the objective basis of perception and of the phases of the subject's passage through chromatic acquisition parallel to linguistic acquisition, to establish the more or less exact psychoanalytic equivalents of a particular subject's color scale. (These phases would include the perception of such and such a color at a given stage; the state of instinctual drive cathexes during this period; the relationship to the mirror phase, to the formation of the specular "I"; relationship to the mother; et cetera.) Given the present state of research, we can only outline certain general hypotheses on the basis of our observations concerning painting's relationship to the subject's signifying mode. In all likelihood, these hypotheses involve the observer much more than they can lay any claim to objectivity.

Forma Lucis: The Burlesque

Therefore, speak to them, and hear, and believe,
Since the light of the truth which requites them
Does not let them turn from itself.

—Dante, *Paradiso*, III, 31–33

That specific economy of color can perhaps explain why metaphysical speculations on light and its variations go back to the very oldest of beliefs. Within Indo-European civilizations, for instance, they are implicit in the fundamentals of Zoroastrianism; later, through Hellenistic civilization,[15] and Plotinism,[16] they reach the center of Christian doctrine (in Saint Augustine, for example), opening up within Christianity an opportunity for the plastic arts, for a flowering of images, never before achieved. The twelfth century occupies a key position in this process because of the humanist reform it brought to Christianity: this affects the metaphysics of color in the work of Saint Bonaventura, when it linked *light* with the *body*. As the other of the body, light gives it its *form* and thus becomes the privileged intermediary between substance and its effect—or the essential element of imagination: "If light names or articulates form, then light cannot possibly be a body; it must be a *something-else-than* body. [. . .] Augustine says that humor and the earth's soil are fundamental counterparts, and philosophers say that warmth is a certain subtle kind of substance. [. . .] Therefore, it seems clear that light, both strictly and figuratively speaking, is not a body, but a corporeal form":[17] *forma lucis.*

This statement entails a liberating scope difficult for us to appreciate today: it aims at contesting the *luminous unicity* of the idea and opens it up to the *spectrum* of the subject's "artistic" experience, the place of the imagination. Formative light is nothing but light shattered into colors, an opening up of colored surfaces, a flood of representations.

Yet, at the same time, we must insist on the ambiguity of such a statement: if it contests a rigid, unitary theology, arrested in the dazzling whiteness of meaning, then, by the same token, it co-opts the chromatic scale (with its basis of drives crossing through the subject), into theological space, as I suggested earlier.

Within this ambiguity and by playing with this contradiction, Western painting professed to serve Catholic theology while betraying it at the same time; it eventually left behind, first, its themes (at the time of the Renaissance), and later, its norm—representation (with the advent of Impressionism and the ensuing movements). Several theological statements bear witness to high spiritual leaders' distrust of painting, which they perceive as "not elevated enough" spiritually, if not simply "burlesque." Hegel evinces this kind of attitude when, after having recognized Giotto's original use of color, and pursuing his reasoning in the same paragraph, he observes that the painter leaves behind spirituality's higher spheres:

> Giotto, along with the changes he effected in respect to modes of conception and composition, brought about a reform in the art of preparing colors. [. . .] The things of the world receive a stage and a wider opportunity for expression; and this is illustrated by the way Giotto, under the influence of his age, found room for burlesque along with so much that was pathetic [. . .] in this tendency of Giotto to humanize and towards realism he never really, as a rule, advances beyond a comparatively subordinate stage in the process.[18]

Thus, in changing color style, Giotto might have given a graphic reality to the "natural" and "human" tendencies of the ideology of his time. Giotto's colors would be "formal" equivalents of the burlesque, the visual precursors of the earthy laugh that Rabelais only translated into language a few centuries later. Giotto's joy is the sublimated jouissance of a subject liberating himself from the transcendental dominion of One Meaning (white) through the advent of its instinctual drives, again articulated within a complex and regulated distribution. Giotto's joy burst into the chromatic clashes and harmonies that guided and dominated the architectonics of the Arena Chapel frescoes at Padua. This chromatic joy is the indication of a deep ideological and subjective transformation; it descreetly enters the theological signified, distorting and doing violence to it without relinquishing it. This joy evokes the carnivalesque excesses of the masses but anticipates their verbal and ideological translations, which came to light later, through literary art (the novel, or, in philosophy, the heresies). That this chromatic experience could take place under the aegis of the Order of Merry Knights commemorating the Virgin is, perhaps, more than a coincidence (sublimated jouissance finds its basis in the forbidden mother, next to the Name-of-the-Father).

Padua's Blue

Blue is the first color to strike the visitor as he enters into the semi-darkness of the Arena Chapel. Unusual in Giotto's time because of its brilliance, it contrasts strongly with the somber coloring of Byzantine mosaics as well as with the colors of Cimabue or the Sienese frescoes.[19]

The delicate, chromatic nuances of the Padua frescoes barely stand out against this luminous blue. One's first impression of Giotto's painting is of a colored substance, rather than form or architecture; one is struck by the light that is generated, catching the eye because of the color blue. Such a blue takes hold of the viewer at the extreme limit of visual perception.

In fact, Johannes Purkinje's law states that in dim light, short wavelengths prevail over long ones; thus, before sunrise, blue is the first color to appear. Under these conditions, one perceives the color blue through the rods of the retina's periphery (the serrated margin), while the central element containing the cones (the fovea) fixes the object's image and identifies its form. A possible hypothesis, following André Broca's paradox,[20] would be that the perception of blue entails not identifying the object; that blue is, precisely, on this side of or beyond the object's fixed form; that it is the zone where phenomenal identity vanishes. It has also been shown that the fovea is indeed that part of the eye developed latest in human beings (sixteen months after birth).[21] This most likely indicates that centered vision—the identification of objects, including one's own image (the "self" perceived at the mirror stage between the sixth and eighteenth month)—comes into play after color perceptions. The earliest appear to be those with short wavelengths, and therefore the color blue. Thus all colors, but blue in particular, would have a non-centered or decentering effect, lessening both object identification and phenomenal fixation. They thereby return the subject to the archaic moment of its dialectic, that is, before the fixed, specular "I," but while in the process of becoming this "I" by breaking away from instinctual, biological (and also maternal) dependence. On the other hand, the chromatic experience can then be interpreted as a repetition of the specular subject's emergence in the already constructed space of the understanding (speaking) subject; as a reminder of the subject's conflictual constitution, not yet alienated into the set image facing him, not yet able to distinguish the contours of others or his own other in the mirror. Rather, the subject is caught in the acute contradiction between the instincts of self-preservation and the destructive ones, within a limitless pseudoself, the conflictual scene of primary narcissism and autoerotism[22] whose clashes could follow any concatenation of phonic, visual, or spectral differences.

Oblique Constructions and Chromatic Harmony

The massive irruption of bright color into the Arena Chapel frescoes, arranged in soft but contrasting hues, gives a sculptural *volume* to Giotto's figures, often leading to comparisons with Andrea Pisano. That is, color tears these figures away from the wall's plane, giving them a depth related to, but also distinct from, a search for perspective. The treatment and juxtaposition of masses of color, transforming surface into volume, is of capital importance to the architectonics of the Padua frescoes; the surface is cut into prisms whose edges clash but, avoiding the axial point of perspective, are articulated as obliquely positioned, suspended blocks.

This conflictual aspect of Giotto's pictorial space has already been noted.[23] In fact, 75 percent of the Padua frescoes display obliquely set blocks: a room viewed from an angle, a building depicted from outside at a given angle, a profile of a mountain, the diagonal arrangement of characters, and so on. These examples attest to Giotto's geometric investigations on the properties of squares and rectangles. Frontal settings are relatively rare, whereas oblique spatial constructions dominate the entire narrative cycle, although to varying degrees, frequently tending to merge with the plane of the wall (as in *The Last Supper*).

In short, Giotto avoids frontal settings as well as vanishing points: conflicting oblique lines indicate that the central viewpoint is not in any fresco, but rather in the space of the building where the painter or viewer is standing. These frescoes, with evanescent or exterior centers, articulated by means of the orthogonals' *aggressive patterns*, reveal a spatial organization very unlike the one adopted by perspective-dominated "realist" art. According to John White, this conflictual organization of pictorial space appears only in Islamic or Chinese art—and there only rarely—in the form of "carpets" or "tables" seen from above, the normal viewpoint being avoided within such "spatial" organizations.[24] On the other hand, Giotto's oblique compositions are sustained by the subject's axial point outside of the image. The fresco is thus without autonomy, impossible to isolate from the narrative series; but neither can it be separated from the building's volume, or severed from the hand tracing it. Each fresco, therefore, is the transposition of this volume and subject into an act that is not yet alienated to the facing facet, within the image in perspective.

This conflict within pictorial space is even more clear cut at Assisi. In the fresco *The Expulsion of the Demons from Arezzo* (figure 5) there are broken spaces, shifted and repeated blocks set side by side at different angles. In *Dream of the Palace and Arms*, the frame, seen from the front, appears as a square; inside, however, there are two blocks

Figure 5. Giotto, *The Expulsion of the Demons From Arezzo*. Basilica of St. Francis, Assisi.

Photo: Scala

seen at a forty-five-degree angle, one next to the other, transparent, with each rectangular surface once again divided in order to generate other blocks and tiered columns. A block is set at an angle to the frame, broken and exploded on the far-side wall, culminating in the triangle at the top (pyramid) or in the green cupola; or, conversely, pyramid and cupola are articulated by means of nested, broken blocks (*The Crucifix of St. Damian Speaks to St. Francis*). *St. Francis Renouncing the World* presents open blocks, pressed onto each other, slightly askew; another diagonal overlapping echoes them within the square fresco. In the *Dream of Pope Innocent III*, a raised and imbalanced block collapses onto another facing it within the square of the frame. In *The Apparition to the Brothers of Arles*, another block, opening from the back towards the viewer, would be almost in perspective except for the friezes and ogives near the top, deepening and multiplying the surfaces and preventing the lines from converging at one point.

In *Visions of Friar Augustine and the Bishop of Assisi* there are blocks open on the right, soaring over a large block oriented towards the left, to which is added, similarly oriented, a triptych of blocks with their far sides shot through with blue ovals.

A similar working of square surfaces may be seen in the Church of Santa Croce in Florence. An interesting variation of Giotto's geometrical investigations of the rectangle appears in *St. Francis Preaching before Honorius III* at Assisi. The surface of the square cut out by the frame is translated into two volumes, one set on top of the other (the seat); but this antagonistic treatment of space is softened by the curves of the three ribbed vaults, as if the square, confronted with the circle, produced an oval lining, a depth set off from the frame, a Field curving inwards, but avoiding the vanishing point of perspective. This particular treatment of space is worth noting, since it reappears at Padua in two figureless frescoes. Situated over the altar, they inaugurate the narrative series and program it, providing its graphic matrix, in three stages: first there is a solid rectangular base; second, above this an angle appears (slanted to the left in one fresco, to the right in the other)—a confrontation of surfaces cut into squares, a conflictive module for space; third, the conflict is nevertheless harmonized in the upper part of the fresco, where the intersecting arcs of the ogives meet in the ribbed cupola's three focal points. A spiral is clinched before the window as if to emphasize the unstoppable and inexhaustible movement going from square to circle.

How do colors participate in this both antagonistic and harmonized space?

Two workings of color may easily be distinguished at Padua: first, in the scenery (field, landscape, architecture); and second, in the make up of human figures and interiors.

The blue field dominates the scenery. The oblique or frontal planes of the blocks stand out from this background either through the use of colors close to blue (green, grayish-green: for example, in *The Annunciation to Anna*) or contrasting with it (rose and pinkish gray, for example, in *The Meeting at the Golden Gate*; or gold and golden-rose in *The Betrothal of the Virgin*). Interiors that are set frontally are surrounded by square or lateral planes painted rose or yellow

(*The Mocking of Christ*). The blue-green relation dominates the upper frescoes, whereas the blue-rose or blue-gold one appears more frequently in the lower registers. Once again, Giotto seemingly wants to facilitate the natural perception of a viewer standing at the center of the somber church. The less visible upper registers are consequently done in blue-green, while the lower ones, more accessible to daylight, accentuate gilded-rose colors, which are, in fact, the first perceived under increased lighting.

In every case, however, the antagonistic space of the overlapping, fragmented blocks is achieved through the confrontation of colored surfaces: either through colors of the same hue with the addition of complementary tones (for example, the pink roof in *The Annunciation to Anna*), or directly through complementary chromatic scales.

What is important is that, except for the basic blues, all other hues are particularly refined and *very light.* It seems as if the distribution of colored masses reflected a search for the *smallest possible difference* capable of shattering a homogeneous background. Such a difference is precisely what causes spatial conflictivity to be perceived without violence—as harmony and transition.

This becomes even more evident in the treatment of human figures.

On the one hand, each mass of color is unfolded into its variants. For example, the colors of clothing are opened out through the realistic effect of drapery folds into variations of pink absorbing gray, white, and green, thus molding a cape. These variants are infinitesimal differentials within the already subtly different light hues of Giotto's palette. In some instances they recall the subdued colorings of Chinese prints, where a text supports the signified, while color seeks out barely perceptible differences, minute retinal sensations charged with the least "semantic latency." These "folds of color" are confrontations between one color and the complete chromatic scale: while each color remains dominant in its various mixtures, it is also *differently* and *indefinitely attenuated.* The conflict within a color moving toward white—an effect of pure brilliance—provides each color and, therefore, each framed surface, with a sense of volume. This rounded, sculptural aspect of Giotto's figures strikes one immediately.

The curves of the drawing (oval shape of the heads, rounded fullness of the bodies) repeat the oval-shaped, colored masses (deformed and drawn out spheres and cylinders). Roundness becomes chromatic and independent of the curved drawing itself. The line seems guided by unfolding color and merely follows it, accentuates it, settles it, identifies it when color defies fixed objects, and in short, distinguishes it from adjoining spheres and colors. These masses of color become spherical through their own self-differentiation; set within an angular space of blocks and squares, they serve as transition between clashing surfaces. In fact, and more effectively than the clashing surfaces, these masses of color generate the volume of the painted surface. The colors of colliding surfaces thus delineate the edges of such cubed space, while the colors of each figure give volume to and round out this conflict between blocks. Color thus succeeds in shaping a space of conflicts, a space of noncentered, unbordered and unfixed transitions, but a space turned inward.

In addition and at the same time, these voluminous colors, as they come into being by intermixing and detaching themselves from the entire spectrum, become articulated with one another either by close contrast (at the same end of the spectrum) or by truly diverging contrast (complementary colors). Thus, in *The Massacre of the Innocents* at Assisi we have the following sequence: brick red—pink—bordeaux—green—white—lavender—white—green—red—pink—lavender—blue (like the field)—red—gold. To simplify, if we designate red by A, blue by B, and yellow by C, the following arrangement may be seen.

Relatively limited differences appear at the beginning (red—pink): A; there is then a jump to the other end of the spectrum (green): B; an echo of the beginning (lavender): A_1; again, a return to the opposite side (green): B_1; its opposite (red): A_2 will be varied until it reaches only a slight difference in hue (pink-lavender): $A_3 = B_3$ before another return to the opposite (blue): B_4 (= field) opposed in turn by red: A_4 before the final C.

Thus, we have: $A—B—A_1—B_1—A_2—A_3 = B_3—B_4—A_4—C$.

The arrangement, whose "model" could very well be a multifaceted gem, is both conflictual and serial. In fact, the geometry represented in the same fresco includes two prismatic towers with their facets obliquely set.

The chromatic treatment of characters produces a plastic effect confirming this geometry. It also adds a harmonization of delineated surfaces and an impression of volume within the colored surfaces themselves. This is done solely by virtue of the colors' own resources, without recourse to geometric determination. Volume is produced by juxtaposing unfolding chromatic differences alone without the assistance of rigid contours. The painter uses drawings and lines, but he coats them, suffuses them with colored matter so that they break away from strictly chromatic differentiation.

By overflowing, softening, and dialecticizing lines, color emerges inevitably as the "device" by which painting gets away from identification of objects and therefore from realism. As a consequence, Giotto's chromatic experiments prefigure a pictorial practice that his immediate followers did not pursue. This practice aspires not to figural representation, but rather, to the resources of the chromatic scale, which then extrapolate, as we have suggested, the instinctual and signifying resources of the speaking subject. For this chromatic system—so crowded with figures, landscape, and mythical scenes—appears void of figuration if viewed at length and attentively. It is like a setting side by side of chromatic differences that throb into a third dimension. Such a chromatic working, therefore, erases angles, contours, limits, placements, and figurations, but reproduces the *movement* of their confrontation.

Color, arranged in this manner, is a compact and plurifunctional element, not conforming to the localization-identification-placement of phenomena and/or their (or any) ultimate meaning; it acts upon the subject's station point outside of the painting rather than projecting him into it. This painting, then, reaches completion within the viewer. It steers the subject towards a systematic cutting through its foreclosure, because it has been set in motion starting from "retinal sensation," their instinctual basis, and the superimposed signifying apparatus. Is this not precisely the "mechanism" of jouissance whose economy Freud locates in the process of removing prohibition by making one's way through it (in his studies on another phenomenon of "bewilderment": witticism, in *Jokes and their Relation to the Unconscious*)?

Let me emphasize, in summing up, that this working one's way through is rigorously regulated by a juxtaposition of differences in volume that operates along two converging paths. On the one hand, it brings into play the geometric possibilities of squares and blocks (their conflict); on the other, it explores the infinitesimal chromatic difference that produces a three-dimensional effect from a colored surface and the opposing or serial alternation of such volumes due to an "element" already indicating volume: the triple register of color (as suggested above) in relation to the sign.

The signifying economy thus made up partakes of an *ideological function*: Giotto's painting as an element of the early fourteenth century societal "superstructure." This raises a fundamental problem, that is, the inclusion of a signifying economy within a social context. By its very nature, artistic practice is indeed doubly articulated: through the inclusion of a "subjective" signifying economy within an "objective" ideological functioning; and through the production of meaning through its subject, in terms of (and liable to the constraints of) concrete social contradictions. In other words, a (subjective) signifying economy becomes an artistic signifying practice only to the extent that it is articulated through the social struggles of a given age. Along such lines, I might suggest that the sociopolitical and ideological position of the painter within the social contradictions of his time ultimately determines a concrete signifying economy, turning it into an artistic practice that will play a given social and historical role. A signifying economy within an artistic practice, therefore, not only operates through the individual (biographical subject) who carries it out, but it also recasts him as *historical subject*—causing the signifying process that the subject undergoes to match the ideological and political expectations of his age's rising classes.

Thus, Giotto's own work-jouissance in color and space and the specific role incumbent on the subject therein, which merge with the ideology of the time: subjectivist and humanist renewal of Christianity; liberating, "secularizing," modern, even "materialist" morality (in the forms of Averroism and nominalism). This ideology corresponds to what Frederick Antal calls the "securely established Florentine upper middle class,"[25] which happens to be the financial basis but also the ideological patron not only of Giotto, but, more generally, of the ensuing pictorial renewal. Antal's study should be consulted for a detailed analysis of the economic and ideological foundations behind the pictorial experience examined here. I would simply emphasize that one cannot understand such practice without taking its socioeconomic foundations into account; nor can one understand it if one chooses to reduce it solely to these foundations, thereby bypassing the signifying economy of the subject involved.

I began with a discussion of color in terms of light, and therefore, of frequency. Applied to an object, however, the notion of color can only have topological value: it expresses precise structures of atoms and molecules. Therefore, what can be described in terms of frequency (light) can only be analyzed in terms of geometry (coloring matter).

Nevertheless, concerning the painting's signification, these topological or frequential differences are of no import in their own specificities and precisions. They are important only as structural differences allowing a spatial distribution. As diacritical markings inside a system (the system of a painting), these differences provide a structural constraint, a general outline, that captures significance as well as its specific subject looking at the painting. Beyond the threshold of structural necessity, however, color plays, as I have shown, on a complex register: the instinctual cathexis of chromatic elements and the ideological values that a particular age places on them. What escapes structural constraint is nonetheless sizable, and it is this area that contemporary semiology, aided by psychoanalysis, is investigating.

I have made use of certain elements in Giotto's painting in order to present several problems relevant to painting as signifying practice. Neither the whole of Giotto's work nor the complexity of the questions raised about it are addressed directly by these reflections. Their object has been, rather, to encourage a return to the ("formal" and ideological) history of painting's subject within its contemporary production; to present the avant-garde with a genetic-dialectical reflection on what produced it and/or that from which it sets itself apart. As Walter Benjamin said of literature: "It is not a question of presenting works [. . .] in correlation to their own times, but rather, within the framework of the time of their birth, to present the time that knows them, that is, our own."[26]

9

MOTHERHOOD ACCORDING TO GIOVANNI BELLINI

The Maternal Body

Cells fuse, split, and proliferate; volumes grow, tissues stretch, and body fluids change rhythm, speeding up or slowing down. Within the body, growing as a graft, indomitable, there is an other. And no one is present, within that simultaneously dual and alien space, to signify what is going on. "It happens, but I'm not there." "I cannot realize it, but it goes on." Motherhood's impossible syllogism.

This becoming-a-mother, this gestation, can possibly be accounted for by means of only two discourses. There is *science*; but as an objective discourse, science is not concerned with the subject, the mother as site of her proceedings. There is *Christian theology* (especially canonical theology); but theology defines maternity only as an impossible elsewhere, a sacred beyond, a vessel of divinity, a spiritual tie with the ineffable godhead, and transcendence's ultimate support—necessarily virginal and committed to assumption. Such are the wiles of Christian reason (Christianity's still matchless rationalism, or at least its rationalizing power, finally become clear); through the maternal body (in a state of virginity and "dormition"[1] before Assumption), it thus establishes a sort of subject at the point where the subject and its speech split apart, fragment, and vanish. Lay humanism took over the configuration of that subject through the cult of the mother: tenderness, love, and seat of social conservation.

And yet, if we presume that *someone* exists throughout the process of cells, molecules, and atoms accumulating, dividing, and multiplying without any *identity* (biological or socio-symbolical) having been formed so far, are we not positing an animism that reflects the inherent psychosis of the speaking Being? So, if we suppose that a *mother* is the subject of gestation, in other words the *master* of a process that science, despite its effective devices, acknowledges it cannot now and perhaps never will be able to take away from her; if we suppose her to be *master* of a process that is prior to the social-symbolic-linguistic contract of the group, then we acknowledge the risk of losing identity at the same time as we ward it off. We recognize on the one hand that biology jolts us by means of unsymbolized instinctual drives and that this phenomenon eludes social intercourse, the representation of preexisting objects, and the contract of desire. On the other hand, we immediately deny it; we say there can be no escape, for mamma is there, she embodies this phenomenon; she warrants that *everything is*, and that it is representable. In a double-barreled move, psychotic tendencies are acknowledged, but at the same time they are settled, quieted, and bestowed upon the mother in order to maintain the ultimate guarantee: symbolic coherence.

This move, however, also reveals, better than any mother ever could, that the maternal body is the place of a splitting, which, even though hypostatized by Christianity, nonetheless remains a constant factor of social reality. Through a body, destined to insure reproduction of the species, the woman-subject, although under the sway of the paternal function (as symbolizing, speaking subject and like all others), more of a *filter* than anyone else—a thoroughfare, a threshold where "nature" confronts "culture." To imagine that there is *someone* in that filter—such is the source of religious mystifications, the font that nourishes them: the fantasy of the so-called "Phallic" Mother.

Because if, on the contrary, there were no one on this threshold, if the mother were not, that is, if she were not phallic, then every speaker would be led to conceive of its Being in relation to some void, a nothingness asymetrically opposed to this Being, a permanent threat against, first, its mastery, and ultimately, its stability.

The discourse of analysis proves that the *desire* for motherhood is without fail a desire to bear a child of the father (a child of her own father) who, as a result, is often assimilated to the baby itself and thus returned to its place as *devalorized man*, summoned only to accomplish his function, which is to originate and justify reproductive desire. Only through these phantasmatic nuptials can the father-daughter incest be carried out and the baby come to exist. At that, the incest is too far removed, bringing peace only to those who firmly adhere to the paternal symbolic axis. Otherwise, once the object is produced, once the fruit is detached, the ceremony loses its effect unless it be repeated forever.

And yet, through and with this desire, motherhood seems to be impelled *also* by a nonsymbolic, nonpaternal causality. Only Ferenczi, Freud, and, later, Marie Bonaparte have spoken about this, evoking the biological destiny of each differentiated sex. Material compulsion, spasm of a memory belonging to the species that either binds together or splits apart to perpetuate itself, series of markers with no other significance than the eternal return of the life-death biological cycle. How can we verbalize this prelinguistic, unrepresentable memory? Heraclitus's flux, Epicurus's atoms, the whirling dust of cabalic, Arab, and Indian mystics, and the stippled drawings of psychedelics—all seem better metaphors than the theories of Being, the logos, and its laws.

Such an excursion to the limits of primal regression can be phantasmatically experienced as the reunion of a woman-mother with the body of *her* mother. The body of her mother is always the same Master-Mother of instinctual drive, a ruler over psychosis, a subject of biology, but also, one toward which women aspire all the more passionately simply because it lacks a penis: that body cannot penetrate her as can a man when possessing his wife. By giving birth, the woman enters into contact with her mother; she becomes, she is her own mother; they are the same continuity differentiating itself. She thus actualizes the homosexual facet of motherhood, through which a woman is simultaneously closer to her instinctual memory, more open to her own psychosis, and consequently, more negatory of the social, symbolic bond.

The symbolic paternal facet relieves feminine aphasia present within the desire to bear the father's child. It is an appeasement that turns into melancholy as soon as the child becomes an object, a gift to others, neither self nor part of the self, an object destined to be a subject, an other. Melancholy readjusts the paranoia that drives to action (often violent) and to discourse (essentially parental, object-oriented, and pragmatic discourse) the feminine, verbal scarcity so prevalent in our culture.

The homosexual-maternal facet is a whirl of words, a complete absence of meaning and seeing; it is feeling, displacement, rhythm, sound, flashes, and fantasied clinging to the maternal body as a screen against the plunge. Perversion slows down the schizophrenia that collapsing identities and the delights of the well-known and oft-solicited (by some women) pantheist fusion both brush up against.

Those afflicted or affected by psychosis have put up in its place the image of the Mother: for women, a paradise lost but seemingly close at hand, for men, a hidden god but constantly present through occult fantasy. And even psychoanalysts believe in it.

Yet, swaying between these two positions can only mean, for the woman involved, that she is within an "enceinte" separating her from the world of everyone else.[2] Enclosed in this "elsewhere," an "enceinte" woman loses communital meaning, which suddenly appears to her as worthless, absurd, or at best, comic—a surface agitation severed from its impossible foundations. Oriental nothingness probably better sums up what, in the eyes of a Westerner, can only be regression. And yet it is jouissance, but like a negative of the one, tied to an object, that is borne by the unfailingly masculine libido. Here, alterity becomes nuance, contradiction becomes a variant, tension becomes passage, and discharge becomes peace. This tendency towards equalization, which is seen as a regressive extinction of symbolic capabilities, does not, however, reduce differences; it resides within the smallest, most archaic, and most uncertain of differences. It is powerful sublimation and indwelling of the symbolic within instinctual drives. It affects this series of "little differences-resemblances" (as the Chines logicians of antiquity would say). Before founding society in the same stroke as signs and communication, they are the precondition of the latter's existence, as they constitute the living entity within its species, with its needs, its elementary apperceptions and communication, distinguishing between the instinctual drives of life and death. It affects primal repression. An ultimate danger for identity, but also supreme power of symbolic instance thus returning to matters of its concern. Sublimation here is both eroticizing without residue and a disappearance of eroticism as it returns to its source.

The speaker reaches this limit, this requisite of sociality, only by virtue of a particular, discursive practice called "art." A woman also attains it (and in our society, *especially*) through the strange form of split symbolization (threshold of language and instinctual drive, of the "symbolic" and the "semiotic") of which the act of giving birth consists. As the archaic process of socialization, one might even say civilization, it causes the childbearing woman to cathect, immediately and unwittingly, the physiological operations and instinctual drives dividing and multiplying her, first, in a biological, and finally, a social teleology. The maternal body slips away from the discursive hold and immediately conceals a cipher that must be taken into account biologically and socially. This ciphering of the species, however, this pre- and transsymbolic memory, makes the mother mistress of neither begetting nor instinctual drive (such a fantasy underlies the cult of any ultimately feminine deity); it does make of the maternal body the stakes of a natural and "objective" control, independent of any individual consciousness; it inscribes both biological operations and their instinctual echoes into this necessary and hazardous *program* constituting every species. The maternal body is the module of a biosocial program. Its jouissance, which is mute, is nothing more than a recording, on the screen of the preconscious, of both the messages that consciousness, in its analytical course, picks up from this ciphering process and their classifications as empty foundation, as a-subjective lining of our rational exchanges as social beings.

If it is true that every national language has its own dream language and unconscious, then each of the sexes—a division so much more archaic and fundamental than the one into languages—would have its own unconscious wherein the biological and social program of the species would be ciphered in confrontation with language, exposed to its influence, but independent from it. The symbolic destiny of the speaking animal, which is essential although it comes second, being superimposed upon the biological—this destiny *seals off* (and in women, in order to preserve the homology of the group, it *censures*) that archaic basis and the special jouissance it procures in being transferred to the symbolic. Privileged, "psychotic" moments, or whatever induces them naturally, thus become necessary. Among such "natural" inducements, maternity is needed for this sexual modality to surface, this fragile, secretly guarded and incommunicable modality, quickly stifled by standard palliatives (by viril and "rational" censorship, or by the sentimentality of "maternal" tenderness toward a substitute-object for everything). This process is quite rightly understood as the demand for a penis. Fantasy indeed has no other sign, no other way to imagine that the speaker is capable of reaching the Mother, and thus, of unsettling its own limits. And, as long as there is language-symbolism-paternity, there will never be any other way to represent, to objectify, and to explain this unsettling of the symbolic stratum, this nature/culture threshold, this instilling the subjectless biological program into the very body of a symbolizing subject, this event called motherhood.

In other words, from the point of view of social coherence, which is where legislators, grammarians, and even psychoanalysts have their seat, which is where every body is made homologous to a male speaking body, motherhood would be nothing more than a phallic attempt to reach the Mother who is presumed to exist at the very place where (social and biological) identity recedes. If it is true that idealist ideologies develop along these lines, urging women to satisfy this presumed demand and to maintain the ensuing order, then, on the other hand, any negation of this utilitarian, social, and symbolic aspect of motherhood plunges into regression—but a particular regression whose currently recognized manifestations lead to the hypostasis of blind substance, to the negation of symbolic position, and to a justification of this regression under the aegis of the same Phallic Mother-screen.

The language of art, too, follows (but differently and more closely) the other aspect of maternal jouissance, the sublimation taking place at the very moment of primal repression within the mother's body, arising perhaps unwittingly out of her marginal position. At the intersection of sign and rhythm, of representation and light, of the symbolic and the semiotic, the artist speaks from a place where she is not, where she knows not. He delineates what, in her, is a body rejoicing [*jouissant*]. The very existence of aesthetic practice makes clear that the Mother as subject is a delusion, just as the negation of the so-called poetic dimension of language leads one to believe in the existence of the Mother, and consequently, of transcendence. Because, through a symbiosis of meaning and nonmeaning, of representation and interplay of differences, the artist lodges into language, and through his identification with the mother (fetishism or incest—we shall return to this problem), his own specific jouissance, thus traversing both sign and object. Thus, before all other speakers, he bears witness to what the unconscious (through the screen of the mother) records of those clashes that occur between the biological and social programs of the species. This means that through and across secondary repression (founding of signs), aesthetic practice touches upon primal repression (founding biological series and the laws of the species). At the place where it obscurely succeeds within the maternal body, every artist tries his hand, but rarely with equal success.

Nevertheless, craftsmen of Western art reveal better than anyone else the artist's debt to the maternal body and/or motherhood's entry into symbolic existence—that is, translibidinal jouissance, eroticism taken over by the language of art. Not only is a considerable portion of pictorial art devoted to motherhood, but within this representation itself, from Byzantine iconography to Renaissance humanism and the worship of the body that it initiates, two attitudes toward the maternal body emerge, prefiguring two destinies within the very economy of Western representation. Leonardo Da Vinci and Giovanni Bellini seem to exemplify in the best fashion the opposition between these two attitudes. On the one hand, there is a tilting toward the body as fetish. On the other, a predominance of luminous, chromatic differences beyond and despite corporeal representation. Florence and Venice. Worship of the figurable, representable man; or integration of the image accomplished in its truth-likeness within the luminous serenity of the unrepresentable.

A unique biographical experience and an uncommon, historical intersection of pagan-matriarchal Orientalism with sacred Christianity and incipient humanism was perhaps needed for Bellini's brush to retain the traces of a marginal experience, through and across which a maternal body might recognize its own, otherwise inexpressible in our culture.

Leonardo and Bellini: Fetish and Primal Repression

Giovanni Bellini: 1430?–1516. Approximately two hundred and twenty paintings, basically on sacred topics, are attributed to him or to his school. He taught Giorgione and Titian and founded the Venetian Renaissance, which came somewhat later than the Florentine but was more organically allied to its Byzantine sources and more attracted by the display of the feminine body than by the Grecian beauty of young boys. Bellini's work is a synthesis of Flemish landscape painting, iconography, and Mediterranean architectural manner. He also contributed a completely new element: the luminous density of color (the initial technique of oil painting, which was already being mastered), of shadows and brightness that, more so than the discovery of perspective, introduced volume into the body and into the painting. Historians of art emphasize, in Bellini's manner, the effect; they often neglect what this manner implies as to pictorial experimentation, but worse, they also neglect to observe it down to the most minute details of the painting's surface.

We have almost no biographical details: a nearly perfect discretion. His father was the painter Jacopo Bellini; his brother, the painter Gentile Bellini. His brother-in-law was the painter Andrea Mantegna. He was the official painter for the Ducal Palace, but the paintings executed in that capacity were destroyed. He was married, but his wife Ginevra Bocheta died young, as did his son, and it is uncertain whether he married again. He was urged by Isabella d'Este to paint pagan motifs but he backed out, refusing to do so; finally, he complied only when assisted by his disciples. In 1506, Dürer called him the best of painters. The spoors of his life leave a discrete imprint, and then they disappear. Bellini himself left us no words, no subjective writings. We must read him through his painting.

Bellini's discretion stands in contrast to the profusion of information and biographical notes left behind by his younger contemporary, Leonardo Da Vinci (1452–1519). Relying on biographical evidence and on paintings as *narrative* as *Virgin and Child with St. Anne* and the *Mona Lisa*, Freud could maintain that Leonardo's "artistic personality" was formed, first, by the precocious seduction he was supposed to have experienced at the hands of his mother (the vampire tail of his dreams would represent the tongue of his mother, passionately kissing the illegitimate child); second, by a double motherhood (taken from his mother, Leonardo was raised in his father's family by his stepmother, who had no children of her own); and finally, by the impressive authority of an office-holding father. The father finally triumphed over the drawing power of the mother, which determined the young man's interest in art, and near the end of his life, Leonardo turned toward the sciences. Thus, we have the typical configuration of a homosexual structure. Persuaded by precocious seduction and double motherhood of the existence of a maternal phallus, the painter never stopped looking for fetish equivalents in the bodies of young people, in his friendships with them, in his miserly worship of objects and money, and in his avoidance of all contact with and access to the feminine body. His was a forbidden mother because she was the primordial seducer, the limit of an archaic, infantile jouissance that must never be reproduced. She established the child's diffident narcissism and cult of the masculine body which he ceaselessly painted, even when a mother figures at the center of the painting. Take for example Leonardo's Virgins: *Madonna with the Carnation* and *Virgin and Child with St. Anne*. There we find the enigmatic smile, identical with that of the Mona Lisa, herself furtively masculine; with naive tenderness, face and torso impulsively turn toward the male infant, who remains the real focus of pictorial space and narrative interest. The maternal figure is completely absorbed with her baby; it is he that makes her exist. "Baby is my goal, and I know it all"—such is the slogan of the mother as master. But when Narcissus is thus sheltered and dominated, he can become the privileged explorer of secondary repression. He goes in quest of fantasies that insure any group's cohesion; he reveals the phallic influence operating over everyone's imaginary. Such an attitude incites pleasure, but it dramatically affects a desire that is impossible to satisfy by an abundance of objects, bodies, or behaviors, which ceaselessly excite and disappoint. As long as there is father, a magisterial Lord, an intimate of Power, Leonardo turns to his symbolic power, eclipsing maternal imprint; he stops the gap in repression and surges towards scientific knowledge rather than investigating through graphic arts the pleasure-anguish within unconscious formations.

Within the economy of representation, this kind of structure unfailingly entails a humanist realism. First, there is a fetishism of the body and an extreme refinement of the technique of representation by resemblance. Next comes the staging of psychological episodes centered in the desire for a body—his, a child's, or another's. Finally, all chromatic, luminous, and architectural experimentation, releasing, threatening, torturing, and gratifying the artist subject within its practice, undergoes a figuration wherein it is reduced to a simple, technical device, destined to give the effect of representable, desirable, fetishistic forms.

The fundamental traits of Renaissance painting emerge in such a vision, and they are supported by the story of Leonardo's life that was brought out by Freud. They can be found elsewhere, both earlier and later; but with him better than with others, both in his biography and his painting, causes and effects come together and determine beyond the details of his life and the themes of his paintings, the very *economy* of representation, regardless of its *referent*. It is no accident that the major segments of this economy, which was to determine Western man's vision for four centuries to come, are fitted into place by virtue of the themes of motherhood, the woman's body, or the mother (Mona Lisa and the Virgin). The artist, as servant of the maternal phallus, displays this always and everywhere unaccomplished art of reproducing bodies and spaces as graspable, masterable *objects*, within reach of his eye and hand. They are the eye and hand of a child, underage to be sure, but of one who is the universal and nonetheless complex-ridden center confronting that other function, which carries the appropriation of objects to its limit: science. Body-objects, passion for objects, painting divided into form-objects, painting-objects: the series remains open to centuries of object-oriented and figurable libido, delighting in images and capitalizing on artistic merchandise. Among this machine's resources figure the untouchable mother and her baby-object, just as they appear in the paintings of Leonardo, Raphael, and others.

Both Bellini's enigmatic biography and the technique of his paintings suggest a different interpretation. Are we in fact dealing with projections made possible by our uncertain knowledge? Perhaps. But they seem well supported by the paintings, a veritable proof of the deductions that biographical information only suggested.

Commentators are puzzled. According to Vasari, Bellini, son of Jacopo, died a nonagenarian in 1516, and thus should have been born in 1426. Yet, in 1429, Jacopo's wife Anna Rinversi recorded in her will the birth of a first-born son. If Giovanni was born before this date, he must have been either an illegitimate child or the son of Jacopo or Anna by a previous marriage. Other biographers insist that Vasari was wrong and that Giovanni was the youngest child, after Nicolosia (Mantegna's wife) and Gentile. This hypothesis is corroborated most convincingly by Giovanni's social standing in relation to Gentile, who held the position of Seigniorial painter before Giovanni; in some paintings, Giovanni appears third after Jacopo and Gentile. But that does not explain why Giovanni, unlike his brother and sister, was living alone in 1459, outside the paternal household, at San Lio in Venice. Nor does it explain—and this is most crucial—why Anna's last will, dated November 25, 1471, does not list him among the children heirs, Nicolosia and Gentile. So it seems that Anna Rinversi did not recognize herself as Giovanni's mother, giving credence to speculations concerning an illegitimate birth or obscure marriage.[3]

Such is the situation, the biographical outline, greeting the viewer who confronts the work of this painter of motherhood above all other topics. Indeed, he was the son of a father: he bore his father's name, worked in his studio, and carried on his painterly tradition. He was also a brother; Gentile let him have the position of Seigniorial painter when he left for Constantinople; Giovanni also finished some of Gentile's paintings. But the mother is absent—the mother has been lost. Was he precociously weaned from an illegitimate, abandoned, dead, or concealed genetrix? Does this point to the disavowal of a "sin" committed beyond the law's purview and of which Giovanni was the result? Whatever the truth may be, Anna does not seem to have replaced the "real" mother, as the honorable Leonardo's wife replaced Leonardo's real mother: Anna knew nothing of the painter of Madonnas. But even if we do remain incredulous in the face of biographical lack and commentators' perplexity, let us also behold the distance, if not hostility, separating the bodies of infant and mother in his paintings. Maternal space is there, nevertheless— fascinating, attracting, and puzzling. But we have no direct access to it. As if there were a maternal *function* that, unlike the mother's solicitude in Leonardo's paintings toward the baby-object of all desire, was merely ineffable jouissance, beyond discourse, beyond narrative, beyond psychology, beyond lived experience and biography—in short, beyond figuration. The faces of his Madonnas are turned away, intent on something else that draws their gaze to the side, up above, or nowhere in particular, but never centers it in the baby. Even though the hands clasp the child and bodies sometimes hug each other, the mother is only partially present (hands and torso), because, from the neck up, the maternal body not covered by draperies—head, face, and eyes—flees the painting, is gripped by something other than its object. And the painter as baby can never reach this elsewhere, this inaccessible peace colored with melancholy, neither through the portrayed corporeal contact, nor by the distribution of colored blocks outlining corporeal volumes. It rather seems as though he sensed a shattering, a loss of identity, a sweet jubilation where *she* is not; but without "her"—without eyes or vision—an *infinitesimal division* of color and space rhythmically produce a peculiar, serene joy. To touch the mother would be to possess this presumed jouissance and to make it visible. Who holds this jouissance? The folds of colored surfaces, the juxtaposition of full tones, the limitless volume resolving into a contrast of "hots" and "colds" in an architecture of pure color, the sudden brightness in turn opening up color itself—a last control of vision, beyond its own density, toward dazzling light. *The Ecstasy of Saint Francis* best sums up this search for jouissance, less by its theme than by the architectonics of a mountain colored in watery tones against which the saint stands, staggering; it could even be a Taoist painting. But the search appears wherever color, constructed volume, and light break away from the theme (always banal, canonical, with no psychology, no elaborate individualization), implying that they are the real, objectless goal of the painting.

Given Bellini's profusion of virginal images, we might be tempted to think that the absent, dead, and mute mother, situated beyond the law, determines that fascination, not as it is confronted with a woman-"body" or woman-"subject," but as it is confronted with the very *function* of jouissance. And yet, Giovanni Bellini could reach it only by following the spoors of the father who, unlike the mother, was always present in the real as well as the symbolic life of the painter. For it was from his father that Giovanni took his first lessons in spatial liberation and sacred painting. In fact, Jacopo, neither dignitary nor lawyer, fervently pursued architecture (see his drawings for *Jesus and the Doctors, Christ before Pilate, The Funeral of the Virgin*, etc., in the Louvre; all are monumental displays of Romanesque or Gothic architecture) and venerated conventional notions of Byzantine motherhood (cf. his *Madonna and Child* paintings in the Correr Museum). Yet the dull seriousness of his motherhood scenes cast him as blind to the mother; he paints her as if carried along by the momentum of Byzantine canon. (Jacopo's real fervor, through the influence of his son-in-law Mantegna, seemed to reside in architectural innovation.) Only his son Giovanni was able to awaken this mother, thus instilling a symbolic life less into the father's sexual object than into its undiscovered jouissance.

First, Giovanni wanted to surpass his father, within the very space of the lost-unrepresentable-forbidden jouissance of a hidden mother, seducing the child through a lack of being.

But then, and most importantly, Giovanni could share in this both maternal and paternal jouissance: He aspired to become the very space where father and mother meet, only to disappear as parental, psychological, and social figures; a space of fundamental unrepresentability toward which all glances nonetheless converge; a primal scene where genitality dissolves sexual identification beyond their given difference. This is how breaking through primal repression, as described earlier and evidenced by the psychological drama or its aesthetic sublimation, was to be spelled out within the individual's biographical matrix.

In any case, we have here a different configuration of artistic practice controlling a different economy of representation. Bellini penetrates through the being and language of the father to position himself in the place where the mother could have been reached. He thus makes evident this always-already-past conditional of the maternal function, which stands instead of the jouissance of both sexes. A kind of incest is then committed, a kind of possession of the mother, which provides motherhood, that mute border, with a language; although, in doing so, he deprives it of any right to a real existence (there is nothing "feminist" in Bellini's action), he does accord it a symbolic status. Unfailingly, the result of this attitude (mother-child representation, marketable painting, etc.) is a fetishized image, but one floating over a luminous background, evoking an "inner experience" rather than a referential "object." This experience, detectable in Bellini's paintings, seems to demand a consuming of the heterosexual relationship. The converse, however, does not hold true; the heterosexuality of this particular economy refers only to the specific relationship between the subject and his identity—the possibility of going through sign, object, and object-libido in order to tap and semiotize even the most minute displacements in those instinctual pressures that mark the dividing line between the species and its language. The point is to reach the threshold of repression by means of the identification with motherhood (be it as heterosexuality or symbolic incest), to reach this threshold where maternal jouissance, alone impassable, is arrayed.

If we see this threshold in a painting, we no longer hear words or meanings; not even sounds. (But in order to see it, we need a relationship to the mother other than that of the fetishistic, object-libidio; we must also work intently upon primal repression, which is insurmountable—making the task as tempting as it is risky.) As in the saturnine skies of Dante's *Paradise*, the voice here is silent. It burst forth as a cry only after having gone through colors and luminous spaces, at the end of Canto XXI. Plunged into a loss of signs, a loss of the seducing figure (the compassionate or laughing mother), we finally come upon deliverance:

> "And tell why the sweet symphony of Paradise
> > Which below sounds so devoutly
> > Is silent in this heaven."
> > "Your hearing is mortal, like your vision,"
> > He answered me, "therefore there is no song here,
> > For the same reason Beatrice has no smile."[4]

In general, Bellini's paintings have a common denominator in *sacra conversazione*. It is there that the "sacred" scene of the Western World has been knotted and arrested. It was soon to be replaced by humanism and rational knowledge, achieving the progress with which we are all familiar. But with what loss of jouissance! As such, it reappears only in the work of certain modern painters (Rothko, Matisse) who rediscovered the technique of eclipsing a figure in order to have color produce volume. Bellini was their precursor, trapped as he was in an epoch fraught with divergent trends.

A Trajectory from Madonna to Venus in the Nude

The practice of honoring Christ's Mother, his Nativity, and her "Dormition" comes to Western Christianity from the Orthodox Catholic Church, which succeeded in annexing the Oriental rites of mother goddess and fecundity. It strained biblical and evangelical interpretation to make it seem as if the rites were derived from these texts, as if they had always been inscribed in them. Byzantine apocrypha of the sixth through ninth centuries confirm this tendency, which appears as official doctrine in the writings of theologians such as St. John of Damascus (late seventh, early eighth century). In these texts, Mary takes on again the potential authority of a Greek goddess (despite the writers' claims to the contrary), sanctioned by the themes of her "Dormition" or Assumption. The only human not to die, she revived in body and/or spirit (this point varies according to interpreters) and in so doing, eliminated the distance between her son and herself. Later, a rather "unfeminist" Master Eckhart emphasized Mary's assimilation to Christ, justified by the Assumption, by asserting that Mary is only the image (fantasy?) of Christ himself, to the extent that, although a man (but like a woman?) he belongs to the Father. Another quite revealing Orthodox conception of the Virgin defines her as ἐργαστήριον, ergasterion—privileged *space*, living *area*, *ladder* (of Jacob), or *door* (of the Temple, in Ezekiel's vision)—*dwelling*, in short; she is thus seen as a *union*, a *contact without gap, without separation*, and these functions make of her a metaphor for the Holy Ghost.

She can be seen in the countless icons that proliferated out of the Orient and steadfastly served as models for Italian art. The formal, rigid iconographic canon, which relied on graphic rigor to delineate blocks of dark colors, produced neither mother nor even goddess, but rather a *style of representation* that shifted from human figures to austere idealization with no gap or separation between the two. This style, which was a link between a body and ascetic rigor, did not waver or lose any of its abstract rigidity until Byzantium's importance began to wane in the twelfth century (the time of the Fourth Crusade, the assertion of southern Slavic peoples, and the Musulman invasion of Asia Minor). At that point, the inaccessible grandeur of the earlier Madonnas gave way to the already humanist compassion (*umilenie* in Russian; ἐλεουσια, *heleousia* in Greek) apparent in *Our Lady of Vladimir* (1125–1130).

The twelfth century witnessed the transition from a single, virginal face to a multitude of figures set in a composition oriented toward an increasingly elaborate architecture (cf. the Sopaćani frescoes in Serbia, 1265). It was thus a transformed Byzantine artistry, this famed *maniera greca* that invaded Italy and influenced Guido da Siena, Duccio, Cimabue, Giotto, and others.

Confronting Byzantium, the Venetian Republic enlarged the economic grip of its position as true colonial empire and amassed artistic influences from Europe and the Orient. Among these figured Gothic architecture, Flemish landscape painting, and Moslem and Romanesque tendencies in iconography, ornamentation, sculpture, and building construction. Venetian Gothic style was thus shaped before the arrival of Florentine humanism. In painting, Byzantine's influence prevailed; for example, Paolo Veneziano adhered to it until after 1350.

There were, nevertheless, alien implantations: Mantegna's supposedly Nordic rigidity but also his Roman architectural experience, and especially Antonello da Messina who passed on to Giovanni Bellini the art of oil painting. These lead all of Venice, including the Bellini family and notably Gentile, toward a renascent realism.

Thus, on the one hand, we have the deeply rooted persistance of the Byzantine universe, and on the other the awakening and growing influence of continental humanism. Between the two, there is a Venetian Republic, welcoming the Greek scholars who were fleeing Moslem dominion, and thus opening itself up to the influences of antiquity. At the same time, under pressure from the Turks, the city-state was beginning to lose its hegemony and to turn toward the "terra firma" of Italy. Similarity, and perhaps due to the consequences of foreign-policy failures, popular involvement in government declined to the extent that the term "Venetian Commune" soon fell into disuse. Yet a consciousness of economic and religious communal *unity* persisted, controlled by the Doges, whose power, symbolic as it was, was not sacred, since it was elective (even if only by one particular class, acting in the name of everyone). The cult of the State became the supreme ethical value and its autonomy vis-à-vis the Church grew, thanks to, for example, increasing influence of the lay courts. Nevertheless, that the often realist and popular piety of the people and even the clergy never diminished is clearly evident in the many reliquary celebrations and religious festivals of the time.

As a divide between Byzantium and humanism, between the sacred serenity of old religion and the political and cultural upheaval on the day, Venice changed ethics at the same time it changed aesthetics, in front of and under Bellini's brush.

New Mores: The impoverished patrician class produced hoodlums who chased nuns and adolescents so regularly that courtesans began to complain of being neglected. Patrician ladies next became aroused, demanding of the Pope the right to wear richly ornamented clothing and jewelry. Carnival eclipsed Assumption in importance. Bullfighting and another fascinating game in which cats go at the pates of bald men incited as much interest and probably more cathartic anguish than the feasts of Saint Mark, the Ascension, and Corpus Christi combined.

New Ideas: The Petrarchian and Neo-Platonist Pietro Bembo arranged for Bellini to undertake a commission from Isabelle d'Este to paint pagan scenes and thus spread the Florentine doctrine unseating virgin motherhood in favor of carnal love as the true beginning of any spiritual ascent toward God. But the apotheosis of the sacred's slide toward voluptuousness is without doubt *Hypnerotomachia Poliphili* (1499), attributed to a Dominican monk named Francesco Colonna, who abandoned Reason and Will for the glory of female nudity—a romance illustrated by woodcuts of yet unprecedented eroticism.

Confronted with the subsequent deluge of nudity and eros, a student of the master iconographers must have resembled a contemporary interpreter of Bach faced with the onslaught of pornography. Such novelty is certainly surprising, but not shocking; it is not completely antithetical to what precedes it. A bridge does exist between the two experiences, but it must be found. Such is the course of Bellini's endeavor.

After a few initial paintings in an iconographic style and in the manner of his father (*The Crucifixion*, Civico Museo Correr, Venice), the Madonnas dating from 1450 to 1460 appear coldly distant and impassive. Contact between mother and child is by the tips of fingers alone, barely emerging out of Byzantine canon (*Mother with Child and St. Jerome*, Detroit). Her contemplative look borders on sadness as if the baby were already crucified (*Adoring Madonna before Her Sleeping Child*, Metropolitan Museum, New York). In fact, a series of crucifixions, based on the theme of Christ's Passion and displaying a Mantegnesque organization of color and landscape (*The Dead Christ in the Sepulchre*, Museo Poldi Pezzoli, Milan; *Christ's Agony in the Garden*, National Gallery, London), is firmly settled within the theme of motherhood.

Moreover, the theme of Christ's death often appears coupled with the Nativity theme, as if the son's death were supposed to provide a necessarily tragic and human rendition of this indeterminate passion-anguish-melancholy-joy giving iridescence to the serenity of the maternal body. Such tragic manifestation of a son's death and the placid exasperation of his mother are best united in the eyes of Jesus, as the color blue collapses into light, in *Christ Blessing the People* (1460, Louvre, Paris).

The theme of motherhood reappears in his work between 1455 and 1460, this time with an accent on the maternal hands. Painted with austere and graphic precision, doubtlessly due to Mantegna's influence, they bear witness to a maternal appropriation of the child. There is a crushing hug, a tussle between a possessive mother and her child, who tries in vain to loosen her grip (*Madonna and Child*, Amsterdam and Berlin) (figure 6). There is a shiver of anguish and fear in the child's hand, which grips the mother's thumb, with a Flemish countryside for backdrop. Is this an archaic memory of maternal seduction, a recollection of the hand whose precocious, already sexual caresses are more threatening than comforting?

In the following years (1460–1464), the mother's hands remain at the center of the painting bringing its miniature drama to a head. Although still possessive, they now shift toward the child's buttocks (*Madonna and Child*, New Haven; *Madonna and Child*, Correr Museum) (figure 7) or rest on his sexual member (National Gallery, Washington; Brera). We have a striking cleavage of the maternal body. On one side the mother's hands hold their object tightly (could it be that, in her relationship to the child, the mother experiences the symbiotic clinging syndrome?); on the other, we see the softened, dreamy peasant faces, nearly distressed at having missed an experience that nothing embodies, as if the child were merely a displaced witness. The climax of this series is the *Madonna and Child* in Bergamo (figure 8), a spotlight thrown on a dramatic narrative. Aggressive hands prod the stomach and penis of the frightened baby, who, alone of all his peers, frees himself violently, taking his mother's hands along on his body. All the while, the folds of the virginal gown separate this little dramatic theater from the maternal body, whose illuminated face

Figure 6. Detail of Bellini, *Madonna and Child*. Rijksmuseum, Amsterdam.

Figure 7. Bellini, *Madonna and Child*. Civico Correr, Venice.

alone is revealed. Her characterless gaze fleeting under her downcast eyelids, her nonetheless definite pleasure, unshakable in its intimacy, and her cheeks radiating peace, all constitute a strange modesty. This split character of the maternal body has rarely been so clearly brought forward. Perhaps a brutal, biographical separation from a complicity as striking as suffocating and an inaccessible recollection that keeps lurking behind the curtain were all necessary for Bellini to accomplish the task.

Figure 8. Bellini, *Madonna and Child*. Accademia Carrara, Bergamo.

Figure 9. Detail of Giovanni Bellini, *The Presentation at the Temple* (*La Presentazione al Tempio*), c. 1460.
Courtesy of the Fondazione Querini Stampalia Onlus, Venice.

The Presentation in the Temple (1460–1464) (figure 9) is considered by some today to be the model, rather than a copy, of Mantegna's similar painting. It presents with less narrative suggestion (but no less clearly, precisely because of the arrangement of bodies) the theme of mother/child separation. The Virgin is holding and lifting her swaddled child, who adheres to the hollow of her body, skin against skin, flesh against flesh, branches of the same trunk. On the left stands the community of women. On the right at a slight distance, an old man, surrounded by other men, holds out his arms to receive the baby, which she does not proffer. According to law, the baby will obviously be separated from its mother, but within this pictorial experience, the symbiosis of the two appears to allow no possible separation. Their embrace evokes the embrace binding the dead Christ to the bosom of his mother, a twin body, while Saint John waits slightly to the side (*Dead Christ Supported by His Mother and Saint John*, Brera).

A long and fruitful period of spatial experimentation in triptychs, altar pieces, and collective scenes followed this forced separation. It is, so to speak, a representation in the plastic arts of the disengagement of the painter from an image—from the Image, which was essentially maternal. Representations of Madonna and Child accompany these spatial investigations, repeating the characteristics of earlier maternal paintings with the exception, perhaps, that distance is more firmly marked into the painting. Air (*Adoring Madonna and Child*, National Gallery, London; Contini Bonacossi, Florence) and landscape (*Madonna and Blessing Child*, Academy Galleries, Venice) abound to the extent that the maternal embrace loosens its vise. It seems as if Bellini had to experience, but especially to surpass, the trauma of maternal seduction in order to insert space into his organization of chromatic markings, and thereby, better to approach the ineffable jouissance transcending the mother. During this period, 1475–80, the painter oriented his interest, first, toward representing other images than that of the mother and sacred subjects (cf. the series of portraits), and second and foremost, toward positioning a basically minimalized body within landscapes or structures that are always architecturally structured. *St. Francis in Ecstasy* (1480 and 1485, Frick Collection, New York) is probably the most striking example of this movement from figuration toward pure spatialization of color.

In the next series of paintings (1480–1490), the split between mother and child becomes thematically as well as concretely accentuated.

The beaming, enigmatic features of the Bergamo *Madonna* (which the child is fleeing) now reverberate in the reticent *Madonna with Two Trees* (1487, Academy Museum, Venice) or in the *Madonnas* of Lugano or São Paolo. Almost serious, probably disappointed, mistrustful, or hurt, it is she who appears ready to flee. Yet, what fills her is less an inaccessible placidity than a certain stiffness, if not a hostile sideglance canceling the always protected, calm appearance of the *Madonna with Two Trees*. The "possessive mother" of the previous period moves toward the representation of a "hostile mother." And the sacred,

Figure 10. Bellini, *Madonna and Child*. Museu de Arte, Sao Paolo.

combining retention and instinctual drive, transforms the former distance-pleasure balance into distance-anguish. It appears as though this aggressivity were rising to the mother's throat, but, in fact, it is the infant that abruptly reveals it when, eluding the hands of the henceforth weary mother, he grabs her by the neck as if to strangle her—the guilty mother (*Madonna and Child*, 1487, São Paolo) (figure 10).

This change in maternal psychology communicated through facial expression and body stance once again accompanies painterly change.

First, there is an increased use of landscape, already present with the trees used to frame the *Madonna with Two Trees*; it unfolds with mountains, countrysides, and turrets, emerging from behind an increasingly revealing backdrop of drapery. This background material, framing either side or both, occupies from one-sixth to two-thirds of the painting. In the painting of the preceding period, the folds of clothing cut the canvas in two, leaving maternal hands with the child on one side, and on the other the jouissance of an enigmatic face. Now, all of the bodies move to one side of the drapery—no longer cape or gown but curtain—leaving behind this screen, which divides the painting, that is, in the place of the Virgin of Bergamo's ecstatic [*jouissant*] features, for example, the colored volume of a gratuitous space. Nowhere else but here, it seems, in the luminous folds and secret depths of the sacred that painting strives to capture; with regard to it, the myth of the maternal figure is nothing but a screen, a foreground, or an obstruction to be broken through. *Second, but simultaneously*, there is an increased use of numerous figures: angels pulling the infant out of a narcissistic solitude (*Madonna and Child with Cherubs*, Academy Galleries, Venice); saints impinging upon the couple's isolated position (*Madonna and Child with Saints Peter and Sebastian*, Louvre, Paris).

Color is the central agent in this production of volume, which is becoming more important than figuration. The thick blues over transparent whites of Mary's cape in *The Madonna with Two Trees*, superimposed over the lighted green of the background panel, hollow out a sense of volume in the foreground. By a "false bottom" effect, this volume engenders, as if by some cinematographic effect, another volume in which an additional dimension of landscape in perspective finds its place. Thus, by virtue of color (the superposition of related hues with contrasting saturation) and perspective, two separate volumes rise up out of the same surface. Or consider the cherubs' red hue (*Madonna and Red Cherubs*, Academy Galleries, Venice), which acts both as link and separation between the foreground, including Mary (and her red dress), and the green landscape of the background, which echo and attenuate the folds of her cape. The total space of the painting thus seems to unfold into three planes.

Yet, this juxtaposition of colored masses, producing a sense of space, gives way in turn to differentiation within chromatic matter itself. Tending toward pure light, Bellini's colors demonstrate that even what always remains multihued and compact figuration inevitably floats in empty space. Precisely by means of such a chromatic outcome, Bellini can *in reality* replace the radiant or anguished maternal face, caught in the grips of primal repression (even if its image persists in his paintings) with a subtle differentiation of vision and of what is figurable and identifiable (cf. *Madonna with the Child Jesus and Saints Catherine and Magdalene*, Academy Galleries, Venice).

Through his frequent use of altar pieces and by positioning the maternal throne in his paintings under architectural vaults, which he himself has sculpted or painted, Bellini produces the same spatial outlook, relativizing the importance of figuration. Whether in the *Madonna, Child, Saints, and Angelic Musicians* (1487, Academy Galleries, Venice), or placed more appropriately into a real architectural setting, as in the triptychs of the Churches of Santa Maria dei Frari (1488) and San Zaccaria (1505), the painter sets himself off from his work. From a distance, the viewer's eye scans from top to bottom a mother who is projected from the painting but who does not dominate. As in Dante's eighth circle of heaven, music can henceforth be heard; the shout has burst through, and it is orchestrated following the greatest blossoming of luminous space. Angelic musicians are present, and other increasingly realistic and numerous characters multiply the frontal surface of the painting. Behind them, the background surface curves around the group, rounding out near the top, but, illuminated by a dark, transparent yellow, it seems to open up infinitely toward another spatiality that no longer needs delineation or stratification; it seems to float luminously, supported by the power of its own chromatic composition. These are the limits of representation, but also of geometrical framework, attained through a saturation of objects and architecture. But there is also a soaring movement beyond this over-fullness perfectly mastered through realistic representation.

Perhaps it would be impossible, or even useless, to search for the biographical landmarks of this journey leading from the "iconographic" mother to the fascinating mother-seductress, and then, passing through a threatening and fleeing mother to the luminous space where she surrogates herself. After the painter's "mysterious" birth, there remains, however, one intriguing biographical fact that may be significant. During the same years between 1480 and 1490 that mark the transformation of mystery, figuration, and the mother-child narrative into a search for space and light encircling and dominating them, Giovanni married and had a son. In 1485, he recorded the dowry of his wife Ginevra Bocheta, and in 1489, Ginevra lists a son Alvise as heir in her will. Between these two dates the child's birth must have occurred. Then did Ginevra die at that time? In any case, when Alvise died ten years later in 1499, he was already orphaned of his mother.

In the fifteen years between 1485 and 1499, Bellini's familial and paternal experiences along with the deaths of his wife and son accompanied, if they did not lead to, the upheaval involving both the psychology of Motherhood and his style. One will recall that the Madonnas in Lugano, São Paolo, the Academy Galleries in Venice, and the church at Frari were painted after his marriage. His newly acquired and soon lost family and paternity reversed the idealized notions of a Byzantine and greatly seductive mother of the years 1450 to 1480; from 1480 until 1500, this fascination changed into the feelings of controlled hostility or disappointment evident in the *Madonna with Two Trees* or the divisive vengeance of the little strangler in São Paolo; finally, without maternal mediation, it produced the ecstasy of Saint Francis, set off by a background of ecstatic green color. It is as if *paternity* were necessary in order to relive the archaic impact of the maternal body on man; in order to complete the investigation of a ravishing maternal jouissance but also of its terrorizing aggressivity; in order somehow to admit the threat that the male feels as much from the possessive maternal body as from his separation from it—a threat that he immediately returns to that body; and finally, in order, not to demystify the mother, but to find her an increasingly appropriate language, capable of capturing her specific imaginary jouissance, the jouissance on the border of primal repression, beyond, although always coexistent with, the imagery of full, mimetic, and true signs.

The final series of motherhood paintings, including the Madonna in Detroit (1500–1509), carries on and perfects Bellini's mastery of the style he created between 1480 and 1500. The mother's face again falls into calmness/absence, dreams of an unsignifiable experience. The infant's body, parallel and close to hers, nonetheless appears more easily separable. Light inundates the canvas; figures increase in number and landscapes extend deeper into the painting, sometimes splitting into different scenes, always divided by a central curtain or one covering two-thirds of the canvas on one side, thus producing two different perspectives: a shallow, frontal perspective and a deeper, converging perspective. The maternal figure increasingly appears as a *module*, a process, present only to justify this cleaved space; she is again the ἐργαστήριον (*ergasterion*), privileged space and living area. Moreover, the very human, that is, *psychological* passion between adult and child seems to be displaced from woman toward a man. The infant Jesus now clings to a saint with more dramatic confidence than he ever displayed for any of the Madonnas, as may be seen in the St. Christopher panel of the Saint Vincent Ferrer polyptych (1464–1468, San Giovanni e Paolo, Venice); or in the Saint Christopher Child Jesus couple in *Saints Christopher, Jerome* [or Saint John Chrysostome?] *and Augustine* (1513, Church of Saint John Chrysostome, Venice). Is not the object-oriented libido always masculine?

What becomes of this movement through maternal jouissance, once it has arrived at its luminous, colored imprint, devoid of object, figure, or spectacle? What happens to it in a Venice just discovering antiquity, humanism, the female body, carnal passion as supreme grace, Bembo's theories, and Polyphilus's dreams?

Bellini accepted secular or pagan commissions (portraits, allegorical studies, paintings lost in the Ducal Palace fire, and so on). But his reticence towards the new was shown when he procrastinated on Isabella d'Este's request despite Bembo's intervention on her behalf and even though his patron eventually asked merely for a simple *presepio*—an adoration of the shepherds which lent itself to a sacred-secular mixture. He yielded to fashion and probably to his patrons, however, when he painted *The Feast of the Gods* (1514, Washington); but its style is already that of Giorgione, and it includes obvious strokes by Titian. Nonetheless, those partaking in the feast still have the awkward appearance of guests at a carnival.

The most surprising of the paintings of his later years is probably the *Venus* in Vienna (1515). It shares the same division of pictorial space of the last Madonnas: one-third landscape, two-thirds fabric panel. But now, instead of the traditionally clad mother in the foreground, we have the nudity of a full-bodied young woman, sheltered by shadows against a luminous background landscape. Even though the style is Giorgione's and the body radiates no less sensuality than do the paintings of Bellini's young disciple, it is not the flesh's iridescence that captures our attention. Rather, it is still the unique light of Bellini's style, emanating not from the juxtaposition of volumes nor the isolation of forms (Leonardo's style), but from the luminous treatment of color itself, sparkling in its matter and through interplay with its counterpart, the complementary hues of the shadows. The colored light thus produces curved and open space, which is easily differentiated from the masses of light carving up the bodies and volumes in the canvases of other contemporary painters. This device, unique to Bellini and especially to this painting, manifests itself even more fully because of the interplay of mirrors, surrounding the body of the Nude, revealing by ricochet her face and neck. Through the perpendicular juxtaposition of mirrors, there appears a crack down the shadowed frontal part of the canvas, producing a bend in the representation and engendering a third space. Neither background nor foreground, it is the opening of one vista of the painting towards the viewer; it appears as inverted perspective, a reversal of the viewer-viewed point of view—enough to make every cubist dream. It is a reflexive glance, a circular look, careful to fragment space as much as possible by following the refraction of light rays.

Her face comes from the *Madonna with Blessing Child* (1509, Detroit), the *Madonna with Two Saints* (1490, Academy Galleries, Venice). The averted, modest, ecstatic, melancholic, or reticent gaze of the Madonnas here projects from the depths of the pupils to see itself, to encounter itself, not in the object-for-others that is the infant, nor even in the viewer (as the angle of the two mirrors opening towards the viewer might suggest), but in the pseudo-object made up by the mirror itself. And the mirror can do nothing more than to return the gaze. Face to face with primary narcissism, restraint persists along with a kind of statement of insurmountable limits: "This is how it is." The Virgin has come down from her clothed exile in an elsewhere that racked her. But the uncovered woman nevertheless remains split. On the one hand, there is the nude and passably erotic body; on the other, its fundamental entrapment by the mirror image, certainly her own, but whose slack, motherly stomach reminds us that she is only one point of view, an interplay of lights, unrepresentable, fleeting.

Through this *Woman and Mirror*, Bellini, now ninety years old, entered easily into the sex shop of his age. In two or three paintings (if we also count the *Allegory* in the Academy Galleries and the *Feast of the Gods* in Washington), he exhibited a connoisseur's mastery of the subject matter equal to that of Giorgione and Titian. Yet, he added his own special discovery, which the fashion of his time never let him display as such: a luminous coloration surpassing any representation of the nude body. This "sacred" element had long accompanied the image of his maternal bodies; since it was thus engendered by, but also already detached from, virginal figurations, as it was from all representations, Bellini was following, like a critic from the future, the object-oriented ostentation of his time, which nevertheless encountered and revealed his main preoccupation (jouissance)—but in still too thematic a manner, essentially tied to objects and deeply fetishistic, since he attached it to a body, in this instance the female body. In the end, the sex shop fulfilled its role for the old master, clearly conveying to the secular world just exactly what worked upon it, what affected it through a Madonna's veils. And still, his use of light vastly surpasses this thematic; it could not be fully appreciated until after Poussin, Cézanne, and Rothko.

Spaces and Glimmers

Saint Francis in Ecstasy (1480–1485, Frick Collection, New York) portrays the saint against a cascade of aquamarine volumes, almost entirely engulfed by their morning glow, fading into semidarkness at lower right. On the left, near the top of the painting, diagonally across from pulpit, book, and skull of the lower right corner, there appears another space, where a landscape, a donkey, and a great deal of light suggest the divine presence. This unfolding of the painting's surface into two planes, each with its own volume, is typical of Bellini's work. Each volume bends, twists, breaks, and fragments itself separately, producing a sense of torment among the represented forms. Yet, they are also homogenized into a single luminous mass by the green hues of the foreground and the orange hues of the background. This splitting/laminating of the surface is heightened by, among other elements, curving and broken lines, winding into a green spiral (a hill) in the lower-left foreground. Yet another spiral balances the first, near the top center, constituting the lower right angle of the backdrop. Consequently, the split/laminated surface of the painting, tormented by the luminous color of each section, finds in its left half a spiral movement that surges upwards, in contrast to the verticality of rocks on the right. Graphic constructions that divide, covered with iridescent colored masses that bind together this multiple surface: foreground/background, upper left-hand diagonal/lower right-hand diagonal, lower diagonal spiral on the left/centered diagonal spiral near the top, undulating left half-vertical right half. Perhaps the saint's ecstasy is precisely this union between the drawing's implacable fragmentation and a soft lining encompassing the fragments within two masses of luminous hues: green and orange. There is interplay among cutting traces, together with infinitesimal differentiations within one color, seeking itself within its own range, up to the borders of its complementarity, until it becomes lost in pure light.

In the *Madonna with the Child Jesus, Saints Catherine and Magdalene* (1490, Academy Galleries, Venice), angular, bending space no longer arises out of the graphic carving out of the drawing. Here the painting's surface constitutes a vault, as did the Frari triptych. But while the triptych's sense of curvature is produced by the curved back wall and arched ceiling, here the cupola effect is produced by the dark color becoming luminous. The outline of the robe covering head and rounded shoulders of the Virgin gives support to it, and the infant's upward gaze suggests it as well—one sees this at once. But the curvature is achieved essentially by the turning of the more saturated colors, filling the painting's forms and volumes, toward yellowish-white.

The brick reds or purples of the saints' garments, Mary's bluish-green robe, the deep orange of their flesh and the rust-maroon tint of their hair deepen or fade with each fold, running through the spectrum, within their own hue, between two invisible limits, from black, where color is extinguished, to bright yellow, where it dazzles. This treatment of color as such is accentuated by an elliptical placement of blinding flashes—exposed flesh changing to yellowish-pink, as in the upper curves of the three women's heads and lower curve of their hands and the baby. The brown background is one of Bellini's fundamental discoveries. Saturated with black, green, and red, the compactness of this brown tint inverts into its opposite—a vague, liquid, invisible color, a sparkling medium engendering and suspending bare brightness. The curved space, repeating the curves of a nude body, results from subdued color moving across the limits of its scale to the two extremes of the spectrum. A high level of sublimation is reached at the very point where anguish appears—an anguish that nudity might otherwise have provoked and that we call eroticism.

In *The Sacred Allegory* (1490–1500, Uffizi, Florence), the tormented graphic nature of forms, fragmented by outlines but bound together by color, is present in the background. That reminder of the graphic space of *Saint Francis in Ecstasy*, however, here becomes geometrical; more Greek, more rational in the painting's foreground, where a terrace railing opens up three sides of a rectangular volume in front of the viewer. The floor is broken up into red and black squares and hexagons, while the tree of life delineates three-fourths of its surface. Light here is not engendered, as in *Madonna with the Child Jesus, Saints Catherine and Magdalene* to create the impression of vaulted space; nor does it burst forth from a corner in order to spiral, twist, and harmonize at the same time, as it did in *Saint Francis in Ecstasy*. It simply exists as an incandescence within the dominating orange that lights up the browns, reds, and whites, from right to left and merges into blue sky at the top center of the painting—flight, hearth, and azure opening. Because of the dominance of variegated yellows, the wavelike or broken features of the many planes of the background, as well as the regular geometry of the foreground, open up on infinity. There are no bent surfaces and no domes. Pure luminosity bathes each figuration, including those that firmly mark the fragmented spaces, and thus allows blinding light to predominate through the yellows. It marks the limits of representation in and for which a few colored-object elements condense—unfailingly, but so as to escape all the more easily—as reds, greens, blacks, and blues, in lieu of robes, trees, sky, mountains, human and animal figures. Now all figural representation appears as a mirage under a yellow, desert sun. This allegorical painting is said to represent Saint Bernard's commentary on the first fourteen verses of Psalm 84, the "restoration of Israel." As Grace, Truth, Justice, and Peace discuss humanity's salvation through the Incarnation, a finally nonthreatening Yahweh himself appears, announcing the arrival of justice and peace. The three women in the painting incorporate three aspects of this *sacra converzatione*: on the left, Maria Aeterna represents Grace and Peace; on the right, a second figure represents a condensation of Truth and Justice; and on the throne, Mary assumes the place of the Father. If this interpretation of the painting is correct, we are in fact confronted with a both thematic and chromatic representation of harmony. Far from suppressing spatial or color differences, such harmony distributes them within an open infinity as integration of the limits separating figures, drawings, and nuances in color and as their endless bonding together. This is the sublimation of a totalizing power, pushed to the limits of representability: form *and* color.

The interplay of mirrors confronting the nude Venus, as understood through Bellini, shows that primary narcissism is the threshold on which pictorial experience ceases and whence it works its effects. If primal repression is just another expression for primary narcissism, then provoking one and the other, working on them, and analyzing them—without ever being able to remove them—must be the *cause* of *jouissance*, and here, more precisely, of jouissance through and within pictorial representation. It can only result in a shattering of figuration and form in a space of graphic lines and colors, differentiated until they disappear in pure light.

Our long biographical and historical, sacred and figural journey has shown that for Bellini, motherhood is nothing more than such a luminous spatialization, the ultimate language of a jouissance at the far limits of repression, whence bodies, identities, and signs are begotten.

10

PLACE NAMES

Childhood Language, Infantile Language

Twice during the past few centuries Western reason perceived that its role of being a servant to meaning was imprisoning. Wishing to escape, it turned toward and became haunted by childhood. Witness Rousseau and Freud—two crises of classical and positivist rationality. And two revolutions loomed on its horizon: one in political economy (seeking its status in Marx), the other in the speaking subject (articulated today by modern literature's disruption of the Christian Word). Before Sade and Solzhenitsyn, who spell out jouissance and horror, analytic discourse was given a privileged foil, a nexus of life and language (of species and society)—the child.

It was as if Reason were suddenly neither satisfied simply to test its restraining bonds by confronting texts, nor to strain meaning by writing the speaking being's identity as fiction; it was forced, instead, to face reproduction of the species (the boundary between "nature" and "culture") and the varied attitudes toward it. Reason was thus transcended by a *heterogeneous element* (biology: life) and by a *third party* (*I/you* communication is displaced by *it*: the child). These challenge the speaker with the fact that he is not whole, but they do so in a manner altogether different from that in which the obsessed person's wretched consciousness ceaselessly signifies his bondage to death. For if death is the Other, life is a third party; and as this signification, asserted by the child, is disquieting, it might well unsettle the speaker's paranoid enclosure. Without this advent of the real (imposed by the child but blocked by the myth of the child), one belief still persists: either men and women exist in and for the romantic or surrealist exchange of ideas or sex; or else sublimation can occur with nothing left over, instinctual drive being totally committed (in Existentialist fashion) to Lifework or History—when it does not foster perversion as the final guarantee of order.

Two thousand years ago the child Jesus came to circumvent these two dead ends, but having become a ritual, like all rituals he quickly became a substitute. He even became a whole history—Christianity. By uncovering childbirth from beneath kinship structures, whose subjective and political outgrowths are traced in the Bible, Christianity may have interfered with Judaism's attraction to obsessional and paranoid confinement. At the same time, it gave a place to women—not necessarily a symbolic progress but certainly a biological and social necessity. And yet, by celebrating Man in the child, that is, by making the child into a universal fetish, Christianity foreclosed the possibility (of which it nevertheless had an inkling) of breaking the cycle of religion; just the same, it was the last possibility of doing so. For where life and discourse come together, that is where the destiny of subjects is caught up in the chain of civilization. Today, the pill and the Pope know this indeed.

The discovery of the Freudian unconscious severs the always possible umbilication of man to the child; the notion of "infantile sexuality" allows for the examination, not of he who does not speak (*in-fans*) but of what within the speaker is not yet spoken, or will always remain unsaid, unnamable within the gaps of speech. It is true that the child buttresses the fundamental premises of Freudian thought (the theory of instinctual drives, rejection-negativity, the emergence of symbolism, the stages marked by the Oedipus complex, et cetera). The child was, however, by Freud's own admission, the place of an "error" that we shall now try to read more closely. Such an error cannot be righted when the mind allows itself to be taken in by the inextricable alternative of "cause" and "effect," as Freud rarely did; compared with which Freud's "errors" have the advantage of showing his thought to be rooted in the eternal return of parent/child: "Am I parent or child, cause or effect, chicken or egg?" So that one might observe, perhaps, that the child is a myth (Oedipal) told by parents to their parents, without which there would be nothing but children, that is, Oedipi unbeknownst to themselves. Were the Greeks, who talked among themselves of having been children, the most lucid parents of history? This might have permitted them to circumscribe aggression (childlike, hereafter termed Oedipal) in order to proceed towards *law* in the *City*.

Let us restate a few facts. Freud married in 1886 and had six children (three girls and three boys) between 1887 and 1895. During this period he completed his neurological research, published his findings on aphasia and infantile paralysis (1891), and began his research on hysteria, through hypnosis at first, leading to the publication in 1895, with Breuer, of *Studies on Hysteria*. That same year marked the birth of Anna (whose analytical research would essentially center on childhood), the end of the family's reproductive cycle, and the beginning of Freud's friendship with Fliess. He would soon begin a self-analysis within the framework of that relationship whose homosexual tenor he later emphasized. He used the word *psychoanalysis* one year later, in 1896. Yet, it was only after the death of his father in 1897 that Freud wrote the inaugural work of psychoanalysis, which set it free of the substantialism, medicine, and catharsis that were still perceptible in *Studies on Hysteria; The Interpretation of Dreams*, of 1897, which situates it within the field of signifying articulations, was published in 1898.

At this moment, Freud introduced a change in the conception of what he had thought to be the *cause* of hysteria: *parental seduction*.[1] FIRST ASSUMPTION: hysteria is set off by parental seduction during childhood. Freud promoted that theory until 1896, the year of his father's death, suggesting that Jacob Freud must have seduced him (letter to Fliess, Feb. 11, 1897), and recognizing that his eldest daughter, Mathilde, was possibly the object of his own attempts at seduction (letter to Fliess, May 31, 1897, several months before his father's death).[2] SECOND ASSUMPTION: that seduction was only a hysterical fantasy merging with a paranoid attitude, and thus serving as a screen for his childhood autoeroticism. Thus the conception of an essentially autoerotic childhood sexuality emerged. THIRD MOVEMENT: Freud also allowed for the child's genital desires and proceeded towards the conception of the Oedipus complex. Although this happened in the last years of the century, written evidence for such a stand does not emerge until 1905 ("Sexuality in the Aetiology of the Neuroses") and in 1906 (*Three Essays on the Theory of Sexuality*).

Between the first assumption (the parent seduces the child and leads it to neurosis) and the second (the seducer is the autoerotic and polymorphous perverse child), two events occurred: Freud ceased having children and his father died. The reversal of his position with respect to the parent-child relationship (the child becoming the agent of seduction), thus corresponding to those events, is dramatically evoked in two subsequent texts: *On the History of the Psychoanalytic Movement* (1914) and *An Autobiographical Study* (1925). Here, Freud terms parental seduction an "erroneous idea" that could have been "fatal to the young science."[3] The distress provoked by the discovery of that mistaken path was so great that he wrote, "Like Breuer, I almost gave up analysis." Why did he nevertheless continue? The explanation is succinct, to say the least: "Perhaps I persevered because I no longer had any choice and could not then begin again at something else. At last came the reflection that, after all, one had no right to despair because one has been deceived in one's expectations; one must revise those expectations."[4]

Acknowledging an end ("one cannot begin again": to have children?) and a feeling of despair (the father is dead: no more seducer?), he at the same time recovered control ("one does not have the right": to abandon the father, no longer to be father, to abdicate paternity?). Such a reading seems to be supported by an examination of his later text, *An Autobiographical Study* (1925): "When, however, I was at last obliged to recognize that these scenes of seduction had never taken place . . . I was for some time completely at a loss [from 1897 to 1900 approximately] . . . I had in fact stumbled for the first time upon the Oedipus complex [in its disguise of seduction fantasy]."[5] Could the discovery of the Oedipus complex, and thereby of infantile sexuality, and thus the beginning of the modern conception of the child, have been produced through an inverted Oedipal complex? Could the "Oedipus complex" be the discourse of mourning for his father's death? As neurosis is the negative of perversion, could that discourse represent, in like manner, the negative of the guilt experienced by a son who is forced by the signifier to take his father's place? The Freudian conception of the child would thus provide the basis for paternal discourse, the solid foundation for the paternal function, and consequently the guarantee, both present and ultimate, of socialization. That may be a paternal vision of childhood and thus a limited one; it is, however, lucidly presented to support the inevitability of the symbolic and/or social code. It is, therefore, an ethical, biblical vision.

So, after having fathered six children *in eight years*, loving them as a devoted father (there seems to be agreement on this), having admitted to being the possible seducer of his daughter but also the victim of his father's seduction, "one can no longer begin again." In addition to this recognition of closure, of disillusionment with respect to the hysterical body, the libido as substance, and "seductive eroticism"— is it the recognition of a sexual dead end?—there came his father's death and Freud's feelings of guilt toward him (no, the seducer cannot be my father, the seducer is me, the child of this father; now I am also the father [of Mathilde]; therefore the seducer can only be the child); this is accompanied at once by the desire to take his place, to assume the moral, paternal function ("One has no right to despair because he has been disappointed," Freud writes). The father is dead, long live the father that I am: *there where it (id) was shall I (ego) come to be.*[6] The "child" is what remains of such a becoming, the result of subtracting the utterance of guilt from the utterance of mastery: "Seduction during childhood retained a certain share, though a humbler one, in the etiology of neuroses. But the seducers turned out as a rule to have been older children."[7] We thus come to the shaping of this image of the child-parent, the seducing child, a child always already older, born into the world with compound drives, erogenous zones, and even genital desires. With the end of the reproductive cycle and spurred by his father's death, Freud's self-analysis led him to that telescoping of father and child, resulting in none other than Oedipus: "I had in fact stumbled for the first time upon the Oedipus complex."[8]

The child-parent or the parent-child, thus presented to analytical practice, joins cause and effect, origin and becoming, space and time, to produce that specific twist of psychoanalytic discourse that brings to mind the Heraclitan αἰών: cyclical time and also space where the Greek thinker happened to see the poet at play—the poet who alone maintains the discourse of a child giving birth (to a father?).[9] Instinctuality is simultaneously revealed as innate and hereditary, but, within the Freudian framework, it is already protected from substantialist interpretations. For although the child enters the world with polymorphous instinctual drives, these conflict with repression and the latter produces the several variants of libido fixation ("subjective structures"). It follows that neurosis—or the speaking subject—can never be dealt with at the level of drive, or through a child at zero degree of symbolism, but rather always through a narrative "texture," that is, a texture of language and phantasm: "It was only after the introduction [within childhood's instinctual experience] of this element of hysterical fantasies [the parental seduction fantasy] that the *texture* of the neurosis and its relation to the patient's life became intelligible."[10]

Nevertheless, this dismantling of the Christian-Rousseauist myth of childhood is accompanied by a problematic endorsement. Projected into the supposed place of childhood, and therefore universalized, one finds the features that are particular to adult discourse; the child is endowed with what is dictated by adult memory, always distorted to begin with; the myth of human continuity persists (from child to parent, Sameness prevails). In like manner, the function of the familial context in the *precocious* development of the child (before puberty, before Oedipus, but also before the "mirror stage") tends to be minimized. This is only too evident in ego-centered trends in child psychology, but also in a psychoanalytic practice that posits the subject as dating from the "mirror stage." The most important debates and innovations in psychoanalysis have consequently and necessarily been centered in this problem. The point is indeed to emphasize the heterogeneity between the libidinal-signifying organization in infancy (let us call it the "semiotic disposition") and the "symbolic" functioning of the speaker following language acquisition and the consequent parental identifications. On the other hand, and at the same time, this precocious, presymbolic organization is grasped by the adult only as regression—jouissance or schizophrenic psychosis. Thus, the difficulty, the impossibility that beset such an attempt at gaining access to childhood: the real stakes of a discourse on childhood within Western thought involve a confrontation between thought and what it is not, a wandering at the limits of the thinkable. Outside of poetic practice (thinking a dissipated language, Heraclitan limit, reinvention of materialism), the analytical solutions to this question (this Freudian "error") always appear problematic: Jung's dead end with its archetypal configurations of libidinal substance taken out of the realm of sexuality and placed in bondage to the archaic mother; the empiricist precision of Melanie Klein's "partial objects" and subsequently the effort, by Winnicott and his followers to posit within the "potential space" between mother and nursing infant a libido without drive, therefore without object, goal, or time—all of which remain specific attributes of the adult speaker's libido; the desiring machines of schizophrenics without signifiers; or finally, in a new and radical way that nevertheless remains all-encompassing within the Name-of-the-Father (as with Lacan), removing the unnamable from childhood and placing it within the *real*, which is at the same time impossible and inevitably persistent within the real-imaginary-symbolic triad.

As distinguished from speculation, *transference*, however, seems to indicate that the signifying disposition that Winnicott calls the "pre-objective libido" (therefore not the Freudian libido),[11] which can be detected in the nonspeaking child, persists beneath the secondary repression imposed as soon as language is acquired; it also continues, through the formation of the Oedipus complex, in all speaking beings, establishing their psychotic foundation or their capacity for jouissance—of which the aesthetic is one among several. This disposition is set out and articulated, from its very beginning (which remains with us as space become permanent time), by *the solutions that parents recently discovered in answer to the sexual inanity manifested by the child.* For the hysteric child to attribute its neurosis to parental seduction is probably an instance of paranoia. But, through the seduction myth, it sees itself as being attached by drive (even before desire) to this object of love extolled by its parents in their denial of the sexual nonrelation that the child's coming punctuates.

Freud's error, however, has still not affected linguistics, which remains universal and Cartesian in its study of individual "languages," phenomenological in its approach to discourse. "Childhood language"—a theoretical mirage—has become for psycholinguistics the privileged ground where the contradictions and dead ends of linguistic rationality are attested. Some see in "childhood language" an empirical demonstration of generative grammar's pertinence (deep structure exists because it functions as such in the child). Others posit a difference between language and logic in children, on the one hand, and in adults on the other. But, in trying to describe the former, they use categories and even unqualified models (always more or less taken from generative grammar) contingent upon the latter. This leads, in the first instance, to the use of childhood language as an illustration of theory, probably amputated, but intended to be completed through maturation. The result, in the second, is a floundering in empiricism, for no concept of the subject, other than one bound to Cartesian logic, is available to account for the differences one supposedly detects in the child's logic or syntax. The presyntactic phases of childhood *semiosis* remain outside of this investigation; but also excluded are all semantic latencies due to sexual and family differences, which are integrated or short-circuited, each time in specific fashion, within the syntactic repression constituting the grid of any language as universal system, and which become manifest in either syntactic liberties or lexical variations of childhood discourse.[12]

It might, on the other hand, be possible to posit as "object" of analysis not "childhood language" but rather "infantile language," in the sense that Freud speaks of infantile sexuality—a telescoping of parent and child. We would then be concerned with the attentiveness that the adult, through his still infantile sexuality, is able to perceive in the discourse of a child (boy or girl) while it refers him to that level where his "own" language is never totally rationalized or normated according to Cartesian linguistics, but where it always remains an "infantile language." Thus it would constitute an analytical attentiveness to language, within the dual relationship transference between adult and child; an analysis that is applied through phantasmic or mythical contents (which have been until now the sole objects of psychoanalysis and child psychology) to the "minimal" components of language (phonic, lexical, and syntactic operations; logico-syntactic categories). The child therefore becomes the real from which we begin our analysis, through minimal components, of our (any) language's *infantile* attributes.

This particular attentiveness to the psychoanalytic conditions underlying language structures might invite a probably *transferential*, or more precisely, maternal attitude toward the child. Cannot the history of post-Freudian child psychology, culminating in the works by Spitz and Winnicott, be summarized as a shift from the paternal, Freudian attentiveness to a maternal attention? With all the progress and setbacks such a phantasmatic attitude induces in men and women analysts . . .

For a woman, the arrival of a child breaks the autoerotic circle of pregnancy (when her jouissance recalls the saint who becomes one with her god, inaccessible and yet consubstantial with her instinctual drive during her passion) and brings about what, for a woman, is the difficult account of a relationship with an other: with an "object" and with love. Is it not true that a woman is a being for whom the One, and therefore the Other, is not taken for granted? And that in order to reach this constantly altered One, to have access to the symbolic-thetic level, which requires castration and object, she must tear herself from the daughter-mother symbiosis, renounce the undifferentiated community of women and recognize the father at the same time as the symbolic? . . . It is precisely the child that, for a *mother* (as opposed to a *genetrix*), constitutes an *access* (an excess) toward the Other. The child is the removal of what was only a graft during pregnancy: an *alter ego* capable (or not) of replacing a maternal narcissism henceforth integrated within a "being for it." Neither for itself nor in itself, but for it . . . The mother of a son (henceforth the generic "infant" no longer exists) is a *being* confronted with a *being-for-him*. The mother of a daughter replays in reverse the encounter with her own mother: differentiation or leveling of beings, glimpses of oneness or paranoid primary identification phantasized as primordial substance. In both cases, the well-known relationship with an object—which exists only as object of love—is founded only as a third-person relationship: neither *I* nor *you* within a relationship of identification or lust, but *he* (*she*). Love replaces narcissism in a third person that is external to the act of discursive communication. Hence, "God is love": it is for this very reason that he does not exist, except to be imagined as child for a woman. Here again one acknowledges the brilliant inspiration of Christian tradition.

From this point on, for the mother—not for the genetrix—the child is an *analyzer.* He releases the hysteric woman's anguish, often hidden, denied, or deferred in its paranoid course, directing it toward others or toward the array of consumer goods. It is an anguish that brings the mother to grips with castration (that very castration that a number of "women" or genetrices deny, because for them the child is the cork that stops, seals the community of the species, and allows for the usurpation of the father's place while refusing to recognize it). The death drive is loosened across its entire dramatic gamut extending from the fury of Lady Macbeth to self-sacrifice, always for the same love object, the third person, the child. Throughout these meanderings where the analyzer leads his mother, acknowledgment of castration prevents murder; it is its opposite and opposes it. For this very reason the mother is able to analyze where the genetrix fails (by blocking, with the "baby," any access to the symbolic disposition through the fantasy of a substantialist fusion within that generative matter where mothers incorporate their children) and where the saint succeeds (when, in her passion for the symbolic, her own body becomes the exalted, sanctioned sign of denial): she keeps open the enclosures where paranoid persons anchor themselves. Maternity knots and unknots paranoia—the ground on which hysterics stand.

It is clear that "neuropsychological maturation" and language acquisition cannot be taken for granted under these conditions. In all likelihood, the structures of any language inevitably carry the imprint of the mother-analyzer relationship. And that is enough to confound any linguistic theory.

Space Causes Laughter

Current attempts to put an end to human subjecthood (to the extent that it involves subjection to meaning) by proposing to replace it with *spaces* (Borromean knots, morphology of catastrophies), of which the speaker would be merely a phenomenal actualization, may seem appealing. We must not forget, however, that such *formants* (even if their refinements lead only to the addressee's catharsis, and they do not function as "models" of a referent-object) have their particular source in the "logical activity specifically linked to language."[13] Husserl's considerations on the spatial intuitions of the Greeks leading up to Euclid have lost none of their epistemological force: the history of human *forming* is rooted in language as a system of propositions.[14] No forming can transcend its origin—meaning, as it is posited by that predication peculiar to language. If the metaphysical solidarity of "meaning," "origin," and "forming" is thus posited as the limit of any attempt at clarification (and also, therefore, of linguistics), and perhaps also of all analysis (and perhaps of psychoanalysis), it still seems clear that any spatial representation provided for within a universal language is necessarily subject to teleological reason, contrary to what "romantic minds" might maintain, attracted as they are to the "mythico-magical."[15]

The history of the speaking being (spatially bound precisely because he speaks) is only spatial variation,[16] never shattering the limits of the speaking/forming, but rather displacing it by means of a *praxis* or a *technè*. It is henceforth clear that meaning's closure can never be challenged by another *space*, but only by a different way of *speaking*: another enunciation, another "literature." There exists, on the other hand, an epistemological bent toward elucidation that is not, as Husserl postulates, the "destiny" of the speaking being; rather, it is *one* of its practices, *one* variation of signifiance not limited to what is "universally intelligible"—madness and literature are its witnesses. If we remain with this tendency, we must choose between two directions: either we delineate the history of spaces (we practice epistemology), or we investigate what Husserl calls "human forming." The second alternative inevitably merges with Freudian preoccupations: the analysis of the "origins" of forming/speaking follows the path of the Freudian "error" mentioned above.

Any attentiveness to "infantile language" (as defined above) seems to be located at that ambiguous point where psychoanalysis opens up the limits of phenomenological meaning by indicating its conditions of production, and where phenomenology encloses the transferential disintegration of meaning—as soon as the latter is being articulated as either demonstrative or simply "universally intelligible" clauses.

To repeat the question that the infant-analyst puts to maternal attentiveness before any mirror shows him any representation whatsoever, before any language begins to encode his "idealities": what about the paradoxical *semiosis* of the newborn's body, what about the "semiotic *chora*,"[17] what about this "space" prior to the sign, this archaic disposition of primary narcissism that a poet brings to light in order to challenge the closure of meaning ("nothing will have taken place but the place," certainly, if not "at heights so far removed that a place fuses with the beyond [. . .] the bewildering successive clash of a whole account in formation . . ."—Mallarmé).

Neither request nor desire, it is an invocation, an anaclisis.[18] Memories of bodily contact, warmth, and nourishment: these underlie the breath of the newborn body as it appeals to a source of support, a fulfillment of care that Spitz properly termed the "diatrophic mother." Vocal and muscular contractions, spasms of the glottis and motor system—all make up for the absence of intrauterine life components. Voice is the vehicle of that call for help, directed at a frustrated memory, in order to insure, first through breath and warmth, the survival of an ever premature human being; and this is undoubtedly significant for the acquisition of language, which will soon be articulated along the same vehicle. Every cry is, psychologically and projectively, described as a cry of distress, up to and including the first vocalizations, which seem to constitute distress calls, in short: anaclises. The newborn body experiences three months of such anaclitic "facilitations" without reaching a stable condition.

Faced with these anaclises, the adult—essentially the mother—offers a disturbed reception, a mobile receptacle, which fashions itself on the invocation, follows its winding course, and eventually accents it with a surge of anguish that the newborn analyzer's body produces in the analysand. From this time on, we must reckon with the mother's desire, beyond which it is hard for her to go, to maintain the newborn child within the invocation: the child as adjunct to the breast, a wealth of her own, may be an analyzer, but it is an analyst lacking any interpretation and who thus locks mother and child within the regression of primary masochism. This is the precise moment for either the "optimal frustration" that Spitz requires of the mother with regard to the child, or Winnicott's mysterious "good enough mother": they are intended to break the primary narcissism within which mother and child are wrapped up, from *anaclisis* to *diatrophy*, so that, with the advent of autoeroticism, the door is finally open to a relationship with the object, at the same time as representation and language make their appearance.

Before this step becomes effective, however, and within the subtle drift from primary narcissism to autoeroticism, the "good enough mother" with her "optimal frustration" scores a point: laughter.

It is perhaps enough that the mother knows both how to *respond to* and to *stop* the anaclisis, so that she might stall, settle, and anchor herself there. Providing an axis, a projection screen, a limit, a curb for the infant's invocation may be what, in the maternal function, relates to the paternal one, probably characterized, at best, by *absence* or *refusal* encoded in presence itself. As the nervous system matures, it probably assumes (and sometimes takes over) the mobile support function provided by the mother/the father, while being influenced by it in other instances.

Voice, hearing, and sight are the archaic dispositions where the earliest forms of discreteness emerge. The breast, given and withdrawn; lamplight capturing the gaze; intermittent sounds of voice or music—all these meet with anaclisis (according to a temporal sequence probably programmed, too, by the particular aptitude of each child), hold it, and thus inhibit and absorb it in such a way that it is discharged and abated through them: early "defenses" against the aggressivity of a (pseudo-) drive (without goal). At that point, breast, light, and sound become a *there*: a place, a spot, a marker. The effect, which is dramatic, is no longer quiet but laughter. The imprint of an archaic moment, the threshold of space, the "chora" as primitive stability absorbing anaclitic facilitation, produces laughter. There is not yet an outside, and the things that made the newborn laugh at about two and one-half months (after the satisfaction of immediate needs produced the hallucinatory laughter of the first weeks) are simply markers of something in the process of becoming stability. But neither external nor internal, neither outside nor inside, such markers are noticeable only because they slow down anaclisis: they do not stop it. One might detect in them the inception of spatiality as well as *sublimation*.

Those scattered and funny moments become projected—archaic synthesis—onto the stable support of the mother's face, the privileged receiver of laughter at about three months. It is then that the narcissism of the initial mother-child symbiosis slips toward autoeroticism; here one observes the emergence of a body parcelled into eroticizable "objects" (essentially oral). Oral eroticism, the smile at the mother, and the first vocalizations are contemporaneous: Spitz's well-known "first point of psychic organization"[19] is already one complex semiotic phenomenon presaged by others.

The inaugural sublimation, in most cases visual, brings us not only to the foundations of narcissism (specular gratification) but to the riant wellsprings of the imaginary. The imaginary takes over from childhood laughter: it is a joy without words. Chronologically and logically long before the mirror stage (where the Same sees itself altered through the well-known opening that constitutes it as representation, sign, and death),[20] the semiotic disposition makes it start as riant spaciousness. During the period of indistinction between "*same*" and "*other*" infant and mother, as well as between "subject" and "object," while no space has yet been delineated (this will happen with and after the mirror stage—birth of the sign), the semiotic *chora* that arrests and absorbs the motility of the anaclitic facilitations relieves and produces laughter.

Orality plays an essential role in this primary fixation-sublimation: appropriation of the breast, the so-called "paranoid" certainty of the nursing infant that he has been in possession of it, and his ability to lose it after having had his fill. What should not be obscured is the importance of the anal "instinctual drive" from this period on: the child has a secure anal discharge while, balancing that loss, it incorporates the breast. Anal loss, accompanied by considerable expenditure of muscular motility, combined with the satisfaction of incorporating the breast, probably encourages projecting facilitation into this visible or audible point that gives the infant a glimpse of space and produces laughter.

The simultaneity of laughter with first vocalizations has long been recognized.[21] And the visual motility/fixation articulation as substratum of archaic semiotic spaciousness as well as laughter seems, moreover, to be borne out by belated childhood laughter. As we know, children lack a sense of humor (humor presupposes the superego and its bewildering). But they laugh easily when motor tension is linked to vision (a caricature is a visualization of bodily distortion, of an extreme, exaggerated movement, or of an unmastered movement); when a child's body is too rapidly set in motion by the adult (return to a motility defying its fixation, space, and place); when a sudden stop follows a movement (someone stumbles and falls). The speed-continuity of movement and its checks—punctuation of the discontinuous: an archaic topos that produces laughter and probably supports Bergson's psychology of laughter and Freud's jokes as well. The *chora* is indeed a strange "space": the rapidity and violence of the facilitations are localized at a point that absorbs them, and they return like a boomerang to the invoking body, without, however, signifying it as separate; they stop there, impart the jolt—laughter. Because it was bounded but not blocked, the rate of facilitation discards fright and bursts into a jolt of laughter. Instability, "bewildering clash," "a whole account in formation" . . . We have either a riant, porous boundary, or a blocking barrier of earnest sullenness—the child gets one or the other from its mother. Either a hysterical mother defying her own mother through parental identification, or a mother subjugated to her's, perpetually seeking symbolic recognition. Either one determines, as early as this "first point of psychic organization," attitudes whose peaks lie in imaginative freedom on the one hand, and ritualistic obsession on the other.

Even more belated dispositions of laughter[22] seem to commemorate stages of this archaic laughter-space—the ambivalence of facilitation (fright/peace, invocation/discharge, motility/check) as well as the porousness of boundaries or of the point of fixation. A sense of humor seems to build up, beginning with such semiotic underpinning, both upon the inhibition of autoeroticism (prescribed by parents) and upon its removal within childhood situations where parental authority or its substitute is weakened. The superego recognizes the ego as faltering vis-à-vis inhibition but, by a leap—shattered movement, space—reconstitutes it as invulnerable and therefore laughing. The *personal* (ego, body) depends on or is constituted by a counterpoise (the point of projection: lamp, mother, parents) that burdens and dominates it but, without being definitively separated (neither barring nor blocking facilitation), by its permissive distance allows the body to discover itself again, relaxed and free of anguish, which is removed elsewhere; a nimble sort of fun is what remains. An inhibition is thus built up for laughter, but as *existing elsewhere*: a set place, always there, but separate from the body, which can, only under these conditions, constitute itself as "personal" and reach jouissance at a distance. At this stage we have the necessary conditions that, avoiding inhibition through laughter, constitute the semiotic disposition and insure its maintenance within the symbolic. The preconditions for language acquisition are given at this point; their modulations involve the entire neurotic gamut of inhibitions and anguish that characterizes the speaking being's destiny.

This distant place that absorbs, defers,[23] and therefore sublimates anguish is the prototype of the *object* much as it is of the "personal":

the body that removes fear to a constant and distant location (the mother) can transfer its place over to what had been an amorphous mass and henceforth becomes a territory of markers, points of fixation, and discharges: the autoerotic body, the body proper.

In order, however, that this point of discharge might acquire another, different existence, one which will form a space, it must be repeated. Rhythm, a sequence of linked instants, is immanent to the *chora* prior to any signified spaciousness: henceforth, *chora* and rhythm, space and time coexist. Laughter is the evidence that the instant *took place*: the space that supports it signifies time. Located elsewhere, distant, permissive, always already past: such is the *chora* that the mother is called upon to produce with her child so that a semiotic disposition might exist. In the same way, later, after the acquisition of language, the child's laughter is one of a past event: because a prohibition has existed it can be overcome and relegated to the past—thus a weakened and masterable replica represents it from then on.

Infantile Space Names

Winnicott's "potential space,"[24] elaborated by a "transitional object,"[25] perfects the necessary conditions for semiotic functioning and transition to language acquisition.

One might, following M. A. K. Halliday,[26] say that prior to the appearance of a truly articulated language, vocalizations are used and endowed with "linguistic functions." Halliday calls them "meaning" functions, but a reformulation of Winnicott's position with respect to language could supply a better phrase: "potential meaning functions." A potential meaning, then, supported in its analytic circumstances by transitional objects, would be, somewhere between the ninth and sixteenth months, differentiated into a full range of functions, described in adult terms as instrumental, regulatory, interactive, personal, heuristic, and imaginative.[27] "Potential meaning" appears phonically in a variety of vocalizations (in varying and specific degrees, according to the child),[28] which eventually grow weaker and are reduced to a rising-falling intonation approximating that of the adult sentence.

According to Halliday, two new functions appear before the second year—the *pragmatic* function (a fusion of instrumental and regulatory functions) and the *mathetic* function (fusion of the personal and heuristic ones). That already implies a complex process of ideation and transformation of the "potential space," after the "mirror stage," into a signifiable space of representation. The child, *intervening* (as it performs one of those functions) and *observing* (as it performs another), encodes them into intonation (rising in the former case, falling in the latter) but, better still, it encodes them into a complex gestural semiotics that is difficult to describe.

While it is true that pseudomorphemes and even pseudophrases emerge during this period, they remain holophrastic: they are vocalizations, they designate the place or object of enunciation (the "topic"), whereas the motor or vocal gesture (intonation) serves as predicate (the "comment").

We note that beginning with the "first point of psychic organization," light-giving marker or mother's face, which produced laughter along with the first vocalizations, the future speaker is led to separate such points into *objects* (transitional at first, then simply objects) and add to them *no longer laughter but phonation*—archetype of the morpheme, condensation of the sentence. As if *the laughter that makes up space had become, with the help of maturation and repression, a "place name."*

Primitive naming very often makes use of adverbs of position, anaphoric demonstratives (*this, that*) or, more generally, "topic" anaphora referring to an object either external or internal to the body proper and to the practical, immediate environment; observable in the first childhood verbalizations, it is always related to a "space"—a *point* that henceforth becomes *object* or *referent*.

Current research on the language of children between two and three years old has shown that 50 percent of the utterances of two-year-olds are of the type, *that's a* followed by a *noun phrase*, the percentage falling to 15 percent at the age of three to three-and-a-half years.[29] The archaic appearance of anaphoric demonstratives is accompanied by other archaic phenomena that have their roots in the first vocalizations and echolalias concomitant to the constitution of the semiotic *chora*: glottal stops and stress (a play on intensity as well as on frequencies of vowel sounds).

Psycholinguists are well aware that the child, before using more or less regular syntax, makes utterances that come closer to the *topic-comment* model than to the *subject-predicate* one.[30] Although admittedly the relevancy of the two syntactic models could be discussed *ad nauseam*, we see here a recurrence of the spatial marker, which not only initiates the semiotic disposition but also shores up the first syntactic acquisitions.

It may be worth going over the semantic functions of the anaphoric demonstratives that are found in the *topic* position in utterances of 50 percent of young French-speaking children. As Damourette and Pichon point out, demonstratives (*ce, cet, cette, celui, celui-ci, celui-là, eux*: from the Latin *ecce*) provide a determination resulting from a state of *presence* and *proximity*; but they also have an *inciting* value, thus relating to the subject of enunciation, beyond what is being signified (such a value informs *ça*: "*Ça, donnez-moi que j'aille acheter votre esclave*"— Molière, *L'Etourdi*, II, 6); the spatial function can become temporal ("*d'ici demain,*" "*en deçà,*" "*en ça*"); finally, demonstratives have a function that could be termed "metalinguistic," for they refer to other signs within the utterance or in the context ("*il faut faire ci, il faut faire ça*"; "*un secret aussi gardé que celui gardé dans ce message*"; "*accepter, dans des circonstances comme celles actuelles, un pouvoir écrasant par son poids*"; or the pleonastic expression, "*c'est le prendre qu'elle veut*"). Finally, let me restate the position of Benveniste, for whom the shifter (*déictique*) is the mark of *discourse* within the system of a particular language—meaning that it is defined essentially through its use by individual speakers. Thus the demonstrative, in modern French, points to the enunciation rather than the utterance (summoning the subject; referring to a place outside of the system of discourse/referent), to a sign (it breaks up the signifying chain and refers to it metalinguistically), or to itself (it can be auto-referential). All these functions, taken collectively, make of the anaphoric demonstrative a complex "shifter," straddling several functions of language, keeping the enunciation at a distance in several ways—away from the subject, the referent, signs, and itself.

A true "catastrophe" in the sense this word has taken on in morphological theories of catastrophes: going over from one enunciative space into another. While it is true that the childhood utterances that have been collated do not all display those semantic latencies of demonstratives, one could posit that they harbor them unconsciously:[31] the child lodges itself within a language, French, that has gathered such modalities of spatialization into one category—"catastrophe." These modalities, however, remain immanent to any usage of the demonstrative, as in all languages, since it is true (as I have observed since the beginning of this investigation) that the archeology of *spatial naming* accompanies the development of autonomy of the *subjective unit*.

The discourse of a two-year-old girl demonstrated what I think is psychoanalytic underpinning of the archaic naming of referential space by demonstratives. Each time she organized the space of the room in which we played together by means of demonstratives or shifters (*c'est, ici, là, haut, bas, ceci, cela*), she felt obliged to "analyze" that place (those places) thus fragmented by giving them a person's name: "mamma" or the mother's first name. Precocious and quite advanced in language learning, extremely attached to her father and, probably, impressed by her mother's new pregnancy (most likely for all of these "reasons," and to assert herself in opposition to her female interlocutor who could not help but remind her of her mother), the little girl established her "mamma" in all the locations designated by these recently acquired spatial terms.

This discourse leads to the hypothesis (which might be confirmed or disproved by other transferences) that spatial naming—including already syntactically elaborated forms such as demonstratives and adverbs of position—retains the memory of the maternal impact already evoked within the constitution of semiotic rudiments. Given the frequency of *topic* demonstrative utterances beginning with the first grammatically constructed sentences, we might submit that the *entry into syntax constitutes a first victory over the mother*, a still uncertain distancing of the mother, by the simple fact of naming (by the appearance of the *topic* and more exactly of the demonstrative *c'est*). The distance seems uncertain, for while the child experiences pleasure in repeating utterances of this type, it also evidences postures of submission, humiliation, and victimization in relation to adults as well as to peers. It is as if a certain masochism appeared, along with the introjection of an archaic mother, which the infant is not yet satisfactorily able to designate, name, or localize.

What is striking is that later, at about three years, the composition of the most frequent utterances changes at the same time as the main behavioral characteristic. The *topic* is henceforth less the anaphoric demonstrative *c'est* than a *personal pronoun* shifter—essentially *Moi je.* While 17 percent of the two-year-old children's utterances exhibit this structure, the figure increases to 36 percent with three-year-old children. At the same time, I note the appearance of the possibility of *negating* the demonstrative: *pas ça, c'est pas*—a game in which the children indulge with a pleasure leading to frequent glossalalias ("*pas ça, c'est cassé, c'est à papa, pas cassé, c'est pas ça, c'est à papa,*" etc.). At the same time that the father is evoked, *negation* and the designation of *protagonists of enunciation* (personal pronouns) begin to appear. This explicit negativity connotes an increased independence within the symbolic and the capacity for auto-designation ("*je*"-object of discourse); aggressiveness is the underpinning of that negativity. An often unmistakable "sadism," which could be interpreted as a devouring of the archaic mother, succeeds the previous "masochism." Significantly, the generic demonstration (*ça c'est*) occurs less frequently at this age: only 15 percent of *ça c'est* followed by a *noun phrase*, as opposed to 50 percent at two years. The psychic cathexis of the child breaks away from the *place* and refines the spatialization of the enunciation as well as that of the signifying chain itself. The well-known "reel game" with its *fort-da*, observed around the age of eighteen months, finds, over a period of time, its linguistic realization first in demonstrative or localizing utterances and finally in personal and negative utterances.

One could relate to this archeology of naming (the spatial reference point, the demonstrative, the "topic," the person's name) and to the equivocal subject/object relationship that is its psychoanalytical counterpart ("potential space," primary narcissism, autoeroticism, sadomasochism), the perplexed notions of logicians on the semantics of proper names. According to some—Stuart Mill, for instance—proper names have no signification (they denote but do not connote): they do not signify but point to a referent. For others like Russell, they are abbreviations of descriptions for a series, class, or system of particulars (and even for a "cluster" of definitions) and are equivalent to demonstratives (*ceci, cela*). For Frege, on the contrary, the shifter does not yet designate an "object." From our point of view, however, the proper name is a substantive of definite reference (therefore similar to the demonstrative) but of indefinite signification ("cognitive" as well as "emotive"), arising from an uncertain position of the speaking subject's identity and referring back to the pre-objectival state of naming. The emergence of personal designation and proper name in close relation to the shifters and semantic latencies (of the "potential space") of this period underpin (and in that sense explain) the dynamic and semantic ambiguity of proper names, their lack of precision as to the notion of identity, and their impact within unconscious and imaginary constructs.

As the *Logique* of Port-Royal points out, *ceci* marks a "confused idea of the immediate thing," while allowing the mind to add ideas "stimulated by circumstances."[32] Hence it provides a presence, posited but indistinct, and an evocation of uncertain multiplicities, which would therefore explain why *this*, in its well-known evangelical usage, is at the same time Bread and Body of Christ: "This is my body." But the believers in the "Cartesian subject," the logicians of Port-Royal, cannot rationalize the passage from one to the other under the same shifter *ceci* except through recourse to *time*: Before, *ceci* was bread and now, *ceci* is my body. Reason is unscathed only at the expense of an obsessional shackling to time and, by the same token, of erasing "mystery" as bodily and/or nominal mutation under the same signifier (despite all the precautions taken with respect to theology in the *Logiques*).

Could trans-substantiation (for this is what we are dealing with, and the child cannot help leading all of us, men and women, to it, for it is indeed such a key fantasy of our reproductive desires) be an indelible theming of this same fold between the "space" of need (for food and survival) and a symbolic space of designation (of the body proper)? Could it be a fold that the archeology of shifters summarizes and is produced in all archaic designations of the mother, as well as in all experiences at the limits of corporeal identity—that is, the identity of meaning and presence?

Childhood language, if we need an "object" of study; infantile language, certainly: it is within our "adult" discourse that these potential meanings and topological latencies are at work. We suggest that naming, always originating in a place (the *chora*, space, "topic," subject-predicate), is a *replacement* for what the speaker perceives as an archaic mother—a more or less victorious confrontation, never finished with her. By indicating, as precisely as possible, how the units and minimal operations of *any language* (and even more so those of discourse) revive, model, transform, and extend the pregnancy that still constitutes the ultimate limit of meaning where, if analysis is lacking, transcendence takes root.

NOTES

Introduction

1. Armando Verdiglione, ed., *Psychanalyse et politique* (Paris: Seuil, 1974), p. 73.
2. Roland Barthes, "L'Etrangère," *Quinzaine Littéraire*, May 1–15, 1970, pp. 19–20.
3. Jean-Paul Enthoven, Interviewer, "Julia Kristeva: à quoi servent les intellectuels?" *Le Nouvel Observateur*, June 20, 1977, p. 99.
4. Jean Piaget, *Structuralism* (New York: Basic Books, 1970), p. 3.
5. *Ibid.*, p. 137.
6. For further details concerning Sollers and *Tel Quel* see the two last chapters of Leon S. Roudiez, *French Fiction Today* (New Brunswick: Rutgers University Press, 1972) and a subsequent article, "Twelve Points from Tel Quel," *L'Esprit Créateur* (Winter 1974), 14(4):291–303.
7. Julia Kristeva, Σημειωτιχὴ/*Recherches pour une sémanalyse* (Paris: Seuil, 1969), p. 19.
8. Cf. Jean Starobinski, *Les Mots sous les mots* (Paris: Gallimard, 1971).

9. Jacques Lacan, *Ecrits/A Selection* (New York: Norton, 1977), p. 155.

10. Essays by Brik and Shklovski are included in Tzvetan Todorov, ed., *Théorie de la littérature* (Paris: Seuil, 1965); phrases quoted are on pp. 151 and 184.

11. Plato, *Timaeus*, 51. I used the Jowett translation.

12. Kristeva, *Des chinoises* (Paris: Editions des Femmes, 1974), pp. 13–14. My translation.

13. Letter to *Le Monde*, Oct. 22, 1976, p. 3.

14. Enthoven, "Julia Kristeva," p. 130.

15. Quoted in Han Suyin, *The Morning Deluge* (Boston: Little, Brown, 1972), p. 55.

16. Enthoven, "Julia Kristeva," pp. 106 and 108.

17. Barthes, "L'Etrangère," p. 19.

18. See, for instance, the Fall 1974 issue of *Diacritics*, which also includes an excellent essay by Philip E. Lewis on Kristeva, entitled "Revolutionary Semiotics."

1. The Ethics of Linguistics

First published in *Critique* 322 (March, 1974), vol. XXX; reprinted in *Polylogue* (Paris: Seuil, 1977).

1. Vladimir Mayakovsky, *How Are Verses Made?* G. M. Hyde, trans. (London: J. Cape, 1970), pp. 36–37. The other Mayakovsky quotations are from *Electric Iron*, Jack Hirschman and Victor Erlich, trans (Berkeley: Maya, 1971), p. 46.

2. From the preface of Velimir Khlebnikov, *Sobranie Sochinenij* (Moscow, 1927–1933).

3. Velimir Khlebnikov, *Oeuvres*, L. Schnitzer, trans. (Paris: Oswald, 1967).

4. In Tzvetan Todorov, ed., *Questions de poétique* (Paris: Seuil, 1973). First appeared as "O pokolenii rastrativshem svoikh poetov," in *Smert' Vladimira Majakovskoga* (Berlin, 1931), pp. 7–45. This essay will appear in English translation in a future volume of Jakobson's *Selected Writings*, published by Mouton in The Hague.

5. *Totem and Taboo* in *The Standard Edition of the Complete Works of Sigmund Freud* (London: Hogarth & The Institute of Psycho-Analysis, 1953), 13:146.

6. "Qu'est-ce que la poésie," in *Questions de poétique*, pp. 124–25.

7. Khlebnikov, *Oeuvres.*

2. The Bounded Text

First published in Σημειωτιχὴ (Paris: Seuil, 1969), pp. 113–42.

1. When considering semiotic practices in relation to the sign, one can distinguish three types: first, a *systematic* semiotic practice founded on the sign, therefore on meaning; conservative and limited, its elements are oriented toward denotata; it is logical, explicative, interchangeable, and not at all destined to transform the other (the addressee). Second, a *transformative* semiotic practice, in which the "signs" are released from denotata and oriented toward the other, whom they modify. Third, a paragrammatic semiotic practice, in which the sign is eliminated by the correlative paragrammatic sequence, which could be seen as a tetralemma—each sign has a denotatum; each sign does not have a denotatum; each sign has and does not have a denotatum; it is not true that each sign has and does not have a denotatum. See my "Pour une sémiologie des paragrammes," in Σημειωτιχὴ: *recherches pour une sémanalyse* (Paris: Seuil, 1969), pp. 196ff.

2. "Literary scholarship is one branch of the study of ideologies [which] . . . embraces all areas of man's ideological creativity." P. N. Medvedev and M. Bakhtin, *The Formal Method in Literary Scholarship: A Critical Introduction to Sociological Poetics*, Albert J. Wehrle, trans. (Baltimore: Johns Hopkins University Press, 1978), p. 3. I have borrowed the term "ideologeme" from this work.

3. I use the term "sememe" as it appears in the terminology of A. J. Greimas, who defines it as a combination of the semic nucleus and contextual semes. He considers it as belonging to the level of manifestation, as opposed to the level of immanence, which is that of the seme. See A. J. Greimas, *Sémantique Structurale* (Paris: Larousse, 1966), p. 42.

4. Within Western scientific thinking, three fundamental currents break away from the symbol's domination, one after another, moving

through the sign to the variable. These three are Platonism, conceptualism, and nominalism. See V. Willard Quine, "Reification of Universals," in *From a Logical Point of View* (Cambridge: Harvard University Press, 1953). I have borrowed from this study the differentiation between two meanings of signifying units: one within the space of the symbol, the other within that of the sign.

5. Émile Mâle, *L'Art religieux de la fin du Moyen Age en France* (Paris: A. Colin, 1908).

6. The following are among the most important: F. Desonay, "Le Petit Jehan de Saintré," in *Revue du Seizième Siècle* (1927), 14:1–48, 213–80; "Comment un écrivain se corrigeait au XVe siècle," in *Revue Belge de Philologie et d'Histoire* (1927), 6:81–121; Y. Otaka, "Etablissement du texte définitif du Petit Jehan de Saintré," in *Etudes de Langue et Littérature Françaises* (Tokyo, 1965), 6:15–28; W. S. Shepard, "The Syntax of Antoine de La Sale," in *PMLA* (1905), 20:435–501; W. P. Soderhjelm, *La Nouvelle française au XVe siècle* (Paris: H. Champion, 1910); *Notes sur Antoine de La Sale et ses oeuvres* (Helsingfors: Ex officina typographica Societatis Litterariae fennicae, 1904). All my references are to the text edited by Jean Misrahi (Fordham University) and Charles A. Knudson (University of Illinois) and published by Droz (Geneva, 1965).

7. Any contemporary novel that struggles with the problems of "realism" and "writing" is related to the structural ambivalence of *Jehan de Saintré*. Contemporary realist literature is situated at the other end of the history of the novel, at a point where it has been reinvented in order to proceed to a scriptural productivity that keeps close to narration without being repressed by it. It evokes the task of organizing disparate utterances that Antoine de La Sale had undertaken at the dawn of the novelistic journey. The relationship between the two is obvious and, as Louis Aragon admits, desired in the case of his own novel, *La Mise à mort* (1965), where the Author (Antoine) sets himself apart from the Actor (Alfred), going so far as to take the name Antoine de La Sale.

8. This term is used by Victor Shklovski in the chapter of his book, *O teorii prozy* (Moscow, 1929), that was translated into French as "La Construction de la nouvelle et du roman" in Tzvetan Todorov, ed., *Théorie de la littérature* (Paris: Seuil, 1965), p. 170.

9. See Georg Henrik von Wright, *An Essay on Modal Logic* (Amsterdam: North-Holland, 1951).

10. I am indebted to Mikhail Bakhtin for his notion of the double and ambiguity as the fundamental figure in the *novel* linking it to the oral carnivalesque tradition, to the mechanism of laughter and the mask, and to the structure of Menippean satire. See his *Problems of Dostoevsky's Poetics* (Ann Arbor: Ardis, 1973), *Rabelais and His World* (Cambridge: MIT Press, 1968), and my essay, "Word, Dialogue, and Novel," in this volume.

11. The notion of "author" appears in Romance poetry about the beginning of the twelfth century. At the time, a poet would publish his verse and entrust them to the memory of minstrels of whom he demanded accuracy. The smallest change was immediately noticed and criticized: "Jograr bradador" (Ramon Menendez-Pidal, *Poesía juglaresca y origines de las literaturas románicas* [Madrid: Instituto de Estudios Politicos, 1957], p. 14, note 1). "'Erron o juglar!' exclamaba condenatorio el trovador gallego y con eso y con el cese del canto para la poesia docta, el juglar queda excluido de la vida literaria; queda como simple musico, y aun en este oficio acabe siendo sustituido par el ministril, tipo del musico ejecutante venido del extranjero y que en el paso del siglo XIV al XV, convive con el juglar" (*Ibid.*, p. 380). In this way, the passage from minstrel as Actor (a character in a dramatic production, an accuser—cf. in juridical Latin: *actor*, the accuser, the controller of the narrative) to minstrel as Author (founder, maker of a product, the one who makes, implements, organizes, generates, and creates an object of which he no longer is the producer but the salesman—cf. in juridical Latin: *auctor*, salesman) is carried out.

12. See my book *Le Texte du roman* (The Hague: Mouton, 1970), a semiotic approach to a transformational discursive structure.

13. For these terms borrowed from structural syntax, see Léon Tesnière, *Esquisse d'une syntaxe structurale* (Paris: Klincksieck, 1953).

14. Michel Granet, *La Pensée chinoise* (Paris: Albin Michel, 1968), chapter 2, "Le Style," p. 50. (Originally published in 1934.)

15. In the epic, man's individuality is limited by his linear relationship to one of two categories: the good or the bad people, those with positive or negative attributes. Psychological states seem to be

"free of personalities. Consequently, they are free to change with extraordinary rapidity and to attain unbelievable dimensions. Man may be transformed from good to bad, changes in his psychological state happening in a flash." D. S. Lichachov, *Chelovek v literature drevnej Rusi* [Man in the Literature of Old Russia] (Moscow-Leningrad 1958), p. 81.

16. See Alois Richard Nykl, *Hispano-Arabic Poetry and Its Relations with the Old Provençal Troubadours* (Baltimore: J. H. Furst, 1946). This study demonstrates how, without mechanically "influencing" Provençal poetry, Arabic poetry *contributed* by contact with Provençal discourse to the formation and development of courtly lyricism in regards to both its content and types, as well as its rhythm, rhyme scheme, internal division, and so on. The Russian academician Nikolai Konrad has demonstrated that the Arab world was in contact, on the other side of Islam, with the Orient and China (in 751, on the banks of the river Talas, the army of the Halifat of Bagdad met the army of the T'ang Empire). Two Chinese collections, "Yüeh-fu" and "Yü-t'ai hsin-yung," which date from the third and fourth centuries A.D., evoke the themes and organization of courtly Provençal poetry of the twelfth through the fifteenth centuries. Chinese songs, on the other hand, constitute a *distinct* series and stem from a different world of thought. Nonetheless, contact and contamination are a fact of those two cultures—the Arabic and the Chinese (Islamization of China, followed by infiltration of Chinese signifying structure [art and literature] into Arabic rhetoric and, consequently, into Mediterranean culture). See Nikolai Konrad, "Contemporary Problems in Comparative Literature," in *Izvestija Akademii nauk SSSR*, "Literature and Language" series (1959), 18:fasc. 4, p. 335.

17. J, Coulet, *Le Troubadour Guilhem Montahagal* (Toulouse: *Bibliothèque Meridionale*, 1928), Series 12, IV.

18. Joseph Anglade, *Le Troubadour Guirault Riquier: Etude sur la décadence de l'ancienne poésie provençale* (Paris: U. de Paris, 1905).

19. Antoine François Campaux, "La Question des femmes au XVe siècle," in *Revue des Cours Littéraires de la France et de l'Etranger* (Paris: I. P., 1864), p. 458ff.; P. Gide, *Etude sur la condition privée de la femme dans le droit ancien et moderne* (Paris: Durand et Pédone-Lauriel, 1885), p. 381.

20. Such are, for instance, the famous "Parisian hawkers' cries"—repetitive utterances and laudatory enumerations that fulfilled the purposes of advertisement in the society of the time. See Alfred Franklin, *Vie privée d'autrefois: I. L'Annonce et la réclame* (Paris: Plon-Nourrit, 1897–1902); and J. G. Kastner, *Les Voix de Paris: essai d'une histoire littéraire et musicale des cris populaires* (Paris: G. Brandus, 1857).

21. See *Le Mystère de Vieux Testament* (fifteenth century), in which the officers of Nebuchadnezzar's army enumerate forty-three kinds of weapons; and *Le Martyr de saint Canten* (late fifteenth century), in which the leader of the Roman troops enumerates forty-five weapons; and so on.

22. Thus, in Grimmelshausen's *Der Satyrische Pylgrad* (1666), there first appear twenty semantically positive utterances that are later restated as semantically pejorative and, finally, as double (neither positive nor pejorative). The blazon appears frequently in mysteries and satirical farces. See Anatole de Montaiglon, *Recueil de poesies françaises des XV et XVIe siecles* (Paris: P. Jannet-P. Daffis, 1865–1878), 1:11–16, 3:15–18; and *Dits des pays*, 5:110–16. In the matter of blazons, see H. Gaidoz and P. Sebillot, *Blason populaire de la France* (Paris: L. Cerf, 1884) and G. D'Haucourt and G. Durivault, *Le Blason* (Paris: Presses Universitaires de France, 1960).

23. Concerning borrowings and plagiarisms by Antoine de La Sale, see M. Lecourt, "Antoine de La Sale et Simon de Hesdin," in *Mélanges offerts à M. Émile Châtelain* (Paris: H. Champion, 1910), pp. 341–50, and "Une Source d'Antoine de La Sale: Simon de Hesdin," in *Romania* (1955), 76:39–83, 183–211.

24. Following a period when books were considered as sacred objects (sacred book = Latin book), the late Middle Ages went through a period when books were devalorized, and this was accompanied by texts being replaced with imagery. "Beginning with the middle of the twelfth century, the role and fate of books changed. As the place of production and exchange, the city had undergone the impact of books and stimulated their appearance. Deeds and words had an echo in them and were multiplied in a proliferating dialectic. The book as a product of prime necessity entered into the cycle of Medieval production. It became a profitable

and marketable product; but it also became a protected product." Albert Flocon, *L'Univers des livres* (Paris: Hermann, 1961), p. 1. *Secular* books soon began to appear: the Roland cycle, courtly novels (the Novel of Alexander the Great, the Novel of Thebes), Breton novels (King Arthur, the Grail), the Romance of the Rose, troubadour and trouvere poems, the poetry of Rutebeuf, fabliaux, the Roman de Renart, miracle plays, liturgical drama, etc. An actual *trade* in manuscript books sprang up and saw considerable expansion in the fifteenth century in Paris, Bruges, Ghent, Antwerp, Augsburg, Cologne, Strasburg, Vienna. In markets and fairs, near the churches, paid copyists would spread out their offerings and hawk their wares. See Svend Dahl, *Histoire du livre de l'antiquité à nos jours* (Paris: Poinat, 1960). The cult of books extended into the court of the kings of Anjou (who were closely linked to the Italian Renaissance) where Antoine de La Sale worked. René of Anjou (1480) owned twenty-four Turkish and Arabic manuscripts, and in his chamber there hung "a large panel on which were written the ABC's with which one can write throughout all the Christian and Saracenic countries."

25. It seems natural for Western thought to consider any writing as *secondary*, as coming after vocalization. This devalorization of writing harkens back to Plato, as do many of our philosophical presuppositions: "There neither is nor ever will be a treatise of mine [on my teaching]. For it does not admit of exposition like other branches of knowledge; but after much converse about the matter itself and a life lived together, suddenly a light, as it were, is kindled in one soul by a flame that leaps to it from another, and thereafter sustains itself" (*The Platonic Epistles*, J. Harward, trans. [Cambridge: Cambridge University Press, 1932], 7:135). Such is the case unless writing happens to be assimilated to an authority figure or to an immutable truth, unless it manages "to write what is of great service to mankind and to bring the nature of things into the light for all to see" (*ibid.*). But idealist reasoning sceptically discovers that "further, on account of the weakness of language [. . .] no man of intelligence will venture to express his

philosophical views in language, especially not a language that is unchangeable, which is true of that which is set down in written characters" (*ibid.*, pp. 136–37). Historians of writing generally agree with that thesis. See James G. Février, *Histoire de l'écriture* (Paris: Payot, 1948). On the other hand, some historians insist on writing's preeminence over spoken language. See Chang Chen-ming, *L'Ecriture chinoise et le geste humain* (Paris: P. Geuthner, 1937), and J. Van Ginneken, *La Reconstitution typologique des langages archaïques de l'humanité* (Amsterdam: Noord-Hollandsche uitgevers-maatschappij, 1939).

26. See Medvedev and Bakhtin, *The Formal Method in Literary Scholarship.*

27. "'Short story' is a term referring exclusively to plot, one assuming a combination of two conditions: small size and the impact of plot on the ending" (B. M. Eikhenbaum, "O. Henry and the Theory of the Short Story," I. R. Titunik, trans., in *Readings in Russian Poetics: Formalist and Structuralist Views* [Ann Arbor: University of Michigan Press, 1978], pp. 231–32).

28. The poetry of troubadours, like popular tales, stories of voyages, and other kinds of narratives, often introduces at the end the speaker as a witness to or participant in the narrated "facts." Yet, in novelistic conclusions, the author speaks not as a witness to some "event" (as in folk tales), not to express his "feelings" or his "art" (as in troubadour poetry); rather, he speaks in order to assume ownership of the discourse that he appeared at first to have given to someone else (a character). He envisions himself as the actor of *speech* (and not of a sequence of events), and he follows through the loss of that speech (its death), after all interest in the narrated events has ended (the death of the main character, for instance).

29. An example of this would be Philippe Sollers's book, *The Park,* A. M. Sheridan-Smith, trans. (New York: Red Dust, 1969), which inscribes the production of its writing before the conceivable *effects* of an "oeuvre" as a phenomenon of (representative) discourse.

30. As to the impact of phonetism in Western culture, see Jacques Derrida, *Of Grammatology* (Baltimore: Johns Hopkins University Press, 1976).

3. Word, Dialogue, and Novel

First published in Σημειωτιχὴ (Paris: Seuil, 1969), pp. 143–73.

1. The point of departure for this essay lies in two books by Mikhail Bakhtin: *Rabelais and His World*, Helene Iswolsky, trans. (Cambridge: MIT Press, 1965), and *Problems of Dostoevsky's Poetics*, R. W. Rotsel, trans. (Ann Arbor: Ardis, 1973). Bakhtin died in 1975, the year of the publication of his collection of essays, *Voprosy literatury i estetiki* (Moscow), published in French as *Esthétique et théorie du roman* (Paris: Gallimard, 1978).

2. Derrida uses the word *gram* (from the Greek *gramma*, "that which is written") to designate the irreducible material element of writing, as opposed to the vast amount of extraneous connotations currently surrounding that word. See his *Of Grammatology*, Gayatri Spivak, trans. (Baltimore: Johns Hopkins Press, 1976). [Ed.]

3. "Language is as old as consciousness, language *is* practical consciousness that exists also for other men, and for that reason alone it really exists for me personally as well." Karl Marx, *The German Ideology*, S. Ryazanskaya, trans., in *The Marx-Engels Reader*, Robert C. Tucker, ed. (New York: Norton, 1972), p. 122. (The French translation quoted by Kristeva is less faithful to the German text, although, in the latter part of the sentence, the German word for "genuine" does modify "consciousness": " . . . auch für mich selbst echt existierende Bewußtsein." The French version begins "Le langage *est* la conscience réelle . . ."—Ed.)

4. I shall refer to only a few of Bakhtin's notions insofar as they are congruent with the conceptions of Ferdinand de Saussure as related to his "anagrams" (see Jean Starobinski, *Les Mots sous les mots* [Paris: Gallimard, 1971]) and suggest a new approach to literary texts.

5. See Julia Kristeva, *La Révolution du langage poétique* (Paris: Seuil, 1974), pp. 59–60, and the "Notes on the Translation and on Terminology" in this volume. [Ed.]

6. Indeed, when structural semantics refers to the linguistic foundations of discourse, it points out that "an expanding sequence is recognized as the equivalent of a syntactically simpler communication" and defines "expansion" as "one of the most important aspects

of the operation of natural languages." A. J. Greimas, *Sémantique structurale* (Paris: Larousse, 1966), p. 72. I conceive of the notion of expansion as the theoretical principle authorizing me to study in the structure of genres an exteriorization (an expansion) of structures inherent to language.

7. E. F. Boudé, *K istorii velikoruskix govorov* (Toward a History of Russian Dialects) (Kazan, 1869).

8. L. V. Czerba, *Vostotchno-luzhickoe narechie* (The Eastern Loujiks' Dialect) (Petrograd, 1915).

9. V. V. Vinogradov, "O dialogicheskoj rechi" (On Dialogical Discourse), in *Russkaja rech*, 1:144.

10. V. V. Vinogradov, *Poetika* (Moscow: Nauka, 1926), p. 33.

11. It seems that what is persistently being called "interior monologue" is the most indomitable way in which an entire civilization conceives itself as identity, as organized chaos, and finally, as transcendence. Yet, this "monologue" probably exists only in texts that pretend to reconstitute the so-called physical reality of "verbal flux." Western man's state of "interiority" is thus a limited literary effect (confessional form, continuous psychological speech, automatic writing). In a way, then, Freud's "Copernican" revolution (the discovery of the split within the subject) put an end to the fiction of an internal *voice* by positing the fundamental principles governing the subject's radical exteriority in relation to, and within, language.

12. Bakhtin, *Problems of Dostoevsky's Poetics*, pp. 151–52.

13. "Shifters, Verbal Categories and the Russian Verb," in *Selected Writings II* (The Hague: Mouton, 1971), pp. 130–47.

14. Bakhtin, *Problems of Dostoevsky's Poetics*, p. 151.

15. I should emphasize that introducing notions of set theory into considerations on poetic language has only metaphorical value. It is legitimate to do so because one can draw an analogy between the Aristotelian logic/poetic logic relationship on the one hand, and the quantifiable/infinite relationship on the other.

16. See Luce Irigaray, "Communication linguistique et communication speculaire," in *Cahiers pour l'Analyse*, no. 3 (May 1966): pp. 39–55.

17. I should like to stress the ambiguous role of Western individualism. Involving the concept of identity, it is linked to the substantialist,

causal, and atomist thought of Aristotelian Greece and has strengthened throughout centuries this activist, scientistic, or theological aspect of Western culture. On the other hand, since it is founded on the principle of a difference between the "self" and the "world," it prompts a search for mediation between the two terms, or for stratifications within each of them, in order to allow the possibility of a correlative logic based on the very components of formal logic.

18. It was perhaps this phenomenon that Bakhtin had in mind when he wrote, "The language of the novel can be located neither on a surface nor on a line. It is a system of surfaces that intersect. The author as creator of everything having to do with the novel cannot be located on any of these linguistic surfaces. Rather, he resides within the controlling center constituted by the intersection of the surfaces. All these surfaces are located at varying distances from that authorial center" ("Šlovo o romane," in *Voprosy literatury* [1965], vol. 8, pp. 84–90). Actually, the writer is nothing more than the *linking* of these centers. Attributing a single center to him would be to constrain him within a monological, theological position.

19. This point of view is shared by all theorists of the novel: A. Thibaudet, *Réflexions sur le roman* (Thoughts on the Novel; Paris: Gallimard, 1938); Koskimies, "Theorie des Romans" (Theory of the Novel), in *Annales Academiae Scientiarum Finnicae*, I, series B (1935): 35:5–275. Georg Lukács, *Theory of the Novel* (Cambridge: MIT Press, 1971), and others.

    An interesting perspective on the concept of the novel as dialogue is provided by Wayne Booth's *The Rhetoric of Fiction* (Chicago: University of Chicago Press, 1961). His ideas concerning the *reliable* and *unreliable writer* parallel some of Bakhtin's investigations into dialogism in the novel, although they do not posit any specific relationship between novelistic "illusionism" and linguistic symbolism.

20. Such a mode shows up in modern physics as well as in ancient Chinese thought, as the two are equally anti-Aristotelian, anti-monological, and dialogical. See S. I. Hayakawa, "What Is Meant by Aristotelian Structure in Language," in *Language, Meaning, and Maturity* (New York: Harper, 1959); Chang Tung-sun, "A Chinese Philosopher's Theory of Knowledge," in S. I. Hayakawa, ed., *Our Language and Our World* (New York: Harper, 1959); Joseph Needham,

Science and Civilization in China, vol. 2 (Cambridge: The University Press, 1965).

21. See the important collection of studies on narrative structure in *Communications*, no. 8 (1966), which includes contributions by Roland Barthes, A. J. Greimas, Claude Bremond, Umberto Eco, Jules Gritti, Violette Morin, Christian Metz, Tzvetan Todorov, and Gérard Genette.

4. How Does One Speak to Literature?

First published in *Tel Quel* 47 (Fall 1971); reprinted in *Polylogue* (Paris: Seuil, 1977), pp. 23–54.

1. References to books by Roland Barthes appear in the body in the text, followed by page numbers. The following editions have been used:

   Critical Essays. Richard Howard, trans. Evanston, Ill.: Northwestern University Press, 1972. [Translation of *Essais Critiques.* Paris: Seuil, 1964.]

   Critique et vérité. Paris: Seuil, 1966.

   Elements of Semiology. Annette Lavers and Colin Smith, trans. New York: Hill and Wang, 1968. [Translation of *Eléments de sémiologie.* Paris: Editions du Seuil, 1964.]

   Michelet par lui-même. Paris: Seuil, 1954.

   Mythologies. Annette Lavers, trans, and ed. New York: Hill and Wang, 1972. [Translation of *Mythologies.* Paris: Seuil, 1957.]

   Sade, Fourier, Loyola. Richard Miller, trans. New York: Hill and Wang, 1976. [Translation of *Sade, Fourier, Loyola.* Paris: Seuil, 1971.]

   Système de la mode. Paris: Seuil, 1967.

   S/Z. Richard. Miller, trans. New York: Hill and Wang, 1974. [Translation of *S/Z.* Paris: Seuil, 1970.]

   Writing Degree Zero. Annette Lavers and Colin Smith, trans. New York: Hill and Wang, 1967. [Translation of *Le Degré zéro de l'écriture.* Paris: Seuil, 1953.]

2. "The concepts of 'psychical energy' and 'discharge' and the treatment of psychical energy as a quantity have become habitual in my thought since I began to arrange the facts of psychopathology

philosophically." Sigmund Freud, *Jokes and Their Relation to the Unconscious*, James Strachey, trans. (New York: Norton, 1960), p. 147.

The reference to Freud is recent and never elaborated in Barthes's works. It does not involve the economic conception of psychic activity in Freud (theories in instinctual drive, metapsychology); rather, *dialectical semantics*, which controls the notion of writing, and its explicit relationship with the speaking subject arguably place Barthes's undertaking within a thinking that is congruent (or could be made congruent) with these Freudian positions.

3. ". . . a mythology that may be causally linked to history by each of its elements, but that, considered in its entirety, resists the course of the latter and continually readjusts its own grid to offer the least resistance against the torrent of events, which, experience has shown, is rarely strong enough to smash it and carry it away in its momentum." Claude Lévi-Strauss, "Le Temps du mythe," *Annales* (May-August 1971), 26(3):540.

4. "Perhaps the power of the maternal figure derives its explosivity from the very power of fascination. We could also say that if the Mother implements her fascinating attraction, it is only because the child previously lived entirely under fascination's glance; it concentrated in itself all the power of enchantment. [. . .] Fascination is fundamentally linked to the neutral and impersonal presence of the indeterminate One, the immense faceless someone [. . .] To write is to enter into an affirmation of solitude where fascination operates as a threatening element." Maurice Blanchot, *L'Espace littéraire* (Paris: Gallimard, 1955), p. 24.

5. The notion of "paragram" is related to Saussure's "anagrams." Kristeva discusses this in her essay, "Pour une sémiologie des paragrammes" in Σημειωτιχή. [Ed.]

6. Blanchot, page 22.

7. "The work poses questions to the life. But we must understand in what sense; the work as the objectification of the person is, in fact, *more complete, more total* than the life. It has its roots in the life, to be sure; it illuminates the life, but it finds its total explanation only in itself. *Yet is is still too soon for this total explanation to*

become apparent to us. [Emphasis mine.] The life is illuminated by the work as a reality whose total determination is found outside of it, both in the conditions that bring it about and in the artistic creation that realizes it and finishes it off by expressing it. Thus, the work—when one has searched it—becomes a hypothesis and a research tool to clarify the biography. [. . .] But we must know also that the work *never* reveals the secrets of the biography." Jean-Paul Sartre, *Search For a Method*, (New York: Knopf, 1967), pp. 142–43.

8. "Language as the practical relation of one man to another is *praxis*, and *praxis* is always language (whether truthful or deceptive) because it cannot take place without signifying itself. [. . .] 'Human relations' are in fact interindividual structures whose common bond is language and which *actually* exists at every moment of History." Jean-Paul Sartre, *Critique of Dialectical Reason*, I, Alan Sheridan-Smith, trans. (London: New Left Books, 1976), p. 99.

9. "That first reflection out of immediacy is the subject's process of distinction of itself from its substance." Georg Wilhelm Friedrich Hegel, *Phenomenology of Mind*, J. B. Baillie, trans. (New York: Macmillian, 1949), p. 804.

10. *Ibid.*, p. 315.

11. Hegel, *Science of Logic*, A. V. Miller, trans. (New York: Humanities Press, 1969), p. 725.

12. Hegel, *Phenomenology of Mind*, p. 195.

13. *Ibid.*, p. 202.

14. "[T]his absolute notion of distinction must be set forth and apprehended purely as inner distinction, self-repulsion of the self-same as self-same, and likeness of the unlike as unlike. We have to think pure flux, opposition within opposition itself, or Contradiction. For in the distinction, which is an internal distinction, the opposite is not only one of two factors—if so, it would not be an opposite, but a bare existent—it is the opposite of an opposite, or the other is itself directly and immediately present within it. No doubt I put the opposite here and the Other, of which it is the opposite, there; that is, I place the opposite on one side, taking it by itself without

the other. Just on that account, however, since I have here the opposite all by itself, it is the opposite of its *own* self, that is, it has in point of fact the other immediately within itself. Thus the supersensible world, which is the inverted world, has at the same time reached out beyond the other world and has in itself that other; it is to itself conscious of being inverted (für sich verkehrte), i.e., it is the inverted form of itself; it is that world itself and its opposite in a single unity. Only thus is it distinction as internal distinction, or distinction *per se*; in other words, only thus is it in the form of *Infinity*." *Ibid.*, pp. 206–7.

15. Tel Quel, *Théorie d'ensemble* (Paris: Seuil, 1968), pp. 25–39.

16. I. Fonagy, "Double Coding in Speech," *Semiotica* (1971), 3(3): pp. 189–222.

17. On the subject of the inscription of instinctual drives through and across language in a unique text controlled by a precise situation of the subject in relation to castration, cf. Philippe Sollers, "La matière et sa phrase," *Critique*, July 1971.

18. Mao Zedong is the only man in politics and the only communist leader since Lenin to have frequently insisted on the necessity of working upon language and writing in order to transform ideology. He obviously considered working on language as a fundamental element of any ideological impact, and thus, of ideology and politics. His remarks are certainly motivated by the particularities of the Chinese language and its literature, by their *distanciation* from writing and by an inequality between the old and the new on these two levels. Yet, beyond these concrete implications, Mao's remarks have a more general worth that we cannot grasp without a theoretical reevaluation of the subject within signifying practice. Thus, for example: "Caring little for grammar or rhetoric, they relish a style which is a cross between the literary and the colloquial." "On Literary Style" in *Mao Tse-Tung on Literature and Art* (Peking: Foreign Language Press, 1960), p. 132; "Whenever a man speaks to others, he is doing propaganda work. Unless he is dumb, he always has a few words to say. It is therefore imperative that our comrades should all study language." "Oppose Stereotyped Party Writing," *ibid.*, p. 102.

5. From One Identity to an Other

Originally a paper read at a seminar organized by Jean-Marie Benoist and directed by Claude Lévi-Strauss at the Collège de France, January 27, 1975; first published in *Tel Quel* (Summer 1975), no. 62; reprinted in *Polylogue* (Paris: Seuil, 1977), pp. 149–72. "D'une identité l'autre," the original title of Kristeva's essay, reflects and makes use of the title of Céline's novel *D'un château l'autre*. Although this has been translated as *Castle to Castle*, the more literal "From One Identity to an Other" has been chosen in order to keep the ambiguous feeling of the French as well as the word "other," an important one in philosophy since Hegel and also in Kristeva's work.

1. Claude Lévi-Strauss, *l'Homme nu* (Paris: Plon, 1971), p. 615.
2. Kristeva's French phrase is *mise en procès*, which, like *le sujet en procès*, refers to an important, recurring concept—that of a constantly changing subject whose identity is open to question. Cf. "Notes on the Translation," p. 17, and note 6. [Ed.]
3. Ernest Renan, *Oeuvres Complètes*, (Paris: Calmann-Lévy, 1947–58) 3:322.
4. Ernest Renan, *The Future of Science* (Boston: Roberts Brothers, 1891), p. 402.
5. Lévi-Strauss, *L'Homme nu*, p. 614.
6. See Jean Starobinski, *Les Mots sous les mots* (Paris: Gallimard, 1971). [Ed.]
7. Edmund Husserl, *Logical Investigations*, J. N. Findlay, trans. (London: Routledge & Kegan Paul, 1970), pp. 276–77.
8. Edmund Husserl, *Ideas: General Introduction to Pure Phenomenology*, W. R. Boyce Gibson, trans. (London: Collier-MacMillan, 1962), pp. 93–94, 101.
9. Edmund Husserl, *Erste Philosophie*, VIII, in *Husserliana* (The Hague: Hrsg. von R. Boehm, 1956).
10. Husserl, *Ideas*, p. 313.
11. Antonin Artaud, "l'Anarchie sociale de l'art," in *Oeuvres complètes* (Paris: Gallimard), 8:287.
12. See Kristeva, *La Révolution du language poétique* (Paris: Seuil, 1974), pp. 274ff. [Ed.]
13. Louis-Ferdinand Céline, *Death on the Installment Plan*, Ralph Manheim, trans. (New York: New Directions, 1966), p. 78.

6. The Father, Love, and Banishment

First published in *Cahiers de l'Herne* (1976); reprinted in *Polylogue* (Paris: Seuil, 1977), pp. 137–47.

1. The references to Racine, Baudelaire, and Dante exist only in the French version of *First Love* (*Premier Amour* [Paris: Minuit, 1970]). The French equivalent of "chamber pot" is *pot de chambre*, but Beckett used the more "elegant" version, *vase de nuit*, which, if the denotation is put aside, could indeed have various poetic connotations. Quotations are from *First Love and Other Shorts* (New York: Grove Press, 1974). [Ed.]

7. The Novel as Polylogue

First published in *Tel Quel* 57 (Spring 1974); reprinted in *Polylogue* (Paris: Seuil, 1977), pp. 173–220. *H* is a novel by Philippe Sollers.

1. In French slang, the letter *H* refers to hashish as well as to heroin, whereas in our slang it refers mainly to heroin. The American slang word *hash* would thus correspond to Sollers's *H*; that connotation of his title should be kept in mind—but there are, of course, a number of others. [Ed.]

2. References to Sollers's novel *H* (Paris: Seuil, 1973) will be made in the body of the text; roman figures within parentheses indicate the page, italics the line. Quotations have been translated except when the discussion is closely textual, as in the following pages, and the points made by Kristeva would not apply to an English version. [Ed.]

3. In French, the pronunciation of *ex-schize* is the same as that of *exquise*, the words meaning respectively "being a former schizoid" and "exquisite." The Surrealist reference is obvious in Sollers's text, where the word *cadavre* precedes *ex-schize*. [Ed.]

4. The "phonic differential," which is a "signifying differential" (Leibnitz hovers in the background), is, briefly put, the place and the means by which the genotext penetrates the phenotext at the level of the signifier; each element of the signifier is thereby overdetermined by the meaning of the lexical item or of the sentence, and by the drives

working through phonation. The phenotext is the printed text, but it is legible in the full sense of the term only when one explores its complex genesis. These notions are developed in the essay, "L'Engendrement de la formule," in *Σημειωτική* (Paris: Seuil, 1969), and *La Révolution du langage poétique* (Paris: Seuil, 1974), pp. 209ff. [Ed.]

5. The reference is to Schreber's *Grundsprache*, which has been translated as "basic language" in the *Standard Edition* of Freud's works. Because of the connotations of "basic" (e.g., "basic English"), I have chosen to translate it as "fundamental language." The French phrase is *langue de fond.* [Ed.]

6. "La raison du plus mort" parodies the well-known line by La Fontaine, "La raison du plus fort est toujours la meilleure" from the fable *The Wolf and the Lamb.* It is a rough equivalent of "Might makes right." [Ed.]

7. "I anus," implying that the noun has become a verb, renders the French *J'anus* but leaves out the obvious pun; "I bring you the child of an inhumed guy's night" feebly attempts to suggest the sound of the English translation of a line by Mallarmé, "I bring you the child of an Idumean night." In French, the analogy is closer: "Je t'apporte l'enfant d'une nuit d'Idumée/Je t'apporte l'enfant d'une nuit d'inhumé." [Ed.]

8. The French, "vous êtes tous collés à l'oral" can mean both, "you have all flunked your orals" or, "you are all glued to orality." [Ed.]

9. Two earlier novels by Sollers: *Drame* (Paris: Seuil, 1965; New York: Red Dust, 1980) and *Nombres* (Paris: Seuil, 1968). *Nombres* was the starting point of Kristeva's essay, "L'Engendrement de la formule" (Cf. note 4). [Ed.]

10. Pierre Overney was a worker killed by a security guard during an antiracist demonstration outside the Renault plant at Billancourt (a Paris suburb) on February 26, 1972; Jalal ed-Din Rumi was a thirteenth-century Sufist poet whose main work is the *Mathnawi*; Jean-Baptiste Charcot (1867–1936) was a French neurologist and explorer of the Antarctic regions and of Greenland, the latter in his ship named *Pourquoi pas?* (*Why not?*); the Biturige were one of the tribes of Gaul, dwelling in what later became the Berry province with some (according to Sollers) wandering to the Bordeaux

region; Gorgias (c. 485–c. 380 BC) was a Greek Sophist born in Sicily who was sent as ambassador to Athens where he settled and taught rhetoric; Johan Jakob Bachofen (1815–1887) was a Swiss jurist and classical scholar who is perhaps best known for his studies on social evolution and matriarchy as developed in his book, *Das Mutterrecht* [Matriarchal law] (Basel: B. Schwabe, 1861); while there were princes in the former duchy and kingdom of Aquitaine, the phrase "Prince of Aquitaine" evokes, for a contemporary cultured French person, the well-known lines from Gérard de Nerval's poem *El Desdichado, "Je suis le ténébreux,—le veuf, l'inconsolé, / Le prince d'Aquitaine à la tour abolie."* [Ed.]

11. Pierre Messmer is a hard-line Gaullist who was appointed premier in 1972 by conservative French President Georges Pompidou; at the Olympic Games in Munich (1972), nine Israeli athletes were seized by the Black September Organization and later killed during a gun battle between the Palestinian terrorists and German police; clearly, Kristeva includes, under the general term, "fascist," the German Nazis and French collaborators who were responsible for massacring French Jews. [Ed.]

8. Giotto's Joy

First appeared in *Peinture* (January 1972), no. 2–3; reprinted in *Polylogue* (Paris: Seuil, 1977), pp. 383–408.

1. "Giotto's paintings do represent a step towards the artificial perspective of the fifteenth century. At the same time the oblique constructions used in the majority of his designs reveal a movement in a *different direction.*" John White, *Birth and Rebirth of Pictorial Space* (London: Faber & Faber, 1973), p. 75 (emphasis mine).

2. We should keep in mind that the Padua frescoes are located in the Scrovegni Chapel, generally known as the Arena Chapel. Dante put Scrovegni's father, Reginald, in the seventh circle of Hell. Scrovegni himself was a patron of Giotto and thus figured in the frescoes. He belonged to the Order of Cavalieri Gaudenti or the "Merry Knights," so called because of the wealth and behavior of its

members, and upheld the existence and dignity of the Virgin Mary. Giotto himself, who worked under the aegis of the Franciscans, seemed to be at odds with the doctrine of Saint Francis (unless he be in agreement with its specifically Florentine decadent form) when he wrote a poem against poverty, "Molti son quei che laudan povertade." (Historians, however, do not all agree that he wrote that poem.) In addition, Giotto appears to have been the only Florentine artist at the beginning of the fourteenth century to have amassed a true fortune. Cf. Frederick Antal, *Florentine Painting and Its Social Background* (New York: Harper, 1947). There is also an anecdote concerning Giotto's pictorial practice. In reply to Pope Benedict XI, who was looking for a painter for Saint Peter's Basilica, Giotto is said to have sent a single proof of his expertise—a perfect circle drawn in red paint—whence the expression "a more perfected art than Giotto's O." Cf. John Ruskin, *Giotto and His Work in Padua* (London: Levey, Robson and Franklyn, 1854).

3. Sigmund Freud, *Papers on Metapsychology: The Unconscious* in *The Standard Edition of the Works of Sigmund Freud* (London: Hogarth Press & The Institute of Psycho-Analysis, 1953), 14:201–2.

4. Freud, *Metapsychology*, p. 202.

5. Freud explains this passage from perception to symbolic function by the economy of *unification* and *rejection* engendering the symbolic function, the separation between subject and object, and the imposition of repression; it is confirmed in its role by the creation of the symbol of negation (cf. *Negation* in *The Standard Edition*, 19:235–39).

6. Freud, *Metapsychology*, p. 202.

7. *Ibid.*, p. 202.

8. Henri Matisse, *Matisse on Art*, Jack Flan, trans. (New York: Phaidon, 1973), Statements to Tériade, 1929–30, p. 58 (emphasis mine).

9. Matisse, Statements to Tériade, 1936, p. 74.

10. Marcelin Pleynet has shown, in the case of Matisse, the connection between chromatic experience, relation to the mother, and above all, the oral phase of infantile eroticism that dominates not only the pre-Oedipal experience, but also the phase preceding the "mirror stage" (and therefore, the constitution of the specular "I"), whose role proves to be capital, not only in elucidating the genesis of the

symbolic function, but even more so, in structuring the "artistic function." Cf. Marcelin Pleynet, "Le Système de Matisse," in *L'Enseignement de la peinture* (Paris: Seuil, 1971), pp. 67–74. Reprinted in Pleynet, *Système de la peinture* (Paris: Seuil, 1977), pp. 66–75.

11. Matisse, Statements to Tériade, 1936, p. 74 (emphasis mine).

12. By that token, its function is related (in the domain of sight) to rhythm's function and, in general, to the musicality of the literary text, which, precisely in this way, introduces instinctual drive into language.

13. *Physical* theories of color have at times embraced this point of view. According to wave theory, each material atom is made up of a sub-atom of color or sound whose connections are immaterial: *dharmas* or *laws.* Anaxagoras held that colors represent the interplay of an infinity of seeds corresponding to the infinity of luminous sensations.

14. Plato maintained that "what we say 'is' this or that color will be neither the eye which encounters the motion nor the motion which is encountered, but something which has arisen between the two and is peculiar to each percipient." *Theaetetus,* F. M. Cornford, trans., in Edith Hamilton & Huntington Cairnes, eds., *Collected Dialogues,* (Princeton: Princeton University Press, 1978), pp. 858–59. Epicurus seems to suggest through his theory of simulacra a connection between color and what we now call the "unconscious." The mind builds a wall against the mass of simulacra that assails it, selecting only those that pique its interest. Cf. M. A. Tonnelat, *Evolution des idées sur la nature des couleurs.* Lecture given at the Palais de la Découverte, 1956.

15. "And knowing that of all things light is best, He made it the indispensable means of sight, the best of the senses; for what the intellect is in the soul, the eye is in the body; for each of them sees, one the things of the mind, the other the things of the senses." Philo, *On The Creation of the World,* passage 53, in *Philosophia Judaica,* Hans Lewy, trans. (Oxford: Oxford University Press, 1946), page 61. See also passage 17. "For the eye of the Absolutely Existent needs no other light to effect perception, but He Himself is the archetypal essence of which myriads of rays are the effluence, none visible to sense, all to the mind. And therefore, they are the instruments of that same God alone, who is apprehended by the mind, not of any who have part and lot in the world of creation. For the created is approached

by sense, which can never grasp the nature which is apprehended by mind." Philo, *On The Cherubim*, passage 97, in *Philo*, F. H. Colson & G. H. Whitaker, trans. (New York: Putnam, 1923), 2:67–69. See also passage 28.

16. "We must imagine a center, and around this center a luminous sphere that radiates from (Intelligence). Then around this sphere, lies a second one that also is luminous, but only as a light lit from another light (the universal Soul). [...] The great light (Intelligence) sheds its light though remaining within itself, and the brilliancy that radiates around it (on to the soul) is 'reason.'" Plotinus, *Enneades*, K. Guthrie, trans. (Philadelphia: Monsalvat Press, 1910), Book IV, 3, 17.

17. "Si ergo lux formam dicit, non potest esse lux ipsum corpus, sed aliquid corporis [...] sicut dicit Augustinus quod humor et humus sunt elementa, et philosophi dicunt quod calor est substantia quaedam subtilis [...] sic igitur ex praedictiis patet, quod lux, proprie et abstracte loqeundo, non est corpus, sed forma corporis." Sanctus Cardinalis Bonaventurae, *Librum Secundum Sententiarum* [Commentary on the sentences, II] in *Opera Omnia* (Paris: Ludovique Vivès: 1864, 1864), Dist. XIII, Art. 2, Quaest. 2; pp. 552–53.

18. Georg Wilhelm Friedrich Hegel, *The Philosophy of Fine Art*, F. P. Osmaston, trans. (New York: Hacker Art Books, 1975), 3:322–24.

19. Ruskin notes that before Giotto, "over the whole of northern Europe, the colouring of the eleventh and early twelfth centuries had been pale: in manuscripts, principally composed of pale red, green, and yellow, blue being sparingly introduced (earlier still, in the eighth and ninth centuries, the letters had often been coloured with black and yellow only). Then, in the close of the twelfth and throughout the thirteenth century, the great system of perfect colour was in use; solemn and deep; composed strictly, in all its leading masses, of the colours revealed by God from Sinai as the noblest;—blue, purple, and scarlet, with gold (other hues, chiefly green, with white and black, being used in points or small masses, to relieve the main colours. In the early part of the fourteenth century the colours begin to grow paler; about 1330 the style is already completely modified; and at the close of the fourteenth century, the colour is quite pale and delicate." Ruskin, *Giotto*, p. 21.

20. "To see a blue light, you must not look directly at it."

21. I. C. Mann, *The Development of the Human Eye* (Cambridge: Cambridge University Press, 1928), p. 68.

22. In this context, it seems that notions of "narcissism" (be it primary) and autoeroticism suggest too strongly an already existing identity for us to apply them rigorously to this conflictual and imprecise stage of subjectivity.

23. White, *Birth and Rebirth of Pictorial Space*, p. 75.

24. *Ibid.*, p. 68.

25. Antal, *Florentine Painting and its Social Background.*

26. Walter Benjamin, "Literaturgeschichte und Literaturwissenschaft" in *Gesammelte Schriften* (Frankfurt/am/Main: Suhrkamp, 1972), 3:290.

9. Motherhood According to Giovanni Bellini

First published in *Peinture* (December 1975), no. 10–11; reprinted in *Polylogue* (Paris: Seuil, 1977), pp. 409–35.

1. "Dormition" refers to the period of the Virgin Mary's death, which is viewed merely as a period of sleep, before she was carried to heaven (Assumption). The word originated in the *Transitus Maria*, a fifth-century Byzantine apocrypha. [Ed.]

2. The French word "enceinte" has been kept as the only way to preserve the pun: "enceinte" is a protective wall around a town; "femme enceinte" is a pregnant woman. [Ed.]

3. Cf. G. Fiocco, *Giovanni Bellini* (Milan: Silvana, 1960); R. Longhi, *Viatico per cinque secoli di Pittura veneziana* (Florence: Sansoni, 1946); L. Coletti, *Pittura veneta del quattro cento* (Novara: 1953); and others.

4. Dante, *Paradisio*, XXI, 58–63.

10. Place Names

Place Names was first published as *Noms de Lieu* in *Tel Quel* 68 (Winter 1976); it appeared in a revised version, from which this translation was made, in *Polylogue* (Paris: Seuil, 1977), pp. 467–91.

1. Ernest Jones, *The Life and Work of Sigmund Freud* (New York: Basic Books, 1953), 1:263.

2. The "seduction" is perhaps directed towards Fliess, through the children as intermediaries (the young Sigmund and Mathilde); notice that Freud changes position in mid-route (from seduced to seducer; from son to father) while the object of seduction changes sex (from boy to girl). This should be added to the dossier of the Freud-Fliess analysis.

3. Sigmund Freud, *The Standard Edition of the Works of Sigmund Freud* (London: Hogarth Press & The Institute of Psycho-Analysis, 1953), 14:7.

4. *Ibid.*

5. *Ibid.*, 20:34.

6. *Wo Es war, soll Ich werden.*

7. Freud, *Standard Edition*, 20:34–35.

8. *Ibid.*

9. Heraclitus, 52; *Αἰὼν παῖς ἐστι παίζων, πεσσεύων*—"Life is a newborn who bears, who plays" (from the Wissman-Bollack French translation), *Héraclite ou la séparation* (Paris: Editions de Minuit, 1972). *Paizon* (*παίζων*), the present participle of the verb *to play*, used with *pesseuon* (*πεσσεύων*: pushing pawns) can only be redundant, as the standard translation shows; the writers allow themselves to differentiate between the signifiers in order to break this redundance and to reveal an etymological meaning of *paizon*: "making a child, engendering, bearing children."

10. "Sexuality in the Neuroses," Freud, *Standard Edition*, 7:274 (emphasis added).

11. "Libido" devoid of object or goal, a paradoxical state of facilitation, thus prior to the constitution of subject, object, and sign. Note the ideological and feminizing anthropo-morphizations of Winnicott's argument: the object's existence presupposes "separation" and "doing" and is defined as the "male element" of sexuality; the object's uncertainty (the "transitional object," to which we shall return later), in which "identity requires so little mental structure" emerges from "Being" whose "foundation . . . can be laid from the birth date" and which, contrary to the male element programmed by frustration, is susceptible to mutilation and is defined as the

"female element." D. W. Winnicott, *Playing and Reality* (New York: Basic Books, 1971), p. 80.

12. Cf. "Psycholinguistique et grammaire générative," the theme of a special issue of *Langages* edited by Jacques Mehler, vol. 16 (December 1969), and "Apprentissage de la syntaxe chez l'enfant," edited by Laurence Lentin for *Langue Française*, vol. 27 (September 1975), which also includes an interesting article by Christine Leroy on presyntactic intonation. For an historical survey of the principal linguistic works on language, cf. Aaron Bar-Adon and Werner F. Leopold, eds., *Child Language, a Book of Readings* (New York: Prentice Hall, 1971).

13. "Here we must take into consideration the peculiar logical activity which is tied specifically to language as well as to the ideal cognitive structures that arise specifically within it." Edmund Husserl, "The Origin of Geometry" in *The Crisis of European Sciences and Transcendental Phenomenology*, David Garr, trans. (Evanston, Ill.: Northwestern University Press, 1970), p. 364.

14. "It is clear that the method of producing original idealities out of what is prescientifically given in the cultural world must have been written down and fixed in firm sentences prior to the existence of geometry" (*ibid.*, p. 366). And further: "Every explication and every transition from making explicit to making self-evident (even perhaps in cases where one stops much too soon) is nothing other than historical disclosure; in itself, essentially, it is something historical (*ein Historiches*), and as such it bears, with essential necessity, the horizon of its history (*Historie*) within itself" (*ibid.*, pp. 370–71). While "we can also say now that history is from the start nothing other than the vital movement of the coexistence and the interweaving of original formations and sedimentations of meaning" (*ibid.*, p. 371).

15. *Ibid.*, p. 378.

16. Is it not true that the only (historical) events today, outside of murder (that is, war) are scientific events: the invention of spaces, from mathematics to astronomy?

17. Cf. "La Chora sémiotique," in *La Révolution du langage poétique* (Paris: Seuil, 1974), pp. 23–30. For a brief account, see the introduction to this volume. [Ed.]

18. R. Spitz, "Autoeroticism re-examined," *Psychoanalytical Study of the Child* (1962), 17:292.

19. R. Spitz, *The First Year of Life: A Psychoanalytic Study of Normal and Deviant Development of Object Relations* (New York: International Universities Press, 1965). Some interesting developments in pediatrics and child psychology are discussed by I. Kreisler, M. Fain, and M. Soulé in *L'Enfant et son corps* (Paris: Presses Universitaires de France, 1974), and S. Lebovici and M. Soulé in *La Connaissance de l'enfant par la psychanalyze* (Paris: Presses Universitaires de France, 1970).

20. Cf. Jacques Lacan, "The Mirror Stage as Formative of the Function of the I," in *Ecrits: A Selection*, Alan Sheridan, trans. (New York: Norton, 1977), pp. 1–7.

21. Darwin notes that after the first cries of suffering, laughter appears towards the third month, accompanied by imitation of sound, before the appearance of gestures expressing desires (at about one year) and finally intonations, all of which are archaic, preverbal modalities (Charles Darwin, "A Biological Sketch of an Infant," *Mind*, 2:285–308 [1877]). W. Wundt notes the dependence that I have mentioned between vocalization and vision: imitative articulation is determined by sounds heard as well as by sounds seen to be articulated, but there is a predominance of visual perception over acoustic perception in the initial stages, and this might explain the precocity of labial and dental consonants (*Volkerpsychologie* [1900], 1911, 1:314–19).

22. Cf. Edith Jacobsen, "The Child's Laughter," in *The Psychoanalytic Study of the Child* (1946), 2:39–60.

23. This deferring facilitation of "instinctual drive" before the letter has been considered, from a philosophical perspective, by Jacques Derrida in *Of Grammatology*, G. Spivak, trans. (Baltimore: Johns Hopkins University Press, 1977).

24. "I refer to the hypothetical area that exists (but cannot exist) between the baby and the object (mother or part of mother) during the phase of the repudiation of the object as not-me, that is, at the end of being merged in with the object" (Winnicott, *Playing and Reality*, p. 107).

25. "The transitional object represents the mother's ability to present the world in such a way that the infant does not at first know that the object is not created by the infant" (*ibid.*, p. 81).

26. M. A. K. Halliday, *Learning How to Mean: Explorations in the Development of Language* (London: Edward Arnold, 1975).

27. *Ibid.* pp. 18ff.

28. Cf. my "Contraintes rythmiques et langage poétique" in *Polylogue* (Paris: Seuil, 1977), pp. 437–66.

29. This research involves two groups of children: for children observed from age three months to three years, and for children observed from age two to three years. The results, statistically meager and solely applicable as hypotheses for future work, must be tested against analyses of a large number of cases. Verbal exchanges are recorded during collective games where an individualized relationship potentially grows between adult analyst and each of the children. The analysis also involves the regression that this play-attentiveness induces in the researchers and students as a prerequisite for the deciphering and interpretation of childhood-infantile discourse.

30. On *topic-comment* interpretation of infant syntax, see Jeffrey S. Gruber, "Topicalization in Child Language," in *Foundations of Language* (1967) 3:37–65; as well as Martin Braine, "The Ontogeny of English Phrase Structure," in *Language* (1961), 39:1–13; Braine notes that the first infant utterances are determined by relationships of order falling into two categories (*pivot words* plus "X") which include pronouns, prepositions, and auxiliaries, and that children first learn *localization* of units before being able to associate them, through a process of "contextual generalizations," into morphemic pairs and finally into normative syntax. Thomas G. Bever, Jerry A. Fodor, and William Wexsel, in "Theoretical Notes on the Acquisition of Syntax: Critique of 'Contextual Generalization,'" *Psychological Review* (1965), 72:476–82, criticize this position and stress that positionality is only the result of innate grammatical classes; in the beginning would be classes, not places. Whatever the methodological and psychological interest of this discussion in its own right, I should like to point out that the spatiality supporting the semiotic function (which I referred to above) is echoed, at the time of the symbolic, linguistic, functioning of the subject, in that positionality determines the organization of the signifying chain itself. The semiotic *chora* at the potential space that, within the equivocal aspect of primary narcissism, played between

fluid "terms" (I/other, inside/outside), is henceforth replaced by terms with precise positions, which draw their logical and syntactic value from that very position. But is the genesis of the positionality of terms (I am outlining a few of its psychoanalytic aspects) as conferring value, a supplementary argument in favor of this theory, to the detriment of the theory (currently widely debated) of the universality of grammatical categories?

31. Cf. J. Petitot, "Identity and Catastrophe," a paper read at the seminar of Claude Lévi-Strauss on *Identity*, January 1975.

32. A. Arnauld and P. Nicole, *Logique* (Paris: Presses Universitaires de France, 1965), p. 101.

INDEX

Index   333

May 1968, 162

Mayakovsky, Vladimir Vladimirovich, 24, 27–35, 70, 125, 211; *Electric Iron*, 28; *How Are Verses Made*, 28, 35

meaning: meaning, structure, and transcendence, 124; nonsense and surmeaning, 102; structure and the production of meaning, 103; subject's relation to, x

Medvedev, P. N., 301*n*., 307*n*.

Mehler, Jacques, 324*n*.

Melville, Herman, 179, 207

Menéndez-Pidal, Ramón, 303*n*.

Menippean discourse, 81–90

Menippean satire, 303*n*.

Menippean tradition, 67, 72, 76, 79

Menippus of Gadara, 81

Messmer, Pierre, 208, 318*n*.

Metz, Christian, 311*n*.

Michelangelo Buonarroti, 158

Michelet, Jules, 105, 107

Mill, John Stuart, 295

Miller, A. V., 313*n*.

Miller, Richard, 311*n*.

Misrahi, Jean, 302*n*.

Mondrian, Piet, 226

monologism. *See* novel

monologue, interior, 309*n*.

monotheism: and art, 215–20, 228–30, 255–56; and writing, 33

Montaiglon, Anatole de, 305*n*.

Monteverdi, Claudio, 207

Morin, Violette, 311*n*.

motherhood: Christianity, 157–59, 276; and paranoia, 244, 285

Mozart, Wolfgang Amadeus, 178, 207

Napoleon, 207

narcissism, 164, 167, 278. *See also* primary narcissism

narrative: analysis of, 63; modes, 65–67; pictorial, 215–18; as

prohibition, 69, 71–76, 79, 85; representation without narrative, 219; specularization in, 216; units, 65, 66

Needham, Joseph, 310*n*.–311*n*.

negation: as affirmation, 68; and the double, 68–70; and non-disjunction, 77–78, 82–83; non-disjunction in the novel, 49–51

negativity: defined, 18; and heterogeneity, 165, 189, 211–12; language as, 108–10; and negation, 163; in writing, 112

Nerval, Gérard de, 161, 195, 207, 212, 318*n*.

neurosis. *See* subject

Nicole, Pierre, 327*n*.

Nietzsche, Friedrich, 24, 78, 80, 195, 207

Notre Dame of Avioth, 41

novel: modern, antirepresentational, 85–87; monological, 66, 67, 69, 71, 73, 76, 85, 87; polyphonic, 67, 70, 79, 84–86; realist, 302*n*., 69, 84, 85. *See also* Text

Nykl, Alois Richard, 304*n*.

obsession in writing, 151

Oedipus: Oedipal aggression, 277; Oedipus complex, 277–82; Oedipal experience, 200, 204; Oedipal maternal body, 199–200; Oedipal mother, 104, 196, 197; Oedipal myth, 277; Oedipal narrative, 177, 196–97, 200; Oedipal stage, 162, 199

Orestes, 196, 200

Orpheus, 196

Otaka, Y., 302*n*.

Overney, Pierre, 206, 208, 317*n*.

Ovid, 82

Pānini, 127

paradox, 40

Raoul de Cambrai, 51
Raphael Santi, 251
realism. *See* novel
Reich, Wilhelm, 141
Reilly, Ann, 22n.
Renan, Ernest, 126–27, 129, 141;
    Averoès et l'Averroïsme, 126; *The Future*
    of Science, 315n.
Renaissance representation in
    painting, 250–51
repression, 24, 96, 137, 141, 146–47,
    155, 158, 210, 211, 212, 219, 222, 224,
    225, 250, 254; primal, 20, 245, 247,
    248–55, 267, 268, 274
Revolution, Soviet, 28, 33, 34, 70
Ricardou, Jean, 8
Richards, I. A., 12
Rinversi, Anna, 251
Risset, Jacqueline, 8
Robespierre, Maximilien, 164
Roche, Denis, 8
Roman de Renart, 77
Rothko, Mark, 226, 255, 271
Rotsel, R. W., 308n.
Rottenberg, Pierre, 8
Round Table, Cycle of, 50
Rousseau, Jean-Jacques, 275, 280
Roussel, Raymond, 185
Rumi, Jalal ed-Din, 207, 317n.
Ruskin, John, 319n., 321n.
Russell, Bertrand, 296
Ryazanskaya, S., 308n.
Rysselbergh, Maria van, 168

Sade, D. A. F. de, 6, 79, 86, 100, 105,
    113, 119, 139, 164, 168, 188, 207, 275;
    Idées sur les romans, 137
Saint Mark's Church (Venice), 158
Salomé, Lou, 168
San Francesco (Assisi), Giotto's
    frescoes in, 232–34, 236
Santa Croce (Florence), 234
Santa Maria Maggiore (Rome), 216
Sant' Apollinare Nuovo (Ravenna), 216

Sartre, Jean-Paul, 8, 100,
    104, 106; *Critique of Dialectical*
    Reason, 313n.
Saussure, Ferdinand de, viii, 4, 14, 16,
    24, 36, 68, 70, 99, 101, 127–29, 141,
    308n., 312n.
Schleicher, August, 126
Schnitzer, L., 300n.
Schreber, *Senatspräsident* Daniel, 30,
    139, 317n.
Scrovegni, Enrico, 218, 318n.
Scrovegni Chapel (Padua), Giotto's
    frescoes in, 215–18, 230–31, 232,
    234, 318n.
Sebillot, P., 305n.
semanalysis, viii, 5, 19; criticism
    and metalanguage, 116–17,
    121–23; criticism and writing,
    affirmation, and irony, 109–10;
    rationalization of the signifying
    process, 106; rhetorical seduction
    vs. style, 140
semantic analysis, 73
sememe, 38, 301n.
semiology, 1, 35; dissolving
    phenomenological signifying and
    mythical entities, 101–3, 106;
    ethics of literary science, 107,
    117; of literature, 93–97, 120–21;
    literature's "absence of place"
    with respect to social sciences,
    96–97; and psychoanalysis, 21;
    semiological negativity, 101–3. *See*
    also semanalysis; semiotics
semiotic disposition: anaclisis,
    286–87; the *chora* and its maternal
    connection, 134; dance, music,
    theater, 134, 142, 145, 178–83;
    defined, 6–7; as determined by the
    symbolic, 21; gestures, 289–90;
    language learning, 286–88; primal
    repression, 224, 243, 247, 254–55;
    semiotic *chora*, 7, 134, 182, 286,
    288–89

semiotics, 4; defined, 19; of literary texts, 66, 69; translinguistic practices, 37, 301n.; *see also* Semiology

Seneca, 55

Seneca the Younger, 82

set theory, 14, 88, 309n.

sexual difference, 152, 155–56, 158, 167–69, 202

Shakespeare, William, 6, 83; *Macbeth*, 284; *Romeo and Juliet*, 203

Shepard, W. S. 302n.

Sheridan-Smith, Alan, 307n., 313n.

Shklovsky, Victor, 6, 300n., 302n.

Sienese frescoes, 230

sign: evolution from symbol to sign, 39–42; non-disjunction within the novel's temporality, 49–50; present tense in inferential enunciation, 57; predication and, 130, 133, 171; Saussurian notion of, 68, 128

signifier/signified: addressee as signifier and signified, 73–74, 129–31, 140–41; word as signifier, 63

signifying differential, 316n.

signifying practice: defined, 20; typology of discourse as, 40–42, 51–52, 134–35

signifying process, ix, 4, 6–8, 125

signifying system, translinguistic, 101

Smith, Colin, 311n.

socialism, 10

Socrates, 55, 84, 207

Socratic dialogue, 80–81

Soderhjelm, W. P., *La Nouvelle française au XVe siècle*, 302n.

Sollers, Philippe, ix, 3, 8, 9; *Drame*, 87, 114, 205; *H*, 161–213; *Lois*, 163, 194, 200, 205; *Nombres*, 205; *The Park*, 307n.; *Sur le matérialisme*, 186

Solzhenitsyn, Aleksandr Isayevich, 275

Song of Roland, 50–51

Sophists, 84

Sopaçani Monastery, 256

Soulé, M., 325n.

sphinx, 196–97

Spinoza, Baruch, 147, 190, 207

Spitz, René A., 283, 286–88; *The First Year of Life*, 325n.

Spivak, Gayatri, 308n., 325n.

Stalin, Joseph V., 2, 163, 207

Stalinism, 24, 163

Starobinski, Jean, 5, 16, 299n., 308n., 315n.

Steinbeck, John, 22

Stockhausen, Karlheinz, 170

Strawson, P. F., 175

structuralism, viii, 3, 4, 6, 24, 63, 128, 132

subject: anal drive, 289; Cartesian subject and generative grammar, 128; defined, 21; as distinct from subject of fetishism, 140; of enunciation, 128; as historical subject, 95–97, 163, 208; and instinctual drives, 143, 164, 179, 280–81; its impossible identity, 124–25, 148, 189, 193; as operating consciousness, 131; oral drive, 288–89; as questionable and in process, 96, 99–100, 124–25, 136, 164, 194–95, 241–48, 254; relation of oral drive to rhythm and music, 178, 194–95; speaking and split subject, 6–7, 23–27, 73; the subject and death drive, 143, 164, 191, 210–11, 226; subject of text as differentiated from subject of neurosis and psychosis, 96, 125, 140, 155, 185, 200, 223; subject of narration, 73; as transcendental ego, 129, 129–30, 289

sublimation, 245, 254, 273–74, 288

surrealism, 8, 134, 174

Suyin, Han, 300n.

Swift, Jonathan, 70, 79, 82, 86, 110, 185

symbolic disposition: defined, 7, 29, 139, 177; as determining the semiotic disposition, their contradiction, 135, 136, 139, 141, 166, 170, 184, 187, 199–200; thesis as predication, 130

Taoist painting, 216, 253
Tel Quel, 3, 8–9, 100
Tesnière, Léon, 303n.
text: defined, 2, 16; fascination and objectification, 104–5; language and biography, 105; the novel as text, *a*) inferential enunciation, 47–48, *b*) bounded text blocked by non-disjunction, 45, 49–53, *c*) programming, 44, *d*) structural and compositional finitude, 58–59, *e*) narrative and literature, 61, *f*) characters as stages in the metamorphosis of the subject of narration, 46–47; the novel as transposition of Menippean ambivalence, 85–86; text and dissolution of Christian ideology, 216–22, 227–28, 259, 271–72; text as fuzzy set, 136; textual logic vs. Hegelian dialectic, 98–99; text vs. kinship rules, 96–97; typology of texts vs. rhetoric of genres, 38
Thales of Miletus, 55
theater: medieval theater, 77–78; text as theater, 77–79, 84
Thebes, 197
Theodoric the Great, 216
Thibaudet, Albert, 310n.
Thibaudeau, Jean, 8
Thom, René, 7
Timides, 55
Titian, 248, 269, 271
Titunik, I. R., 307n.
Todorov, Tzvetan., 2, 12, 311n.; *Théorie de la littérature*, 300n., 302n.; *Questions de poétique*, 300n.

Tolstoy, Leo, monological novels of, 69, 87
Tonnelat, M. A., 320n.
transference, 109, 162, 177, 281, 283, 294
transfinite, 71, 169, 187, 194
transgression of codes, 70
Trotsky, Leon, 29
truth, ix, x–xi, 24, 25
Tucker, Robert C., 308n.
Tynanov, J., 31
Tzara, Tristan, 12

utterance, 36–38, 115, 175–76, 185, 187, 206

Van Ginneken, J., 307n.
Van Gogh, Vincent, 190, 207, 212
Varro, Marcus Terentius, 81–83
Vasari, Giorgio, 215, 251
Vedas, 191
Venetian Gothic style, 257
Veneziano, Paolo, 257
Verdiglione, Armando, 299n.
Vergil, 47; Aeneas and Dido, 47
Vietnam War, 207
Vinogradov, V. V., 309n.
Voltaire, François Marie Arouët de, 82–3, 185

Wahl, François, 9
Webern, Anton, 161
Wehrle, Albert J., 301n.
Wexsel, William, 326n.
Whitaker, G. H., 321n.
White, John, 232, 318n., 322n.
Wilson, Edmund, 13, 22
Winnicott, D. W., 281, 283, 287, 291; *Playing and Reality*, 323n., 324n., 325n.
Wolfson, Louis, 6
woman, xi, 10–11; as other in medieval poetry, 51–52; and theoretical reason, 147; loss of identity in jouissance, 167; her place within Christianity, 276

word: direct, denotative, and object-oriented, 71–72; dialogical, 65, 71; *see also* Signifier/signified

Wright, Georg Henrik von, *An Essay on Modal Logic*, 303*n.*

writing: defined, 21–22; and the law, 111–14, 120; and realism, 302*n.*

Wundt, W. (*Volkerpsychologie*), 325*n.*

Xenophon, 80

Yin-yang, 69

Young, La Monte, 170

Yüeh-fu, 304*n.*

Yü-t'ai hsin-yung, 304*n.*

Zhdanov, Andrei Aleksandrovich, 24

Zoroastrianism, 228